STALLED

STALLED

THE REPRESENTATION OF WOMEN IN CANADIAN GOVERNMENTS

Edited by
Linda Trimble, Jane Arscott,
and Manon Tremblay

UBCPress · Vancouver · Toronto

21 20 19 18 17 16 15 14 13   5 4 3 2 1

Printed in Canada on FSC-certified ancient-forest-free paper
(100% post-consumer recycled) that is processed chlorine- and acid-free.

Library and Archives Canada Cataloguing in Publication

    Stalled: the representation of women in Canadian governments / edited by Linda Trimble, Jane Arscott, and Manon Tremblay.

Includes bibliographical references and index.
Issued also in electronic formats.
ISBN 978-0-7748-2520-7 (bound); ISBN 978-0-7748- 2521-4 (pbk.)

    1. Women legislators – Canada. 2. Women – Political activity – Canada. I. Trimble, Linda. II. Arscott, Jane. III. Tremblay, Manon.

HQ1236.5.C2S73 2013	305.43'3280971	C2013-901628-7

Canadä

UBC Press gratefully acknowledges the financial support for our publishing program of the Government of Canada (through the Canada Book Fund), the Canada Council for the Arts, and the British Columbia Arts Council.

This book has been published with the help of a grant from the Canadian Federation for the Humanities and Social Sciences, through the Awards to Scholarly Publications Program, using funds provided by the Social Sciences and Humanities Research Council of Canada.

UBC Press
The University of British Columbia
2029 West Mall
Vancouver, BC V6T 1Z2
www.ubcpress.ca

Contents

Tables and Figures

Figures

Acknowledgments

Independently of each other, Sylvia Bashevkin and Manon Tremblay approached Linda Trimble to find out if an update of *In the Presence of Women: Representation in Canadian Governments* was in the works (Arscott and Trimble 1997). After all, a lot had happened in the fifteen years since its publication, and, while women's representation in the House of Commons was fairly regularly tracked, in the interim the provinces and territories had been largely overlooked. Determining whether or not the benchmarks observed in 1997 had been surpassed would require more investigation. Linda and co-editor Jane Arscott concluded a new volume was a good idea and convinced Manon to join the editorial team. Sylvia agreed to write a foreword for the book, and we were delighted when leading scholars from across the country quickly and enthusiastically signed on to the project as well.

Producing this volume would not have been possible without a great deal of support and assistance. First drafts of several of the chapters were presented at the 2011 meeting of the Canadian Political Science Association in Waterloo, and we received invaluable feedback from panel participants and audience members. The two anonymous reviewers for UBC Press offered detailed comments on all of the chapters and their thoughtful suggestions were enormously helpful. We were fortunate indeed to work with a fabulous group of authors who produced first-rate work on time and happily agreed to update material when elections occurred. A special thank you must go to

Emily Andrew at UBC Press. Not only did Emily champion the idea of a new book on women's descriptive representation, she and her colleagues deftly steered it through the various stages of the publishing process.

In this volume we show that only a few more women have been elected to public office in Canada over the past few decades. But, ever hopeful that the goal of gender parity in political representation can, eventually, be achieved, we dedicate this volume to the many more women who will seek and win public office in the years to come.

Women, Power, Politics

Surveying the Canadian Landscape

SYLVIA BASHEVKIN

In 1997, the publication of *In the Presence of Women* marked a significant watershed in the development of gender and politics scholarship in Canada. The volume skilfully presented and codified what was known about women's engagement in federal, provincial, and territorial legislative politics. Organized in a way that made a large body of research material accessible to students at all levels, the book proved extremely useful to faculty members teaching a wide range of subjects, including introductory Canadian and comparative politics. That volume stands, nearly fifteen years later, as a landmark accomplishment not only for its editors, Jane Arscott and Linda Trimble, but also for each of the chapter contributors. Together, they mapped the terrain and challenged future researchers to gauge both how the field had evolved and how women's participation had or had not increased.

What do we now know about women's political engagement in Canada that we did not know in 1997? Which areas of enquiry have been most vigorously pursued, and which are in need of closer attention? To what extent has scholarly research in this field challenged broader understandings of Canadian politics?

Among the reasons that we are able to think retrospectively, and to analyze what's known and not known, is that a considerable body of scholarship exists today that was not available in earlier decades. This is no small matter since the professional norms discouraging gender and politics research were, and in many instances remain, quite powerful. One of the major reasons to press forward with scholarship by colleagues at all levels, including graduate and undergraduate students, is to ensure the largest possible reach for their work and to attract both academic talent and public attention towards what remains an intellectually exciting, empirically and conceptually promising, and politically relevant area of enquiry.

This foreword advances two main propositions. First, the empirical gender and politics field has made progress, but not enough. Large stretches of the Canadian terrain remain un- or at least under-explored. To a large extent, we are in the curious position of seeing that the more we know, the less we know. Phrased differently, as more layers of onion are removed, the more interior we find – meaning that what has been learned can directly inspire further research. Second, the academic and public impacts of this scholarship have been measurable and important, but challenges remain. My reflections suggest that we need not only more academic recognition of research in the field but also, given its fundamental link to political representation in democratic systems, more public sharing of that material. Electronic databases provide Canadians with a wealth of contemporary as well as historical information, for example, about patterns of women's election to parliamentary office. Yet public awareness and understanding of this subject remains for the most part frozen in time, having advanced little beyond the level of knowledge that prevailed when research in the field was in its infancy during the 1980s.

One of the obvious ways of assessing a field of enquiry is to think chronologically, going back to the earliest work and then moving forward to the present time. From that perspective we can begin to understand why relatively more is known about some areas – notably election to legislative office – than others. Janine Brodie and Jill Vickers conducted among the very first empirical studies in the area, examining patterns of candidacy and election to public office during the 1970s (see Brodie 1977; Vickers 1978). This research built on what was then a nascent comparative politics literature, which asked how many women served in legislatures, from what socio-economic and professional backgrounds they came, and how political mobility and ambition differed by gender (see Duverger 1955; Gruberg 1968; Jaquette 1974; Kirkpatrick 1974, 1976; Lovenduski and Hills 1981; Vallance 1979).

The major organizing themes in this literature include why so few women were elected to public office, what relationships existed between elected women and women in the general population, and how changes to parties, elections, and legislatures could enhance female political participation.

Decades later, these remain core interests of scholars in the field. More-over, as was the case in the early years, much of the research in this area continues to pivot at a conceptual level around questions of representation. Hanna Pitkin's classic 1967 study titled *The Concept of Representation* set out a key organizing concept, namely, "acting for," or substantive representation, which raised the possibility that elected politicians could be carriers of ideas for broader societal interests and could act, while in public office, on behalf of social movements (Pitkin 1967, 11).

During the 1970s and following, as feminist organizations in Canada began to engage directly with mainstream political institutions, probing linkages between politicians and movements offered a logical next step for this literature. Among gender and politics scholars, especially those study-ing one of the world's most disciplined parliamentary systems, parties be-came an institutional focal point in this story, whether the questions involved how women voted, which parties fielded women candidates and under what competitive circumstances, or how policy issues of particular relevance to women unfolded during as well as between election campaigns.

Vicky Randall's (1987, 108) comparative overview of the field argued that party ideology mattered to each of these questions. Her claim was highly significant in an era dominated by notions of "the end of ideology" in post-industrial society (see Bell 1960), and it demonstrated the extent to which gender and politics research, from a very early point in its development, interrogated prevailing social science wisdom. Randall's conclusion – that left parties seemed more rhetorically congenial towards feminist claims, more willing to field women candidates, and less likely to segregate women members in separate women's auxiliary organizations than did parties of the centre and right – was confirmed in Canadian research dating from the mid-1980s (see Bashevkin 1985).

Progressive parties were also more willing to experiment with formal rule changes designed to increase numbers of female party convention delegates and legislative candidates. Research on quotas, targets, and what was termed a "critical mass" of influential women dates back at least to the 1968 US Democratic Party convention, where criticism of the seeming exclusion of women and racial minorities from traditional party structures prompted the creation of what became known as the McGovern-Fraser Commission (see Kirkpatrick 1976, 43). The willingness of both Democrats and Republicans to introduce important representational reforms between 1968 and 1972 helps to explain why numbers of women delegates to US party conventions increased markedly through the 1970s. This transformation took place during the same period that the United Nations declared 1975 the International Year of the Woman, thus directing global attention towards women's engagement in politics and other fields.

A robust comparative literature exploring quotas and their impact developed during subsequent years. Much of it focused on how large a numerical presence in what kinds of institutions was necessary to alter not just the content of policy rhetoric and decisions but also the tenor of issue debates (see Childs and Krook 2008, 2009; Dahlerup 1988; Krook 2009). In Canada, some research was undertaken in this area, notably by Manon Tremblay on federal MPs (see Tremblay 1998). Yet a number of obvious questions that might have been asked by an alien landing from outer space remain unanswered. For example, given that the federal, British Columbia, and Ontario New Democratic Party (NDP) organizations were at the forefront of pursuing party quota strategies, what was the impact of these reforms on the gender composition of party caucuses? The nature of party issue platforms? The ability of parties to mobilize women voters? The dynamics of party strength between elections? Is it a coincidence that the federal NDP has elected women leaders, as have both the BC and Ontario parties?

The fact that Canada has had an unusually high number of women party leaders, often in organizations far from power, provides another crucial dimension to this story. Researchers have only begun to probe the within-Canada as well as cross-national aspects of this pattern. Published work reveals a preponderance of female party heads in weak opposition organizations on the political left, which suggests that, in the future, closer attention should be directed towards system-wide variables, including electoral rules, as well as party-level factors such as competitive circumstances and ideological positioning (see Bashevkin 2010; O'Neill and Stewart 2009). Analyzing party leadership campaigns also permits scholars to examine the role of individual women elites in acting as transmission belts between feminist movements and mainstream political institutions (Bashevkin 2009).

If we compare the years 1980 and 2010, we see that far more women were elected to Canadian legislatures, even though the proportion reached a stalemate in the one-fifth range (Bashevkin 2011). The reasons that numbers plateaued deserve closer examination since research suggests the causal chain may begin with a hostile media climate that reduces the supply of willing candidates (see Gidengil and Everitt 2003; Goodyear-Grant 2009). In addition, the rural-urban divide is illustrated by the fact that relatively few women politicians are elected in the rural and small-town constituencies that are typically overrepresented in Canadian legislatures (Carbert 2009). Early studies point as well towards such obstacles as the financial and occupational costs of candidacy, discrimination within party organizations (including "dirty tricks" in the course of competitive nomination contests), and the weight of family responsibilities on women generally (see Brodie 1985, 111).

Lisa Young's *Feminists and Party Politics,* published in 2000, explores party/social movement relations with reference to both the United States and Canada. Her conclusions closely parallel those of Vicky Randall in identifying strong ideological drivers whereby left and centre parties were more welcoming towards women activists, particularly those with feminist backgrounds, than were parties of the right (see Young 2000, 169, 206; Randall 1987, 108). In a period of conservative ascendance since 2006, therefore, stalled growth in numbers of elected women seems far from surprising. More systematic longitudinal comparison across provinces and at the federal level will permit researchers to test the relationship between electoral results and women's legislative recruitment.

Above all, scholarship in this area would benefit immeasurably from a comprehensive, up-to-date analysis of the evolution of contemporary feminisms in English Canada and Quebec (published studies include Adamson, Briskin, and McPhail 1988; de Sève 1985; Dumont 2008; Lamoureux 1986; Vickers, Rankin, and Appelle 1993). A thorough political study of the National Action Committee on the Status of Women (NAC), to parallel accounts of the Women's Electoral Lobby in Australia and of the National Organization for Women (NOW) in the United States, could address many significant questions (see Barakso 2004; Sawer 2008). Did NAC's evolution parallel that of peak Canadian Aboriginal, anti-poverty, and environmental groups that emerged during the same wave of "new social movement" ferment? How have organizations in Quebec and the rest of Canada differed in their strategies for engagement with mainstream political institutions? Were elected women more likely to pursue substantive representation activities during the height of extra-parliamentary feminist mobilization? To what extent did levels of cross-party cooperation among women legislators, and the dynamics of party women's caucuses, mirror the ebbs and flows of organized interests operating outside parliaments?

Although Canadian researchers have begun to address feminist movement-political party relations, they have not extensively probed the consequences of electoral outcomes for women in the general population. Cheryl Collier's (2001, 2008) work on anti-violence as well as child care initiatives in Ontario and British Columbia demonstrates the importance of the party in power to the treatment of both policy issues. Turning her question around to interrogate women's collective effectiveness within parties as a phenomenon to be explained would tell us what factors facilitated or, alternatively, discouraged feminist activists from joining various organizations and seeking to mould party platforms. In turn, this scholarship would shed light on the internal party dynamics behind both electoral and substantive representation.

Although relations between organized anti-feminism and political parties form an important part of this narrative, they have for the most part escaped academic scrutiny. Understanding how groups such as REAL Women and other anti-equality interests have established themselves within both party grassroots and elite circles poses a significant challenge, in part because of the difficulties entailed in studying what remain largely closed organizations. Yet Canadian gender and politics scholarship needs to extend its reach to this area, and we are fortunate to have useful models to draw upon in the US literature (see Schreiber 2008) and in earlier work on feminists in Canadian parties (Tremblay and Pelletier 2003).

It is also worth juxtaposing research on movement and legislative involvement with the study of Canadian constitutional and judicial politics. Debates surrounding constitutional reform during the late 1970s and early 1980s, and later in the Meech Lake and Charlottetown periods, stimulated strong interest in how courts interpreted women's rights. The presence of equality language in sections 15 and 28 of the Canadian Charter of Rights and Freedoms led researchers of diverse political persuasions to ask how equality-seeking interests intervened in the courts, how judges made decisions, and whether women judges made much difference (see, for example, Anderson 2001; Manfredi 2004; Razack 1991).

What remains remarkable about this literature is how few linkages have been made between peaks and valleys in movement mobilization, movement interest in mainstream politics, and women's legislative engagement, on one side, and constitutional and judicial outcomes, on the other (for one exception, see Dobrowolsky 2007). In particular, we need to assess relationships among elected women in parliaments and at local and municipal levels, on one side, and extra-parliamentary (including court-focused) mobilization, on the other. Did periods of sustained success by the Women's Legal Education and Action Fund (LEAF) as Canada's lead gender equality litigator correspond with periods of growth in elected numbers? What was the role of the Court Challenges Program not only in supporting equality-seeking interests in the courts but also in stimulating women's interest in pursuing legal and political careers? Why has the Charter not served thus far as the foundation for a successful campaign to secure system-wide quotas for women candidates? Will efforts to vet Canadian judicial appointees in ways that emulate US practices reduce the numbers of women who are willing to be considered for these positions and thus diminish the likelihood of "acting for" behaviour on the bench?

During the past three decades, Canada's major cities have undergone significant transformations not just in terms of de facto jurisdictional responsibilities – given the process of downloading from constitutionally privileged orders of government – but also with respect to population growth and population diversity. Have these shifts created new expectations concerning gender representation in cities, including in urban party organizations? Studies, including Andrew (2009), probe the involvement of local ethno-cultural women's groups in municipal policy making, thus setting in place the groundwork for a more expansive research agenda that asks if and how diverse women are making their way into elective office at federal and subnational levels. Future steps in this area might build on Holli's (2008) comparative theorizing, which considers links among extra-parliamentary feminist interests, elected politicians, and bureaucratic units charged with gender equality responsibilities. According to Holli, studying "feminist triangles" over time and space, even within a single city or region, can illuminate the ways in which organized interests shape institutions and policies.

Finally, it is essential to bear in mind that women's political engagement unfolds in political executive institutions that are likely even more severely gendered than any of those mentioned to this point. In political science generally, senior appointive office remains an under-researched area – perhaps, as MaryAnne Borrelli (2002, 15) observes, "because it seems to lack continuity in its relationships and practices." This point is worth pursuing because several Canadian women from the centre-right Progressive Conservative Party held federal cabinet posts that were uncommon in international terms, including two as external affairs ministers (Flora MacDonald and Barbara McDougall) and one as defence minister (Kim Campbell) between 1979 and the early 1990s. Moreover, women from across the political spectrum were appointed during the 1980s and following to top finance positions in provincial cabinets.

Despite the powerful role of political executives in Canada, relatively little scholarship has explored cabinet office-holding (exceptions include Bauer and Tremblay 2011; Kerby 2009; Studlar and Moncrief 1997, 1999;

Trimble and Tremblay 2005). Published memoirs and biographies of elite women provide useful background material but do not evaluate, for example, the substantive representation discourse and behaviour of appointed female elites, whether comparatively across women in terms of left-right party-in-power considerations or with reference to male predecessors and successors who held the same positions. How did elite-level women relate, or not relate, to organized feminism as well as anti-feminism in civil society?

It is worth concluding with an even tougher question: Has Canadian political science been fundamentally challenged or changed during the past thirty years by gender and politics research? Most gender and politics scholars carefully read what is considered the "general" literature of their respective specializations, whether that material concerns parties, elections, public policy, federalism, or political economy, since currency is a professional expectation in the discipline. It remains doubtful, though, that most "general" scholars invest parallel energies in the gendered scholarship – even if it falls within their own areas of interest. Important opportunities continue to exist to reverse that situation – including by insisting that colleagues, journalists, and our fellow citizens take women and politics scholarship more seriously than they have, and by ensuring the research produced in this subfield is so academically strong (in the sense of conceptually compelling and empirically interesting) that other members of the discipline cannot afford to ignore it. The publication of *Stalled: The Representation of Women in Canadian Governments* presents a valuable chance to attain this goal.

References

Adamson, Nancy, Linda Briskin, and Margaret McPhail. 1988. *Feminist Organizing for Change.* Toronto: Oxford University Press.

Anderson, Ellen. 2001. *Judging Bertha Wilson: Law as Large as Life.* Toronto: Osgoode Society for Canadian Legal History.

Andrew, Caroline. 2009. "Women and Community Leadership: Changing Politics or Changed by Politics?" In Sylvia Bashevkin, ed., *Opening Doors Wider: Women's Political Engagement in Canada,* 19-32. Vancouver: UBC Press.

Barakso, Maryann. 2004. *Governing NOW: Grassroots Activism in the National Organization for Women.* Ithaca: Cornell University Press.

Bashevkin, Sylvia. 1985. *Toeing the Lines: Women and Party Politics in English Canada.* Toronto: University of Toronto Press.

–. 2009. "Party Talk: Assessing the Feminist Rhetoric of Women Leadership Candidates in Canada." *Canadian Journal of Political Science* 42(2): 345-62.

—. 2010. "When Do Outsiders Break In? Institutional Circumstances of Party Leadership Victories by Women in Canada." *Commonwealth and Comparative Politics* 48(1): 72-90.

—. 2011. "Women's Representation in the House of Commons: A Stalemate?" *Canadian Parliamentary Review* 34(1): 17-22.

Bauer, Gretchen, and Manon Tremblay, eds. 2011. *Women in Executive Power: A Global Overview.* London: Routledge.

Bell, Daniel. 1960. *The End of Ideology: On the Exhaustion of Political Ideas in the Fifties.* New York: Free Press.

Borrelli, MaryAnne. 2002. *The President's Cabinet: Gender, Power, and Representation.* Boulder, CO: Lynne Rienner.

Brodie, M. Janine. 1977. "The Recruitment of Canadian Women Provincial Legislators, 1950-1975." *Atlantis* 2(2): 6-17.

—. 1985. *Women and Politics in Canada.* Toronto: McGraw-Hill Ryerson.

Carbert, Louise. 2009. "Are Cities More Congenial? Tracking the Rural Deficit of Women in the House of Commons." In Sylvia Bashevkin, ed., *Opening Doors Wider: Women's Political Engagement in Canada,* 70-90. Vancouver: UBC Press.

Childs, Sarah, and Mona Lena Krook. 2008. "Critical Mass Theory and Women's Political Representation." *Political Studies* 56(3): 725-36.

—. 2009. "Analysing Women's Substantive Representation: From Critical Mass to Critical Actors." *Government and Opposition* 44(2): 125-45.

Collier, Cheryl. 2001. "Working with Parties: Success and Failure of Child Care Advocates in British Columbia and Ontario in the 1990s." In Susan Prentice, ed., *Changing Child Care: Five Decades of Child Care Advocacy and Policy in Canada,* 117-31. Halifax: Fernwood.

—. 2008. "Neoliberalism and Violence against Women: Can Retrenchment Convergence Explain the Path of Provincial Anti-Violence Policy, 1985-2005?" *Canadian Journal of Political Science* 41(1): 19-42.

Dahlerup, Drude. 1988. "From a Small to a Large Minority: Women in Scandinavian Politics." *Scandinavian Political Studies* 11(4): 275-97.

de Sève, Micheline. 1985. *Pour un féminisme libertaire.* Montréal: Boréal Express.

Dobrowolsky, Alexandra. 2007. "Beyond Winners and Losers? What Has Happened to Women's Equality after 25 Years of Charter Struggles?" Paper presented at CPSA meetings, University of British Columbia. Available at http://www.cpsa-acsp.ca/.

Dumont, Micheline. 2008. *Le féminisme québécois raconté à Camille.* Montréal: Remue-ménage.

Duverger, Maurice. 1955. *The Political Role of Women.* Paris: UNESCO.

Gidengil, Elisabeth, and Joanna Everitt. 2003. "Conventional Coverage/ Unconventional Politicians: Gender and Media Coverage of Canadian Leaders' Debates, 1993, 1997, 2000." *Canadian Journal of Political Science* 36(3): 559-77.

Goodyear-Grant, Elizabeth. 2009. "Crafting a Public Image: Women MPs and the Dynamics of Media Coverage." In Sylvia Bashevkin, ed., *Are Doors Opening Wider? Studies of Women's Political Engagement in Canada,* 147-66. Vancouver: UBC Press.

Gruberg, Martin. 1968. *Women in American Politics*. Oshkosh, WI: Academia.

Holli, Anne Maria. 2008. "Feminist Triangles: A Conceptual Analysis." *Representation* 44(2): 169-85.

Jaquette, Jane S., ed. 1974. *Women in Politics*. New York: Wiley.

Kerby, Matthew. 2009. "Worth the Wait: Determinants of Ministerial Appointment in Canada, 1935-2008." *Canadian Journal of Political Science* 42(3): 593-611.

Kirkpatrick, Jeane J. 1974. *Political Woman*. New York: Basic Books.

–. 1976. *The New Presidential Elite*. New York: Russell Sage.

Krook, Mona Lena. 2009. *Quotas for Women in Politics: Gender and Candidate Selection Reform Worldwide*. New York: Oxford University Press.

Lamoureux, Diane. 1986. *Fragments et collages: Essai sur le féminisme québécois des années 70*. Montréal: Remue-ménage.

Lovenduski, Joni, and Jill Hills, eds. 1981. *The Politics of the Second Electorate*. London: Routledge and Kegan Paul.

Manfredi, Christopher P. 2004. *Feminist Activism in the Supreme Court: Legal Mobilization and the Women's Legal Education and Action Fund*. Vancouver: UBC Press.

O'Neill, Brenda, and David K. Stewart. 2009. "Gender and Political Party Leadership in Canada." *Party Politics* 15(6): 737-57.

Pitkin, Hanna F. 1967. *The Concept of Representation*. Berkeley: University of California Press.

Randall, Vicky. 1987. *Women and Politics: An International Perspective*. London: Macmillan.

Razack, Sherene. 1991. *Canadian Feminism and the Law: The Women's Legal Education and Action Fund and the Pursuit of Equality*. Toronto: Second Story Press.

Sawer, Marian, with Gail Radford. 2008. *Making Women Count: A History of the Women's Electoral Lobby in Australia*. Sydney: University of New South Wales Press.

Schreiber, Ronnee. 2008. *Righting Feminism: Conservative Women and American Politics*. New York: Oxford University Press.

Studlar, Donley T., and Gary F. Moncrief. 1997. "The Recruitment of Women Cabinet Ministers in the Canadian Provinces." *Governance* 10(1): 67-81.

–. 1999. "Women's Work? The Distribution and Prestige of Portfolios in the Canadian Provinces." *Governance* 12(4): 379-95.

Tremblay, Manon. 1998. "Do Female MPs Substantively Represent Women? A Study of Legislative Behaviour in Canada's 35th Parliament." *Canadian Journal of Political Science* 31(3): 435-65.

Tremblay, Manon, and Réjean Pelletier. 2003. "Feminist Women in Canadian Politics: A Group Ideologically Divided?" *Atlantis* 28(1): 80-90.

Trimble, Linda, and Manon Tremblay. 2005. "Representation of Canadian Women at the Cabinet Table, 1917-2002." *Atlantis* 30(1): 31-45.

Vallance, Elizabeth. 1979. *Women in the House: A Study of Women Members of Parliament*. London: Athlone Press.

Vickers, Jill McCalla. 1978. "Where Are the Women in Canadian Politics?" *Atlantis* 3(2): 40-51.

Vickers, Jill, Pauline Rankin, and Christine Appelle. 1993. *Politics as If Women Mattered: A Political Analysis of the National Action Committee on the Status of Women.* Toronto: University of Toronto Press.
Young, Lisa. 2000. *Feminists and Party Politics.* Vancouver: UBC Press.

STALLED

Introduction

The Road to Gender Parity

MANON TREMBLAY, JANE ARSCOTT, AND LINDA TRIMBLE

Stalled: The Representation of Women in Canadian Governments maps women's political representation across Canada and over time by tracking the numbers of women elected to municipal councils, provincial and territorial legislatures, and the House of Commons as well as women appointed to the Senate. In addition to documenting women's representation as candidates, office-holders, cabinet ministers, party leaders, and representatives of the Crown, each of the chapters in this volume offers explanations for the continuing under-representation of women in these categories. The authors consider what is being done by political parties, governments, and women's organizations to recruit more, and more diverse, women candidates and to promote women into executive positions. Prospects for gender parity – roughly equal numbers of women and men in political office – are assessed in each jurisdiction and institution. The conclusions are disappointing. In 1990 Chantal Maillé projected that, at then current rates of increase, equal representation of women in political office would take forty-five years. More than two decades later, the achievement of gender balance in Canada's legislatures remains as distant as before due to lower than anticipated rates of feminization (increases in the percentage of women elected) (Praud 2003).

The present volume extends and updates earlier work conducted on women's descriptive representation across Canada (Arscott and Trimble 1997; Trimble and Arscott 2003). Some political levels have been better documented than others. Parliament and a few of the provincial legislative assemblies (notably in Ontario and Quebec) have been relatively closely examined, whereas research about the presence of women in municipal governance, the Senate, and the territories has barely begun. This volume helps fill the gap by incorporating chapters on women's representation in these under-explored jurisdictions. In addition to offering a systematic array of data on women's electoral representation in federal, provincial and territorial, and municipal politics, the chapters map the progression of women in party leadership roles and appointed positions such as cabinet and Senate posts. With the exception of the municipal politics chapter, each of the chapters begins with an information box that presents the most recent data on women's representation in elected and appointed political positions. The chapters on Canada's national and subnational elected legislatures each follows a common template, beginning with key cultural, historical, socio-economic, or political factors that shape women's political representation in that jurisdiction before offering longitudinal data on numbers of women legislators, candidates, party leaders, cabinet ministers, first ministers, and representatives of the Crown. Each chapter analyzes these data, identifying the factors that best explain the observed trends. In particular, authors address the puzzle of the stalled electoral project for women. Why, after significant increases in the 1980s (Studlar and Matland 1994), has women's electoral representation stagnated since the mid-1990s? Finally, each of the chapters assesses the prospects for gender equality in the individual jurisdiction or institution.

Based on the traditional dominance of scholarship at the federal level, readers might expect to see the national institutions given priority by being placed at the front end of the book, or to see the chapters grouped regionally or thematically. Because city politics is, quite literally, "politics where we live," the newest material on the municipal level appears first. Chapter 1 explores the argument that election to city politics is somehow "easier" than winning a legislative position. The lens then shifts to the subnational legislatures, with Chapters 2 to 12 detailing women's political presence in each of Canada's provinces and territories. Rather than organizing these chapters from west to east, a conceptual configuration that ignores the North and misleadingly implies that there are geographic explanations for women's under-representation, the jurisdictions are arranged in alphabetical order, beginning with Alberta and ending with the territories. As these chapters illustrate, there are leaders and laggards in each region of Canada. The remaining chapters present information on the federal level of governance, examining women's progress in the House of Commons (Chapter 13) and the Senate (Chapter 14). The final chapter, an integrative conclusion, assesses trends over time and across jurisdictions and gauges the overall prospects for gender parity.

This introductory chapter answers two questions. First, what do we already know about the recruitment, integration, and impact of women in institutions of representative democracy? In the first section of the chapter, we provide a brief overview of the evolving literature on women's representation in Canada. While the knowledge base has expanded considerably over the past three decades, many questions about women's descriptive representation remain unanswered. But this gives rise to another question: Why should we care about women's continued under-representation in positions of political authority? As we explain in the final section of the chapter, the representation of women in elected and appointed offices continues to be an important measure of both gender equality and the overall health of democratic governance.

The State of Knowledge about Women and Political Representation in Canada

Numerous studies have been written about women and politics, including analyses of their integration into the institutions of representative democracy. Thomas (1994, 4) divides the evolution of works on women in politics in the United States into three distinct periods, starting with the first women elected, followed by the electoral project that may have been driven by feminism, and rounded out by considerations about substantive representation. This division is reflected in the development of research on the subject in Canada.

The first period of research on women and politics was instigated by the election of women at various levels of government. While very few academic researchers studied women's political participation in Canada at this time, articles by Bashevkin (1983), Brodie (1977), Cochrane (1977), Kohn (1984), Kopinak (1985), Langevin (1977), Tardy (1982), Vickers (1978), and Vickers and Brodie (1981) laid the initial groundwork. These authors compared female legislators with male legislators, emphasizing socio-demographic profiles, including age when first elected; marital status, employment status, education, occupation or profession; and participation in civil society organizations. Studies took note of where women were elected – in rural or urban communities, and in municipal, provincial, or federal arenas – and examined women's positioning and responsibilities when they gained access to ministerial posts.

The small number of women in political institutions, and their necessarily exceptional character, inspired the first reflections about why there were so few women in politics. Early explanations maintained that political parties were reluctant to select women candidates in competitive ridings (Brodie and Vickers 1981, 1982; Hunter and Denton 1984), that the media depicted female politicians as actors belonging mainly to the private sphere (Archibald et al. 1980), or that socialization and female gender roles did not encourage women to think of themselves as political beings. Research on women in politics in Canada has been preoccupied with explaining the disproportionately low levels of election and appointment of women to public office ever since.

The second and third periods of research on women in politics have been set against the background of a feminist electoral project. In general, the goal of this project is to increase the presence of women in Canadian politics and to use women's presence in governing institutions to change and improve women's living conditions. As Iris Marion Young (1994, 116) notes, "identity-based representation requires both the presence of women in legislatures [descriptive representation] as well as the inclusion of women's perspectives, beliefs, interests and diversity in the representational process [substantive representation]" (see also Pitkin 1967, 60-143). The idea of critical mass links descriptive and substantive representation by arguing that, if there are more women in politics, they will be in a better position to move the process of public decision making in a direction that is favourable to the interests of women (Dahlerup 1988; Kanter 1977). A number of feminist theorists, including Phillips (1995), Williams (1998), and Young (1989, 1990, 1994, 2000), have expanded the contours of the feminist electoral project (in Canada, see Vickers 1997; Young 1997). The notion that elected women represent all women has also generated a number of different opinions and critiques (see, among others, Ship 1998; Trimble 2006).

The second period of research, which began during the early 1980s, gave some attention to substantive representation. In addition to documenting continued obstacles to the election of women, researchers asked whether elected women were more likely than their male counterparts to support feminist ideas and policies. For instance, Erickson (1997) analyzed the opinions of a sample of female and male candidates in the 1993 federal election. She found that female candidates were significantly more likely than male candidates to support the election of more women members of Parliament. As well, women were more likely to favour the implementation of measures designed to remediate gender imbalances. Similar research was conducted at the provincial level. In 1982, Bashevkin (1985a) investigated feminist attitudes among delegates to the conventions of the three main political parties in Ontario. Women in each party were more likely than were their male counterparts to support the women's movement and affirmative action measures (Praud 1995, 1998), and more of them detected discrimination against women in politics. Tremblay (1992, 1995) made the same observation in Quebec: female politicians had more firmly feminist convictions than did their male colleagues. Although the Atlantic provinces are often described as being more traditional with regard to women's participation in politics (Brodie 1977; Carbert 2002), O'Neill and Erickson (2003) and Arscott (1997) have challenged this assumption. Arscott (1997, 330) discovered that "women legislators [in Newfoundland and Nova Scotia] began taking a more openly woman-positive political stance in debates over the prospect of institutionalizing the government's concern for the status of women."

The second period of research on women and politics in Canada has also been typified by "barriers" research. A number of works were inspired by Norris's (1996) model, which addresses obstacles to women's success by dividing the pathway to political power into four steps: eligibility, recruitment, selection, and election. In other words, to sit in the legislature a person must: have the right (or legal capacity) to do so, decide to become a candidate, be selected by a political party, and be chosen by the electors to represent them. Norris's pathway to a legislative mandate is analogous to being hired: eligibility corresponds to the group of people who are qualified to apply for a job vacancy; recruitment refers to those who apply; selection is similar to the short list of applicants chosen for an interview with the employer; and election is equivalent to hiring one of the applicants. The process occurs in an environment made up of socio-cultural regimes (such as socialization and gender roles), economic regimes (for example, employment structure by sex), and political regimes (the party system and the voting system, for example).

Eligibility alone does not explain the under-representation of women in politics in Canada since, like men, women are now entitled to vote and to run for office. Recruitment, selection, and election, however, are not universally available and, as a result, have generated a good deal of research. In Tahon's (1997) view, maternity is at the core of the political exclusion of women. Among the factors that MacIvor (1996, 235-41) advances to explain the low presence of women in Canadian politics, three are linked to recruitment: first, the public-private split; second, the gendered division of labour in the home and the workplace; and, third, the negative impacts of parent-hood. Women's sense that they can understand politics, which certainly is a precondition for envisaging a political career, remains salient, as a recent study by Gidengil, Giles, and Thomas (2008) shows.

It is one thing for a woman to see herself in politics but another for her to be seen by others as capable of assuming a mandate of political rep-resentation. For political parties, selection consists of choosing the candi-dates who will run for election under their banner; as such, the demand for candidates is orchestrated by party elites. The selection process is not neu-tral as it is based on a group of values regarding the ideal profile of a candi-date (Norris and Lovenduski 1989). The candidate profile differs from one party to another; moreover, parties that historically have monopolized the political scene (the Conservatives and the Liberals) tend to favour candi-dates whose features correspond more to masculine socialization and roles than to women's experiences (Erickson 1993; Pitre 2003a, 2003b; Tremblay and Pelletier 2001).

The processes used by political parties for selecting candidates have posed additional difficulties for women, one related to the position of women within parties, the other to incumbent female candidates. In Bashevkin's (1985b, 53-79) view, the position of women within English-Canadian political parties could be summarized as "the higher the fewer" – that is, the higher the positions, the fewer women fill them. As they did not hold key positions, women were less likely to be identified as potential can-didates by selection committees. In a survey of MPs conducted in 2000, Young and Cross (2003) observed that women had a less prestigious profile than did their male counterparts, a gap that certainly militated against their selection as candidates.

Moreover, the number of terms an elected official may serve is unlimited. Incumbent politicians seeking re-election are almost automatically selected by their political party. Incumbent female candidates have clearly higher suc-cess rates than do female candidates seeking a first term in office, and men are proportionally more numerous than are women within federal, provin-cial, territorial, and municipal political institutions; this situation represents a major barrier to women who wish to win a first mandate (Gidengil and Vengroff 1997; Tremblay 2009). However, Young (1991) found that the high turnover rate for members of Parliament favoured the election of women.

Election, the last step in the path to political power, may pose a number of difficulties for women, starting with the voting system. The first-past-the-post voting system poses obstacles to the election of women because parties present only one candidate per riding, whereas proportional voting systems encourage a diversified list of candidates in each riding (Matland 2003, 2005; Norris 2000, 2004). In Canada, MacIvor (2003) and Studlar and Moncrief (1999) have demonstrated the negative impact of the first-past-the-post system for women.

Women running for office are further disadvantaged by campaign financing and treatment by the media. Although Canada has public election campaign funding, Brodie (1991) found that lack of money was a major obstacle reported by the (then) few women candidates. In contrast, Young (2006, 57) more recently notes "that candidate gender has only a minimal effect on ability to raise funds and rates of campaign spending." Media treatment of women aspirants to political office has been a well-documented issue since the mid-1980s (see, among others, Gingras 1995; Robinson and Saint-Jean 1995; Sampert and Trimble 2003), including in high-visibility political party positions (Everitt and Camp 2009a, 2009b; Everitt and Gidengil 2003; Gidengil and Everitt 1999; Tremblay and Bélanger 1997; Trimble and Everitt 2010).

Obstacles to women's quest for political power have changed over time. Such changes have inspired an evolving research agenda. Bashevkin (2009, 11) characterizes the current situation as: "women plus power equals discomfort," which "refers to a specific normative climate that says either no woman is good enough to be a public leader, or else no normal woman is (or would ever want to be) powerful." For example, women party leaders confront the "discomfort equation" highlighted by Bashevkin. O'Neill and Stewart (2009) demonstrate that major parties are less likely to select women than are less competitive parties. Moreover, female leaders' careers are shorter than men's, and male leaders are more likely to achieve greater electoral victory. Bashevkin's (2010, 87) examination of ten party leadership campaigns in Canada since the mid-1970s "found electoral competitiveness, defined with reference to the firmness of a party's grip on power or its proximity to power in opposition, to be negatively related to women's leadership success." The reluctance of competitive political parties to select a female leader may be counterproductive. As O'Neill (1998) has shown in the case of the 1993 Canadian federal elections, a female leader may attract female electors, offering parties the potential to strengthen their electoral base of support (see also Bashevkin 2011; for a divergent point of view see Goodyear-Grant 2010 and Goodyear-Grant and Croskill 2011).

The third, and newest, period of research on women in politics is distinctive in three ways. First, in addition to analyzing obstacles, researchers in this phase have documented opportunities for enhancing women's representation in political life. Gauvreau (2011) interviewed female candidates in the 2010 New Brunswick election and found that fixed-date elections were seen as an opportunity for women to prepare their campaigns. Kerby's (2009) analysis of ministerial careers in Ottawa from 1935 to 2008 found that women have been 50 percent more likely than men to sit in the federal cabinet. Drawing on earlier scholarship by Studlar and Matland (1996), Moncrief and Studlar (1996), Studlar and Moncrief (1997), and Byrne (2009, 1997), several chapters in this book suggest similar trends in provincial cabinets.

Second, researchers in the third phase challenge the totalizing category of "woman" (Arend and Chandler 1996; Black and Erickson 2000, 2003). While a great deal of work in this area remains to be done, the gross under-representation of Aboriginal and racialized women has been documented and scholars are beginning to identify the particular obstacles to elected office posed by race and ethnicity (Andrew et al. 2008; Black 2000, 2003, 2008; Ship 1998). As the chapters in *Electing a Diverse Canada* (Andrew et al. 2008, 255) illustrate, there is "an archetype of the Canadian elected official – male, White, middle-class, middle-aged, Christian, Canadian-born, and majority-language speaking." However, research is beginning to reveal opportunities as well as barriers to the election of women who do not fit the archetype. For example, the assumption that visible minority women are less likely to be elected than are Caucasian women is challenged by recent data on women's election to the House of Commons and in eleven cities across Canada (Andrew et al. 2008, 265; Black 2008, 247).

Third, the research agenda has evolved beyond descriptive representation to determine whether or not women's presence in political spaces changes ways of performing politically (Tremblay and Trimble 2004; Trimble and Tremblay 2005). Whereas authors in the second period investigated whether feminist ideas could make female politicians allies with the women's movement in a pro-woman electoral project, authors in the third period ask whether female politicians have been translating words into actions. The basic question was: Do women change politics? There is some evidence to suggest that they do, albeit only under certain conditions (Tremblay 1998; Trimble 1993, 1997). Factors other than the presence of women in legislatures constrain the ability of women to substantively represent women's interests in legislative discussions, including feminist consciousness, role within the legislature, party affiliation, and parliamentary procedure. The critical mass theory's argument that, below the level of 30 percent women, legislators are collectively silenced has been called into question as well (Burt, Horton, and Martin 2000). Trimble (1993, 1997) and Lore (2008) analyzed statements by MLAs in Alberta and British Columbia, respectively, and found that even a small number of women can make a difference in legislative discussions. Hence a question for future investigation remains: Which factors (institutional and others) empower a minority composing less than the 30 percent critical mass threshold within an organization to substantively represent a group or a cause within specific representational bodies?

Four decades of research has shown that descriptive representation, or being there, is a necessary but insufficient condition for substantive representation – that is, voicing ideas and making claims on behalf of women and other previously excluded or marginalized groups. But there can be no doubt that symbolic representation, or the very presence of women in political roles from which they were once formally excluded, is a crucial marker of equality. While women are no longer formally barred from contesting or holding elected or appointed office, the problem of under-representation remains, especially for marginalized and racialized women. This book was prompted by the seemingly intractable nature of this problem in Canada.

The Count Continues: Women, Representation, and Equality

Why do numbers matter? Why are scholars still counting the women in elected and appointed office in Canada and around the world? Very simply, the numbers still do not add up to fairness in political representation for women. How can a democracy be legitimate if it fails to represent up to half its population? Gender parity is defined as the attainment of roughly equal numbers of women and men in elected and appointed political offices. Parity remains a remote prospect for women. At present women hold approximately one in five seats in national parliaments around the world (IPU 2013a). As of February 2013, women are 40 percent or more of the representatives in fewer than a dozen countries, comprising the majority of representatives in only one nation: Rwanda. Nowhere in the world do women predominate at the level of 60 percent or more of the legislative positions as men do in more than 90 percent of countries (IPU 2013b). In Canada's House of Commons the numbers of women present have increased over time, from 18 percent fifteen years ago to 25 percent in 2012 (IPU 1997a, 2013b). But while Canada is above the international average, its global ranking has fallen from a three-way tie for twenty-first in 1997 to a tie for forty-fifth place in 2013 (IPU 1997a, 2013b).

Counting the number of women elected and appointed to national legis-lative bodies is internationally recognized as a measure of women's equality globally. Over the last half-century, attentiveness to the gender dimension of representation has been variously used to compare and analyze women's involvement in the life of nations. Starting in the 1950s, the United Nations (UN) has encouraged women's participation at the national level (Duverger 1955), and UN agencies and programs have sponsored and promoted edu-cational campaigns for this purpose (United Nations Development Pro-gramme 2011). The global relevance of the issue is illustrated by the efforts of international organizations such as the Inter-Parliamentary Union (IPU), the World Economic Forum (WEF), and the International Knowledge Net-work of Women in Politics. As noted above, the IPU (1997a, 2013a, 2013b) tracks women's numbers in elected national legislatures worldwide. The WEF goes further, ranking countries according to their ability to close gen-der gaps, including gender gaps in legislative representation (Hausman, Tyson, and Zahidi 2011). The International Knowledge Network of Women in Politics (iKNOW 2011) coordinates knowledge exchanges among polit-ical activists. More sophisticated measures of women's equality – most recently, the indices of women's "empowerment" – have been produced for the World Economic Forum (Hausman, Tyson, and Zahidi 2011).

However, the problem of women's under-representation is not merely a matter of numbers or formal equality (Gotell and Brodie 1991). The legitim-acy of democratic institutions and decision-making practices is challenged by the scarcity of women in elected office. The argument that the under-representation of women in public life constitutes a democratic deficit has gained wide acceptance internationally (Cool 2010, 4). Since the 1990s, international organizations have highlighted the relationships between women's political participation and equality, empowerment, and democ-racy: "Democracy, security, development, human rights and gender equal-ity are inextricably linked" (World Conference of Speakers of Parliament 2010). As the *Universal Declaration of Democracy* affirms, the "achievement of democracy presupposes a genuine partnership between men and women in the conduct of the affairs of society in which they work in equality and complementarity, drawing mutual enrichment from their differences" (IPU 1997b). The very act of making representational claims by and for women serves to improve the quality of democratic deliberation and decision mak-ing (Saward 2006, 2008; Rehfeld 2006).

The Report of the Royal Commission on the Status of Women (1970, 339-41) initiated systematic counting of women's election and appointment to political office in Canada. Since then the figures have increased from under 2 percent to nearly 25 percent, or about half a percent a year on average. Two leaps forward have occurred. The first took place in the mid-1980s when the 10 percent watershed was broken at the federal level, and the second happened a decade later when the level of women's representation federally approached 20 percent. Alarmingly, the evidence shows no significant overall increases since then. It is clear that the pattern in Canada exemplifies incremental rather than fast-paced growth (Dahlerup and Freidenvall 2005, 27). Gender parity is possible, but without awareness, public education, advocacy (Equal Voice 2011), affirmative action measures, and political will it is unlikely to be achieved for another half century. With no further great leaps forward in sight, explaining the gender malaise in representation becomes all the more important.

The number of women in the highest public decision-making roles in national public life has long been emblematic of how far women's equality has come, and how far it has yet to go. As the individual chapters in this volume demonstrate, the addition of a few more women over time has not yet realized the goal of an equal partnership between women and men in democratic governance.

References

Andrew, Caroline, John Biles, Myer Siemiatycki, and Erin Tolley. 2008. *Electing a Diverse Canada: The Representation of Immigrants, Minorities, and Women.* Vancouver: UBC Press.

Archibald, Linda, Leona Christian, Karen Deterding, and Dianne Hendrick. 1980. "Sex Biases in Newspaper Reporting: Press Treatment of Municipal Candidates." *Atlantis* 5(2): 177-84.

Arend, Sylvie, and Celia Chandler. 1996. "Which Distinctiveness? Major Cleavages and the Career Paths of Canadian Female and Male Politicians." *Women and Politics* 16(1): 1-29.

Arscott, Jane. 1997. "Between the Rock and a Hard Place: Women Legislators in Newfoundland and Nova Scotia." In Jane Arscott and Linda Trimble, eds., *In the Presence of Women: Representation in Canadian Governments*, 308-37. Toronto: Harcourt Brace and Company.

Arscott Jane, and Linda Trimble, eds. 1997. *In the Presence of Women: Representation in Canadian Governments.* Toronto: Harcourt Brace and Company.

Bashevkin, Sylvia B. 1983. "Social Background and Political Experience: Gender Differences among Ontario Provincial Party Elites, 1982." *Atlantis* 9(1): 1-12.

–. 1985a. "Political Participation, Ambition and Feminism: Women in the Ontario Party Elites." *American Review of Canadian Studies* 15(4): 405-19.

–. 1985b. *Toeing the Lines: Women and Party Politics in English Canada.* Toronto: University of Toronto Press.

–. 2009. *Women, Power, Politics: The Hidden Story of Canada's Unfinished Democracy.* Don Mills: Oxford University Press.

–. 2010. "When Do Outsiders Break In? Institutional Circumstances of Party Leadership Victories by Women in Canada." *Commonwealth and Comparative Politics* 48(1): 72-90.

–. 2011. "Women's Representation in the House of Commons: A Stalemate?" *Canadian Parliamentary Review* 34(1): 17-22.

Black, Jerome H. 2000. "Entering the Political Elite in Canada: The Case of Minority Women as Parliamentary Candidates and MPs." *Canadian Review of Sociology and Anthropology* 37(2): 143-66.

–. 2003. "Differences That Matter." In Manon Tremblay and Linda Trimble, eds., *Women and Electoral Politics in Canada*, 59-74. Don Mills: Oxford University Press.

–. 2008. "Ethnoracial Minorities in the 38th Parliament: Patterns of Change and Continuity." In Caroline Andrew, John Biles, Myer Siemiatycki, and Erin Tolley, eds., *Electing a Diverse Canada: The Representation of Immigrants, Minorities, and Women*, 229-54. Vancouver: UBC Press.

Black, Jerome H., and Lynda Erickson. 2000. "Similarity, Compensation or Difference? A Comparison of Female and Male Office-seekers." *Women and Politics* 21(4): 1-38.

–. 2003. "Women Candidates and Voter Bias: Do Women Politicians Need to Be Better?" *Electoral Studies* 22(1): 81-100.

Brodie, Janine. 1977. "The Recruitment of Canadian Provincial Women Legislators, 1950-1975." *Atlantis* 2(2) (Part 1): 6-17.

Brodie, Janine, with the assistance of Celia Chandler. 1991. "Women and the Electoral Process in Canada." In Kathy Megyery, ed., *Women in Canadian Politics: Toward Equity in Representation*. Research Studies, Royal Commission on Electoral Reform and Party Financing, vol. 6, 3-59. Toronto: Dundurn Press.

Brodie, Janine, and Jill Vickers. 1981. "The More Things Change ... Women in the 1979 Federal Campaign." In Howard R. Penniman, ed., *Canada at the Polls, 1979 and 1980: A Study of the General Elections*, 322-36. Washington, DC: American Enterprise Institute for Public Policy Research.

–. 1982. *Canadian Women in Politics: An Overview.* Canadian Research Institute for the Advancement of Women Paper 2. Ottawa: Canadian Research Institute for the Advancement of Women.

Burt, Sandra, Alison Horton, and Kathy Martin. 2000. "Women in the Ontario New Democratic Government: Revisiting the Concept of Critical Mass." *International Review of Women and Leadership* 6(1): 1-11.

Byrne, Lesley. 1997. "Feminists in Power: Women Cabinet Ministers in the New Democratic Party (NDP) Government of Ontario, 1990-1995." *Policy Studies Journal* 25(4): 601-12.

–. 2009. "Making a Difference When the Doors Are Open: Women in the Ontario NDP Cabinet, 1990-95." In Sylvia B. Bashevkin, ed., *Opening Doors Wider: Women's Political Engagement in Canada*, 93-107. Vancouver: UBC Press.

Carbert, Louise. 2002. "Historical Influences on Regional Patterns of the Election of Women to Provincial Legislatures." In William Cross, ed., *Political Parties,*

Representation, and Electoral Democracy in Canada, 201-22. Don Mills: Oxford University Press.

Cochrane, Jean. 1977. *Women in Canadian Politics*. Toronto: Fitzhenry and Whiteside.

Cool, Julie. 2010. *Women in Parliament*. Ottawa: Library of Parliament. Available at http://www.parl.gc.ca/.

Dahlerup, Drude. 1988. "From a Small to a Large Minority: Women in Scandinavian Politics." *Scandinavian Political Studies* 11(4): 275-99.

Dahlerup, Drude, and Lenita Freidenvall. 2005. "Quotas as a 'Fast Track' to Equal Representation for Women: Why Scandinavia Is No Longer the Model." *International Feminist Journal of Politics* 7(1): 26-48.

Duverger, Maurice. 1955. *The Political Role of Women*. Paris: UNESCO.

Equal Voice. 2011. EV Mission. Available at http://www.equalvoice.ca/.

Erickson, Lynda. 1993. "Making Her Way In: Women, Parties and Candidacies in Canada." In Joni Lovenduski and Pippa Norris, eds., *Gender and Party Politics*, 60-85. London: Sage.

—. 1997. "Might More Women Make a Difference? Gender, Party and Ideology among Canada's Parliamentary Candidates." *Canadian Journal of Political Science* 30(4): 663-88.

Everitt, Joanna, and Michael Camp. 2009a. "One Is Not Like the Others: Allison Brewer's Leadership of the New Brunswick NDP." In Sylvia B. Bashevkin, ed., *Opening Doors Wider: Women's Political Engagement in Canada*, 127-44. Vancouver: UBC Press.

—. 2009b. "Changing the Game Changes the Frame: The Media's Use of Lesbian Stereotypes in Leadership versus Election Campaigns." *Canadian Political Science Review* 3(3): 24-39.

Everitt, Joanna, and Elisabeth Gidengil. 2003. "Tough Talk: How Television News Covers Male and Female Leaders of Canadian Political Parties." In Manon Tremblay and Linda Trimble, eds., *Women and Electoral Politics in Canada*, 194-210. Don Mills: Oxford University Press.

Gauvreau, Marilyne. 2011. "The Nomination of Women in the 2010 New Brunswick Election." *Canadian Parliamentary Review* 34(2): 43-47.

Gidengil, Elisabeth, and Joanna Everitt. 1999. "Metaphors and Misrepresentation: Gendered Mediation in News Coverage of the 1993 Canadian Leaders' Debates." *International Journal of Press/Politics* 4(1): 48-65.

Gidengil, Elisabeth, Janine Giles, and Melanee Thomas. 2008. "The Gender Gap in Self-Perceived Understanding of Politics in Canada and the United States." *Politics and Gender* 4(4): 535-61.

Gidengil, Elisabeth, and Richard Vengroff. 1997. "Representational Gains of Canadian Women or Token Growth? The Case of Quebec's Municipal Politics." *Canadian Journal of Political Science* 30(3): 513-37.

Gingras, François-Pierre. 1995. "Daily Male Delivery: Women and Politics in the Daily Newspapers." In François-Pierre Gingras, ed., *Gender and Politics in Contemporary Canada*, 191-207. Don Mills: Oxford University Press.

Goodyear-Grant, Elizabeth. 2010. "Who Votes for Women Candidates and Why?" In Cameron D. Anderson and Laura B. Stephenson, eds., *Voting Behaviour in Canada*, 43-64. Vancouver: UBC Press.

Goodyear-Grant, Elizabeth, and Julie Croskill. 2011. "Gender Affinity Effects in Vote Choice in Westminster Systems: Assessing 'Flexible' Voters in Canada." *Politics and Gender* 7(2): 223-50.

Gotell, Lise, and Janine Brodie. 1991. "Women and Parties: More than an Issue of Numbers." In Hugh G. Thorburn, ed., *Party Politics in Canada*. 6th ed., 53-67. Scarborough: Prentice-Hall Canada.

Hausman, Ricardo, Laura D. Tyson, and Saadia Zahidi. 2011. *The Global Gender Gap Report 2011*. Geneva: World Economic Forum. Available at http://www3.weforum.org/.

Hunter, Alfred A., and Margaret A. Denton. 1984. "Do Female Candidates 'Lose Votes'? The Experience of Female Candidates in the 1979 and 1980 Canadian General Elections." *Canadian Review of Sociology and Anthropology* 21(4): 395-406.

iKNOW (International Knowledge Network of Women in Politics). 2011. iKnow Politics. Available at http://www.iknowpolitics.org/.

IPU (Inter-Parliamentary Union). 1997a. Statistical Archive. Women in National Parliaments as of 1 January 1997. Available at http://www.ipu.org/.

–. 1997b. Universal Declaration of Democracy. Declaration adopted without a vote by the Inter-Parliamentary Council at its 161st session (Cairo, 16 September 1997). Available at http://www.ipu.org/.

–. 2013a. Women in Parliaments: World and Regional Averages. Women in National Parliaments as of 1 February 2013. Available at http://www.ipu.org/.

–. 2013b. Women in National Parliaments as of 1 February 2013. Available at http://www.ipu.org/.

Kanter, Rosabeth Moss. 1977. "Some Effects of Proportions on Group Life: Skewed Sex Ratios and Responses to Token Women." *American Journal of Sociology* 82(5): 965-90.

Kerby, Matthew. 2009. "Worth the Wait: Determinants of Ministerial Appointment in Canada, 1935-2008." *Canadian Journal of Political Science* 42(3): 593-611.

Kohn, Walter S.G. 1984. "Women in the Canadian House of Commons." *American Review of Canadian Studies* 14(3): 298-311.

Kopinak, Kathryn. 1985. "Women in Canadian Municipal Politics: Two Steps Forward, One Step Back." *Canadian Review of Sociology and Anthropology* 22(3): 372-89.

Langevin, Liane. 1977. *Missing Persons: Women in Canadian Federal Politics*. Ottawa: Advisory Council on the Status of Women.

Lore, Grace. 2008. "Women Legislators and Women's Issues in British Columbia." *Canadian Parliamentary Review* 31(4): 26-27.

MacIvor, Heather. 1996. *Women and Politics in Canada*. Peterborough: Broadview Press.

–. 2003. "Women and the Canadian Electoral System." In Manon Tremblay and Linda Trimble, eds., *Women and Electoral Politics in Canada*, 22-36. Don Mills: Oxford University Press.

Maillé, Chantal. 1990. *Primed for Power: Women in Canadian Politics*. Ottawa: Advisory Council on the Status of Women.

Matland, Richard. 2003. "Women's Representation in Post-Communist Europe." In Richard E. Matland and Kathleen A. Montgomery, eds., *Women's Access to Political Power in Post-Communist Europe*, 321-42. New York: Oxford University Press.

—. 2005. "Enhancing Women's Political Participation: Legislative Recruitment and Electoral Systems." In Julie Ballington and Azza Karam, eds., *Women in Parliament: Beyond Numbers: A Revised Edition*, 93-111. Stockholm: International IDEA.

Moncrief, Gary F., and Donley T. Studlar. 1996. "Women Cabinet Ministers in Canadian Provinces 1976-1994." *Canadian Parliamentary Review* 19(3): 10-13.

Norris, Pippa. 1996. "Legislative Recruitment." In Lawrence LeDuc, Richard G. Niemi, and Pippa Norris, eds., *Comparing Democracies: Elections and Voting in Global Perspective*, 184-215. Thousand Oaks, CA: Sage.

—. 2000. "Women: Representation and Electoral Systems." In Richard Rose, ed., *The International Encyclopedia of Elections*, 348-51. Washington, DC: Congressional Quarterly Press.

—. 2004. *Electoral Engineering: Voting Rules and Political Behavior.* Cambridge: Cambridge University Press.

Norris, Pippa, and Joni Lovenduski. 1989. "Pathways to Parliament." *Taking Politics* 1(3): 90-94.

O'Neill, Brenda. 1998. "The Relevance of Leader Gender to Voting in the 1993 Canadian National Election." *International Journal of Canadian Studies* 17: 105-30.

O'Neill, Brenda, and Lynda Erickson. 2003. "Evaluating Traditionalism in the Atlantic Provinces: Voting, Public Opinion and the Electoral Project." *Atlantis* 27(2): 113-22.

O'Neill, Brenda, and David K. Stewart. 2009. "Gender and Political Party Leadership in Canada." *Party Politics* 15(6): 737-57.

Phillips, Anne. 1995. *The Politics of Presence.* Oxford: Clarendon Press.

Pitkin, Hanna Fenichel. 1967. *The Concept of Representation.* Berkeley: University of California Press.

Pitre, Sonia. 2003a. "Political Parties and Female Candidates: Is There Resistance in New Brunswick?" In Manon Tremblay and Linda Trimble, eds., *Women and Electoral Politics in Canada*, 110-24. Don Mills: Oxford University Press.

—. 2003b. "Women's Struggle for Legislative Power: The Role of Political Parties." *Atlantis* 27(2): 102-9.

Praud, Jocelyne. 1995. "The Beginnings of Affirmative Action for Women in the Ontario New Democratic Party." In Jean-Pierre Beaud and Jean-Guy Prévost, eds., *La social-démocratie en cette fin de siècle/Late Twentieth-Century Social Democracy*, 201-22. Ste-Foy: Presses de l'Université du Québec.

—. 1998. "Affirmative Action and Women's Representation in the Ontario New Democratic Party." In Manon Tremblay and Caroline Andrew, eds., *Women and Political Representation in Canada*, 171-93. Ottawa: University of Ottawa Press.

—. 2003. "The Parti Québécois, Its Women's Committee, and the Feminization of the Quebec Electoral Arena." In Manon Tremblay and Linda Trimble, eds., *Women and Electoral Politics in Canada*, 126-37. Don Mills: Oxford University Press.

Rehfeld, Andrew. 2006. "Towards a General Theory of Political Representation." *Journal of Politics* 68(1): 1-21.

Robinson, Gertrude, and Armande Saint-Jean. 1995. "The Portrayal of Women Politicians in the Media: Political Implications." In François-Pierre Gingras, ed., *Gender and Politics in Contemporary Canada*, 176-90. Don Mills: Oxford University Press.

Royal Commission on the Status of Women (Bird Commission). 1970. *Report of the Royal Commission on the Status of Women*. Ottawa: Information Canada.

Sampert, Shannon, and Linda Trimble. 2003. "'Wham, Bam, No Thank You Ma'am': Gender and the Game Frame in National Newspaper Coverage of Election 2000." In Manon Tremblay and Linda Trimble, eds., *Women and Electoral Politics in Canada*, 211-26. Don Mills: Oxford University Press.

Saward. Michael. 2006. "The Representative Claim." *Contemporary Political Theory* 5(3): 297-318.

–. 2008. "Introduction: The Subject of Representation." *Representation* 44(2): 93-97.

Ship, Susan Judith. 1998. "Problematizing Ethnicity and 'Race' in Feminist Scholarship on Women and Politics." In Manon Tremblay and Caroline Andrew, eds., *Women and Political Representation in Canada*, 311-40. Ottawa: University of Ottawa Press.

Studlar, Donley. 1999. "Will Canada Seriously Consider Electoral System Reform? Women and Aboriginals Should." In Henry Milner, ed., *Making Every Vote Count: Reassessing Canada's Electoral System*, 123-32. Peterborough: Broadview Press.

Studlar, Donley T., and Richard E. Matland. 1994. "The Growth of Women's Representation in the Canadian House of Commons and the Election of 1984: A Reappraisal." *Canadian Journal of Political Science* 27(1): 53-79.

–. 1996. "The Dynamics of Women's Representation in the Canadian Provinces: 1975-1994." *Canadian Journal of Political Science* 29(2): 269-93.

Studlar, Donley T., and Gary F. Moncrief. 1997. "The Recruitment of Women Cabinet Ministers in the Canadian Provinces." *Governance: An International Journal of Policy and Administration* 10(1): 67-81.

–. 1999. "Women's Work? The Distribution and Prestige of Portfolios in the Canadian Provinces." *Governance: An International Journal of Policy and Administration* 12(4): 379-95.

Tahon, Marie-Blanche. 1997. "La maternité comme opérateur de l'exclusion politique des femmes." In Manon Tremblay and Caroline Andrew, eds., *Femmes et représentation politique au Québec et au Canada*, 19-31. Montreal: Remue-ménage.

Tardy, Évelyne. 1982. *La politique: Un monde d'hommes? Une étude sur les mairesses au Québec*. Montréal: Hurtubise HMH.

Thomas, Sue. 1994. *How Women Legislate*. New York: Oxford University Press.

Tremblay, Manon. 1992. "Quand les femmes se distinguent: Féminisme et représentation politique au Québec." *Canadian Journal of Political Science* 25(1): 55-68.

–. 1995. "Gender and Support for Feminism." In François-Pierre Gingras, ed., *Gender and Politics in Contemporary Canada*, 31-55. Don Mills: Oxford University Press.

—. 1998. "Do Female MPs Substantively Represent Women? A Study of Legislative Behaviour in Canada's 35th Parliament." *Canadian Journal of Political Science* 31(3): 435-65.

—. 2009. "Women in the Quebec National Assembly: Why So Many?" In Sylvia B. Bashevkin, ed., *Opening Doors Wider: Women's Political Engagement in Canada*, 51-69. Vancouver: UBC Press.

Tremblay, Manon, and Nathalie Bélanger. 1997. "Femmes chefs de partis politiques et caricatures éditoriales: L'élection fédérale de 1993." *Recherches féministes* 10(1): 35-75.

Tremblay, Manon, and Réjean Pelletier. 2000. "More Women or More Feminists? Descriptive and Substantive Representations of Women in the 1997 Canadian Federal Election." *International Political Science Review* 21(4): 381-405.

—. 2001. "More Women Constituency Party Presidents: A Strategy for Increasing the Number of Women Candidates in Canada?" *Party Politics* 7(2): 157-90.

Tremblay, Manon, and Linda Trimble. 2004. "Still Different after All These Years? A Comparison of Female and Male Canadian MPs in the Twentieth Century." *Journal of Legislative Studies* 10(1): 97-122.

Trimble, Linda. 1993. "A Few Good Women: Female Legislators in Alberta, 1972-1991." In Catherine A. Cavanaugh and Randi R. Warne, eds., *Standing on New Ground: Women in Alberta*, 87-118. Edmonton: University of Alberta Press.

—. 1997. "Feminist Politics in the Alberta Legislature, 1972-1994." In Jane Arscott and Linda Trimble, eds., *In the Presence of Women: Representation in Canadian Governments*, 128-53. Toronto: Harcourt Brace and Company.

—. 2006. "When Do Women Count? Substantive Representation of Women in Canadian Legislatures." In Marian Sawer, Manon Tremblay, and Linda Trimble, eds., *Representing Women in Parliament: A Comparative Study*, 120-33. Abingdon (Oxon)/New York: Routledge.

Trimble, Linda, and Jane Arscott. 2003. *Still Counting: Women in Politics across Canada*. Peterborough: Broadview Press.

Trimble, Linda, and Joanna Everitt. 2010. "Belinda Stronach and the Gender Politics of Celebrity." In Shannon Sampert and Linda Trimble, eds., *Mediating Canadian Politics*, 50-74. Toronto: Pearson.

Trimble, Linda, and Manon Tremblay. 2005. "Representation of Canadian Women at the Cabinet Table, 1917-2002." *Atlantis* 30(1): 31-45.

United Nations Development Programme. 2011. Empowering Women. Available at http://www.beta.undp.org/.

Vickers, Jill. 1978. "Where Are the Women in Canadian Politics?" *Atlantis* 3(2) (Part 2): 40-51.

—. 1997. "Toward a Feminist Understanding of Representation." In Jane Arscott and Linda Trimble, eds., *In the Presence of Women: Representation in Canadian Governments*, 20-46. Toronto: Harcourt Brace and Company.

Vickers, Jill, and M. Janine Brodie. 1981. "Canada." In Joni Lovenduski and Jill Hills, eds., *The Politics of the Second Electorate: Women and Public Participation*, 52-79. London: Routledge and Kegan Paul.

Williams, Melissa S. 1998. *Voice, Trust, and Memory: Marginalized Groups and the Failings of Liberal Representation*. Princeton: Princeton University Press.

World Conference of Speakers of Parliament. 2010. Declaration adopted by the conference adopting Securing Global Democratic Accountability for the Common Good. Available at http://www.ipu.org/.

Young, Iris Marion. 1989. "Polity and Group Difference: A Critique of the Ideal of Universal Citizenship." *Ethics* 99(2): 250-74.

−. 1990. *Justice and the Politics of Difference*. Princeton: Princeton University Press.

−. 1994. "Gender as Seriality: Thinking about Women as a Social Collective." *Signs* 19(3): 713-38.

−. 2000. *Inclusion and Democracy*. Oxford: Oxford University Press.

Young, Lisa. 1991. "Legislative Turnover and the Election of Women to the Canadian House of Commons." In Kathy Megyery, ed., *Women in Canadian Politics: Toward Equity in Representation*. Research Studies, Royal Commission on Electoral Reform and Party Financing, vol. 6, 81-99. Toronto: Dundurn Press.

−. 1997. "Fulfilling the Mandate of Difference: Women in the Canadian House of Commons." In Jane Arscott and Linda Trimble, eds., *In the Presence of Women: Representation in Canadian Governments*, 82-103. Toronto: Harcourt Brace and Company.

−. 2006. "Women's Representation in the Canadian House of Commons." In Marian Sawer, Manon Tremblay, and Linda Trimble, eds., *Representing Women in Parliament: A Comparative Study*, 47-66. Abingdon (Oxon)/New York: Routledge.

Young, Lisa, and William Cross. 2003. "Women's Involvement in Canadian Political Parties." In Manon Tremblay and Linda Trimble, eds., *Women and Electoral Politics in Canada*, 92-108. Don Mills: Oxford University Press.

1

Truly More Accessible to Women than the Legislature?

Women in Municipal Politics

MANON TREMBLAY AND ANNE MÉVELLEC

A widespread idea in writings on women and municipal politics is that decision-making bodies elected at the local level are more accessible to women than are federal, provincial, and territorial legislative political institutions (Brodie 1985, 21; Vickers 1978). Many reasons are given for this. One is that involvement in local politics is easier to reconcile with family life, whereas elected positions at the federal, provincial, and territorial levels entail frequent absences and long-distance travel (Andrew 1984, 1991; Brodie 1985, 82). Another is that the nature of municipal politics corresponds better to women's policy concerns (Maillé 1997; Trimble 1995). Indeed, provincial, territorial, and federal politics seem to deal with issues remote from the daily lives of ordinary people, whereas an important aspect of municipal politics consists of meeting the population's daily needs through delivery of basic services. Other reasons include the low level of competitiveness in municipal politics compared to provincial, territorial, and federal politics; the absence of political parties (which are suspected of erecting barriers to women candidates); and the lower cost of election campaigns (Vickers 1978). Finally, thanks to the principle of no taxation without representation, female landowners were able to vote in municipal elections earlier (in many cases in the nineteenth century) than in legislative elections,[1] thus adding support to the argument of those who see the municipal level of government as more accessible to women.

This chapter compares women's representation in city halls with their presence in Canadian legislatures. It challenges the idea that election to municipal governments is somehow "easier" for women. We believe that many of the obstacles faced by women who seek power at the federal, provincial, and territorial levels of government also line the pathways to political representation at the municipal level, especially in large cities. Moreover, we believe some of the explanations for the alleged accessibility of local elected bodies are essentialist. It is problematic to assume that women's political interests, activities, and choices are governed by traditional gender roles. For instance, the argument that women seek office "closer to home" assumes that women are by nature and inclination attracted to child care and other household duties and likely to see such roles as obstacles in the path to political office. The idea that women perform femininity – that is, that women in politics are concerned with issues defined as being associated with their sex – contributes to the construction and maintenance of inflexible gender codes.

In the first part of this chapter, we give an overview of the institutional framework of municipal politics in Canada. In the second part, we paint a statistical portrait of the presence of women in municipal and legislative politics in Canada. In the third part, we address some of the explanations for under-representation of women in Canada's legislative bodies and explore whether they shed light on women's under-representation in municipal politics in Canada. Finally, we present several strategies implemented by Canadian municipalities to attain a better balance of representation between women and men, and we conclude by suggesting further avenues for research.

Background

Municipal politics is the poor relative of political science in Canada. One reason may be that the municipal level is often considered minor, and it is situated somewhat at the margin of the political field as traditionally conceived. For instance, political parties are largely absent from the municipal scene, and the absence of large partisan organizations tends to individualize and personalize election campaigns: all candidates must finance their campaigns on their own (Young 2008). Perhaps this is why voter participation in municipal elections tends to be lower than in provincial, territorial, and federal votes. Municipal voter turnout hovers around 45 percent, but it may be as low as 35 percent in large cities. In Toronto in 2000, for example, participation was 36 percent (Hicks 2006). The political level "closest to the citizens" is thus not necessarily the one about which electors are the most enthusiastic, especially because a large proportion of candidates are elected by acclamation in several provinces (i.e., more than 60 percent in Quebec, Saskatchewan, and Prince Edward Island).[2] The only notable exceptions to the lack of party mobilization at the municipal level are in Quebec and British Columbia, where municipal political parties exist. These parties, a traditional presence in the large cities in these provinces, have participated in institutionalizing the municipal level as a third political category, distinct from the provincial, territorial, and federal ones.

Canadian municipalities are run by municipal councils, the members of which are usually elected in first-past-the-post voting systems, whether by ward (generally for municipal councillors) or by the entire municipality (for mayors). Any debate over voting systems focuses on the advantages and disadvantages of election by ward or by the entire municipality. Depending on the jurisdiction, municipal mandates last for terms of three or four years. Most provincial governments have sought to reform their municipal systems, especially in metropolitan areas. It is notable that more than half of all Quebecers, Ontarians, and British Columbians live, respectively, in the Montreal, Toronto, and Vancouver metropolitan regions. Several provincial governments have enacted municipal amalgamations in an attempt to reduce the number of municipalities, improve the performance of municipal administrations and fiscal equity, or fight urban sprawl. Amalgamations have, in fact, reduced the number of municipal elected representatives without fundamentally changing these representatives' functions and working conditions (Kushner and Siegel 2003). Some reforms have also modified, to various extents, the distribution of jurisdictions between the province and the municipalities, particularly in Ontario and Quebec. In general, however, the reforms have essentially affected the municipal map without really transforming the finances, jurisdictions, or terms of local democracy.

Women's Political Representation: The Numbers
Although the social sciences, unlike the physical sciences, do not easily lend themselves to the formulation of laws, they can nevertheless lead to certain general observations. One of these is that women are under-represented in politics, in both legislative and executive bodies of state power (Bauer and Tremblay 2011).[3] Some scholars suggest that, although women have not reached parity of representation in municipal politics, they are present in

TABLE 1.1

Proportion (%) of women in municipal and legislative politics, by province and territory, 2002 and 2009

	Municipal[1]			Legislative[2]		
	2002	2009	% change[3]	2002	2009	% change
Alberta	23	25	+10	21	16	−23
British Columbia	26	31	+20	24	29	+22
Manitoba	10	14	+35	23	32	+39
New Brunswick	21	26	+26	18	13	−30
Newfoundland & Labrador	25	26	+4	17	21	+25
Northwest Territories	25	39	+54	11	16	+49
Nova Scotia	19	21	+13	10	17	+70
Nunavut	24	34	+42	5	5	0
Ontario	21	24	+15	18	28	+55
Prince Edward Island	24	29	+21	22	26	+17
Quebec	21	24	+16	23	30	+29
Saskatchewan	12	14	+17	22	22	0
Yukon	24	39	+61	29	11	−63
Canada, total	20	23	+16	21	22	+7
Mean	21	26	25	19	21	10

1 The percentages merge female mayors and female councillors.

2 The numbers are as of the most recent federal, provincial, or territorial general election around 2002 and 2009.

3 This column expresses the substantial variation in the proportion of women in 2009 compared with 2002. For example, the proportion of women in municipal politics in Alberta was 25% in 2009, a 10% increase over 2002, when it was 23% (i.e., 23 + 10% = 25).

Sources: For the municipal level in 2002, Canadian Women Voters Congress (2004); in 2009, Federation of Canadian Municipalities (2009). The legislative data were collected from the several provincial and territorial legislative assembly websites.

higher proportions at this level (Brodie 1985, 21; Vickers 1978). Things may have changed, however, because more recent figures force us to consider such a reading with caution.[4]

Looking at the first decade of the twenty-first century, we explored the hypothesis that women are more present on the municipal than legislative political scene in the ten provinces and three territories that make up the Canadian federation. Our results are given in Table 1.1. In general, this reading is well founded: the Canadian municipal scene had an average feminization rate (defined as the proportion of women among a given group of politicians) of 21 percent in 2002 and 26 percent in 2009, while proportions on the legislative scene were 19 percent and 21 percent, respectively. What is more, the growth in the proportion of women in municipal elective bodies from 2002 to 2009 was clearly greater than it was in legislative bodies: 25 percent versus 10 percent. Finally, Table 1.1 shows that the presence of women in municipal politics grew between 2002 and 2009 in all jurisdictions considered, although unequally (between 4 and 59 percent), whereas a number of provincial and territorial legislatures saw their proportion of women representatives drop over this period. As it happens, some provinces and territories showed a clear contrast with regard to changes in proportions of women in municipal and legislative politics in 2002 and 2009, the most notable being Yukon, which saw an increase of 61 percent of women on the municipal scene but a drop of 63 percent in the legislature.

In short, the idea that a higher proportion of women are elected in local than in legislative politics seems to have some truth to it, at least when municipal data are aggregated to the provincial and territorial scale.[5] Is it possible that the path towards municipal power involves fewer obstacles for women than does the path leading to a legislative assembly? The answer is far from simple.

Explanations

Since the 1990s, a number of studies have been published throughout the world, especially in the West, examining the under-representation of women in politics, notably in national parliaments.[6] Women's participation in municipal politics has generated much less research, however, with the consequence that theoretical and conceptual tools are less fully developed. Since this chapter assesses the representation of women in municipal and legislative political institutions, the models developed to study female legislative representatives have been used to make this comparison and are adapted as needed.

Anyone who wants to become a legislator must be eligible to be a candidate, possess certain qualities, gain the support of a political party, and be elected. These requirements also apply to someone who wishes to be elected in municipal politics, except for the step of selection by a political party, which comes into play only in municipalities in which such actors exist.

Eligibility is not a factor in the exclusion of women from legislative or municipal politics. Electoral statutes in Canada no longer limit the rights to vote and run for office to men, and they no longer explicitly forbid women to do so.

Recruitment refers to the capacity of an individual to submit her or his candidacy for a legislative or municipal position. This capacity is measured by the yardstick of theories on political representation and the concept of social capital. Representation brings up the dilemma of distinction: Should representatives resemble the represented or is it unimportant if they are different? A panoply of studies shows that legislative politicians in Canada have a clearly more elitist profile, in terms of education and profession, than do people in the population; they are rich in social capital because they are involved in associative and civic networks, and a number of them are professional politicians (Brodie 1985, 44-54; Docherty 2005, 26-46; Franks 1987, 66-71; Oakes 1994, 148-92; Studlar et al. 2000). Put succinctly, legislative politicians in Canada are different from the population with regard to their socio-demographic features and their social and political capital. Is it different for politicians at the municipal level, where elected decision-making bodies are often described as closer to the people? Are municipal councils perhaps less elitist?

A number of studies show that municipal politicians in Canada, like their provincial, territorial, and federal counterparts, have an elitist profile in comparison to the population in general (among others, Andrew et al. 2008; Simard 2004; Tardy 2002, 37-53). For example, as Siegel, Kushner, and Stanwick (2001) observed in 1998, mayors in thirty-two large Canadian cities (those with a population of 100,000 or more) had attained a level of education clearly above that of the populations that they represented since almost two-thirds of them had a university degree.[7] Far from abating, this trend seems to have become more pronounced over time. Bloemraad (2008) finds that 92 percent of representatives in Vancouver in the mid-2000s held a university degree, a proportion in line with those observed in other large Canadian cities (Andrew et al. 2008). That said, Simard (2004) hypothesizes that municipal politicians are less elite than are legislative representatives in comparison to the population. Research has yet to be done on this question.

Although there is no doubt that many women in Canada possess the attributes to be elected to municipal office, they must still make the decision to take the leap into politics. On the legislative level, a number of factors have been advanced to explain why women do not put their name forward, including family responsibilities (MacIvor 1996, 236-38; Tremblay 2005) and the lack of financial resources (Brodie 1991; Young 2006). At first glance, these factors may not seem to be such major obstacles at the municipal level, for two reasons: first, proximity makes it easier to reconcile family and political career; second, a municipal election campaign might be less costly than a federal, provincial, or territorial campaign. However, it is important to put the influence of the family on political ambitions in perspective be-cause many women simply do not have (or no longer have) children to supervise or because the other parent or a third party takes an active part in their upbringing (Brodie 1991; Tremblay 2008, 93-94).

Furthermore, it is not certain that an election campaign in a large city is less expensive than a provincial, territorial, or federal campaign, notably due to the lack of financial support from the state and political parties. In her study of about three hundred female candidates for legislative and mu-nicipal elections in Canada from 1945 to 1975, Brodie (1985, 103) high-lights the important role played by personal financial assets in financing municipal election campaigns (see also Bherer et al. 2008, 43; Briggs 2000; Vickers and Brodie 1981). What is more, in their study of factors that shape electoral success in Ontario municipal politics, Kushner, Siegel, and Stanwick (1997) find that financing a campaign is a major obstacle, espe-cially in cities with a population of at least ten thousand. Gavan-Koop and Smith (2008) put figures to the financial barrier: in the Vancouver metro-politan region, a campaign for a seat on the council of a small- or medium-sized city involves expenditures on the order of $5,000 to $8,000, while a campaign for the position of mayor costs around $50,000. In Toronto in 2006, the average expenditure for councillors was $48,500, and two candi-dates spent $100,000, which is well beyond legal limits (MacDermid 2009, 13).[8] Bherer et al. (2008, 11) note a disturbing practice: Montreal parties, far from financially supporting the election campaigns of women candi-dates running for them, sometimes ask them (as well as male candidates) to make a contribution. Such a request may discourage some potential candi-dates, especially women, from deciding to run for municipal office.

The decision whether to take the leap into the electoral arena also de-pends in part on a sense of political competency, which, in turn, can certain-ly be stimulated by encouragement to aspire to office. However, it seems that women, even those who are highly qualified and have a rich network of political contacts, are less likely to receive such encouragement than are men (Fox and Lawless 2010; Niven 2006). The results are contradictory for municipal politics. For instance, Brodie (1985, 102) observed that women engaged in municipal politics in Canada between 1945 and 1975 (i.e., at a time when very few women were encouraged to seek electoral office) re-ceived their main support from close friends and members of their family – another factor mitigating the negative influence of family on women's pol-itical ambitions. On the other hand, in her study of female municipal coun-cillors in Quebec in 1997, Tardy (2002, 64) found that more than half of them had been solicited by a person already sitting on the municipal council. In short, additional research is called for to provide a clearer picture of the role of encouragement in recruiting women to municipal politics.

Encouragement to enter politics involves the concept of political opportunity structure – that is, the broader context that encourages or discourages collective action. Several factors affect the ability (and perhaps willingness) of women to assume a legislative mandate of representation. Many of these factors emerge during the selection and election stages. Research has brought to light a range of factors, many of them institutional in nature, to explain the under-representation of women in Canada's parliamentary spaces. What is their value for understanding women's participation in municipal politics?

The political parties are blamed for the deficit of women in legislative positions, accused of not selecting female candidates or, if they do select them, running them in ridings in which victory seems unlikely (Bashevkin 1993, 84-85; Brodie 1977; Brodie and Vickers 1981; Hunter and Denton 1984; Vickers 1978).[9] Political parties are not as important on the municipal political scene, which may explain the lack of information available on their effects on women's access to local government. However, it seems that the municipal-level parties do not restrict women candidates to less promising ridings. Studying the profile and electoral success of some 450 mayors in Canada between 1982 and 1997, Siegel, Kushner, and Stanwick (2001) found that 31 percent of the female mayoral candidates were victorious, as opposed to 21 percent of the male mayoral candidates (see also Kushner, Siegel, and Stanwick 1997). Bherer et al. (2008, 17, 22) also note higher success rates for women in the Montreal elections of 2001 and 2005, and Champagne (n.d.) does so for the 2009 election. Kopinak (1985) makes the same observation on a Canada-wide scale, and, more recently, Bourgeois and Strain (2009) do so for New Brunswick. In contrast, the study by Gavan-Koop and Smith (2008) reveals that fewer women sit on the councils of Vancouver localities in which political parties exist, which may lead to the supposition that the parties pose obstacles to the election of women. Finally, examining women's participation on the councils of some 260 Quebec municipalities between 1984 and 1995, Gidengil and Vengroff (1997) conclude that there is no link between the presence of political parties and the proportion of female municipal councillors.[10]

A second institutional factor responsible for the under-representation of women in Canada's parliamentary spaces is the voting system. A number of studies come to the conclusion that first-past-the-post voting systems are

less favourable to the election of women than are proportional voting systems (among others, Matland 2005; Norris 2000, 2004; Rule 1994). Even
though a handful of Canadian municipalities used proportional voting procedures to elect their representatives during the twentieth century,[11] the
first-past-the-post voting system currently has a stranglehold on legislative
and municipal elections in Canada – a preponderance that few general
works on municipal politics in Canada call into question (Sancton and Young
2009; Tindal and Tindal 2008). Despite much deliberation about the municipal amalgamations that occurred in Canada since the 1990s, the literature
remains virtually silent, surprisingly so, concerning the appropriateness of
adopting proportional voting systems.

In any case, whereas the negative effects of the first-past-the-post voting
system on the election of women to the House of Commons and to legislative assemblies in Canada are well known (among others, MacIvor 2003;
Pilon 2007, 127-30; Studlar 1999; Tremblay 2010b; Young 1994), there is
little research on this issue for municipalities. In fact, it has generated a
few hypotheses, but these remain to be verified. Sampert (2008, 100), for
instance, maintains: "The two councillors per ward system in Edmonton
may be the reason that women hold a slightly higher percentage of seats on
city council in Edmonton compared to Calgary" (emphasis added). The
two-member constituency was used for the Prince Edward Island Legislative
Assembly up to the second half of the 1990s, and Crossley (1997) believes
that this may help to explain why that province's legislature had higher feminization rates than did other provincial and territorial legislative assemblies. Bird (2008, 151) posits: "The representation of ethnic minorities and
women *would arguably be* better served by a mixed member proportional
(MMP) system" (emphasis added). Evaluating the impact on women of municipal restructuring in London (UK) and Toronto, Bashevkin (2006, 28-50)
argues that the higher numerical representation of women reached in
London (about 40 percent) compared with Toronto (about 30 percent) results in part from the partial proportionality voting system used for electing
members of the Greater London Authority.

The opportunity for female and male politicians to run for re-election is
another factor that helps to explain the under-representation of women in
legislative politics in Canada. In fact, outgoing representatives have a number of assets that should help with their re-election – name recognition and
a dense network of contacts strengthened during the legislative career
among them – and these assets are not available to candidates who have
never been elected (Brodie 1985, 106-19; Young 1991). Their higher success

rates attest to the very clear advantage that outgoing representatives have in legislative elections (Tremblay 2009). Since incumbent candidates are mostly men, the incumbency factor also seems to exert a negative influence on the election of women in municipal politics, and it may be even stronger than in legislative politics due to the "longstanding power of incumbency" (Andrew et al. 2008, 263) on the municipal political scene and to the high turnover rates of politicians in the House of Commons and provincial and territorial legislatures (Matland and Studlar 2004; Moncrief 1998). In their study conducted in the 1990s on the Ontario municipal scene, Kushner, Siegel, and Stanwick (1997) show that incumbent candidates often had a clear advantage over non-incumbent candidates, particularly in large cities. Simard (2004) and Champagne (n.d.) make the same observation for Quebec, and Gidengil and Vengroff (1997, 533) write: "Put bluntly, the more men seek a second (or third) term, the fewer opportunities there are for women to gain even token representation." And since it is mainly men who are incumbent candidates, and considering the under-representation of women in local politics as both candidates and councillors, the advent of gender parity in municipal political institutions seems to be on the distant horizon.

Other factors suspected of playing a role in women's under-representation in municipal politics have emerged from several Canadian studies, including size of the locality (Gavan-Koop and Smith 2008; Gidengil and Vengroff 1997) and the number of candidates per seat (Kushner, Siegel, and Stanwick 1997). These two factors raise the question of whether the amalgamations of municipalities that occurred in recent years in Canada have had a negative impact on women's presence in municipal politics, as some posit (Tardy, Tremblay, and Legault 1997, 17-18). Once again, the answers given by different authors to this question are not unanimous. Bherer et al. (2008, 5) and Simard (2004) feel that amalgamations have not led to a drop in the presence of women in Quebec municipal politics, whereas Bird (2008) maintains the reverse for Hamilton. Both responses are no doubt correct as the feminization rate of municipal political institutions is the result of a political opportunity structure specific to each respective municipality.

In short, the path to city hall in no way resembles a long, tranquil river; rather, it resembles an obstacle course, similar to the paths towards the federal Parliament and the legislative assemblies of provinces and territories. Thus, the argument that municipal political institutions are more accessible to women than are their federal, provincial, and territorial counterparts is not at all convincing.

Conclusion: Prospects for Gender Parity

At the end of this brief reflection on women and municipal politics in Canada, the answer to the question of whether this decision-making elective body is more accessible to women than are provincial, territorial, and federal political institutions is not clear. The dearth of research on local politics in Canada in general, and on participation by women in municipal institutions in particular, no doubt contributes to this ambiguity. Given the obstacles strewn on the path towards city hall, as well as on the trajectory leading to parliamentary representation, one might answer no. In fact, there appear to be more material, normative, and institutional obstacles to women's election at the municipal level than previously assumed. Several of these obstacles are similar to those existing at the provincial, territorial, and federal levels, such as the difficult decision to take the leap into politics and the lack of encouragement in pursuing this ambition, the ambivalent position of political parties with regard to women's involvement in legislative and local politics, and the presumed negative effect of the first-past-the-post voting system on the election of women. Yet other barriers are unique to municipal politics, notably the lack of financial support from the state and political parties, the hypothesized adverse effect of incumbency, and the size of the locality and the number of candidates per electoral district. On the other hand, given the higher proportions of women in municipal politics than in legislative bodies one might answer yes – a response that must be mitigated in light of the lower proportion of women in a mayoral position compared to the proportion on municipal councils on the whole (16 percent versus 25 percent).[12]

In spite, or perhaps because, of the lack of knowledge on women's participation in municipal politics in Canada, many strategies have been designed and deployed – seemingly more than at the legislative level – to raise the feminization rate in local elective institutions. Some of these strategies come from the provincial level.[13] For example, in 1999 the government of Quebec instituted *À égalité pour décider,* "a financial assistance program that aims to increase the number of women in decision-making positions in local and regional bodies and to reduce the obstacles keeping women from participating fully in the exercise of power."[14] Some cities have also taken initiatives to attract women to local politics. For example, the Regional

Municipality of Waterloo and the City of Kitchener set up the Women's Municipal Campaign School.[15] The City of Ottawa joined with a series of women's groups to form the City for All Women Initiative, the general mission of which is "to strengthen the capacity of the full diversity of women and the City of Ottawa to work in partnership so as to create a more inclusive city and promote gender equality."[16] Finally, a myriad of women's groups are active in the field; for example, Equal Voice/À voix égales is active in several provinces.[17]

Numerous initiatives have been developed by different political actors, with various goals: to inform, demystify, and raise awareness; to provide initiation into politics, recruitment, and training; and to offer support during election campaigns. Nevertheless, without minimizing the relevance and range of this type of initiative, the micro-sociological, even individualistic, approach helps to feed the prejudice that if there are no women in politics it is because they do not have the resources to get themselves elected but that once they are trained they can win. In other words, not only are these initiatives endorsing the rules of the political game that are responsible, at least in part, for the under-representation of women in politics, but they are also strengthening them by advising women to adapt to them. Yet without a profound transformation of the rules of the political game, such as adoption of quotas to balance the candidacies of women and men and to equalize their chances of success, female/male parity is an objective as distant on the municipal scene as it is in the federal Parliament and within provincial and territorial legislatures.

Notes

1 Female landowners were able, however, to vote in legislative elections in Lower Canada from 1791 to 1849 (see Tremblay 2010a, 12-15).
2 See Intergovernmental Committee on Urban and Regional Research, "Municipal Elected Officials – Acclaimed vs Elected," Muniscope: An ICURR Service, available at http://www.muniscope.ca/.
3 See Inter-Parliamentary Union, "Women in National Parliaments," available at http://www.ipu.org/.
4 See, for instance, the results presented in the recent book edited by Andrew et al. (2008).
5 However, it should be mentioned that, while it seems that women are doing better overall at the municipal level than at the federal, provincial, and territorial levels, there is a similar "leadership gap" between the number of rank-and-file elected representatives and the number in the highest and most important positions.

6 See Inter-Parliamentary Union, "Women in Politics, Bibliographic Database," available at http://www.ipu.org/.

7 Siegel, Kushner, and Stanwick (2001) note, however, a substantial difference between women and men: the latter are more likely to have attended university, the former are more likely to have attended college.

8 In comparison, in Toronto Danforth, in the 2006 federal elections the spending limit was $76,419 and two candidates spent more than $74,000, while in the 2006 provincial by-election the Liberal candidate spent $154,000, the NDP candidate about $100,000, and the Progressive Conservative about $50,000. For the federal elections see Elections Canada, "Financial Reports: Candidate's Electoral Campaign Return," available at http://www.elections.ca/; for the provincial elections see Elections Ontario, "2006 Candidate By-Election Campaign Period Return," available at http://www2.elections.on.ca/.

9 It should be noted that more recent studies have shown that women were no longer running in no-chance ridings (Studlar and Matland 1996; Young 2006).

10 This observation may be open to question today as there are now twice as many municipal political parties in Quebec; Tardy (2002, 57) counted 97 in 1998, whereas the chief electoral officer of Quebec counted 193 for the 2009 election, 170 of which presented both female and male candidates.

11 Essentially the single transferable vote. See Pilon (1999, 2006, 2007, 79-82).

12 See Federation of Canadian Municipalities, "Municipal Statistics, Elected Officials Gender Statistics, 2011," available at http://www.fcm.ca/.

13 For examples of such strategies undertaken in Nova Scotia, see Carbert (2011); for Quebec, see Tremblay (2010a, 166-89).

14 See Québec, Secrétariat à la Condition féminine, "Programmes et prix," available at http://www.scf.gouv.qc.ca/.

15 See "Women's Municipal Campaign School," available at http://www.learnhowtorun.com/.

16 See "City for All Women Initiative," available at http://www.cawi-ivtf.org/.

17 See Equal Voice/À voix égales, available at http://www.equalvoice.ca/.

References

Andrew, Caroline. 1984. "Les femmes et la consommation collective: Les enjeux de l'engagement politique." *Politique: Revue de la Société québécoise de science politique* 5: 107-22.

–. 1991. "Le pouvoir local: Stratégie de pouvoir ou nouvelle impasse pour les femmes?" In Québec, ed., *L'égalité: Les moyens pour y arriver*, 63-75. Québec: Les Publications du Québec.

Andrew, Caroline, John Biles, Myer Siemiatycki, and Erin Tolley. 2008. "Conclusion." In Caroline Andrew, John Biles, Myer Siemiatycki, and Erin Tolley, eds., *Electing a Diverse Canada: The Representation of Immigrants, Minorities, and Women*, 255-69. Vancouver: UBC Press.

Bashevkin, Sylvia B. 1993. *Women and Party Politics in English-Canada*. 2nd ed. Toronto: Oxford University Press.

–. 2006. *Tales of Two Cities: Women and Municipal Restructuring in London and Toronto*. Vancouver: UBC Press.

Bauer, Gretchen, and Manon Tremblay, eds. 2011. *Women in Executive Power: A Global Overview*. London: Routledge.

Bherer, Laurence, and Jean-Pierre Collin et al. 2008. *La participation et la représentation politique des femmes au sein des instances démocratiques municipales.* Montréal: Institut national de la recherche scientifique, Centre – Urbanisation Culture Société, Groupe de recherche sur les innovations municipales (GRIM). Available at http://www.vrm.ca/.

Bird, Karen. 2008. "Many Faces, Few Places: The Political Under-Representation of Ethnic Minorities and Women in the City of Hamilton." In Caroline Andrew, John Biles, Myer Siemiatycki, and Erin Tolley, eds., *Electing a Diverse Canada: The Representation of Immigrants, Minorities, and Women*, 136-55. Vancouver: UBC Press.

Bloemraad, Irene. 2008. "Diversity and Elected Officials in the City of Vancouver." In Caroline Andrew, John Biles, Myer Siemiatycki, and Erin Tolley, eds., *Electing a Diverse Canada: The Representation of Immigrants, Minorities, and Women*, 46-69. Vancouver: UBC Press.

Bourgeois, Daniel, and Frank Strain. 2009. "New Brunswick." In Andrew Sancton and Robert Young, eds., *Foundations of Governance: Municipal Government in Canada's Provinces*, 186-222. Toronto: University of Toronto Press.

Briggs, Jacqui. 2000. "'What's in It for Women'? The Motivations, Expectations and Experiences of Female Local Councillors in Montreal, Canada and Hull, England." *Local Government Studies* 26(4): 71-84.

Brodie, Janine. 1977. "The Recruitment of Canadian Provincial Women Legislators, 1950-1975." *Atlantis* 2(2) (Part 1): 6-17.

–. 1985. *Women and Politics in Canada*. Toronto: McGraw-Hill Ryerson.

Brodie, Janine, with the assistance of Celia Chandler. 1991. "Women and the Electoral Process in Canada." In Kathy Megyery, ed., *Women in Canadian Politics: Toward Equity in Representation*. Research Studies, Royal Commission on Electoral Reform and Party Financing, vol. 6, 3-59. Toronto: Dundurn Press.

Brodie, M. Janine, and Jill Vickers. 1981. "The More Things Change ... Women in the 1979 Federal Campaign." In Howard R. Penniman, ed., *Canada at the Polls, 1979 and 1980: A Study of the General Elections*, 322-36. Washington, DC: American Enterprise Institute for Public Policy Research.

Canadian Women Voters Congress. 2004. *Women and Electoral Reform: Submission to VERC*. Appendix A. Available at http://womenvoters.ca/.

Carbert, Louise. 2011. "Making It Happen in Practice: Organized Efforts to Recruit Rural Women for Local Government Leadership." In Barbara Pini and Paula McDonald, eds., *Women and Representation in Local Government: International Case Studies*, 76-94. London: Routledge.

Champagne, Patrick. N.d. *Femmes et élections municipales 2009: Portrait statistique*. Québec: ministère des Affaires municipales, Régions et Occupation du territoire. Available at http://www.electionsmunicipales.gouv.qc.ca/.

Crossley, John. 1997. "Picture This: Women Politicians Hold Key Posts in Prince Edward Island." In Jane Arscott and Linda Trimble, eds., *In the Presence of*

Women: Representation in Canadian Governments, 278-307. Toronto: Harcourt Brace and Company.

Docherty, David C. 2005. *Legislatures*. Vancouver: UBC Press.

Federation of Canadian Municipalities. 2009. *FCM Municipal Statistics, Male-Female Gender Statistics*. Available at http://www.fcm.ca/.

Fox, Richard L., and Jennifer L. Lawless. 2010. "If Only They'd Ask: Gender, Recruitment, and Political Ambition." *Journal of Politics* 72(2): 310-26.

Franks, C.E.S. 1987. *The Parliament of Canada*. Toronto: University of Toronto Press.

Gavan-Koop, Denisa, and Patrick Smith. 2008. "Gendering Local Governing: Canadian and Comparative Lessons: The Case of Metropolitan Vancouver." *Canadian Political Science Review* 2(3): 152-71.

Gidengil, Elisabeth, and Richard Vengroff. 1997. "Representational Gains of Canadian Women or Token Growth? The Case of Quebec's Municipal Politics." *Canadian Journal of Political Science* 30(3): 513-37.

Hicks, Bruce M. 2006. *Are Marginalized Communities Disenfranchised? Voter Turnout and Representation in Post-merger Toronto*. IRPP Working Paper Series 2006-03.

Hunter, Alfred A., and Margaret A. Denton. 1984. "Do Female Candidates 'Lose Votes'? The Experience of Female Candidates in the 1979 and 1980 Canadian General Elections." *Canadian Review of Sociology and Anthropology* 21(4): 395-406.

Kopinak, Kathryn. 1985. "Women in Canadian Municipal Politics: Two Steps Forward, One Step Back." *Canadian Review of Sociology and Anthropology* 22(3): 372-89.

Kushner, Joseph, and David Siegel. 2003. "Effect of Municipal Amalgamation in Ontario on Political Representation and Accessibility." *Canadian Journal of Political Science* 36(5): 1035-51.

Kushner, Joseph, David Siegel, and Hannah Stanwick. 1997. "Ontario Municipal Elections: Voting Trends and Determinants of Electoral Success in a Canadian Province." *Canadian Journal of Political Science* 30(3): 539-53.

MacDermid Robert. 2009. *Funding City Politics: Municipal Campaign Funding and Property Development in the Greater Toronto Area*. Toronto: CJS Foundation for Research and Education. Available at http://www.scribd.com/.

MacIvor, Heather. 1996. *Women and Politics in Canada*. Peterborough: Broadview Press.

–. 2003. "Women and the Canadian Electoral System." In Manon Tremblay and Linda Trimble, eds., *Women and Electoral Politics in Canada*, 22-36. Don Mills: Oxford University Press.

Maillé, Chantal. 1997. "Gender Concerns in City Life." In Timothy L. Thomas, ed., *The Politics of the City: A Canadian Perspective*, 103-13. Toronto: Nelson.

Matland, Richard E. 2005. "Enhancing Women's Political Participation: Legislative Recruitment and Electoral Systems." In Julie Ballington and Azza Karam, eds., *Women in Parliament: Beyond Numbers*. Rev. ed., 93-111. Stockholm: International IDEA.

Matland, Richard E., and Donley T. Studlar. 2004. "Determinants of Legislative Turnover: A Cross-National Analysis." *British Journal of Political Science* 34(1): 87-108.

Moncrief, Gary F. 1998. "Terminating the Provincial Career: Retirement and Electoral Defeat in Canadian Provincial Legislatures, 1960-1997." *Canadian Journal of Political Science* 31(2): 359-72.

Niven, David. 2006. "Throwing Your Hat Out of the Ring: Negative Recruitment and the Gender Imbalance in State Legislative Candidacy." *Politics and Gender* 2(4): 473-89.

Norris, Pippa. 2000. "Women's Representation and Electoral Systems." In Richard Rose, ed., *The International Encyclopedia of Elections*, 348-51. Washington, DC: CQ Press.

–. 2004. *Electoral Engineering: Voting Rules and Political Behavior*. Cambridge: Cambridge University Press.

Oakes, Judith McKenzie. 1994. "The Honourable Members: Parliamentary Careers in Canada, 1958-1993." PhD diss., University of Toronto.

Pilon, Dennis. 1999. "The History of Voting System Reform in Canada." In Henry Milner, ed., *Making Every Vote Count: Reassessing Canada's Electoral System*, 111-21. Peterborough: Broadview Press.

–. 2006. "Explaining Voting System Reform in Canada: 1874 to 1960." *Journal of Canadian Studies* 40(3): 135-61.

–. 2007. *The Politics of Voting: Reforming Canada's Electoral System*. Toronto: Emond Montgomery Publications.

Rule, Wilma. 1994. "Parliaments of, by, and for the People: Except for Women?" In Wilma Rule and Joseph F. Zimmerman, eds., *Electoral Systems in Comparative Perspective: Their Impact on Women and Minorities*, 15-30. Westport: Greenwood Press.

Sampert, Shannon. 2008. "More than Just Cowboys with White Hats: A Demographic Profile of Edmonton and Calgary." In Caroline Andrew, John Biles, Myer Siemiatycki, and Erin Tolley, eds., *Electing a Diverse Canada: The Representation of Immigrants, Minorities, and Women*, 92-110. Vancouver: UBC Press.

Sancton, Andrew, and Robert Young. 2009. *Foundations of Governance: Municipal Government in Canada's Provinces*. Toronto: University of Toronto Press.

Siegel, David, Joseph Kushner, and Hannah Stanwick. 2001. "Canadian Mayors: A Profile and Determinants of Electoral Success." *Canadian Journal of Urban Research* 10(1): 5-23.

Simard, Carolle. 2004. "Qui nous gouverne au municipal: Reproduction ou renouvellement?" *Politique et Sociétés* 23(2-3): 135-58.

Studlar, Donley T. 1999. "Will Canada Seriously Consider Electoral System Reform? Women and Aboriginals Should." In Henry Milner, ed., *Making Every Vote Count. Reassessing Canada's Electoral System*, 123-32. Peterborough: Broadview Press.

Studlar, Donley T., Dianne L. Alexander, Joanna E. Cohen, Mary Jane Ashley, Roberta G. Ferrence, and John S. Pollard. 2000. "A Social and Political Profile of Canadian Legislators, 1996." *Journal of Legislative Studies* 6(2): 93-103.

Studlar, Donley T., and Richard E. Matland. 1996. "The Dynamics of Women's Representation in the Canadian Provinces: 1975-1994." *Canadian Journal of Political Science* 29(2): 269-93.

Tardy, Évelyne. 2002. *Les femmes et les conseils municipaux du Québec*. Montréal: Hurtubise.

Tardy, Évelyne, Manon Tremblay, and Ginette Legault. 1997. *Maires et mairesses: Les femmes et la politique municipale.* Montréal: Liber.

Tindal, Robert Charles, and Susan Nobes Tindal. 2008. *Local Government in Canada.* 7th ed. Toronto: Nelson.

Tremblay, Manon. 2005. "Canada." In Yvonne Galligan and Manon Tremblay, eds., *Sharing Power: Women, Parliament, Democracy,* 139-57. Aldershot: Ashgate.

–. 2008. *100 questions sur les femmes et la politique.* Montréal: Remue-ménage.

–. 2009. "Women in the Quebec National Assembly: Why So Many?" In Sylvia B. Bashevkin, ed., *Opening Doors Wider: Women's Political Engagement in Canada,* 51-69. Vancouver: UBC Press.

–. 2010a. *Quebec Women and Legislative Representation.* Translated by Kathe Röth. Vancouver: UBC Press.

–. 2010b. "Bilan des réformes électorales au Canada: Quelle place pour les femmes?" *Canadian Journal of Political Science* 43(1): 25-47.

Trimble, Linda. 1995. "Politics Where We Live: Women and Cities." In James Lightbody, ed., *Canadian Metropolitics: Governing Our Cities,* 92-114. Toronto: Copp Clark.

Vickers, Jill. 1978. "Where Are the Women in Canadian Politics?" *Atlantis* 3(2) (Part 2): 40-51.

Vickers, Jill McCalla, and M. Janine Brodie. 1981. "Canada." In Joni Lovenduski and Jill Hills, eds., *The Politics of the Second Electorate: Women and Public Participation,* 52-79. London: Routledge and Kegan Paul.

Young, Lisa. 1991. "Legislative Turnover and the Election of Women to the Canadian House of Commons." In Kathy Megyery, ed., *Women in Canadian Politics: Toward Equity in Representation.* Research Studies, Royal Commission on Electoral Reform and Party Financing, vol. 6, 81-100. Toronto: Dundurn Press.

–. 1994. *Electoral Systems and Representative Legislatures: Consideration of Alternative Electoral Systems.* Ottawa: Canadian Advisory Council on the Status of Women. Available at http://www.law-lib.utoronto.ca/.

–. 2006. "Women's Representation in the Canadian House of Commons." In Marian Sawer, Manon Tremblay, and Linda Trimble, eds., *Representing Women in Parliament: A Comparative Study,* 47-66. London: Routledge.

–. 2008. "Political Finance in City Elections: Toronto and Calgary Compared." *Canadian Political Science Review* 2(3): 88-102.

2

The Alberta Advantage?

Women in Alberta Politics

BRENDA O'NEILL

In many ways Alberta presents a number of contradictions. After all, the province boasts a number of political firsts for women. Alberta's was the first among the Canadian provincial legislatures and the House of Commons to elect women in 1917. The Famous Five, who successfully fought for and won the right of women's recognition as persons, allowing them to sit in the Senate, hailed from Alberta. One of these women, Emily Murphy, went on to become the first woman magistrate in Canada and the British Empire. However, women's more recent political achievements in the province are more difficult to identify. Notwithstanding the results of the April 2012 election, the province has had relatively few women party leaders and a poor record of electing women to the legislature when compared to the other provinces. The "Alberta Advantage," it seems, does not apply to all things.[1]

The most recent election might be seen as an indication that women's political representation in the province is, however, improving. For one thing, the election resulted in the province's first woman premier, Alison Redford, leader of the Progressive Conservative Party (PCP). A woman, Danielle Smith of the Wildrose Party, also leads the Official Opposition, making Alberta the first province to have women sitting in these top two positions. Moreover, the election resulted in a slight increase in the percentage of women candidates and MLAs. These are important milestones, to be sure. History shows, however, that progress in one election can be followed

POLITICAL REPRESENTATION OF WOMEN IN
ALBERTA

FIRSTS

Right to vote and stand for election

▪ Most women win right to vote and stand for election	1916
▪ Aboriginal women win right to vote	1965

Contesting office

▪ First women to contest office: Louise McKinney (Non-Partisan League) and Roberta MacAdams (Soldiers' Representative)	1917
▪ First women to win office: Louise McKinney and Roberta MacAdams	1917-21
▪ First Aboriginal woman to win office: Pearl Calahasen (PC)	1989 to present
▪ First visible minority to win office: Theresa Woo-Paw (PC) (Chinese)	2008 to present
▪ First woman appointed to cabinet: Irene Parlby (UFA government), minister without portfolio	1921-35
▪ First woman premier: Alison Redford (PC)	2011 to present

CURRENT REPRESENTATION AT A GLANCE

		Women elected	
	Date of election	Number	Percent
Women in legislature	2012/04/23	23 of 87	26
Women in cabinet	2012/04/23	4 of 19	21

Women political party leaders
- ▪ Alison Redford (PC), 2011 to present
- ▪ Danielle Smith (Wildrose Alliance Party), 2009 to present

Lieutenant governor
- ▪ None at present

Advisory council on the status of women
- ▪ The Advisory Council on Women's Issues was created in 1986 and disbanded in 1996.
- ▪ The council was created by the Getty Conservatives after fourteen years of lobbying by women's groups. It had fourteen board members from across the province, appointed by cabinet, and it reported to the minister responsible for the status of women. The council was mandated as an advisory body and was not empowered to conduct research. A sunset clause in the council's enabling legislation led to its disbandment in 1996.
- ▪ At the present time, David Hancock, minister of human services, is responsible for women's issues.

by a setback in the next, and, this being the case, gains cannot be taken for granted.

Key to understanding the trends in women's representation in the province are the strength of the Progressive Conservative Party in a one-party dominant system, the province's cultural and political ethos, and the limited influence of feminists on official politics in the province. This chapter examines women's political representation in Alberta and provides explanations for existing trends. It begins with a review of the province's political, social, and cultural environments.

Background

An understanding of Alberta must begin with an understanding of its political and cultural ethos. Alberta sits at the conservative end of the political spectrum in Canada; its economic roots, historical immigration patterns from the United States, and periodic economic booms have combined with the "cowboy" mythology to create a cultural and political milieu geared less towards supporting the less well off in society and more towards rewarding those who are capable of pulling themselves up by their boot straps and "gettin' her done." According to Wesley (2011, see Chapter 3), Alberta's political ethos consists of three key values: first, a laissez-faire brand of frontier liberalism – individualism; second, a populist impulse; and third, a "synthetic form of anti-colonialism vis-à-vis central Canada," which he labels provincial autonomy. These cultural and political underpinnings have translated into strong electoral support for parties on the right at both the provincial and federal levels, unlike anywhere else in the country. In the 2011 general election, for example, 66.8 percent of voters in the province gave their support to the Conservative Party of Canada, resulting in its taking twenty-seven of the province's twenty-eight seats (Elections Canada 2011). And in 2012, 34 percent of voters supported the Wildrose Party in the provincial election, one further to the right on the ideological spectrum than any other in Canada.

The province has a long history of one-party dominance. Since 1971, the dominant party has been the Progressive Conservatives. In recent political history, Premier Ralph Klein's approach to governing provides an important window into Alberta politics. In office from 1992 to 2006, "Klein had a populist, 'tough love' approach to governing that stressed individual responsibility, collective solidarity, and provincial autonomy as the best means of reviving Alberta's economy and society" (Wesley 2011, 100). Moreover, his government believed that governments should be kept in check and "get out of the way and let people do what they do best" (106). This strong belief in individualism combined with support for a limited state has meant the virtual absence in Alberta governments of discussions surrounding women's issues, the status of women, or women's political representation. Although the election of Ed Stelmach and, most recently, Alison Redford to lead PC governments has strengthened the progressive element of the party, it remains solidly right of centre, especially on fiscal matters.

A strand of social conservatism also exists in the province, reflected in part in the importance assigned to the family. In its statement of principles, for example, the Progressive Conservative Party emphasizes: "The family is paramount in the development of social responsibility and a sense of self-worth. The family, as defined by its individual members, is of vital importance to our communities" (PC Alberta 2011). Indeed, in 1990 Premier Getty established the Premier's Council in Support of Alberta Families and declared that its objective was "to strengthen the family, to provide reasons why the family is stronger, why mothers will stay in the house, in the family while not having care outside of the house" (quoted in Harder 2003, 5). This focus on the family combines with strong Christian evangelicalism and a Christian fundamentalism that fits in with the province's individualist ethos (Wiseman 2007, 255).

This cultural and political ethos has meant little fertile ground for attention to women's issues and programs designed to assist women. According to Harder (2003, 159): "Since the early 1970s, pay- and employment-equity programs, increases to the minimum wage, and the establishment of training programs for women on social assistance have been almost uniformly rejected by the Alberta government. This rejection has been made on the basis that individuals have responsibility for their own well-being and that the opportunities exist for women to realize equality within the labour market." Indeed, while the Advisory Council on Women's Issues was created in 1986 after pressure from women in the province, the way in which it was instituted ensured its inability to effect real change for women in province. It was disbanded ten years later.

Some statistics can help to illuminate the status of Alberta's women relative to women in the rest of the country. Alberta is by all measures one of Canada's "have provinces," leading the provinces in real economic growth and fiscal performance over the past twenty years (Alberta Finance and Enterprise 2011; Hale 2006, 394) and possessing a very low tax structure (including no provincial sales tax) (Hale 2006, 378). Such wealth belies, however, some relatively poor rankings across the provinces on a number of measures of particular importance for women.

According to Statistics Canada, for example, both women and men in the province earn higher average total incomes, men at $61,700 and women at $34,000, than do women and men in any of the remaining provinces (Statistics Canada 2010c, 7). The gender gap in earnings – $27,700 – is, however, larger than that found in any other province. Women in Alberta earn only fifty-five cents for every dollar earned by men.

Similarly, spending on childcare in the province pales in comparison with that of the other provinces and territories. In 2007-08, the province spent $195 per child aged between 0 and 12 years on regulated child care, in last place among the provinces and territories (Beach et al. 2009, 207). By comparison, Quebec ranked at the top of the list, with spending at $1,694 per child; it remains, however, an outlier on this score. Instead, compare Alberta with Nunavut, which ranks just above Alberta, with spending at $272 per child; and New Brunswick, at eleventh overall, with spending at $274 per child. A relatively strong economy need not always translate into a strong and comprehensive set of social welfare programs, particularly for women, especially when the status of women and gender equality are concepts absent from the dominant political discourse.

The relative absence of gender from political discourse, a limited political opportunity structure within the state given the long-standing ideological orientation of the government, and a state that has at times been openly "hostile to feminist demands" (Rankin and Vickers 2001, 9), have provided very little opportunity for feminists in the province to effectively influence official politics and policy. When such a climate is combined with a government funding framework that has not only significantly reduced the funding offered to women's groups in recent years but also made this funding contingent on the absence of any advocacy work, the relative weakness of women's organizations in the province vis-à-vis the state machinery is understandable. Moreover, as Collier (1995) shows, minority women's advocacy can be particularly ineffective under such conditions (see also Rankin 1996). As the province with the third highest proportion of visible minorities in the country, at 13.9 percent of the population (Statistics Canada 2010b), and the third highest proportion of Aboriginals, at 5.8 percent (Statistics Canada, 2010a), the impact of impenetrable and unresponsive state structures is acutely felt by a significant number of women in Alberta, especially the most marginalized.

Women's Political Representation: The Numbers

On the whole, women's political representation in Alberta is relatively poor on a number of different measures when compared to the remaining provinces or the federal level of government. A look at the data suggests that, overall, the number of female legislators, candidates, cabinet ministers, party leaders, and lieutenant governors provides little in the way of evidence to suggest that women have reached anything close to parity in the political arena.

Women's political representation in the Alberta legislature has grown significantly since most women earned the right to vote in 1916, but the largest consistent gains have been limited to the 1980s and 1990s. From 1917 to 1975, women never held more than 6 percent of the seats in the legislature, and there were never more than one or two women sitting among the men in the chamber. Increases in representation for women began in 1979; the overall level of representation increased from 3 to 8 percent – a five percentage point jump. This level of representation was then repeated in the next election in 1982. Consistent increases over the next four elections resulted in a high-water mark once the ballots were counted in the 1997 election: at that time, one in four members sitting in the Alberta legislature was a woman. One could not be faulted if one had concluded at the time that such increases were likely to continue and that parity might eventually be reached.

We now see, however, that the steady increases were short lived. The high-water mark for representation achieved in 1997 has yet to be repeated. Drops of five and then four percentage points over the next two elections brought the level of representation back down to 16 percent – roughly equivalent to its level in 1989 – following the 2004 election. A small increase in the number of women elected in the 2008 election and then another in the 2012 election have meant that women's legislative representation in the province currently stands at 26 percent. One in four members of the chamber is a woman, a level above the worldwide average of 19.9 percent for national lower houses (Inter-Parliamentary Union 2012) and fifth overall among the provinces. Pipeline arguments that women's levels of representation will continue to increase as women gain advanced education and enter the workforce – often used as an argument against the adoption of formal measures to increase their number – are less convincing given back to back decreases in 2001 and 2004 in women's level of legislative representation (Lawless and Fox 2005, 26). Such decreases may well be repeated.

TABLE 2.1

Women in the Alberta legislature, by election

Election date	Party elected	Total number of legislators	Women elected Number	%
1917/06/07	Liberal	56	2	4
1921/07/18	United Farmers	61	2	3
1926/06/08	United Farmers	61	1	2
1930/06/19	United Farmers	63	1	2
1935/08/22	Social Credit	63	2	3
1940/03/21	Social Credit	57	1	2
1944/08/08	Social Credit	57	3	5
1948/08/17	Social Credit	57	2	4
1952/08/05	Social Credit	60	2	3
1955/06/29	Social Credit	61	2	3
1959/06/18	Social Credit	65	4	6
1963/06/17	Social Credit	63	2	3
1967/05/23	Social Credit	65	1	2
1971/08/30	PC	75	2	3
1975/03/26	PC	75	2	3
1979/03/14	PC	79	6	8
1982/11/02	PC	79	6	8
1986/05/08	PC	83	10	12
1989/03/20	PC	83	13	16
1993/06/15	PC	83	16	19
1997/03/11	PC	83	22	27
2001/03/12	PC	83	17	21
2004/11/22	PC	83	13	16
2008/03/03	PC	83	17	21
2012/04/23	PC	87	23	26

Note: Conducting research on women's political representation in Alberta is tremendously frustrating, especially for candidate nominations. The long list of sources included in the tables reflects the fact that there is no policy at Elections Alberta of collecting data on election candidates beyond name, riding, and political party. As a result, information on the gender of candidates has to be identified from a number of various sources, depending on the date of each election, including academic treatments, media coverage, the Canadian Parliamentary Guide, political party websites (although they rarely keep information beyond the most recent election), individual MLA websites, and political parties themselves.

Sources: Palamarek (1989); *Canadian Parliamentary Guide* (1993-2001); Trimble and Arscott (2005); CBCnews (n.d.); Elections Alberta (2008); Equal Voice (2012b); and individual party and MLA websites.

Parties play a key role in determining the number of women who make it into legislatures; their willingness to approach women to contest elections and their commitment to gender balance have been argued to be a key factor in increasing women's political numbers (Caul 1999; Lawless and Fox

TABLE 2.2
Women candidates in Alberta, by party and election

Election date	PC		Liberal		NDP		Alberta Alliance/ Wildrose Alliance	
	Number	%	Number	%	Number	%	Number	%
1982/11/02	6 of 79	8	4 of 29	14	15 of 79	19	–	
1986/05/08	10 of 83	12	10 of 63	16	18 of 83	22	–	
1989/03/20	12 of 83	15	16 of 83	19	19 of 83	23	–	
1993/06/15	17 of 83	21	21 of 83	25	29 of 83	35	–	
1997/03/11	20 of 83	25	27 of 83	33	29 of 77	38	–	
2001/03/12	16 of 83	19	19 of 83	23	27 of 83	33	–	
2004/11/22	12 of 83	15	19 of 82	23	26 of 83	31	14 of 83	17
2008/03/03	17 of 83	21	23 of 82	28	33 of 83	40	8 of 61	13
2012/04/23	22 of 87	25	20 of 87	23	41 of 87	47	11 of 87	13

Sources: Palamarek (1989); *Canadian Parliamentary Guide* (1993-2001); Trimble and Arscott (2005); CBCnews (n.d.); Elections Alberta (2008); Equal Voice (2012a); and individual party and MLA websites.

2005, chap. 5). To evaluate how the number of women nominated to run in Alberta elections varies with political party, Table 2.2 provides information on the number of candidates nominated in each election since 1982 broken down by political party (note that the table only includes political parties that have successfully elected members to the legislature).

The first conclusion to be drawn from the data is that not all political parties have been equally successful at placing women as candidates in elections. Following trends that have been found elsewhere, political parties on the ideological right in the province tend to nominate fewer women than do political parties found on the left (Black and Erickson 2000; Caul 1999; Young 2000). More specifically, the Progressive Conservatives, and more recently the Alberta Alliance and the Wildrose parties, have been less successful than have the New Democrats and the Liberals, with the exception of the 2012 election, at nominating women to contest elections. Research suggests that women tend to fare better overall in parties that are less successful at the ballot box (O'Neill and Stewart 2009).

Without a doubt, the winner in this contest is the New Democratic Party. In every election since 1993, its share of women candidates has exceeded 30 percent. And in every election since 1982, its share of women candidates has exceeded that recorded for each of the remaining major parties, and often by a significant margin. In the most recent provincial election, for example, the party's percentage of women candidates – 47 percent – was twenty-two percentage points higher than that of the Progressive Conservatives (25 percent) and a full thirty-four percentage points higher than that recorded for the Wildrose Party (13 percent). The explanation for the party's record reflects its commitment to gender equality more generally. The NDP has adopted voluntary quotas that set a target of having women constitute half of all nominees in elections, as many as possible of them in winnable ridings. Although difficult to meet given the decentralized nature of candidate selection in the single-member plurality system, the commitment can nevertheless be identified as an explanation for the party's success on this score. The Alberta New Democrats additionally have a dedicated fund – the Olga Blondheim Fund – whose function is to help women defray the costs associated with standing for election in the province (Alberta NDP n.d.).

Ideologically to the right of the Alberta New Democrats, the Alberta Liberal Party has historically been second in its success in nominating women as candidates in Alberta elections. Although committed to working towards the equal representation of women and men in the Alberta legislature (Alberta Liberal Party 2011), it has had less success than the NDP in translating this commitment into concrete results. Only once in the last eight elections has the party nominated women in more than 30 percent of contested constituencies, and that was in 1997. In the last three provincial elections the party's percentage of women candidates has averaged approximately one in four.

Of the three main parties that have consistently contested elections since the 1980s, the Progressive Conservative Party has almost always trailed in terms of the percentages of women that have made up its lists of candidates. In relatively few elections in the period has the percentage of women on its candidate list exceeded 20 percent, and never has it gone beyond 25 percent. Very recently, in 2004, its share of women candidates was a dismal 15 percent, but in the 2012 election the percentage of women candidates once again reached a high of 25 percent, matching that reached in 1997. Given its ideological stance on the centre-right of the ideological spectrum, the party does not endorse policies or programs designed to alleviate systemic barriers to women's political access (PC Alberta 2011).

Recent additions to the political party roster in the province have had a detrimental effect on women's representation at the level of candidate nominations, due largely to the fact that the two political parties are both situated to the right of other political parties in the province. The first, the Alberta

Alliance, contested the 2004 election and fielded candidates in each of Alberta's eighty-three ridings. However, relatively few, only 17 percent, of these candidates were women. The party experienced a disappointing finish overall, electing only a single member to the legislature. Soon thereafter the party merged with the Wildrose Party to form the Wildrose Alliance Party of Alberta, which simplified its name to the Wildrose Party in 2011. As the most conservative party in the province, its platform is libertarian and socially conservative. The new party managed to field candidates in sixty-one of the province's ridings, but only eight of them were women (13 percent). The party failed to elect any members, but subsequent floor crossings and a successful by-election in 2009 swelled its numbers in the legislature to four, one of whom was a woman (Heather Forsyth – Calgary-Fish Creek). In the 2012 election, the Wildrose Party rose to become a serious contender for power, in the end winning seventeen seats and Official Opposition status. Women, however, made up only 13 percent of its eighty-seven candidates.

The second general conclusion to draw from the table is the absence of a trend over time in the percentage of women candidates within each party over the period. Similar to arguments about the number of women elected to the legislature, arguments that women's level of representation among candidates will naturally and continually rise to match that of men are without merit. While there have been periods of growth, these have been followed by periods of sometimes significant decline.

Women's representation in the province can also be evaluated by looking at leadership positions within the parties in the province. Until recently, however, the record was less than stellar and seems to a certain extent to reflect the "revolving door" metaphor coined by Trimble and Arscott (1993, 71). Only four women have led major political parties in the province and only one has yet to turn that position into leading the Alberta government (see Table 1.3). One of the earliest was Betty Paschen (not shown), who led the Green Party of Alberta from 1990 to 1995; the party, however, never won a seat in the provincial legislature.

The first woman to lead a major party in the province was Pam Barrett. Elected to lead the Alberta New Democrats on a single ballot following the resignation of Ross Harvey, she held the position from 1996 until 2000. Barrett was first elected in 1986 in the Edmonton-Highlands riding by somewhat surprisingly defeating a sitting cabinet member, Dave King, for the seat. She was re-elected in 1989, and during her tenure in the legislature was the first woman in the province to hold the position of deputy house leader (Palamarek 1989, 131). She unexpectedly withdrew from politics in

TABLE 2.3
Women party leaders in Alberta

Name	Political party	Period of service
Pam Barrett	NDP	1996-2000
Nancy MacBeth	Liberal	1998-2001
Danielle Smith	Wildrose Alliance	2009 to present
Alison Redford	PC	2011 to present

1993 but returned a few years later to lead the NDP into the 1997 election. Under her leadership the party regained seats in the legislature, going from none to two, despite a small drop in its overall vote share. One of those seats was her own – in the riding of Edmonton-Highlands. Somewhat surprisingly, and unlike the trend for many female party leaders, Barrett resigned as MLA and as leader in 2000 (Goyette 2000).

The second woman to have led a major party in the province is Nancy MacBeth (formerly Betkowski), elected leader of the Liberal Party of Alberta in 1998, a position that she held until 2001. MacBeth's political trajectory is also an unusual one as she began her career with the Progressive Conservatives but ended it with the Liberals. First elected as a Progressive Conservative in the province in 1986, and then again in 1989, she served as a minister in Don Getty's governments. In 1992, she ran for the leadership of the Progressive Conservative Party, eventually losing to Ralph Klein despite her lead on the first ballot (Stewart and Archer 2000, 25). MacBeth subsequently retired from politics but returned in 1998 to contest the leadership of the Alberta Liberals. The move is considered less surprising given her ideological position as a Red Tory. After winning the leadership on the first ballot, she easily won a seat in the legislature in a 1998 by-election in the riding of Edmonton-McClung. A poor showing for the party in the 2001 general election, including her failure to win her own seat, however, resulted in her resignation as leader of the party.

Recent events in provincial politics suggest that the revolving-door metaphor may have less resonance. Described as "the showdown between two Alberta women" (Bashevkin 2012, n.p.), the two strongest parties in the 2012 election were led by women. Danielle Smith was elected leader of the Wildrose Party in 2009 at the age of thirty-eight and currently sits as leader of the Opposition. Her background is varied, including an internship with the Fraser Institute, trustee with the Calgary Board of Education, journalist, and director of provincial affairs for Alberta with the Canadian Federation of Independent Business (Sharpe 2012). The party's significant rise in the polls during the 2012 campaign was strong enough to have many pollsters predicting a Wildrose win (see Wingrove 2012). Although less successful than many predicted, the party's meteoric rise under Smith's leadership is unlikely to lead to calls for her resignation in the short term.

Newly elected premier Alison Redford won the leadership of the Progressive Conservative Party in the fall of 2011 following Ed Stelmach's decision to step down, and then she led her party to win a majority government in the spring 2012 election. Trained as a lawyer, Redford was first elected to the provincial legislature in 2008 and then immediately appointed minister of justice and attorney general, a position she held until she resigned to run for the party leadership. This limited time in government led many to characterize her as an underdog, her run as a long shot, and her subsequent win as a surprise victory (Flanagan 2011; Hirsch 2011). However, an effective campaign that styled Redford as the candidate for change and that appealed directly to public-sector unions, as well as a strong performance in the final leadership debate, allowed her to take the lead on the second ballot.[2]

It is still too early to identify how well women are likely to fare under her leadership. Despite her being characterized as a "feminist human-rights lawyer," her first cabinet included only two other women, a mere 14 percent of all cabinet members, and a step back for women's representation in the province. As discussed below, her 2012 cabinet does not suggest that the political representation of women is a high priority. Moreover, responsibility for women's issues has been handed over to a male member of cabinet, David Hancock, minister of human services. The threat from the Wildrose Party on the right of the political spectrum is unlikely to provide much room for Redford to flex her Red Tory muscles.

An additional measure of women's levels of representation involves considering their numbers in government cabinets. Table 1.4 provides an overview of the share of women in every post-election cabinet in the province since 1982. The share of women nominated to cabinet has closely mirrored the overall share of women in the legislature since 1982 (the latter are found in Table 1.1); the exceptions are 2004 and 2008, when the percentage of women in cabinet exceeded the percentage of women in the legislature by five and nine percentage points respectively, and 2012, when their percentage in cabinet was five points below that in the legislature. Prior to 2012, one might have suggested a trend towards women's increased cabinet representation, a possibility supported by a comparison of the percentage of

TABLE 2.4
Women in cabinet in Alberta, by election

Election date	Party elected	Total number of cabinet ministers*	Women appointed to cabinet		% of women in in governing caucus in cabinet
			Number	%	
1982/11/02	PC	30	2	7	33
1986/05/08	PC	25	4	16	80
1989/03/20	PC	26	4	15	50
1993/06/15	PC	17	3	18	18
1997/03/11	PC	19	4	21	20
2001/03/12	PC	24	5	21	31
2004/11/22	PC	24	5	21	42
2008/03/03	PC	24	7	29	41
2012/04/23	PC	19	4	21	22

* Includes the premier.

TABLE 2.5
Female representatives of the Crown in Alberta

Name	Period of service
W. Helen Hunley	1985-91
Lois E. Hole	2000-5

Source: Legislative Assembly of Alberta (n.d.[a] and n.d.[b]).

women nominated to run by the PCP between 1982 and 2008 and those sitting in cabinet. In 2004 and 2008, for example, the percentage of women in cabinet exceeded that among the party's candidates by six and nine percentage points. Premier Redford's selection of relatively few women, despite a significant number of women from which to choose, puts an end to the trend of women's increasing cabinet representation.

The lieutenant governor serves an important constitutional as well as symbolic role in the province, and Alberta has had two women serve as representatives of the Crown. The first woman to hold the position was the Honourable W. Helen Hunley, who served from 1985 until 1991 (Palamarek 1989, 108-10). The second woman lieutenant governor, the Honourable Lois E. Hole, served in the position from 2000 to 2005.

Explanations

The level of women's representation in Alberta cannot be understood without reference to the dominance of the Progressive Conservative Party for more than forty years. Alberta stands apart from other provinces in having a one-party dominant system, which it has had for much of its history (Stewart and Carty 2006). As shown in Table 1.1, the PCP has formed the government after every election since 1971. More than this, however, it has earned a significant share of the votes in each election, averaging around 50 percent for the period, which in a single-member plurality system translates into clear dominance over the remaining parties in the system (101). This fact is important for explaining women's representation in the province because the PCP has not focused its attention on women's representation (Sampert 2008) and, with the exception of the 2012 election, has one of the poorest records of dominant political parties in the province for nominating women to run in general elections (see Table 1.2).

The combination of the PCP's nominating few women to stand in general elections and its electoral dominance in a single-member plurality system results in a poorer electoral showing for women in the province than might otherwise be the case. Parties on the left are more likely to push for increasing the numbers of women in their ranks at every level; when these parties are successful, women's numbers can increase among elected legislators and leaders (Caul 1999; O'Neill and Stewart 2009). Success for parties on the left can also provide a contagion effect, resulting in pressure on parties on the right to attend to such issues as women's level of representation in the legislature (Matland and Studlar 1996). The lack of such a strong opposition from the left in the province, however, diminishes the likelihood of such an outcome. The rise of the Wildrose Party, on the right of the ideological spectrum, leaves little hope for an increase in women's political representation, given its lack of concern for the issue itself and its poor record to date.

Success can result, however, when a key political actor champions women's representation or when the nomination of women to ridings occurs strategically. The high-water mark for women's representation in the province in 1997 has been argued to stem in part from Liberal leader Grant Mitchell's focused and largely successful efforts to increase the number of women nominated by the party to run in the election: the number of women running under the Liberal banner increased by six from the previous election to a high of twenty-seven. Additionally, it has been argued that the willingness of the Klein Conservatives to recruit women to run in safe seats in that same election helps to explain women's representational gains (Trimble and Arscott 2005, 29). The significant number of women elected under the Progressive Conservative Party banner in 2012, eighteen of twenty-two female candidates overall, defies a simple explanation, particularly in light of the closely contested nature of the election. Safe seats were few in number. The degree to which Alison Redford may have championed women's nominations across the province remains unclear.

Importantly, then, the combination of a one-party dominant system and a centre-right dominant party hinders but does not eliminate the possibility of representational gains. In her review of gender in the province in the 1980s, for example, Trimble (1992) suggests that gender came onto the agenda in Alberta at that time for three reasons: a shift in federal-provincial relations, the apparent end of one-party dominance, and an increased number of women politicians and elites committed to gender equality. While federal-provincial relations remain relatively calm, the continuing dominance of the PCP and the lack of gender champions might help to explain the current lack of attention devoted to women and, in particular, to women's representation in the province.

The shift away from seeing the federal government as the enemy in the 1980s led the provincial government to regard the feminist movement as a legitimate voice; unfortunately, this happened at the same time that the feminist movement in the province was turning away from the state and becoming increasingly fragmented (Harder 2003, 155). This, combined with the Klein government's targeting of feminist groups as "special interests" opposed to the will of the people (Smith 2001, 300), has meant that such groups have been less than successful in advancing women's representational interests. Recent funding cuts and restrictions on advocacy work have further limited the ability of women's groups in the province to effectively voice their interests to government.

Several organizations have since appeared with a goal of electing more women in the province, among them Equal Voice (both a North Chapter and a South Chapter of the organization) and the One Woman One Vote organization run by YWCA Edmonton. Their efforts have included providing information and resources designed to encourage and assist women to become politically engaged and holding campaign schools for women interested in seeking office (see www.onewomanonevote.org and www.equalvoice.ca). Extremely active, these groups' efforts may have helped bring about the rise in the number of elected women in the 2012 election. There is, however, a strong anti-feminist movement in the province. REAL women, a national women's organization devoted to advocating women's traditional role in the family, opened a branch in the province in 2004. The Alberta Federation of Women United for Families, a provincial organization with a similar mandate, also exists.

Conclusion: Prospects for Gender Parity

Evidence from Alberta underscores the important role that political parties play in determining the strength of women's political representation. The long-standing dominance of a party on the centre-right of the ideological spectrum in the province, combined with an electoral system that inflates its dominance among voters in the allocation of seats, makes it increasingly unlikely that concern for women's relative absence in the political arena will make it onto the political agenda at any point in the near future. The surprising rise of the Wildrose Party in the most recent election, a party to the right of the PCP ideologically, increases the degree to which electoral success for women in the province is dependent on their success within the PCP. Limited electoral success for parties on the left, and a disregard for gender balance in the only party in forty years to challenge the PCP's dominance, mean that women's levels of political representation in the province rest largely with the Progressive Conservatives.

The populist and individualist threads that run through Alberta's popular and political cultures further hinder the advancement of policies or programs designed to assist women's political representation. In the short term at least, the Alberta Advantage is unlikely to include gender parity for women. In fact, gender parity, or something close to it, would require a significant shift in the cultural and political ethos in the province or a concomitant shift in party fortunes. There is little evidence that the former is likely to occur anytime soon. The latter – at least in the form of gains for parties to the left of the Progressive Conservatives – seems unlikely given the success of the Wildrose Party in the 2012 election.

Another possibility for change is electoral reform. It has been argued, for example, that a shift from the single-member plurality system to one adopting multi-member ridings represents one possibility for boosting women's political representation in the province (Jansen and Young 2005), although the arrival of the Wildrose Party alters these conclusions somewhat. Because neither the provincial government nor the public has expressed any need for or interest in electoral reform, the status quo is likely to hold for years to come. So long as the governing party continues to benefit from the boost offered by the electoral system, the provincial parties most likely to push for electoral reform remain relatively minor players on the provincial scene,[3] and Albertans continue to be content with the electoral system that is in place, reform remains unlikely.

Notes

I wish to thank Julie Croskill for her research assistance and the political parties in Alberta who responded so generously to her requests for information. I also wish to thank Lisa Lambert for providing her experiential insight on the state of feminist organizing and organizations in Alberta.

1 The "Alberta Advantage" was a slogan used for about fifteen years to "brand" the province. Ironically, it was replaced in 2009 with a slogan aptly summarizing the province's neoliberal political culture: "Freedom to create, spirit to achieve" (see Audette and Henton 2009).

2 The leadership race adopted a preferential vote election method: ballots allowed voters to rank order the three candidates in order of preference. Although Gary Mar, the front-runner, led with 42.5 percent of first preferences, he did not receive the majority required for winning. As a result, Doug Horner, in third place after counting first preferences, was eliminated and his second place preferences transferred to the remaining two candidates. After these votes were counted, Alison Redford was declared the leader of the party, having won 51 percent of the vote.

3 In the 2012 election, both the NDP (some form of proportional representation) and the Liberals (alternative voting) included electoral reform in their election platforms.

References

Alberta Finance and Enterprise. 2011. *Alberta Economic Quick Facts.* Available at http://www.albertacanada.com/.

Alberta Liberal Party. 2011. *Alberta Liberal Action Plan: Open Government.* Available at http://www.albertaliberal.com/.

Alberta NDP. N.d. *Alberta NDP Women's Caucus.* Available at http://women.albertandp.com/.

Audette, Trish, and Darcy Henton. 2009. "Province Launches New Brand after Dumping 'Alberta Advantage.'" *Edmonton Journal,* 24 March.

Bashevkin, Sylvia. 2012. "Ms. Premier in Alberta? No Surprise." *Globe and Mail,* 4 April. Available at http://www.theglobeandmail.com/.

Beach, Jane, Martha Friendly, Carolyn Ferns, Nina Prabhu, and Barry Forer. 2009. *Early Childhood Education and Care in Canada 2008.* Toronto: Childcare Resource and Research Unit.

Black, Jerome H., and Lynda Erickson. 2000. "Similarity, Compensation, or Difference? A Comparison of Female and Male Office-Holders." *Women and Politics* 21(4): 1-38.

Canadian Parliamentary Guide. 1993-2001. Scarborough: Gale Canada.

Caul, Miki. 1999. "Women's Representation in Parliament: The Role of Political Parties." *Party Politics* 5(1): 79-98.

CBCnews. N.d. *Alberta Votes 2008.* Available at http://www.cbc.ca/.

Collier, Cheryl. 1995. "A Tale of Two Provinces: Women, Parties and Governments in Ontario and Manitoba, 1990-1995." MA essay, Carleton University.

Elections Alberta. 2008. *Candidate Summary of Results: General Elections 1905-2004.* Available at http://www.electionsalberta.ab.ca/.

Elections Canada. 2011. *2011 General Election: Preliminary Results.* Available at http://enr.elections.ca/.

Equal Voice. 2012a. *114 Women Seek Election to Alberta Legislature.* Available at http://www.equalvoice.ca/.

–. 2012b. *More Women Win Seats in Alberta Legislature.* Available at http://www.equalvoice.ca/.

Flanagan, Tom. 2011. "The Redford Effect: Stagecraft, Statecraft and Rhetorical Pragmatism." *Policy Options,* November, 18-21.

Goyette, Linda. 2000. "A Search for the Holy Grail." *Elm Street,* May, 25-38.

Hale, Geoffrey. 2006. "Balancing Autonomy and Responsibility: The Politics of Provincial Fiscal and Tax Policies." In Christopher Dunn, ed., *Provinces: Canadian Provincial Politics,* 373-412. Peterborough: Broadview.

Harder, Lois. 2003. *State of Struggle: Feminism and Politics in Alberta.* Edmonton: University of Alberta Press.

Hirsch, Todd. "Alberta's Surprising New Premier." *Policy Options,* November, 16.

Inter-Parliamentary Union. 2012. Women in National Parliaments. Available at http://www.ipu.org/.

Jansen, Harold, and Lisa Young. 2005 "Electoral Democracy in Alberta: Time for Reform." *IAPR Policy Brief* No. IAPR-PB-0502. Available at http://www.ucalgary.ca/.

Lawless, Jennifer L., and Richard L. Fox. 2005. *It Takes a Candidate: Why Women Don't Run for Office.* New York: Cambridge University Press.

Legislative Assembly of Alberta. N.d.(a). The Honourable Lois E. Hole, C.M., 2000-2005. Available at http://www.assembly.ab.ca/.

–. N.d.(b). Lieutenant Governors. Available at http://www.assembly.ab.ca/.

Matland, Richard E., and Donley T. Studlar. 1996. "The Contagion of Women Candidates in Single-Member District and Proportional Representation Electoral Systems: Canada and Norway." *Journal of Politics* 58(3): 707-33.

O'Neill, Brenda, and David K. Stewart. 2009. "Gender and Political Party Leadership in Canada." *Party Politics.* 15(6): 737-57.

Palamarek, Michael. 1989. *Alberta Women in Politics: A History of Women and Politics in Alberta.* A report for Senator Martha P. Bielish. Edmonton: Government of Alberta.

PC Alberta. 2011. Statement of Principles. Available at http://www.albertapc.ab.ca/.

Rankin, L. Pauline. 1996. "Experience, Opportunity and the Politics of Place: A Comparative Analysis of Provincial and Territorial Women's Movements in Canada." PhD diss., Carleton University.

Rankin, L. Pauline, and Jill Vickers. 2001. *Women's Movements and State Feminism: Integrating Diversity into Public Policy.* Ottawa: Status of Women Canada.

Sampert, Shannon. 2008. "More than Just Cowboys with White Hats: A Demographic Profile of Edmonton and Calgary." In Caroline Andrew, John Biles, Myer

Siemiatycki, and Erin Tolley, eds., *Electing a Diverse Canada: The Representation of Immigrants, Minorities and Women*, 92-110. Vancouver: UBC Press.

Sharpe, Sydney. 2012. "Danielle Smith: Is She Alberta's Sarah Palin, or the Future of Canada?" *Globe and Mail*, 16 April. Available at http://www.theglobeandmail.com/.

Smith, Peter J. 2001. "Alberta: Experiments in Governance – From Social Credit to the Klein Revolution." In Keith Brownsey and Michael Howlett, eds., *The Provincial State in Canada: Politics in the Provinces and Territories*, 277-308. Peterborough: Broadview Press.

Statistics Canada. 2010a. Aboriginal Identity Population by Age Groups, Median Age and Sex, Percentage Distribution for Both Sexes, for Canada, Provinces and Territories – 20 Percent Sample Data. Updated 6 October 2010. Available at http://www.statcan.gc.ca/.

–. 2010b. Canada's Ethnocultural Mosaic, 2006 Census: Provinces and Territories. Updated 11 February 2010. Available at http://www.statcan.gc.ca/.

–. 2010c. "Economic Well-Being." In *Women in Canada: A Gender-Based Statistical Report*. 6th ed. Catalogue no. 89-503-X. Available at http://www.statcan.gc.ca/.

Stewart, David K., and Keith Archer. 2000. *Quasi-Democracy: Parties and Leadership Selection in Alberta*. Vancouver: UBC Press.

Stewart, David K., and R. Kenneth Carty. 2006. "Many Political Worlds? Provincial Parties and Party Systems." In Christopher Dunn, ed., *Provinces: Canadian Provincial Politics*, 97-113. Peterborough: Broadview.

Trimble, Linda. 1992. "The Politics of Gender in Modern Alberta." In Allan Tupper and Roger Gibbins, eds., *Government and Politics in Alberta*, 219-45. Edmonton: University of Alberta Press.

Trimble, Linda, and Jane Arscott. 2003. *Still Counting: Women in Politics across Canada*. Peterborough: Broadview Press.

–. 2005. "Barriers to Women: Why Are We So Far from Gender Parity?" *Alberta Views*, June, 28-31.

Wesley, Jared J. 2011. *Code Politics: Campaigns and Cultures on the Canadian Prairies*. Vancouver: UBC Press.

Wingrove, Josh. 2012. "Wildrose Party Set for Sweeping Majority, Latest Poll Shows." *Globe and Mail*, 22 April. Available at http://www.theglobeandmail.com.

Wiseman, Nelson. 2007. *In Search of Canadian Political Culture*. Vancouver: UBC Press.

Young, Lisa. 2000. *Feminists and Party Politics*. Vancouver: UBC Press.

3

When Numerical Gains Are Not Enough

Women in British Columbia Politics

JOCELYNE PRAUD

Since the 1991 breakthrough election that resulted in women winning a quarter of the seats in the legislature, a first in Canadian history, BC women have been well represented as candidates, MLAs, cabinet ministers, and party leaders. As of April 2012, women hold a third of the seats in the legislature and over 40 percent of the posts in the cabinet of the newly elected leader of the Liberal Party and provincial premier, Christy Clark. Therefore, numerically and symbolically speaking, British Columbia can be identified as a vanguard province. However, the dramatic institutional and policy setbacks that women suffered in the first half of the 2000s also indicate that British Columbia is not a vanguard province when it comes to women's substantive representation.

First, I focus on the numerical gains that BC women have made since 1991. While different factors explain the increased presence and visibility of women in BC politics – for instance, a political culture and environment that is more open to women's political involvement as well as the greater proportion of educated professional women – I highlight the importance of party ideology and party contagion. Were it not for the BC New Democratic Party's initiatives to promote women, prompting rivals on the right to recruit more women, women's numerical gains may not have been so noteworthy. I then address the dramatic institutional and policy strides that women made during the 1991-96 NDP government and then lost during the 2001-5 Liberal government. In the end, I propose that, in order for

POLITICAL REPRESENTATION OF WOMEN IN
BRITISH COLUMBIA

FIRSTS
Right to vote and stand for election
- Most women win right to vote and stand for election — 1917
- Asian and South Asian women / Aboriginal women win right to vote and stand for election — 1947 / 1949

Contesting office
- First woman to contest office: Mary Ellen Smith (Independent) — 1918
- First woman to win office: Mary Ellen Smith (elected as an Independent in 1918 and then as a Liberal from 1920 onwards) — 1918-28
- First black woman to win office: Rosemary Brown (NDP) — 1972-88
- First woman MLA of East Indian-Canadian descent to win office: Judi Tyabji (Liberal until 1993 and then Progressive Democratic Alliance) — 1991-96
- First women MLAs of Chinese-Canadian descent to win office: Ida Chong (Liberal) / Jenny Kwan (NDP) — 1996 to present / 1996 to present
- First publicly identified lesbian MLA to win office: Jenn McGinn (NDP) — 2008-9
- First woman MLA with a disability: Stephanie Cadieux (Liberal) — 2009 to present
- First woman appointed to cabinet without a portfolio: Mary Ellen Smith (Liberal) — 1921/03 to 1921/11
- First woman appointed to cabinet with a portfolio: Tilly Jean Rolston (Social Credit), education — 1952-53

CURRENT REPRESENTATION AT A GLANCE

	Date of election	Women elected Number	Percent
Women in legislature	2009/05/12	25 of 85	29
Women in cabinet	2009/06/10	7 of 25	28

Women political party leaders
- Jane Sterk (Green), 2007 to present
- Christy Clark (Liberal), 2011 to present

Lieutenant governor
- Judith Guichon, 2012 to present

Advisory council on the status of women
- The Ministry of Women's Equality was created in 1991 and disbanded in 2001.

substantive policy changes to take place, three conditions need to be present: (1) gender parity, or the equal representation of women and men, in the legislature and cabinet; (2) a governing party that is committed to support women and issues of concern to them; and (3) a progressive and feminist premier who will promote gender parity and policies designed to improve the lives of all women.

Background

British Columbia's early reliance on resource industries such as fishing, logging, and mining, in which male workers have always been the majority, served to establish men as the main economic and, by extension, political actors in the province for at least the first one hundred years of its history.[1] However, major economic and social developments in the latter part of the twentieth century have put other groups, notably women and visible ethnic minorities, in a position to challenge men's dominance of politics. For instance, the much greater importance of the services-producing sector (retail, finance, education, health care, etc.), which employs a majority of women, compared to the declining goods-producing sector (resources, utilities, and manufacturing) as well as the significant increase in the proportion of women university graduates means that the province now has a large pool of educated professional women with the necessary skills to become politicians.[2] Furthermore, one would expect the increased multi-ethnic character of the provincial population and, in particular, the large East and Southeast Asian communities to be reflected among women and men candidates and elected officials.[3]

Observers of BC politics such as Edwards (2008, 22-24) often note that the resource basis of the provincial economy contributed to the emergence and persistence of a class-based left/right divide pitting workers (and thus unions) against managers and owners of resource industries (and thus business interests). Although various political parties have come, gone, and even resurrected in British Columbia, since 1941, the provincial party system has basically functioned as a polarized two-party system, with a party of the left supported by unions, the CCF-NDP (Co-operative Commonwealth Federation-New Democratic Party), and a party of the right supported by business corporations, first the Social Credit (Socred) Party and then the Liberal Party.[4] After winning all the elections between 1952 and 1986 except one, the 1972 election that brought the NDP to power for three years, the Social Credit Party was decimated in 1991 in the wake of a string of scandals in which several of its elected officials, including the premier, were involved.

At present, the provincial party system consists of the left-leaning NDP, which was in power from 1991 until 2001, and the Liberal Party, essentially a coalition party of federal Liberals and Conservatives and former Socreds, which proceeded to implement neoliberal policies shortly after its 2001 victory. The polarization of the party system and, in particular, the acrimonious ideological rhetoric coming from both the left and the right may have been an additional deterrent to women's involvement in politics, especially in the period after the Second World War.

From 1917, the year the newly elected Liberal government granted the rights to vote and run in elections to women, up until the resurgence of feminism in the 1970s, all the above-mentioned parties generally ignored women.[5] For instance, in the post-suffrage period, political parties nominated hardly any women candidates. Not surprisingly, all the elections held between 1920 and 1969 sent five or fewer women to the legislature (Table 3.1). Furthermore, the very few women who were appointed to cabinet during this same period tended not to have portfolios (e.g., Mary Ellen Smith, the first woman elected as an MLA and appointed to cabinet) (Erickson 1997, 114). In short, politics was first and foremost the prerogative of men no matter the party until the 1970s, when feminists within the NDP forced their party to address the under-representation of women and issues of concern to them.

Women's Political Representation: The Numbers

Candidates

With regard to BC women candidates, two factors appear to have been at play since the 1980s: party ideology and party contagion. First, the left-leaning provincial NDP has consistently presented the highest number of candidates in all elections but one held between 1983 and 2009. Second, its efforts to promote women candidates appear to have had a contagion effect, with first the Social Credit Party and then the Liberal Party recruiting women candidates.

As indicated in Table 3.2, in 1983 and 1986, the BC NDP ran, respectively, thirteen and twenty-one women – that is, about three times as many women as did the Social Credit Party, which ran only five and six women. Except for the 2005 election, which saw twenty-five women running under the Liberal banner and twenty-three under the NDP banner, through the 1990s and 2000s, the BC NDP presented the highest number of women candidates. What is particularly striking is that the difference in the two parties' number

TABLE 3.1

Women in the BC legislature, by election

Election date	Party elected	Total number of legislators	Women elected Number	%
1920/12/01	Liberal	47	1	2
1924/06/20	Liberal	48	1	2
1928/07/18	Conservative	48	0	0
1933/11/ 02	Liberal	47	1	2
1937/06/01	Liberal	48	2	4
1941/10/21	Liberal*	48	5	10
1945/10/25	Coalition*	48	2	4
1949/06/15	Coalition*	48	2	4
1952/06/12	Social Credit	48	3	6
1953/06/09	Social Credit	48	1	2
1956/09/19	Social Credit	52	2	4
1960/09/12	Social Credit	52	3	6
1963/09/30	Social Credit	52	1	2
1966/09/12	Social Credit	55	4	7
1969/08/27	Social Credit	55	5	9
1972/08/30	NDP	55	6	11
1975/12/11	Social Credit	55	6	11
1979/05/10	Social Credit	57	6	11
1983/05/05	Social Credit	57	6	11
1986/10/22	Social Credit	69	9	13
1991/10/17	NDP	75	19	25
1996/05/28	NDP	75	20	27
2001/05/16	Liberal	79	19	24
2005/05/17	Liberal	79	17	22
2009/05/12	Liberal	85	25	29

* In the 1945 and 1949 elections, the Liberal and Conservative parties ran as a team so as to ensure the re-election of the coalition government they had formed following the 1941 election. The coalition dissolved in 1952.

Source: Legislative Library of British Columbia (2010, 9-10).

of women candidates, which remained quite small (i.e., one or two) between 1996 and 2005, jumped to sixteen in the 2009 election, with forty-one New Democrat women candidates and twenty-five Liberal women candidates. As will be clarified later, the affirmative action rules for women candidates that the BC NDP adopted in November 2007 largely accounts for the party's presenting a gender-balanced slate of candidates in 2009.

The figures contained in Table 3.2 also point to a pattern of party contagion. Such a pattern is observable when a party's efforts to promote women

TABLE 3.2
Women candidates in BC, by party and election

Election date	Liberal		NDP		Social Credit	
	Number	%	Number	%	Number	%
1983/05/05	–		13 of 57	23	5 of 57	9
1986/10/22	–		21 of 69	31	6 of 69	9
1991/10/17	15 of 71	21	24 of 75	33	19 of 74	24
1996/05/28	20 of 75	27	22 of 75	29	–	
2001/05/16	19 of 79	24	20 of 79	25	–	
2005/05/17	25 of 79	32	23 of 79	29	–	
2009/05/12	25 of 85	29	41 of 85	48	–	

Source: Compiled from Elections British Columbia (1988); Legislative Library of British Columbia (2002); and Equal Voice, British Columbia Chapter (n.d.).

prompt its competitors to do the same, which then leads the former to take additional steps to outdo the latter and reassert its women-friendly image (Meier 2004). The BC NDP's consistent and active promotion of women candidates may have caused the unpopular and scandal-ridden Social Credit Party to choose Rita Johnston as its new leader and premier in April 1991 and also to triple the size of its contingent of women candidates from six to nineteen between 1986 and 1991. Party contagion may have also influenced the Liberal Party to include about the same proportion of women among its candidates as the NDP and vice versa between 1996 and 2005. Finally, the BC NDP's adoption of affirmative action rules for candidacies and their effective implementation in 2009, and perhaps even the recent selection of Christy Clark as Liberal Party leader and premier, could be interpreted as the latest instances of party contagion in British Columbia.

MLAs
The presence of the left-leaning NDP and party contagion appear to account for the significant increase in women MLAs that took place following the 1991 election and thus British Columbia's record of electing women to the legislature going from "unremarkable," to borrow Erickson's (1997, 119) adjective, to noteworthy. Indeed, the Legislative Assembly had five or fewer women until 1969, six from the early 1970s until the early 1980s, and then nine in 1986. The greater number of women candidates presented by the NDP, the Liberal Party, and the Social Credit Party, and the victory of the NDP contributed to the breakthrough of 1991, with nineteen women elected to a legislature of seventy-five (25 percent of whom were women). In

her book *Seeking Balance: Conversations with BC Women in Politics*, former NDP MLA Anne Edwards (2008, 177) notes that, as a result, "BC became the first Canadian assembly to elect women to 25 percent of its seats." In the 1996 and 2001 elections, if women's overall share of seats remained stable despite the 2001 virtual obliteration of the NDP, it is in part due to the Liberal Party's still awarding about a quarter of its candidacies to women, perhaps as a way to signal that it was just as supportive of women as was the NDP. The significant increase that took place between 2005 and 2009 can be attributed to both parties' presenting women candidates and, above all, to the NDP's implementing its new affirmative action rules for candidates and thus presenting a gender-balanced slate of candidates (41/85, or 48 percent).

Party Leaders and Premiers

Up until recently, BC women usually led only either marginal parties or major parties that were facing, or had gone through, a major electoral defeat. The BC Greens, which have never elected a representative to the Legislative Assembly, have had primarily women leaders – Adriane Carr in the first half of the 2000s and Jane Sterk since 2006. The same can be said about the short-lived provincial Conservative Party and Western Reform of the early 2000s and the Liberal Party in the early 1980s.[6] In April 1991, the Social Credit Party chose veteran cabinet minister Rita Johnston to replace Bill Vander Zalm, who had to resign as premier and party leader following the revelation that he had used the premier's office to speed up the sale of his biblical theme park, Fantasy Gardens. Six months later, her party, which had held power for a total of thirty-six years, was soundly defeated by the NDP. Her successor, Grace McCarthy, was unable to revitalize the moribund party.[7] In 2001, Joy MacPhail became interim leader of the NDP after her party lost all its seats but two, hers and that of Jenny Kwan, to the Liberal Party of Gordon Campbell (Edwards 2008, 204, 220-25).

TABLE 3.3

Women leaders of parties with legislative representation in BC

Name	Political party	Period of service
Rita Johnston	Social Credit	1991-92
Grace McCarthy	Social Credit	1993-94
Carole James	NDP	2003-11
Christy Clark	Liberal	2011 to present

TABLE 3.4
Women premiers in BC

Name	Political party	Period of service
Rita Johnston	Social Credit	April to November 1991
Christy Clark	Liberal	2011 to present

Following the resignation of Carole James, another woman, veteran MLA Dawn Black, briefly served as interim NDP leader until the election of Adrian Dix on 17 April 2011.

The more recent selections of Carole James and Christy Clark as leaders of the provincial New Democratic and Liberal parties do not quite fit the pattern of women only being able to lead marginal parties and/or decimated (or about to become decimated) parties. By the time the NDP launched its leadership contest, the party was on its way to recovery, thanks in large part to the rebuilding efforts of Joy MacPhail and Jenny Kwan. In November 2003, James, a former president of the BC School Trustees Association and the only woman candidate, won the NDP leadership on the second ballot. She then led her revitalized party in the 2005 and 2009 elections, regaining Official Opposition status with thirty-three seats and then thirty-five seats (Edwards 2008, 225-27). Nonetheless, the events that led up to her resignation and subsequent replacement by Dix, notably the caucus revolt involving thirteen MLAs, lend some credence to the argument that the closer to power a party is, the less likely it is to have a woman leader. While Kwan, the spokesperson for the caucus revolt against James, mainly decried her leadership style, she also had issues with James's outreach to the business community and support for the banning of corporate and union donations to BC parties. Since the leadership contest that resulted in the selection of the more leftist Dix included no women candidates, one wonders to what extent the unceremonious removal of James may have deterred women from running.

As for Christy Clark, the argument that she won the leadership of a weakened party and government destined to lose the next election appears to be tenuous. First, the Liberal leadership race comprised high-profile cabinet insiders such as Kevin Falcon, George Abbott, and Mike de Jong, who were more than willing to take the helm of the party and government and deal with the harmonized sales tax controversy that had just forced Premier Campbell out of office.[8] Furthermore, Clark defeated her rivals largely because of her broad public appeal (apparent right at the outset of the race), her "Families First" agenda, and her promise to govern differently. Last, due to the 2001 Constitution (Fixed Election Dates) Amendment Act, which provides that BC elections are to be held every four years on the second Tuesday of May, Premier Clark was not required to face voters for another two years (in May 2013). In sum, the fact that British Columbia's two main provincial parties selected women as leaders signals that, in that province, the pattern of women as caretakers of marginal or moribund parties may have been broken.

Cabinet Ministers

Notwithstanding the two cabinets appointed right after the 1983 and 1991 elections, for most of the past three decades, the proportion of women cabinet ministers has been equivalent to that of women MLAs. Social Credit premier Bill Bennett's 1983 cabinet included only one woman (or 5 percent of ministers compared to 11 percent of MLAs), Grace McCarthy, who was reappointed as human resources minister with the added responsibility for urban transit (Table 3.5). Given the under-representation of women among Social Credit candidates (only 9 percent in 1983 versus 23 percent for the NDP), the subsequent under-representation of women in the Socred caucus (two, Grace McCarthy and Rita Johnston, versus four in the NDP caucus) and cabinet was to be expected (Erickson 1997, 113, 115; Table 1.2). By

TABLE 3.5
Women in cabinet in BC, by election

Election date	Party elected	Total number of cabinet ministers*	Women appointed to cabinet		% of women in governing caucus in cabinet
			Number	%	
1983/05/05	Social Credit	19	1	5	50
1986/10/22	Social Credit	18	2	11	50
1991/10/17	NDP	19	7	37	47
1996/05/28	NDP	14	4	29	33
2001/05/16	Liberal	28	8	29[†]	47
2005/05/17	Liberal	23	5	22	45
2009/05/12	Liberal	25	7	28	54

* Includes the premier.
† This cabinet included seven ministers of state without portfolios, three of whom were women.
Source: Compiled from Legislative Library of British Columbia (2011b; 2013) and Tafler (1983, 8).

contrast, the 1991 cabinet of NDP premier Mike Harcourt included seven women ministers (or 37 percent of ministers compared to 25 percent of MLAs) (Table 3.5); in his words: "Women will be responsible for probably 80 percent of our budget, so I think we have made our message clear that women are going to be front and centre and equal in our government" (quoted in Hunter 1991).

In a sense, Premier Harcourt's 1991 cabinet set a precedent for women's presence in the provincial executive. Although the premiers who came to power thereafter, including NDP premier Glen Clark, may not have shared Harcourt's commitment to gender balance, they did nonetheless appoint about the same proportion of women to cabinet as that present in the legislature, thereby signalling that, since 1991, gender (though not gender balance per se) has been a consideration in the premiers' selection of cabinet members. By way of example, the streamlined cabinet of Glen Clark comprised four women (or 29 percent of ministers compared to 27 percent of MLAs), and the 2001 and 2005 cabinets of Gordon Campbell both included five women ministers with portfolios (or about 22 to 24 percent of ministers with portfolios compared to 22 to 24 percent of MLAs) (Table 3.5).[9]

Beside gender, ethnicity appears to have been an additional consideration in the selection of cabinet members, as indicated by Glen Clark's recruitment of Jenny Kwan (municipal affairs and then women's equality), and Gordon Campbell's recruitment of Sindi Hawkins (health planning), Ida Chong (women's and seniors' services), and Naomi Yamamoto (intergovernmental relations) (Legislative Library of British Columbia 2011a).[10] As of the most recent cabinet shuffle, Liberal premier Christy Clark's cabinet contains eight women, including herself, Ida Chong (Aboriginal relations and reconciliation), Naomi Yamamoto (small business), and Stephanie Cadieux (children and family development).[11] It is the most gender-balanced and diverse of all BC cabinets to date ("Executive Council of the Government of British Columbia" 2012).[12]

This overview of women's presence in the provincial executive highlights how a left-leaning premier committed to gender balance proceeded to significantly improve women's visibility, which then led his successors from both the left and the right to include about the same proportion of women ministers as that of women MLAs. With regard to cabinet appointments then, the key factors at play appear to be not only the left-leaning party's holding power and party contagion but also the will of a progressive premier.

TABLE 3.6
Female representatives of the Crown in BC

Name	Period of service
Iona Campagnolo	2001-7
Judith Guichon	2012 to present

Explanations

Political Parties

Why did British Columbia's record for electing women go from being "unremarkable" up until the 1991 election to being noteworthy thereafter? Beginning in the 1970s and 1980s, at the urging of its feminist Women's Rights Committee, the NDP launched several initiatives to enhance the presence of women among its candidates and elected representatives and even went as far as adopting affirmative action rules for party positions in 2001 and for candidacies six years later. While the NDP's early initiatives appear to have prompted the Social Credit Party in 1991 and, above all, the revitalized Liberal Party and its Women's Liberal Commission from the 1990s onwards to be more proactive in their recruitment of women candidates, neither of these two parties from the right ever resorted to their rival's more coercive measures.

Two decades after the Royal Commission on the Status of Women had identified parties' women's auxiliaries, which separated women from the mainstream party organization and confined them to supportive roles, as a major impediment to women's involvement in politics, the Social Credit Party still had one such body in 1990. For Erickson (1997, 117), this auxiliary's "continued existence symbolized a party that found traditional notions of women and politics difficult to shed." Consequently, the sudden surge in Socred women candidates in 1991 could be attributed in part to the fact that many fewer men, including a large number of incumbents, were interested in contesting the election under the banner of a badly damaged party that was almost certainly heading for defeat.

In 1991, after twelve years with no legislative representation, a rejuvenated Liberal Party, which had just replaced its former women's auxiliary with the BC Women's Liberal Commission, managed to win seventeen seats and thus re-enter the legislature as the Official Opposition party. Unlike the previous women's auxiliary of the party, the Women's Liberal Commission was to help women develop their political skills and enhance their role in the political process (Edwards 2008, 38; Erickson 1997, 118). Since the 1990s, together with its Women's Liberal Commission, the Liberal Party has made concerted efforts to recruit women candidates (Edwards 2008, 38). Because of these efforts, Edwards (2008, 38) notes, the Liberal Party has been "the second most successful party in BC at electing women to assemblies [after the NDP]."

The efforts of the BC New Democrats to enhance women's role in politics date back to 1971, when, at the request of party feminists, the defunct women's committee of the 1960s was reconstituted. The new Women's Rights Committee (WRC) was to prepare women to play a more effective role as party "members, active party officers, or as potential representatives" and to "study and work towards implementing the recommendations of the Royal Commission" (Erickson 1997, 114). Through the 1970s, the WRC focused mainly on formulating policy resolutions on women's rights and keeping women's issues on the party agenda. Then, in the mid-1980s, the committee's focus shifted to encouraging women to seek nominations, thus indicating that the 8 percent increase in the proportion of NDP women candidates between 1983 and 1986 (from 23 percent to 31 percent) was not a coincidence. Before the 1991 election, the WRC worked hard to ensure that women received nominations in winnable ridings and convinced the election-planning committee of the NDP to include an "Equality Campaign" (also named "Campaign to Women Voters") designed to draw attention to women's equality issues and women candidates in the party's electoral campaign (Erickson 1997, 114-16). In the end, thanks to the concerted efforts of its feminist women's committee, sixteen of the NDP's twenty-four women candidates were elected. Following this major achievement, the committee successfully lobbied the party to ensure gender balance in party positions and candidacies (Edwards 2008, 38-39). At the 2011 leadership convention, it reasserted its support for "a fair and effective quota system ... the only model worldwide that has proven to achieve greater diversity and gender balance in electoral politics" (BC NDP Women's Rights Committee 2011).

At present, what sets the NDP apart from the Liberal Party is its adoption of affirmative action rules, first for party positions and then for candidacies. Though both parties have shown that they are committed to promoting women candidates, the former is clearly more willing to use coercive measures so as to enhance gender balance and diversity than is the latter. Since 2001, Article 13.01 (c) of the NDP Constitution requires that half of

vice-presidents, members-at-large, regional members, and youth representatives be women and that both genders be represented in the top three positions of party leader, president, and treasurer (BC NDP 2009; Hewlett
2011). Then, at its November 2007 convention, the party adopted a policy
providing that: 30 percent of the ridings not held by the party be set aside
for women candidates; 10 percent of such ridings be reserved "for candidates from 'under-represented groups,' notably youth, persons of colour, the
disabled, aboriginal people and those who are either gay, lesbian, bisexual or
transgender"; and all ridings vacated by retiring NDP MLAs be designated
for women candidates ("BC NDP Passes Affirmative Action Rules for Nominations" 2007). After a spirited debate on the floor of the convention, the
policy, which was endorsed by the party leader at the time (Carole James)
and several MLAs, passed. It was first implemented in the 2009 provincial
election and accounts for the NDP's presenting a gender-balanced slate of
candidates (or 19 percent more women candidates than the Liberal Party)
and, possibly, for women now holding a third of the seats in the legislature.

Despite the objections of some NDP members to their party's affirmative
action rules and, in particular, to those pertaining to candidacies, the BC
NDP's commitment to the selection of a gender-balanced and diverse slate
of provincial candidates appears to have strengthened since 2007. As noted
above, these rules were passed at the November 2007 convention even
though a number of speakers expressed concerns about such rules under-
mining democracy and, in particular, riding associations' autonomous
selection of candidates ("BC NDP Passes Affirmative Action Rules for
Nominations" 2007; "BC NDP to Choose Candidates through Affirmative
Action" 2007). Early in 2011, the blunt criticisms that leadership candidate
Harry Lali made publicly about the party's "equity quotas" for candidates
were not echoed by any of the other leadership contestants.[13] In its November
2011 report to the provincial council, the party's Equity Mandate Committee,
which was set up to review the recruitment and nomination of candidates
from under-represented groups for the 2009 election, recognized that the
implementation of the party rules had been "clumsy and opaque" and that
"better communication and conversation with constituencies, over a longer
period of time, would make the process smoother and less traumatic" (BC
NDP 2011, 5).[14] Furthermore, after stating the party's current gender and
diversity targets of 50 percent women candidates and 25 percent candidates
from equity-seeking (or under-represented) groups, the committee made a
number of recommendations relative to the nomination of candidates for the

upcoming election, such as: the replacement of retiring women MLAs by women candidates and that of retiring men MLAs by either women or equity-seeking candidates; the nomination of women candidates in twenty-five target seats; the establishment of a search committee dedicated to finding diverse candidates; the award of financial incentives to constituencies that selected women and equity-seeking candidates; and a formal review of the party's selection of diverse candidates for the 2013 election (BC NDP 2011, 7-8). In the end, a large majority of New Democrats passed the recommendations at the December 2011 convention ("Thoughts on the BC NDP 50th Anniversary Convention" 2011).

Demand and Supply[15]

The BC New Democrats' and Liberals' consistent efforts over the past two decades to bring women into politics indicate that nowadays neither of them can afford to have less than 20 percent of women among their candidates, elected representatives, and cabinet ministers as this would mean risking losing votes. According to some of the public opinion polls conducted at the time of the latest Liberal leadership contest, BC citizens appear to be quite receptive to women's playing a prominent role in politics (Hunter 2011). However, the fact that both political parties still have to seek out women indicates that, even in British Columbia, women remain more reluctant to embark on a political career than do men. For some of the women interviewed by Edwards, the particularly polarized and adversarial nature of provincial politics is off-putting. According to former MLA Jan Pullinger: "The death-defying antics of BC politics is certainly a deterrent to women – it is so vicious here" (Edwards 2008, 170). For others, including Edwards (170), however, the "polarization and circus atmosphere ... 'create clear-edged issues," which can actually prompt women to get involved. In former MLA Lynn Hunter's view: "You have to be somewhat of a radical in order to gain political office in British Columbia – radical left or radical right" (171). Though the polarization of BC politics can turn off some women, the challenge of balancing family life, especially when children are young, with a political career is probably the most common obstacle for women. Furthermore, in British Columbia, the case of Liberal MLA Judi Tyabji, who, in 1994, was denied custody of her three children on the grounds that her demanding political career prevented her from adequately caring for them, likely put a few women off politics (Erickson 1997, 121; Trimble and Arscott 2003, 109).

On this issue, Edwards's (2008, 179) description of the average woman MLA or MP from British Columbia as a woman who is in her late forties to mid-fifties and has children is illuminating. Indeed, while motherhood does not prevent women from eventually becoming politicians, more often than not it delays their entry into politics. This may be especially true in British Columbia, one of most laggard provinces when it comes to affordable child-care services (Praud and Dowling 2010, 247).[16] Furthermore, as Christy Clark's experience suggests, caring for a young child while in political office is extremely difficult, even when one can afford private childcare. With the help of two caregivers, one in Victoria and one in her riding, Clark, the first BC cabinet minister to deliver a baby, was able to fulfill her responsibilities as deputy premier and cabinet minister for three years before resigning (Edwards 2008, 114-16). Consider Clark's comments on her leaving politics: "My family needs more of me than I have been able to give them." And: "Time is the number one barrier for me at the moment. You need to network to be successful. You need to meet informally, to bring people along to a policy before decision time, but my evenings belong to my son and my husband" (Clark, quoted in Edwards 2008, 116, 97). These comments illustrate how, even in the twenty-first century, the mothering of pre-school children can entail a significant interruption of a woman's political career. For other women, it may delay or even prematurely end it, a possibility that men still rarely have to confront.

Conclusion: Prospects for Gender Parity

In Canada's West Coast province, the 1991 election, which saw women's presence in the provincial legislature double (from 13 percent to 25 percent), was a breakthrough for women's numerical representation. Furthermore, since, for the past two decades, women have been generally well represented among legislators and cabinet members, British Columbia can be identified as a vanguard province when it comes to women's numerical representation. Various factors account for the 1991 breakthrough and women's continued presence in the legislature and cabinet, namely, a political culture and environment that are now more receptive to women's involvement in politics and a larger pool of educated professional women. However, the most significant factors have to do with political parties and, more specifically, party ideology and party contagion. Indeed, the innovative steps that the left-leaning and feminist NDP initially took to enhance the presence of women in politics led its rivals on the right to be more proactive in their recruitment of women candidates, which in turn may have prompted the NDP to adopt affirmative action rules.

Given the dramatic institutional and policy advances and setbacks that BC women have incurred over the past two decades while holding on average a quarter of the legislative and cabinet seats, BC constitutes a fruitful case in which to study the links between women's numerical representation and their substantive representation.[17] On the one hand, the BC case suggests that the increased presence of women alone does not automatically bring about substantive policy gains for women; on the other hand, one needs to be careful about dismissing women's increased presence as irrelevant to women's substantive representation, especially in light of Grace Lore's (2008, 26-27) study of the BC MLAs elected in 2005, which finds that women representatives actually made the majority of statements related to women's issues and thus acted as substantive representatives for women. Consequently, in British Columbia, it appears that, while women's numerical representation and substantive representation (defined as the raising of women's issues) are connected, three conditions are needed for more consequential policy changes to occur: (1) women's holding half of the legislative and cabinet seats, (2) a governing party that considers women and their issues to be key priorities, and (3) a feminist premier who champions gender parity and policies designed to enhance the well-being of all women.

At the time of writing, it is doubtful that Christy Clark's Liberal government will be able to fulfill all of these conditions before the next provincial election in May 2013. While the government can boast having the province's most gender-balanced and diverse cabinet, it cannot really claim having taken significant steps to improve the lot of BC women. To be fair, during the leadership race and after her election, Clark made it clear that families were her priority and made no statements about the need to better the lives of different groups of women. However, thus far, no major policy initiatives have been launched for families. As BC Children's Advocate Mary Ellen Turpel-Lafond and others have pointed out, the 2012 provincial budget appears to focus largely on deficit reduction and contains little for families, especially those hit hardest by the economic crisis ("BC Budget Aims for Fiscal Prudence" 21 February 2012; Hunter, 23 February 2012). Consequently, the tenure of British Columbia's second woman premier may turn out to be an unfortunate example of women's important numerical gains not translating into substantive policy gains for women, families, and children.

Notes

1 On this point, see Erickson (1997, 108-9).

2 On the rise of the service sector, see Howlett, Pilon, and Summerville (2010, 21-23). According to BC Stats (June 2008, 1; September 2008, 2), in 2005, 54 percent of service-sector workers were women, and in 2006, 58 percent of university graduates between the ages of 25 and 34, and 52 percent of university graduates between the ages of 35 and 44, were women.

3 In 2006, 26 percent of census respondents identified their ethnic origin to be East Asian or Southeast Asian (BC Stats July 2008, 1).

4 Before 1941, the two-party system could not be described as polarized since there were no clear substantive differences between the Conservative and Liberal parties. Following the 1941 election, these two parties formed an anti-left coalition so as to prevent their common enemy, the CCF, from winning power. This coalition dissolved in 1952, and the newly created Social Credit Party took its place on the right side of the ideological spectrum. On the history of British Columbia's polarized two-party system, see Phillips (2010, 109-12, 121-23).

5 For detailed accounts of the thirty-year suffrage campaign of BC women, see Cleverdon (1974, 84-100) and Edwards (2008, 25-32).

6 Shirley McLoughlin led the Liberal Party from 1981 until 1983, while Susan Power and Lisa Maskell, respectively, led the Conservative Party between 2001 and 2002 and Western Reform in 2003 (Edwards 2008, 229).

7 On McCarthy's efforts to revitalize her party, see Trimble and Arscott (2003, 80-81) as well as Edwards (2008, 222-23).

8 In 2010, the Liberal government passed the bill providing for the harmonization of the provincial sales tax and the federal goods and services tax (the harmonized sales tax, or HST) after pledging not do so. Following a successful petition campaign against the HST, the government was forced to submit it to a referendum.

9 If the women ministers of state (without portfolios) appointed in 2001 by Premier Gordon Campbell in 2001 are taken into account, the proportion of women ministers rises to 28.6 percent, the exact same proportion of women ministers in the 1996 Glen Clark cabinet (see Table 3.5).

10 For more details on the backgrounds of Ida Chong, Jenny Kwan, and Sindi Hawkins, see Edwards (2008, 134-36).

11 A paraplegic, Cadieux is the second MLA to put accessibility of the legislature to the test since Social Credit MLA Doug Mowat wheeled his way through his duties from 1983 to 1991.

12 The other women in Christy Clark's cabinet are: Mary Polack (transportation and infrastructure), Moira Stilwell (social development), Margaret MacDiarmid (health), and Shirley Bond (justice and attorney general) ("Executive Council of the Government of British Columbia" 2012).

13 With regard to Lali's criticisms, see Bailey (2011).

14 I thank Jenn McGinn and Timothy Chu for clarifying the NDP's affirmative action rules.

15 On the issue of demand and supply, see Ashe and Stewart's (2011, 17) study, which argues that in British Columbia and other systems "demand-side discrimination by

gatekeepers and not undersupply" accounts for the under-representation of women and visible minorities.

16   In 2008, the Canadian Labour Congress gave a "D-" to British Columbia for its child-care performance because of the high cost of childcare, the low salaries of daycare workers, and the lack of licensed childcare spaces in the province (Praud and Dowling 2010, 247). These were likely the result of the 2001-5 Liberal government's deep cuts and its reversal of the New Democrats' childcare initiatives (see Teghtsoonian 2010, 314, 319-320).

17   These advances and setbacks have been well documented by Erickson (1997, 2010), Collier (2008), Teghtsoonian and Chappell (2008), and Teghtsoonian (2010).

References

Ashe, Jeanette, and Kennedy Stewart. 2011. "Legislative Recruitment: Using Diagnostic Testing to Explain Underrepresentation." *Party Politics*, 1-21. Available at http://ppq.sagepub.com/content/.

Bailey, Ian. 2011. "Lali Enters Race, Decries Gender Quotas." *Globe and Mail*, 7 January.

"BC Budget Aims for Fiscal Prudence." 2012. *CBC News*, 15 February. Available at http://www.cbc.ca/.

"BC NDP to Choose Candidates through Affirmative Action." 2007. *Vancouver Sun*, 18 November. Available at http://www.canada.com/.

"BC NDP Passes Affirmative Action Rules for Nominations." 2007. *Bread and Roses*, 18 November. Available at http://breadnroses.ca/.

BC NDP. 2009. The Constitution of the New Democratic Party of British Columbia. Available at http://www.bcndp.ca/.

BC NDP. 2011. *Equity Mandate Committee Report*. November.

BC NDP Women's Rights Committee. 2011. "Equity Mandate Extension Motion." Available at http://www.bcndp.ca/.

BC Stats. June 2008. "BC Census Fast Facts: British Columbia's Labour Force by Industry." Available at http://www.bcstats.gov.bc.ca/.

–. July 2008. "BC Census Fast Facts: Ethnicity and Visible Minority Characteristics of BC's Population." Available at http://www.bcstats.gov.bc.ca/.

–. September 2008. "BC Census Fast Facts: Educational Attainment of British Columbians." Available at http://www.bcstats.gov.bc.ca/.

Cleverdon, Catherine L. 1974. *The Woman Suffrage Movement in Canada*. Toronto: University of Toronto Press.

Collier, Cheryl N. 2008. "Neoliberalism and Violence against Women: Can Retrenchment Convergence Explain the Path of Provincial Anti-Violence Policy, 1985-2005?" *Canadian Journal of Political Science* 41: 19-42.

Edwards, Anne. 2008. *Seeking Balance: Conversations with BC Women in Politics*. Halfmoon Bay, BC: Caitlin Press.

Elections British Columbia. 1988. *Electoral History of British Columbia, 1871-1986*. Available at http://www.llbc.leg.bc.ca/.

Equal Voice British Columbia Chapter. N.d. "Equal Voice BC Notes Percentage of Women Elected Provincially Slowly Trending Upwards." Available at http://www.equalvoice.ca/.

Erickson, Lynda. 1997. "Parties, Ideology, and Feminist Action: Women and Political Representation in British Columbia Politics." In Jane Arscott and Linda Trimble, eds., *In the Presence of Women: Representation in Canadian Governments*, 106-27. Toronto: Harcourt Brace and Company.

—. 2010. "Electoral Behaviour in British Columbia." In Michael Howlett, Dennis Pilon, and Tracy Summerville, eds., *British Columbia Politics and Government*, 131-50. Toronto: Emond Montgomery Publications.

"Executive Council of the Government of British Columbia." 2012. Available at http://www.gov.bc.ca/.

Hewlett, Jason. 2011. "NDP Gender Rules Deemed 'Ridiculous.'" *Kamloops Daily News*, 3 January. Available at http://www.kamloopsnews.ca/.

Howlett, Michael, Dennis Pilon, and Tracy Summerville. 2010. "Introduction." In Michael Howlett, Dennis Pilon, and Tracy Summerville, eds., *British Columbia Politics and Government*, 3-12. Toronto: Emond Montgomery Publications.

Hunter, Justine. 1991. "Women Head Cabinet for Change." *Vancouver Sun*, 6 June.

—. 2011. "A Serious Man: Adrian Dix's Image War with the Liberals." *Globe and Mail*, 22 April.

—. 2012. "Christy Clark's First Budget Not Exactly Family Friendly." *Globe and Mail*, 23 February. Available at http://www.theglobeandmail.com/.

Legislative Library of British Columbia. 2002. *Electoral History of British Columbia, Supplement, 1987-2001*. Available at http://www.llbc.leg.bc.ca/.

—. 2010. "Women Members of the Legislature of British Columbia." 2 July. Available at http://www.llbc.leg.bc.ca/.

—. 2011a. "Campbell Cabinet – 37th Parliament 2001-2005, 38th Parliament 2005-2009, 39th Parliament 2009-2011." 14 March. Available at http://www.llbc.leg.bc.ca/.

—. 2011b. "Cabinets." 11 May. Available at http://www.llbc.leg.bc.ca/.

—. 2013. "A Checklist of Members of the Legislature of British Columbia." 17 January. Available at http://www.llbc.leg.bc.ca/.

Lore, Grace. 2008. "Women Legislators and Women's Issues in British Columbia." *Canadian Parliamentary Review* 3(4): 26-27.

Meier, Petra. 2004. "The Mutual Contagion Effect of Legal and Party Quotas: A Belgian Perspective." *Party Politics* 10(5): 583-600.

Phillips, Stephen 2010. "Party Politics in British Columbia: The Persistence of Polarization." In Michael Howlett, Dennis Pilon, and Tracy Summerville, eds., *British Columbia Politics and Government*, 109-30. Toronto: Emond Montgomery Publications.

Praud, Jocelyne, and Isla Dowling. 2010. "Les services de garde de jeunes enfants au Canada Anglais et au Québec." In Shawna Geissler, Lynn Loutzenhiser, Jocelyne Praud, and Leesa Streifler, eds., *Mothering in Canada: Interdisciplinary Voices/ La maternité au Canada: Voix interdisciplinaires*, 241-56. Downsview, ON: Demeter Press.

Tafler, Sid. 1983. "Bennett Drops Deputy Post." *Globe and Mail*, 27 May.

Teghtsoonian, Katherine. 2010. "Social Policy in Neo-Liberal Times." In Michael Howlett, Dennis Pilon, and Tracy Summerville, eds., *British Columbia Politics and Government*, 309-30. Toronto: Emond Montgomery Publications.

Teghtsoonian, Katherine, and Louise Chappell. 2008. "The Rise and Decline of Women's Policy Machinery in British Columbia and New South Wales: A Cautionary Tale." *International Political Science Review* 29(1): 29-51.

"Thoughts on the BC NDP 50th Anniversary Convention." 2011. 11 December. Available at http://terahertzatheist.ca/.

Trimble, Linda, and Jane Arscott. 2003. *Still Counting: Women in Politics across Canada*. Peterborough: Broadview Press.

4

Complacency and Gender Silence

Women in Manitoba Politics

SHANNON SAMPERT

Winnipeg's historic Exchange District features a two-story mural painted on the side of what used to be called the Walker Theatre.[1] The mural memorializes Nellie McClung's famous mock Parliament speech in which she took Manitoba's premier to task for refusing to grant the vote to women. McClung's tactic was successful: two years later Manitoba women became the first in Canada to win the right to vote. Manitoba has also set the bar for the highest number of women elected in any Canadian legislature. But recent trends suggest a certain level of complacency about ensuring women's fair and equal representation in electoral politics. Indeed, in its 2010 Equity Report Card, the United Nations Platform for Action Committee (UNPAC) – Manitoba determined that "despite women's presence in government, there still seems to be a nervousness around using the W word (Woman) within the halls of power." UNPAC went further: "Without political will, equality will never become entrenched in government practice and policy. We look to our governments to provide leadership on gender equality" (United Nations Platform for Action Committee – Manitoba 2011). Leadership of this sort was not evident in Manitoba's last election, held in 2011, as the number of female candidates, the number of women elected, and the number of women named to cabinet all dropped. Furthermore, women political party leaders are still a rarity. Representational gains made by women in Manitoba are inconsistent at best, and there are few signs of continued

· POLITICAL REPRESENTATION OF WOMEN IN
MANITOBA

FIRSTS

Right to vote and stand for election

▪ Most women win right to vote and stand for election	1916
▪ Aboriginal women win right to vote and stand for election	1952

Contesting office

▪ First women to contest office: Edith Rogers (Liberal), Harriet Dick (Independent), Alice Holling (Independent), A. Pritchard (Labour), and Genevieve Lipsett Skinner (Conservative)	1920
▪ First woman to win office: Edith Rogers (Liberal)	1920-32
▪ First visible minority woman to win office and first visible minority woman named to cabinet: Flor Marcelino (NDP), minister of culture, heritage and tourism	2007 / 2011 to present
▪ First publicly identified lesbian to win office: Jennifer Howard (NDP)	2007 to present
▪ First woman appointed to cabinet: Thelma Forbes (PC), minister of urban development, minister of municipal affairs and public works	1966-69
▪ First woman house leader: Jennifer Howard (NDP)	2010 to present

CURRENT REPRESENTATION AT A GLANCE

		Women elected	
	Date of election	Number	Percent
Women in legislature	2011/04/10	16 of 57	28
Women in cabinet	2011/04/10	7 of 19	37

Women political party leaders
▪ None at present

Advisory council on the status of women
▪ The Status of Women was created in 1982.

commitment to achieving gender parity. Perhaps, having achieved the high-water mark of 32 percent women in the Manitoba legislature in 2007, political leaders assumed that a third of the seats was "good enough" representation for women and have moved on to other issues.

This chapter begins with a look at Manitoba's political context, including a very brief overview of the political parties that helped form the province's political culture. It then examines the representation of women in Manitoba politics, exploring the role the electoral system played in assuring women's first victory at the ballot box, the watershed election for women in Manitoba politics in 1981, and the current status of women in the Manitoba legislature as candidates, MLAs, party leaders, and representatives of the Crown. I contend that, while Manitoba reflects a number of success stories for women in terms of representation, the fact that the electoral project has stalled recently suggests the political will to recruit women has waned. Moreover, the women who have been politically successful do not reflect Manitoba's rich diversity. Finally, I argue that Manitoba's female political leaders have endured gendered criticisms and sexist slurs of the sort that may discourage other women from considering a political career. A diminishing commitment to recruitment of women for party candidacy and leadership positions, coupled with a lack of public discussion of women's political aspirations and policy concerns, suggests the quest for gender parity in Manitoba will continue to be a hard-fought struggle.

Background: Manitoba's Political Culture

Many people tend to lump Manitoba with Alberta and Saskatchewan into one large group dubbed "the West" or "the Prairies." Even worse, Manitoba is often been described (or disparaged) as average, serving as the median in terms of geographic size, economic growth, and political affiliations. However, these depictions of the province show limited appreciation for the interesting political history and culture of Manitoba. The province is truly the centre of the country, serving for centuries as an important transportation hub for interprovincial trade and as the "gateway to the west." Moreover, Manitoba is marked by political contradictions, its unique political culture shaped by periods of conflict.

As Jared Wesley (2010, 62) points out, Manitoba's description as being average reflects the province's "modesty" and "moderation," values that are "embodied in the province's core symbols including its flag, logo, mottos, and slogans." Transformative events have shaped its political culture, beginning with its "violent entry" into Confederation, the Riel Rebellions, the 1919 General Strike, and heated debates regarding bilingualism and biculturalism (54). More recently, the province played a starring role in the failed Meech Lake Accord, which sought to amend the Constitution to reflect Quebec's constitutional aspirations. During the ratification process for Meech Lake, Manitoba became the locus of opposition to the Accord, particularly among First Nations and Aboriginal groups. On the grounds that the Accord did not reflect either the input or the interests of Canada's

Aboriginal peoples, Manitoba MLA Elijah Harper refused to provide the necessary unanimous consent the provincial legislature needed to approve the Accord.[2] Based on these events, Manitoba's political elites recognized "the importance of progressive centrism, pragmatism, and flexible partisanship" (62).

Manitoba's parties did not fully evolve into a modern party system until well into the 1950s. Indeed, coalitions and non-partisanship shaped the political landscape in Manitoba, exemplifying the ideals of compromise and accommodation that were the norm for the first half of the twentieth century. Beginning in the 1950s and from 1969 onward, Manitoba has featured a two-and-a-half-party system, with the battle for control of the provincial legislature alternating between the NDP and the Progressive Conservatives (Adams 2008, 19). The party system plays an important gatekeeping function in the recruitment and nomination of women; thus, the transition from a quasi-competitive, quasi-partisan system into a competitive multi-party system was a significant factor shaping women's representation in the province.

Demographically, Winnipeg is considered one of Canada's most ethnically diverse cities (O'Neill and Wesley 2008, 205). Manitoba has a long history of reliance on immigration policies to boost its population and to consolidate its labour base. Immigrants from eastern Canada, New England, and the United Kingdom began to settle in Manitoba in the 1870s to take advantage of the homestead program. To this day, "Manitoba's labour force growth is heavily reliant on immigrants" (Hum and Simpson 2010, 295) who work in its diverse economy, including its important industrial sector. Manitoba had the fourth highest foreign-born population in the country, according to statistics, with 14 percent of Manitoba's population being born outside Canada (Manitoba 2010, 6). The Philippines and the United Kingdom were the top two source countries of immigration between 1991 and 2006 (ibid.). Overall, visible minorities make up about 10 percent of Manitoba's population.

As well, Manitoba has a large and growing Aboriginal population. In 2004 close to 15 percent of Manitoba's population was Aboriginal, and those numbers were projected to increase largely due to high fertility rates and decreased mortality rates (Manitoba 2005, 11).

Women's Political Representation: The Numbers

In 1916, Manitoba was the first province to grant women the right to vote, and a by-election held in that year provided women with their first opportunity to use the ballot box; however, there was only "one woman in the area eligible to vote" so these new-found rights had no effect (McDowell 1975-76). In the first general election thereafter, in 1920, Liberal Edith Rogers was elected – Manitoba's first female MLA – and she represented Winnipeg until 1932. Prior to her entry into politics, Rogers had played an important role in the war effort, becoming president of the Women's Auxiliary of the Great War Veterans' Association and secretary of the Central Council of the Battalion Auxiliary as well as being awarded the Gold Medal of the Canadian Legion. Her involvement with war work was seen as pivotal to her winning support from veterans and their families in subsequent elections (McDowell 1975-76). It is important to note that Rogers was elected in Winnipeg under a form of proportional representation that was in place only in the city and only from 1920 until 1949 (the ridings outside of Winnipeg did not have this type of PR system). The electoral system utilized a single transferable vote for multiple member constituencies, called a Hare system (Jansen 1998, 61). Winnipeg was, at that time, a ten-member electoral district "and voters cast their ballots by rating their preferences for all candidates involved" (Adams 2008, 12). Rogers was one of five women candidates who ran in the 1920 and 1922 elections in Winnipeg, and, in both elections, she was one of the last candidates to win under the preferential ballot, suggesting that she may not have been as successful if the elections in Winnipeg had been run in a traditional first-past-the-post system.

Indeed, a *Winnipeg Free Press* article suggested that the proportional representation system in place at the time helped women run as candidates because it allowed for "all comers." In contrast, according to the newspaper: "Various parties in the city do not make an effort to have representation from the women electors at their conventions, on their committees and on their tickets" ("Why No Women among Rural Candidates?" *Winnipeg Free Press*, 8 July 1922). Thus, in the early days, the role of the political party as gatekeeper to women's electoral success (already somewhat weakened by the non-partisan nature of early politics) was ameliorated by an electoral system of proportional representation. In 1949, Winnipeg's ten-member constituency was divided into three districts represented by four MLAs each and elected with a preferential ballot system. As a result, the opportunities for women narrowed considerably. From 1941 until 1958, no women were elected, and until 1981 there were never more than two women in the provincial legislature at any point in time.

The seeds of change for women's representation were planted in the contest for the leadership of the NDP, which was the Official Opposition in

TABLE 4.1
Women in the Manitoba legislature, by election

Election date	Party elected	Total number of legislators	Women elected	
			Number	%
1920/06/29	Liberal	55	1	2
1922/07/18	UFM*	55	1	2
1927/06/28	Progressives	55	1	2
1932/06/16	Liberal Progressives	55	0	0
1936/07/27	Liberal Progressives	55	1	2
1941/04/22	Liberal Progressives	55	0	0
1945/10/15	Liberal Progressives	55	0	0
1949/11/10	Liberal Progressives	57	0	0
1953/06/08	PC	57	0	0
1958/06/16	PC	57	0	0
1959/05/14	PC†	57	1	2
1962/12/14	PC	57	2	4
1966/06/23	PC	57	2	4
1969/06/25	NDP	57	1	2
1973/06/28	NDP	57	0	0
1977/10/11	PC	57	1	2
1981/11/17	NDP	57	7	12
1986/03/18	NDP	57	8	14
1988/04/26	PC	57	10	18
1990/09/11	PC	57	10	18
1995/04/25	PC	57	11	19
1999/09/21	NDP	57	13	23
2003/06/03	NDP	57	14	25
2007/05/22	NDP	57	18	32
2011/10/04	NDP	57	16	28

* In Manitoba, when John Bracken was elected premier in 1922 under the United Farmers of Manitoba (UFM) banner, coalition-style government became the norm for provincial politics. The UFM became the Progressives and then the Liberal Progressives formed a coalition government from 1941 until 1953. Thus, under Premier Bracken, candidates ran under distinct party banners but were expected to declare whether they were supporting the governing coalition. According to Chris Adams, party distinctions then became quite unclear.
† In 1960, a by-election resulted in a second woman being elected to the provincial legislature. With the election of Carolyn Alexander Morrison, representation of women grew to 3.5%.
Source: Manitoba Legislative Library.

1979. Muriel Smith, at one time the NDP party president, announced her intention to run as NDP leader, supported by women activists and those associated with the left. Smith ran against Howard Pawley and Russ Doern and, while Pawley easily won the leadership, Smith came in second, signalling to

TABLE 4.2
Women candidates in Manitoba, by party and election

Election date	NDP		PC		Liberal	
	Number	%	Number	%	Number	%
1981/11/17	12	21	5	9	7*	18
1986/03/18	10	18	6	11	13	23
1988/04/26	10	18	7	12	15	26
1990/09/11	16	28	10	18	15	26
1995/04/25	15	26	11	19	16	28
1999/09/21	17	30	15	26	11†	22
2003/06/03	18	32	14	25	22	39
2007/05/22	19	33	16‡	29	17	30
2011/10/04	18	32	12	21	13	24

* Out of 39 seats.
† Out of 51 seats.
‡ Out of 56 seats.
Source: Manitoba Legislative Library.

the party elites that the newly emerging women's movement was beginning
to play a significant role in determining policy direction and party politics.
As a result, Pawley (2011, 85-87) made an important decision to actively
recruit women to run in the subsequent election, and this changed the face
of politics in Manitoba. In the November 1981 election that brought Pawley
and the NDP to office, seven women, including Smith, were elected – the
largest number of women ever elected in the province to that date. A key
ingredient to women's success was Pawley's deliberate decision to ensure
that all ridings, including ridings held by incumbents, actively sought female
candidates. According to Pawley, by doing this, the NDP could recruit strong
women, and, as a result, the party "succeeded in putting forth a number of
first-rank female candidates in winnable ridings for the forthcoming election" (99). Since the 1981 election, power in Manitoba has alternated between NDP and Progessive Conservative governments, and, until the most
recent election in 2011, the number of women elected to the provincial
legislature has risen fairly steadily. Between 1981 and 2011, the percentage
of women in the Manitoba legislature increased in total by sixteen percentage points, with the highest level achieved in 2007 when Gary Doer's NDP
won a third mandate. In that election, 32 percent of the legislators were
women, a provincial record. However, while the NDP was returned to office
in the October 2011 election, the number of female MLAs dropped slightly,

to 28 percent (sixteen women elected). That the number of women elected and the number of women candidates declined in the 2011 election compared to the 2007 election suggests that complacency may have settled in.

Table 4.2 shows that the 2011 election saw all parties run fewer women candidates than in the 2007 election, suggesting that gender was not a primary consideration for party recruitment. The NDP had the highest number of women candidates – eighteen, or 32 percent of its total candidates. The Liberals came in second with thirteen candidates (24 percent) and the PCs had twelve candidates (21 percent). Thus, the steady gains experienced by women in the two dominant parties appear to be at their high-water mark. Moreover, there are very few women candidates who ran outside of the urban centres of Brandon or Winnipeg and few who were visible minorities or Aboriginal.

The NDP, PCs, Liberals, and the Green Party have paid attention to changing demographics, and they ran a diverse field of candidates in the 2011 election, with the percentage of visible minority candidates for the top three parties exceeding 10 percent (Martin 2011). But this has not translated into diversity in representation for women as only one visible minority woman has been elected. The picture is even bleaker for the representation of Aboriginal women. In the 2011 election, no party had many First Nations, Métis, or Inuit candidates: the PC had only 5 percent, the NDP only 7 percent, and the Liberals were highest with 18 percent (Martin 2011). The low numbers translate into a depressing statistic for women: to date, no Aboriginal woman has ever been elected to the Manitoba legislature.

Political Leadership
The Manitoba Liberal Party was responsible for an important "first" for women in Manitoba. In January 1984, Sharon Carstairs, at the time a forty-one-year-old teacher, announced her candidacy for the Liberal Party and became the first female party leader not only in Manitoba but also in western Canada. She easily won the leadership race in a first ballot victory in March 1984 and inherited a party that was in dire shape. According to Trimble and Arscott (2003, 77), Carstairs's leadership of a party that was electorally decimated is not unusual: "Canadian political parties have briefly turned to women leaders for the novelty value, but their inability to parlay the much overplayed 'gender factor' into electoral miracles has led the media and party strategists to conclude, as an Alberta news magazine editor put it, 'we don't do really well with lady political leaders.'" Indeed, Carstairs

TABLE 4.3
Women party leaders in Manitoba

Name	Political party	Period of service
Sharon Carstairs	Manitoba Liberals	1984-93
Ginny Hasselfield	Manitoba Liberals	1996-98
Bonnie Mitchelson	Manitoba Progressive Conservatives (interim leader)	2000

Source: Manitoba Legislative Library.

suggested that being a woman would work to her advantage because women would have a chance to "vote for one of their own" ("Teacher Seeks Liberal Leadership," *Winnipeg Free Press*, 17 January 1984). During her time as Liberal leader, from 1984 until 1993, the percentage of Liberal women candidates grew steadily and the Liberals enjoyed a modicum of success in getting elected to the legislature. However, Carstairs resigned in 1990 after the Liberals lost thirteen seats and after playing a particularly exhausting role in Manitoba's handling of the controversial Meech Lake Accord (Trimble and Arscott 2003, 79). Ginny Hasselfield was the Liberal Party's second woman leader, and she took control of the party in 1996. Like Carstairs she inherited a party that was electorally decimated; however, unlike Carstairs, Hasselfield was unable to improve the party's fortunes and resigned as leader following increasing divisiveness within the party (Gerrard 2006, 164). To this date, the Liberals continue to struggle in Manitoba; that the NDP is a centrist party makes it difficult for the Grits to map out policy areas that set them apart from their primary competitor.

Following his party's loss in the 2011 provincial election, Progressive Conservative leader Hugh McFayden announced he would step down as leader. In April 2012, only one person, Brian Pallister, announced his interest in leading the party, and no women candidates came forwarded to run for the position (CBC 2012). This is perhaps not surprising. While Conservative women MLAs played a key role in PC leader Stuart Murray's resignation in 2005, there was no woman candidate for the post at that time either. Instead, McFayden, a political rookie in 2006 (Rabson 2005), was chosen as leader while more experienced women MLAs like Bonnie Mitchelson, who was first elected in 1986 and was made a cabinet minister under Gary Filmon, sat on the sidelines. Indeed, Mitchelson was the Manitoba Progressive Conservative Party's first female leader in 2000, when she served as interim leader, yet she did not throw her hat into the ring for consideration as leader.

Despite the NDP's record of electing women, when Manitoba premier Gary Doer stepped down to take the position of Canadian ambassador to the United States in 2009, no female candidates stepped forward for the party leadership contest. Theresa Oswald's name was certainly mentioned early on as a replacement for Doer (Owen and Kusch 2009), and she was considered within party circles as "the prototype for the 21st-century politician" ("The Power 30," *Winnipeg Free Press*, 28 October 2007). However, when announcing her decision at a news conference, Oswald cited family reasons and the ongoing H1N1 issue (she was the minister of health at the time) for not seeking the leadership. Instead, she and four other female caucus colleagues supported Andrew Swan's leadership bid. Nancy Allen, then labour minister, said that, while she was "broken-hearted" no female leadership contenders were stepping forward, she was supporting Swan because he was supportive of gender issues (Kusch 2009). However, Swan was incapable of garnering support and he withdrew from the leadership contest early, leaving Steve Ashton and Greg Selinger as the only contenders. Selinger easily won the leadership contest, attracting Swan supporters along the way (Welch 2009).

Obviously, in Manitoba there are a number of dynamic, experienced women who would be capable of taking a leadership role in their party. However, it is also obvious that to date few have stepped forward do so. Perhaps it is because the parties do not seem to be actively recruiting women for leadership positions. Perhaps it is because the women themselves do not want to face the inordinate amount of scrutiny that accompanies these positions. Indeed, as I discuss later in this chapter, the few women who have been elected to leadership positions have faced staggeringly negative attention while in that role.

Women in Cabinet

Between 1981 and 2011, the percentage of women appointed to cabinet has increased, although the record is marked by ups and downs. NDP leader Howard Pawley's attention to gender recruitment did not end with his election in 1981. He named three of the seven women in the NDP caucus to his cabinet (17 percent). He rewarded Muriel Smith with the position of deputy premier (the first Canadian woman to be named to this post), and two other women were also given cabinet postings: Maureen Hemphill in education and Mary Beth Dolin in labour (Pawley 2011, 128). However, in 1986, with Pawley's re-election, only two women were appointed to his cabinet despite the fact that its size increased, resulting in a drop for women's representation to 11 percent. Interestingly, in 1988, when Pawley's government fell to a Conservative minority, party insiders blamed the loss in part on women, who, along with organized labour, were viewed as having too much influence on the party (Santin 1988).

Following the Progressive Conservative win in 1988, Premier Gary Filmon decreased the cabinet in size to sixteen members, and he appointed two women to cabinet posts; thus, women held 13 percent of the overall cabinet. In 1990, women's representation in cabinet dropped to 11 percent because the cabinet size increased by two, while the number of women appointed remained the same. Between 1981 and 1995, the number of women in cabinet never surpassed three, and the overall percentage never went higher than 17 percent.

That all changed, however, when Doer won in 1999. His first cabinet named five women to the inner circle (33 percent), but in the subsequent election in 2003, the numbers dropped back down to three (21 percent). In 2007, six women were named to cabinet, holding a third of the cabinet positions. When Selinger won the leadership, he unveiled a new cabinet in November 2009. Nine women were appointed, including Rosanne Wowchuk, who became Manitoba's first female finance minister (Owen 2009). In 2010, Jennifer Howard was appointed Manitoba's first government House leader. Howard, Manitoba's first lesbian MLA, is also disabled, and in 2011 her ministerial responsibilities included persons with disabilities as well as the post of minster responsible for the status of women. Selinger also named Manitoba's first visible woman minority, Flor Marcelino, the minister of culture, heritage and tourism. In 2011, his new cabinet saw seven women named to it (37 percent), a new record. Overall, under the NDP, the number of women appointed to cabinet has increased in the last decade.

There are other notable firsts for Manitoba women in cabinet. In 1986, NDP MLA Judy Wasylycia-Leis was the first minister to care for her child while at work. Wasylycia-Leis was elected with the Pawley government in 1986, and she cared for her first son, Nick, in her legislature office (Stephenson 1986). Her second son, Joe, was born just a few months after the Pawley government fell, and, as backbencher, she was the first MLA to give birth while in office ("Wasylycia-Leis Gives Birth to Baby Boy," *Winnipeg Sun*, 13 December 1988). Almost twenty years later, the first female cabinet

TABLE 4.4
Women in cabinet in Manitoba, by election

Election date	Party elected	Total number of cabinet ministers*	Women appointed to cabinet		% of women in governing caucus in cabinet
			Number	%	
1981/11/17	NDP/Pawley	18	3	17	60
1986/03/18	NDP/Pawley	19	2	11	50
1988/04/26	PC/Filmon	16	2	13	67
1990/09/11	PC/Filmon	18	2	11	40
1995/04/25	PC/Filmon	18	3	17	60
1999/09/21	NDP/Doer	15	5	33	56
2003/06/03	NDP/Doer	14	3	21	33
2007/05/22	NDP/Doer	18	6	33	46
2011/10/04	NDP/Selinger	19	7	37	44

* Includes the premier.
Source: Manitoba Legislative Library.

minister would give birth while holding office: Healthy Living Minister Theresa Oswald and her husband Sam McCreedy welcomed their son Jack on 20 September 2005 (Saunders 2005). Their experiences challenge the conventional wisdom that women delay entry into political life because of childrearing responsibilities.

Manitoba has had only one female lieutenant governor: Pearl McGonigal, who was the Queen's representative for the province from 1981 until 1986. McGonigal, the second woman lieutenant governor in Canada, was St. James's first female councillor, elected to city council in 1969 (Manitoba 2011a). The fact that McGonigal is Manitoba's lone female lieutenant governor is surprising given that the position is determined by the prime minister in consultation with the premier and is considered non-partisan. As a result, it is the type of appointment that could easily alternate between male and female designates.

TABLE 4.5
Female representatives of the Crown in Manitoba

Name	Period of service
Pearl McGonigal	1981-86

Explanations

Why in a province that has been at the forefront of women's "firsts" is gender parity still out of reach? Why is the rich ethnic diversity of Manitoba not reflected in the legislature? And why have so few women come forward to take an active role in leadership? One of the reasons may be because women Manitoba have organized themselves to work within organizations outside of politics and these organizations have been successful in raising issues about gender equality. There are many feminist organizations in Manitoba that advocate on behalf of women on a number of topics. For example, UNPAC, the Manitoba Farm Women's Conference, and the Manitoba Women's Institute, along with the Manitoba office of the Canadian Centre for Policy Alternatives, the Manitoba Federation of Labour, and the Assembly of Manitoba Chiefs, consider gender in their policy directions. As well, the Province of Manitoba still has a Status of Women Division that operates under the minister of Manitoba labour, and an advisory council operates within that division. This council has a chairperson and a board mandated to work on behalf of women in Manitoba (Manitoba 2011b). As a result, the Manitoba government has demonstrated leadership in the implementation of domestic violence and violence against women programs and has also responded to the gendered implications of health-care policy with the implementation of gender-based analysis in Manitoba Health and the creation of programs for healthy babies and families (United Nations Platform for Action Committee – Manitoba 2011). A community health centre, Klinic, has advocated for women since the 1970s, providing services such as a rape crisis counselling component, pregnancy information, and access to counselling for those who have experienced domestic violence, including children (Klinic 2011). Thus, for some women, political activism from within one of these organizations may be viewed as a more advantageous way to advance concerns about gender equality in Manitoba than engaging in electoral politics.

Another explanation may be that parties no longer feel a need to recruit women. In the last provincial election, none of the political parties seemed to be actively speaking about recruiting more women to run in politics and there was a sense of complacency in dealing with the "woman" problem. In the early days of the women's movement, efforts were made to recruit women to stand as candidates in party nomination contests. However, nominating women candidates has become less important since the NDP returned to power in 1999 under the leadership of Gary Doer. In 2004, NDP party members lashed out at the Doer government for being a "bastion of healthy white males" and demanded a "task force to be formed ... on ways to find more women, Aboriginals, visible minorities and disabled persons as candidates" (Martin 2004). While the push to actively recruit women may have had a small effect in 2007, with just one more female NDP candidate nominated since 2003 (up to nineteen candidates, or 33 percent), the numbers seem to be in decline. All three parties in the 2011 provincial election were relatively mute about their recruitment efforts. That the issue of women running in October 2011 was not discussed was reflected in the number of women candidates nominated.

Finances may also prevent women from running in Manitoba, particularly Aboriginal, minority, and rural women. In an interview with the *Winnipeg Free Press*, Jennifer Howard pinpointed fundraising as a major issue for women who were thinking of running for politics (Martin 2011). Like other women in Canada, Manitoba women are over-represented among the poorest citizens, making on average sixty-nine cents for every dollar men earn. Aboriginal women and women with disabilities earn just 50 percent of the average earnings of all men in Canada. Women who are reliant on social assistance have not seen a significant increase in their support since 1992, and the minimum wage remains the lowest in the country (United Nations Platform for Action Committee – Manitoba 2011). Given women's often tenuous financial circumstances, it is perhaps not that surprising that only certain women are elected – that is, the ones who are financially capable of shouldering the expense of an election. While this is certainly also the case for men of lower social standing, the larger ratio of women living in poverty means that the number of women capable of considering running for provincial politics is smaller than the number of men.

Perhaps more telling, women themselves may make the decision not to run. First, as Howard says, "women tend to undervalue" their skills: "I've never talked to a male candidate and had him express fear that he wasn't smart enough to be a candidate ... but it's a common fear with women" (Martin 2011). As well, women, particularly women leaders, may be looking at the experiences of other high-profile women politicians and deciding to opt out. For example, former Liberal leader Sharon Carstairs, former NDP MLA Marianne Cerilli, former NDP MLA Judy Wasylycia-Leis,[3] and former Winnipeg mayor Susan Thompson all faced derision in their public lives because of their gender. Carstairs's time in office was marred by sexist critiques of her persona and political credibility. In an interview with the *Winnipeg Sun* conducted just before she retired as Liberal leader, Carstairs shared some of the written notes she received from Manitobans during her political career. One questioned her hairstyle, suggesting she looked atrocious. Another suggested that the Liberals needed a new male leader, one who did not "talk and look like Mickey Mouse." One called her "a fat, useless, no-good slob." These personal attacks were one of the reasons Carstairs walked away from the legislature:

> "In the early years, I discounted it (the personal attacks) and then it began to bother me more and more and more. I'm not a negative person, but when I began to find myself becoming more offended, more angry about it, I decided it is time to move on, so I can again become positive ... There's still an unwillingness to accept us (female politicians) as equals," she says. "I get more offended by that, not less." (Stephenson 1993)

Cerilli, an NDP MLA from 1990 until 2003, protested in the Manitoba legislature about the behaviour of a male minister, claiming he said she "needed a slap" (Krueger 1994). Wasylycia-Leis also faced direct personal attacks both during her time as a member of the Legislative Assembly and then later when she ran against incumbent Winnipeg mayor Sam Katz in 2010. She also faced criticism when she brought her sons to work in the 1980s (Flood 1989). In 2010, Wasylycia-Leis was pilloried for never having had a "real job in her life," despite her previous experiences both federally and provincially (Black Rod blogspot 2010). Thompson was Winnipeg's first and only female mayor from 1992 until 1998, and during that time her personal life and status as a single woman was the subject of discussion ("Just a Fighter," *Winnipeg Free Press*, 14 March 1993). In 2010, Thompson described her time in City Hall as "brutal," with personal attacks "so vicious she was glad her parents weren't alive to hear them" (Reynolds 2010). These highly personalized and gendered attacks heaped on women who are in politics send a negative message to women who may be considering a political career.

Conclusion: Prospects for Gender Parity

Manitoba women have enjoyed a number of firsts in Canada: they were the first to receive the vote and to see a woman as leader of a competitive western Canadian provincial party. Manitoba has also led the way in terms of numbers of women in the provincial legislature and in cabinet, setting a trend for other provinces to emulate. However, true equality – a legislature and cabinet within which women hold half of the seats – is a goal that is not being actively pursued. Moreover, efforts to see more diversity among women are apparently not on the agenda. Indeed, a pervasive gender silence suggests a certain level of complacency in Manitoba.

What do I mean by "gender silence"? None of the parties seems to want to talk about women and women's issues in any substantive way. For example, in the 2011 provincial election, none of the political parties talked publicly about efforts to recruit women to run as candidates. Perhaps this should not have been unexpected, given that these types of public disclosures are often met with scorn. Additionally, the gender-neutral term "families" has replaced the more specific term "women" in party policy platforms on issues of childcare, health care, and the economy. It would appear that the high-water mark of success seen in the 2007 election signalled that the representation of women no longer needed attention. In 2011, all three political parties nominated fewer women than they did in 2007, and, as a result, all three saw fewer women win. Thus, women's representation at the nomination level appears to have crested at slightly above 30 percent and certainly well below the fair and equal goal of 50 percent. This is worrisome because it indicates a consensus among party elites that the "woman problem" has been solved and that political parties have moved onto other issues. Hardfought gains for women may well be eroded in future elections if the issue of gender is allowed to fall off the political radar.

Notes

I am grateful for the assistance provided by the reviewers of this chapter. I would also like to thank the wonderful staff at the Manitoba Legislative Library in Archives of Manitoba for their invaluable assistance. And a special thank you to Michelle Falk, my research assistant, who helped with the early stages of my research.
1 The Walker Theatre was renamed the Burton Cummings Theatre in 2002, but some residents of Winnipeg dislike the new name and continue to refer to it as the Walker Theatre.
2 The Accord was not ratified in Newfoundland and Labrador before the deadline, thus Manitoba was one of two provinces that did not approve the Accord before the deadline. As a result, this constitutional amendment package was not passed into law.
3 Wasylycia-Leis went on to become an NDP MP and most recently was a Winnipeg mayoral candidate.

References

Adams, Christopher. 2008. *Politics in Manitoba: Parties, Leaders, and Voters.* Winnipeg: University of Manitoba Press.
Black Rod Blogspot. 2010. 5 May. Available at http://blackrod.blogspot.ca/.

CBC. 2012. "Brian Pallister Sets Sights on PC Leadership." 11 April. Available at http://www.cbc.ca/.

Flood, Gerald. 1989. "MLA Nurses Baby at Work." *Winnipeg Free Press*, 22 February.

Gerrard, Jon, with Gary Girard. 2006. *Battling for a Better Manitoba: A History of the Provincial Liberal Party.* Winnipeg: Heartland Associates.

Hum, Derek, and Larry Simpson. 2010. "Manitoba in the Middle: A Mutual Fund Balanced for Steady Income." In Paul Thomas and Curtis Brown, eds., *Manitoba Politics and Government: Issues, Institutions, Traditions*, 293-305. Winnipeg: University of Manitoba Press.

Jansen, Harold John. 1998. "The Single Transferable vote in Alberta and Manitoba." PhD diss., University of Alberta.

Klinic. 2011. "Our History." Available at http://www.klinic.mb.ca/.

Krueger, Alice. 1994. "Sexism Rife, MLAs Claim: Taunts, Harassment Common – Carstairs." *Winnipeg Free Press*, 16 June.

Kusch, Larry. 2009. "Swan First to Throw Hat into the Ring." *Winnipeg Free Press*, 3 September.

Manitoba. 2005. *Manitoba's Aboriginal Community: A 2001 to 2026 Population and Demographic Profile.* Winnipeg: Government of Manitoba.

–. 2010. *Ethnicity Series: A Demographic Portrait of Manitoba.* Vol. 1: *Foreign Born Population.* Winnipeg: Government of Manitoba.

Martin, Melissa. 2011. "Faces of the Election." *Winnipeg Free Press*, 3 October.

Martin, Nick. 2004. "Doer Government Called Bastion of White Males." *Winnipeg Free Press*, 8 March.

McDowell, Linda. 1975-76. "Some Women Candidates for the Manitoba Legislature." Manitoba Historical Society. Available at http://www.mhs.mb.ca/.

O'Neill, Brenda, and Jared Wesley. 2008. "Diversity and Political Representation in Winnipeg." In Caroline Andrew, John Biles, Myer Siemiatycki, and Erin Tolley, eds., *Electing a Diverse Canada: The Representation of Immigrants, Minorities, and Women*, 205-28. Vancouver: UBC Press.

Owen, Bruce. 2009. "Selinger Overhauls Cabinet." *Winnipeg Free Press*, 4 November.

Owen, Bruce, and Larry Kusch. 2009. "New Premier Arrives October 17." *Winnipeg Free Press*, 1 September.

Pawley, Howard. 2011. *Keep True: A Life in Politics.* Winnipeg: University of Manitoba Press.

Manitoba. 2011a. Lieutenant Governor of Manitoba. History. Past Lieutenant Governors. The Honourable Pearl McGonigal. Available at http://www.lg.gov. mb.ca/.

–. 2011b. Manitoba Labour and Immigration. Status of Women. Available at http:// www.gov.mb.ca/.

Rabson, Mia. 2005. "Murray Not in House, Likely Stepping Down Today." *Winnipeg Free Press*, 8 November.

Reynolds, Lindor. 2010. "Thompson Bears Scars from Her Time in Office." *Winnipeg Free Press*, 6 May.

Santin, Aldo. 1988. "Battered NDP Vows to Start Rebuilding." *Winnipeg Free Press*, 27 April.

Saunders, Carol. 2005. "Minister Takes Time for New Baby." *Winnipeg Free Press,*
    6 October.
Stephenson, Wendy. 1986. "Corridors of Power: Uniting Family with Politics." *Win-
    nipeg Sun,* 27 July.
—. 1993. "Red Sails in the Sunset." *Winnipeg Sun,* 2 May, 30-31.
Trimble, Linda, and Jane Arscott. 2003. *Still Counting: Women in Politics across
    Canada.* Peterborough: Broadview Press.
United Nations Platform for Action Committee – Manitoba. 2011. *Manitoba
    Equality Report Card.* Available at http://www.unpac.ca/.
Welch, Mary Agnes. 2009. "Selinger Wins NDP Race." *Winnipeg Free Press,* 17
    October.
Wesley, Jared. 2010. "Political Culture in Manitoba." In Paul Thomas and Curtis
    Brown, eds., *Manitoba Politics and Government: Issues, Institutions, Traditions,*
    43-72. Winnipeg: University of Manitoba Press.

5

A Province at the Back of the Pack
Women in New Brunswick Politics

JOANNA EVERITT

In the 2010 New Brunswick provincial election, eight women were elected: together they comprised almost 15 percent of the seats in the Legislative Assembly. Slightly better than the seven elected previously, neither result was a high-water mark for women's representation in the province. That feat occurred in 1999 when women held ten (18 percent) of the fifty-five seats. Since then levels have dropped to an approximation of those in the late 1980s and have not improved substantially. Thus, while New Brunswick sat near the middle of the pack in terms of provincial political representation of women in the mid-1990s (Desserud 1997, 256), other provinces have now pulled ahead and New Brunswick has fallen into last place in Canada.

This chapter considers the situation of women in New Brunswick politics and attempts to account for why so few women have been elected in recent years. It examines the impact of the party system, the electoral system, role models, and the presence of advocacy organizations such as the NB Advisory Council on the Status of Women and Equal Voice on women's success (or lack thereof) in provincial election campaigns. I conclude that the traditional two-party system and the single-member plurality electoral system are the primary explanations for why women's representation has remained so low. Further, I counsel caution regarding the potential for change, despite the increase in the number of female candidates in the last provincial election and the creation of a New Brunswick chapter of Equal Voice.

POLITICAL REPRESENTATION OF WOMEN IN
NEW BRUNSWICK

FIRSTS

Right to vote and stand for election
- Most women win right to vote and stand for election   1919
- Aboriginal women win right to vote   1963

Contesting office
- First woman to contest office: Dr. Frances Fish (Conservative)   1935
- First woman to win office: Brenda Robertson (PC)   1967-84
- First woman appointed to cabinet: Brenda Robertson (PC),   1970-74
  minister of youth, minister of health, minister responsible for
  social program reform
- First woman political party leader: Elizabeth Weir (NDP)   1988-2005
- First publicly identified lesbian to lead a political party: 2005-6
  Allison Brewer (NDP)

CURRENT REPRESENTATION AT A GLANCE

		Women elected	
	Date of election	Number	Percent
Women in legislature	2010/09/27	8 of 55	15
Women in cabinet	2010/10/12	5 of 15	33

Women political party leaders
- None at present

Lieutenant governor
- None at present

Advisory council on the status of women
- The Advisory Council on the Status of Women was created in 1975 and disbanded
  in 2011.

Background

New Brunswick, Canada's only bilingual province, is the home of almost
730,000 individuals. Between 85,000 and 125,000 people reside in each of
its three main cities and their surrounding communities; approximately half
the population lives in small towns or rural communities. The rural economy has been driven by forestry, mining, fishing, and mixed farming, while

the urban economies vary, with oil refining and paper mills in Saint John, transportation and distribution in Moncton, and government, universities, and the military in Fredericton.

The north is predominately French-speaking Acadian (27 percent), whereas the south is composed mainly of individuals of English, Irish, and Scottish ancestry (60 percent). Other ethnic identities, almost all European, have increased in recent years but remain limited (around 10 percent). Less than 2 percent have South Asian, East Asian, Middle Eastern, or African backgrounds, limiting their numerical impact on the province's political culture. The First Nations population is also small (around 3 percent) and is located primarily in the north and along the St. John River. As a result, the major demographic cleavage in the province is language, with the population divided north-south on linguistic lines. These linguistic identities are overlaid by religious identities, and religion continues to play an important role in New Brunswick. Over half of the population identify themselves as Catholic, and another approximately 30 percent identify as Protestant (Baptists, United Church of Canada, Anglicans, and Pentecostals).

The rural, economic, and cultural make-up of New Brunswick accounts in part for its slow progress towards women's political equality. Such locales are less likely to see women running as political candidates because of the patron-client role played by local politicians within rural economic settings (Carbert 2006, 2010; Pitre 2004). As Darcy, Welch, and Clark (1994) note, blue-collar, working-class cultures are traditionally male-dominated and often provide limited roles for women. While a working-class heritage alone does not lead to a rejection of gender equality, in combination with a more static culture, such as that found in New Brunswick, it can create an environment resistant to changes that may be perceived as disruptive to the established social and political orders within political parties. Women's representation tends to be low in traditionalistic cultures in which there is an "emphasis on the continuity of elite control in social, economic and political affairs" (56).

For much of the province's history it has been possible to classify New Brunswick as a traditionalistic culture due to its clear class divisions and social hierarchy, along with the presence of a small number of notable families – such as the Irvings, McCains, and, to a lesser extent, the Olands and Ganongs – that hold key economic and political decision-making positions within the province. While Conrad (2003, 84) suggests that New Brunswick and Atlantic Canada are no more socially conservative than are other parts of the country, when factors such as support for the New

Democratic Party, the rural-urban mix, the incidence of incumbents, and political culture are taken into account, there is evidence of a more traditional political culture that is less open to the election of women.

The French-English divide, along with a more subtle, yet nonetheless important, Catholic-Protestant distinction have tended to focus attention away from other identity-based cleavages, making gender representation less prominent than language or religious diversity. Finally, the rigid two-party system (New Brunswick has never had a minority government) has continued to resist the efforts of the New Democratic Party, a party that is more open to women's political representation (Young 2002) than others, to gain a foothold in the province.[1] Taken together, these factors result in a political culture that, while not blatantly hostile to women's political involvement (O'Neill and Erickson 2003), has not worked effectively from within to become more inclusive. Accordingly, the status quo remains unchallenged.

Women's Political Representation: The Numbers

Members of the Legislative Assembly

Save for a period in the 1990s, New Brunswick has lagged behind other provinces in terms of the representation of women. It was the seventh province to grant women the right to vote (in 1919) and the ninth (second to last) to grant them the right to run for provincial office (in 1934). The first woman to run for a seat in the provincial Legislative Assembly was Dr. Frances Fish, a Progressive Conservative, who ran unsuccessfully in the election of 1935. Few women stood for provincial office over the next few decades, and it was not until 1967 that Brenda Robertson made history by becoming the first woman elected to the Legislative Assembly of New Brunswick.[2] In 1970, she also became the first female cabinet minister in the province, appointed by Progressive Conservative premier Richard Hatfield to the youth portfolio.

In the twenty years following Robertson's first election in 1967, only three other women were successful in New Brunswick politics: Liberal Shirley Dysart (1974-95), Progressive Conservative Mabel DeWare (1978-87), and Progressive Conservative Nancy Teed (1978-87). With the McKenna Liberal sweep in 1987, the number of women in the Legislative Assembly almost doubled, jumping from four to seven. While all three PC women lost their seats, six new women joined Dysart on the government benches, pointing to the impact that landslides can have in improving women's representation. As can be seen from Table 5.1, since 1987 the number of women elected to the Legislative Assembly has ranged from a low of seven (1987, 2003,

TABLE 5.1

Women in the New Brunswick legislature, by election

Election date	Party elected	Total number of legislators	Women candidates		Women elected	
			Number	%	Number	%
1935/06/27	Liberal	58	1	1	0	0
1939/11/20	Liberal	58	0	0	0	0
1944/08/28	Liberal	58	0	0	0	0
1948/06/28	Liberal	58	1	0.1	0	0
1952/09/22	PC	58	0	0	0	0
1956/06/18	PC	58	0	0	0	0
1960/06/27	Liberal	58	0	0	0	0
1963/04/22	Liberal	58	2	2	0	0
1967/10/13	Liberal	58	3	3	1	2
1970/10/26	PC	58	3	2	1	2
1974/11/18	PC	58	13	7	2	3
1978/10/23	PC	58	13	7	4	7
1982/10/12	PC	58	19	10	4	7
1987/10/12	Liberal	58	31	17	7	12
1991/09/23	Liberal	58	52	23	10	17
1995/09/11	Liberal	55	47	21	9	16
1999/06/07	PC	55	46	24	10	18
2003/06/09	PC	55	34	19	7	13
2006/09/18	Liberal	55	33	20	7	13
2010/09/27	PC	55	72	31	8	15

Source: Elections New Brunswick, various years.

2006) to a high of ten (1991 and 1999). The results of September 2010 improved slightly but not enough to alter the province's position at the back of the pack in terms of gender representation.

The situation municipally and federally in New Brunswick is just as bleak. Politicians often use municipal experience as a stepping stone to other levels of office. However, if few women hold municipal office, a potential pool of provincial or federal aspirants is lost. In 2001 women made up 23 percent of city councillors, and that number increased to 32 percent only in 2012. The situation for female mayors, at 18 percent, is worse, having only increased by three percentage points since 1992. Women's representation in the federal House of Commons is even lower there than it is at the provincial and municipal levels. In 2004, two women represented New

TABLE 5.2
Women's success in different New Brunswick parties, 1970-2010

Party	Number of women MLAs	% of all women MLAs	Total number of MLAs	% of party's MLAs who were women
PC	17	52	146	12
Liberal	14	42	148	10
NDP	1	3	3	33
CoR	1	3	9	11
Total	33	100	306	

Source: Elections New Brunswick, various years.

Brunswick in Ottawa, accounting for 20 percent of the MPs. In 2011, there was only one female New Brunswick MP (10 percent). In other words, as at the provincial level, federal and municipal data show a persistent pattern of under-representation of New Brunswick women in political decision-making bodies.

As Table 5.2 indicates, since Robertson's election forty years ago, seventeen (52 percent) of the women who have been elected to the Legislative Assembly were members of the Progressive Conservative party. A slightly smaller number, fourteen (or 42 percent), were members of the Liberal Party. Both the NDP and the Confederation of Regions (CoR) parties elected one female MLA, each representing 3 percent of the overall number of women elected. These numbers are understandable given that the Progressive Conservatives had won seven of the eleven elections since 1970, holding office for twenty-five years. The Liberals won four elections, forming the government for only fifteen years. Surprisingly, a slightly larger percentage of Progressive Conservative MLAs have been women. Slightly more women MLAs have been Progressive Conservatives (12 percent) than Liberals (9 percent) over the past four years.

Candidates
As Table 5.3 indicates, both the Liberal Party and the Progressive Conservative Party have run roughly the same number of candidates, and in five of the last eight elections the latter has run the fewest female candidates. As classic brokerage parties, they share similar ideological space, differentiating themselves by their personnel rather than by their policies. Both parties also situate themselves to the right of centre, making them less likely to nominate women than are parties of the left.

TABLE 5.3
Women candidates in New Brunswick, by party

	PC		Liberal		NDP		CoR		Green		Other*		Total	
	N	%	N	%	N	%	N	%	N	%	N	%	N	%
1982	6	11	3	5	9	17	–	–	–	–	1	10	19	10
1987	6	10	7	12	16	28	–	–	–	–	–	–	30	16
1991	8	14	9	16	25	43	10	21	–	–	–	–	52	23
1995	5	9	8	15	20	36	5	19	–	–	8	47	47	21
1999	10	18	9	16	24	44	1	6	–	–	2	22	46	24
2003	9	16	9	16	15	27	–	–	–	–	1	11	34	19
2006	8	15	10	18	15	31	–	–	–	–	–	–	33	21
2010	14	25	12	22	18	33	–	–	23	45	5	29	72	31
Total	66	20	67	20	142	43	16	5	23	7	17	5	333	21

* The "Other" category includes the Parti Acadien (1982), the Natural Law Party (1995 and 1999), the Grey Party (2003), and the People's Alliance of NB (2010). The minor parties frequently do not run full slates and their percentages are calculated by using the actual total number of candidates presented.

Source: Elections New Brunswick, various years.

This classic two-party system helps explain New Brunswick's dismal record in electing women. The New Democratic Party has never had more than two members sitting in the Legislative Assembly, leaving "the dynamic force" (Young 2002) in Canadian politics absent. Although since 1987 between 27 and 44 percent of the NDP candidates have been women, the party's weak standing in the polls has meant that the other parties have been able to ignore its example. Indeed, as Sonia Pitre's (2003a, 2003b) work shows, the Progressive Conservative and Liberal parties in New Brunswick have no formal regulations to assist women in running for riding nominations. Only in the most recent provincial election have the Conservatives or the Liberals run female candidates in over 20 percent of the ridings.

Table 5.3 indicates that little change has occurred in the number of women running for election since the mid-1990s. The appearance of the Green Party in 2010 accounts for the most substantial increase in female candidates. The Greens, like the NDP, promote equality within their party; a new but politically weak party, the Greens are unlikely to win a seat. Women are less likely to be found in more competitive positions within strong political parties (Bashevkin 1993, chap. 3), and they are often run as sacrificial lambs in what might be considered lost-cause ridings (Brodie 1985, 117). Minor parties such as the Parti Acadien (1982), the Confederation of Regions party (1991), the Natural Law Party (1995 and 1999), the Grey Party (2003), and, most recently, the People's Alliance of New Brunswick (2010) and the Green Party, have generally run a proportionately larger number of women than have the more established parties.

Factors such as the single-member plurality electoral system and the challenge of incumbency also contribute to the poor representation of women. Plurality systems enable each constituency to determine that its best candidate is a male, something unlikely to happen under a more proportional electoral system in which party lists can receive greater scrutiny and therefore party elites are pressured to ensure a better gender balance. For this reason the New Brunswick Advisory Council on the Status of Women (NBACSW) recommended that the electoral system be changed during the public hearings of the New Brunswick Commission on Legislative Democracy (NBCLD) in 2004 (NBACSW 2004).

Unfortunately, despite the fact that the NBCLD eventually recommended changing the provincial electoral system to a mixed-member proportional system, there has been little movement in the province to consider this option (New Brunswick 2004). The commission's recommendations languished after the 2006 election. The incoming Liberals had little interest in electoral reform, and even with the return of the Progressive Conservatives to government it is unlikely that any change will occur.

Incumbency also contributes to the low number of women elected in New Brunswick. The position of MLA confers significant benefits in a relatively poor province like New Brunswick, in terms of both income and prestige. Once elected, few individuals willingly step down from office unless they are retiring. Most leave office due to electoral defeat. As a result, in any given election most "winnable" seats for any given party are already taken, and they are probably held by a man. In the 2010 provincial election, only seven of the fifty-five ridings had no incumbent running. In six of seven ridings the party that held the seat replaced the incumbent with a man. In the seventh, the female incumbent was replaced by another woman. All the women non-incumbents challenged in ridings in which their party had previously lost. Such an unlevel playing field makes it difficult to increase the number of female candidates and the number of women MLAs elected. If parties increase the number of female candidates that they run, but only run them in ridings in which the party is unlikely to win, there is little chance of increasing the overall number of female MLAs. The McKenna landslide in 1987 produced an immediate jump in the number of women in the Legislative Assembly, though many of these seats were lost when the Lord PCs defeated the Liberals in 1999. This replacement of Liberal women with Conservative women happened again in 2010. This suggests that the two main parties would need to make a concerted effort to replace incumbents with women for any increase in the number of women elected to occur.

The data in Table 5.4 indicate the number of terms in office held by the male and female MLAs in the various New Brunswick political parties. A substantial portion of MLAs hold their seats for multiple terms. Female MLAs tend to have shorter political careers than do their male counterparts. This is particularly the case for the Liberal MLAs as almost 43 percent of female MLAs are defeated after just one term compared to 29 percent of male MLAs. An even larger number of both male and female Conservative MLAs are defeated after just one term; however, the gender gap in this experience is much smaller.

About 10 percent more women than men in both parties serve only one or two terms. Women are especially electorally vulnerable and are more likely to run in ridings in which their party has a lower level of support, giving them little chance of winning. The flip side of this observation is that a similarly disproportionate number of men are likely to run in constituencies

TABLE 5.4

Term lengths for MLAs in New Brunswick

	1 term	2 terms	3 terms	4 terms	5 or more	Total
PC						
Women	9 (53%)	3 (18%)	2 (12%)	2 (12%)	1 (6%)	17
Men	61 (47%)	17 (13%)	18 (14%)	20 (16%)	13 (10%)	129
Difference	6%	5%	-2%	-4%	-6%	
Total	70	20	20	22	14	146
Liberal						
Women	6 (43%)	3 (21%)	4 (29%)	0	1 (7%)	14
Men	39 (29%)	34 (25%)	31 (23%)	14 (10%)	16 (12%)	134
Difference	14%	-4%	6%	-10%	-5%	
Total	45	37	35	14	17	148
NDP						
Women	–	–	–	1 (33%)	–	1
Men	2 (67%)	–	–	–	–	2
Total	2	–	–	1	–	3
CoR						
Women	1 (13%)	–	–	–	–	1
Men	7 (88%)	–	–	–	–	7
Total	8	–	–	–	–	8

Note: Data in this table include all MLAs who have held office since the first female MLA was elected to office in 1967.
Source: Elections New Brunswick, various years.

that are electoral strongholds for their party. Overall, male candidates are generally better positioned to win than are female candidates.

Part of the explanation for this tendency may be linked to the relatively informal recruitment process that is in place in the Liberal Party and, to a lesser degree, in the Progressive Conservative Party (Pitre 2003a). In both parties little targeted recruitment of women or other under-represented groups occurs. The NDP has a much more institutionalized approach, which relies more heavily on candidate search committees that actively seek out potential candidates (Pitre 2003a). As Tremblay and Pelletier (2001) have found, women holding positions as riding presidents (and possibly in other senior positions) can often have an influence on who runs as a candidate. Furthermore, party elites perceive that women have a more difficult time running in rural areas than do men due to the additional barrier of having to overcome traditional gender biases (Pitre 2004, 228). This leads a large number of rural riding associations to be unwelcoming to female candidates.

The degree to which parties adhere to an egalitarian or feminist ideology is perhaps the most important factor. Pitre (2003a, 122) notes that the competitive parties are not prepared to act decisively to recruit women, perhaps because of a misplaced "perception that the recruitment and selection of candidates is an entirely neutral process, which is not the case." As a result, female candidates are more likely to run in seats where their party is traditionally less successful (Pitre 2004; Erickson 1991).

Party Leaders

Five women have served as party leader: Louise Blanchard (1981) for the Parti Acadien; Shirley Dysart (as interim leader in 1995) for the Liberals; Elizabeth Weir (1988-2005) and Allison Brewer (2005-6) for the NDP; and Barbara Baird-Filliter (1989-91) for the Progressive Conservatives. While the role played by each of these women in New Brunswick politics differs, their experiences as leaders of minor parties, as interim leaders, or

TABLE 5.5
Women party leaders in New Brunswick

Name	Political party	Period of service
Barbara Baird-Filliter	PC	1989-91
Elizabeth Weir	NDP	1988-2005
Allison Brewer	NDP	2005-6

as leaders of parties that have just suffered a crushing defeat were similar to those of female party leaders elsewhere.

Louise Blanchard,[3] leader of the Parti Acadien, was the first female leader of a political party in New Brunswick. However, since the Parti acadien was a minor party in decline at the time of her election, little attention has been given to her achievement (see Desserud 1997). Since its formation in 1972, the party has promoted bilingualism and social and educational reform for the Acadian community. Blanchard was its fourth leader, and despite running candidates in several elections the party never won any seats. After the 1982 election, in which Blanchard ran unsuccessfully, the party became inactive, officially dissolving in 1986.

Shirley Dysart was the first woman to lead a party in the Legislative Assembly. She served as interim leader of the Liberal Party in the mid-1990s when the Official Opposition held only eighteen of fifty-eight seats. Dysart stepped down when Frank McKenna took over the leadership, and she subsequently became one of his senior cabinet ministers.

Barbara Baird-Filliter assumed the leadership of the New Brunswick Progressive Conservatives in 1989 after the party's crushing defeat in the 1987 election. She had never run for office and had no direct links to the former Hatfield government. This forty-year-old family lawyer provided a fresh start for a party that had lost every seat in the Legislative Assembly. However, like other women party leaders, she suffered from intense and critical scrutiny that portrayed her as "a lightweight, unable to understand complex issues" (Desserud 1997, 273). She resigned within a year and a half, saying she had received poor advice and that the party was looking for a scapegoat to blame for its state of disarray. Reluctant though she was to attribute her experiences to sexism and a male-dominated political culture, her experiences within her party and with the New Brunswick media are similar to those of women elsewhere (see Everitt 2003; Robinson and Saint-Jean 1991, 1995).

The New Democratic Party has the most experience with female party leaders, fitting with its reputation for openness to female candidates as well as its weak electoral status in the province (Bashevkin 2009). It first selected Elizabeth Weir in 1988. Weir won her seat in Saint John in 1991 by a slim margin but held it until she retired from politics in 2005. She was an important force in New Brunswick politics, playing an active role in the Legislative Assembly and attracting substantial media attention. However, for the duration of her term she was the sole NDP MLA. Unlike in the case of Alexa McDonough in Nova Scotia, the weakness of the NDP support in New Brunswick made it difficult to build a viable party infrastructure, and the concentration of the party's limited resources in her own riding during each election minimized other candidates' ability to get elected.

In 2005, Weir was replaced by Allison Brewer, Canada's first publicly identified lesbian party leader (Everitt and Camp 2009a, 2009b). Brewer's experience as party leader was affected by her status as a woman and as a lesbian. She was not given credit for her previous experience and was frequently and incorrectly presented as a single-issue candidate. Not unexpectedly, given her party's weak support in the province, she failed to win her seat in the 2006 provincial election and resigned as party leader shortly thereafter.

Lieutenant Governors

Two women have served as lieutenant governor in New Brunswick, a high-profile (albeit a powerless) political role. Margaret Norrie McCain, a well-known social activist and philanthropist married to Wallace McCain, co-founder of McCain Foods Limited, served between 1994 and 1997. She had a background in social work and was actively involved in organizations that championed women's rights, social equality, the elimination of family violence, education, and the arts.

McCain was replaced by Marilyn Trenholme Counsell, who served between 1997 and 2003. Trenholme Counsell, a family physician from Sackville, New Brunswick, served as MLA for Tantramar between 1987 and 1997 and held two minister of state portfolios under Frank McKenna. She was appointed to the Senate in 2003.

The appointment of the women lieutenant governors gave a symbolic nod towards the political representation of women and issues of concern to women without any accompanying policy change (see Gotell and Brodie 1991); nonetheless, these women served as important political role models in New Brunswick. Each was a social activist in her own way and saw part of her role as drawing attention to issues concerning women, children, and families.

TABLE 5.6
Female representatives of the Crown in New Brunswick

Name	Period of service
Margaret Norrie McCain	1994-97
Marilyn Trenholme Counsell	1997-2003

TABLE 5.7
Women in cabinet in New Brunswick, by election

Election date	Party elected	Total number of cabinet ministers*	Women appointed to cabinet Number	%	Number of women in governing caucus	% of women in governing caucus in cabinet*
1982/10/12	PC	23	3	13	3	100
1987/10/12	Liberal	21	3	14	7	43
1991/09/23	Liberal	18	4	22	7	57
1995/09/11	Liberal	21	5	24	7	71
1999/06/07	PC	15	3	20	8	38
2003/06/09	PC	18	5	28	5	100
2006/09/18	Liberal	19	2	11	4	50
2010/09/27	PC	16	5	31	8	63

* Includes the premier.
Source: Materials from the NB Legislative Library.

Cabinet

Along with leading political parties or serving as lieutenant governor, female politicians have been able to serve as role models through their positions in cabinet. Pressures for inclusivity have resulted in at least one woman sitting at the cabinet table since 1977. Robertson was joined by Mable DeWare in 1978 and by Nancy Teed in 1982. During the McKenna years the numbers grew from three women in his first cabinet to five in the cabinets established after the 1991 and the 1995 elections. During this period five of the seven women in the Liberal caucus also had a seat in cabinet.

Bernard Lord's Progressive Conservatives elected eight new PC women after their 1999 victory but defeated six of the seven Liberal women. Despite having more women in its caucus, the PC government only had three women in its first cabinet. However, since Lord appointed a smaller cabinet, women retained 20 percent of its seats. After the 2003 election all five women were appointed to Lord's second cabinet.

The low point for women in New Brunswick came with the election of the Shawn Graham Liberal government in 2006. Only seven women were elected – three Liberals and four Progressive Conservatives. A few months later Joan McAlpine-Stiles crossed the floor to the government side. Graham chose Carmel Robichaud and Mary Schryer, who together comprised 11 percent of the cabinet seats. For eighteen months in the middle of the Liberal's term New Brunswick had only one female cabinet minister (5 percent of the cabinet seats), the poorest representation it had had in thirty years. The election of the David Alward Progressive Conservatives in 2010 increased the number of women in the government caucus, giving him the opportunity to appoint five of his eight female MLAs to cabinet.

Simply looking at the numbers of women in cabinet would lead one to conclude that, except for the Graham interlude, New Brunswick's premiers have done a fairly good job of appointing women to cabinet over the last forty years. The Progressive Conservatives under Richard Hatfield set the example: all three of their female MLAs sat in cabinet during his last government. Bernard Lord repeated this experience in his second government in the mid-2000s, and Frank McKenna and David Alward surpassed this number with five women at their cabinet tables in 1995-99 and 2010, respectively. The chance of a woman who sits on the government side of the Legislative Assembly being appointed to cabinet would appear to be stronger in New Brunswick than in other provinces: "Women have done better, proportionately, in cabinet appointments than in legislative elections" (Studlar and Moncrief 1997, 73). Given this trend, and given the concern that many of these female cabinet ministers have expressed over the years concerning female political representation,[4] it is discouraging that more women have not been recruited to political life in recent years.

The responsibility and the profile that comes with cabinet positions makes a female cabinet minister a role model. As other scholars have indicated (Bashevkin 1993, 87-89; Studlar and Moncrief 1997), women tend to have less influential positions in cabinet (e.g., local government or environment), hold portfolios that are "housekeeping files" (e.g., ministers of state) or that are stereotypically gendered, such as family and community services, status of women, or seniors. Desserud (1997) argues that this was not necessarily the case in New Brunswick; however, a forty-year review of the various cabinet portfolios held by women in successive New Brunswick governments suggests otherwise as women are frequently appointed to the less prestigious and lower-profile areas of responsibility or portfolios. When a woman was appointed to higher-prestige positions, her tenure was often brief, as was the case for Aldéa Landry, minister responsible for intergovernmental affairs (1987-91), or during periods in which the position is of lesser importance.

Table 5.8 indicates that only 36 percent of the portfolios held by women could be defined as senior portfolios, including justice/attorney general, health, education, labour, or family and community services, whereas 64 percent of the female cabinet ministers were in more junior, relatively

TABLE 5.8
Portfolios held by women in New Brunswick cabinets

	High prestige	Medium prestige	Low prestige	Total
Senior	Deputy premier (1) Inter-governmental affairs (1) Justice/attorney general (2) Health (5) Education (3)	Labour (3) Transportation (1) Fisheries (1) Solicitor general (1)	Family and community services (11)	29 (11%)
Junior		Environment (7) Postsecondary education (5) Energy (3) Housing (2) Human resource development (2) Public safety (1) Supply and services (1) Income assistance (2)	Local government (8) Non-profit organizations (3) Aboriginal affairs (1) Tourism (1) Status of women (7) Seniors (4) Childhood (3) Literacy and adult education (1)	51 (89%)
Total	12 (15%)	29 (36%)	39 (49%)	80

Source: Materials from the NB Legislative Library.

low-profile portfolios. No woman has served as minister of finance or economic development. When women held more powerful portfolios, as is the case in other provinces, they tended to be responsible for more traditionally feminine areas associated with social spending, such as health and education, reflecting a gendered division of labour in cabinet responsibility. While women have held cabinet positions in New Brunswick since the early 1970s, their overall presence has not been large, prominent, or powerful. This situation has limited their ability to serve as important role models for other women considering a future in politics.

Explanations

New Brunswick remains one of the laggards in the country in women's representation, falling at the back of the pack in terms of seats held by women in the Legislative Assembly. Stocktaking of women's participation in provincial political office in the mid-1990s found that the majority of the provinces' levels of representation fell in the range of 15 to 19 percent, with New Brunswick sitting at slightly over 16 percent. Fifteen years later, levels of representation have increased in the majority of the provinces, whereas New Brunswick has actually dropped slightly to just below 15 percent.

It is understandable that New Brunswick trails behind the more urban provinces such as Ontario, British Columbia, or Quebec; or the western provinces, which are more likely to support left-wing parties. That it has fallen so far behind other Atlantic provinces with similar social, economic, and political cultures is surprising. To understand women's representation in New Brunswick, however, we must continue to look to its rural nature, its persistent two-party system supported by the first-past-the-post electoral system, and a political discourse that sees representation more in terms of language or religion rather than in terms of gender. This conclusion is accentuated by a high degree of incumbency and the lack of internal pressures to see that parties reform their structures to make them more open to women.

In addition, with few women holding seats in the Legislative Assembly few female role models have existed in New Brunswick politics. Women leaders of political parties and members of provincial cabinets have tended to follow patterns found elsewhere in the country. Women leaders tend to have held their leadership positions when their party held little power in the legislative assemblies or when their party had been electorally decimated (Bashevkin 2009; Trimble and Arscott 2003). Similarly, women have tended to play a limited role around New Brunswick's cabinet table, and when they do play a role, they hold traditionally feminine portfolios or ones that have little power and influence.

In the early 2000s Premier Bernard Lord established a commission to examine democratic structures in the province and possibilities for improving them. Academics (Everitt and Pitre 2007; Cross and Young 2007), the New Brunswick Advisory Council on the Status of Women (NBACSW 2004), and other interested parties addressed the issue of the representation of women, making suggestions for changes to the system that would increase the opportunities for women to be politically involved. The final report of the New Brunswick Legislative Democracy Commission included recommendations found in their submissions. These involved: increased tax refunds for parties that ran female candidates in at least 35 percent of their seats; the production and publication of reports on measures taken by the parties to increase the representation of women; and the active recruitment and appointment of women to agencies, boards, and commissions (NBCLD 2004). Unfortunately, the Conservative government did not move on these recommendations, and they were then completely ignored by the Graham Liberal government after its election in 2006. Only the recommendation for fixed-date elections was adopted, and, while female candidates in 2010 agreed that this was helpful in giving them time to prepare their campaigns, it seemed to have little impact on their decision to run for office (Gauvreau 2011, 44).

Political parties have been able to ignore the province's low representation of women in the past because there have been few external pressures on them to change. Early feminist organizing in the province was strongest among Acadian women who had been involved in the Acadian rights movement. La Fédération des dames d'Acadie formed in 1968 to promote the rights of women and francophones. In 1973, LES FAM (Liberté, Égalité, Sororité – Femmes Acadiennes de Moncton) lobbied governments to establish a provincial advisory council for women and to implement the recommendations of the Royal Commission on the Status of Women. Initially most of the women's groups took a general approach to the promotion of women's interests and concerns. By the late 1970s and early 1980s, when the women's movement's focus on greater political representation was strongest, the recruitment and election of women to politics received more attention (Young 2000). Groups like the Saint John Women for Political Action promoted women's political awareness and involvement, as did the New Brunswick Women's Political Caucus and FRAPPE (Femmes regroupées pour l'accessibilité au pouvoir politique et économique). FRAPPE organized the first and only party leaders' debate in the 1987 provincial election in Moncton. A two-day forum on women's participation in politics was also held that year. Since the early 1990s, however, the electoral project has faltered, with feminist organizing focusing more on grassroots politics. Only the now defunct New Brunswick Advisory Council on the Status of Women championed electoral change as it supplemented and supported the limited number of female voices in the Legislative Assembly,[5] keeping women's concerns in the public eye.

In the fall of 2009, New Brunswick established a chapter of Equal Voice, a multi-partisan organization dedicated to electing more women to politics. This organization had had chapters in other provinces for almost a decade. After a spate of media attention about the poor representation of women in the New Brunswick Legislative Assembly, the provincial chapter quickly grew to almost eighty members. It hosted a training session that drew seventy participants to prepare them to seek the nomination and to run in the 2010 provincial election. Several participants subsequently ran in band council elections, the 2010 provincial election, and the 2011 federal election. Further activity resulted in a record number of women running and being elected in the May 2012 municipal elections. The organization challenged provincial parties to recruit more female candidates and commented on the results of elections at all levels.[6] With this organization still in its infancy, it is difficult to assess the degree to which it will be able to work with the parties to increase attention to the need to elect more women.

Conclusion: Prospects for Gender Parity

New Brunswick women remain significantly under-represented in their Legislative Assembly and in key leadership roles in all branches of government. Their political advancement has been hampered by a political culture preoccupied with regional, linguistic, and to some extent religious differences, a party system and patterns of party support that shift power between two centre-right political parties, and a weakly organized women's movement that, in recent years, has not placed a priority on electing women to public office.

Change, when it has occurred, is the result of unanticipated swings in party support whereby women running in ridings in which their party is not expected to win are swept into office. Unfortunately, as was the case in 2010, electoral upsets also mean that women incumbents located in swing seats are defeated. Until political parties make deliberate efforts to recruit women to winnable seats significant increases in the representation of women remain unlikely. Even if they do this, possibly as a result of external pressures such as government-legislated incentives (as was proposed by the NB Commission on Legislative Democracy) or the lobbying of Equal Voice New Brunswick, the records of other provinces are also likely to improve, making it probable that New Brunswick will remain at the back of the pack in terms of women's representation in Canada.

Notes

1 This two-party system may be weakening as a result of the surge in support for the NDP in the province during the 2011 federal election.
2 In a 1964 by-election Margaret Rideout won a seat in the House of Commons for the riding of Westmoreland. She replaced her husband, who had died while in office.

She doubled his vote from the previous year, despite having been challenged for the nomination by ten men.

3 Blanchard's mother, Mathilda Blanchard, ran against Richard Hatfield for the leadership of the Progressive Conservative Party in 1969, making her the first woman to run for the leadership of a political party in New Brunswick.

4 I attended early meetings of Equal Voice NB, which were also attended by politicians, including Aldéa Landry, Joan Kingston, Madeline Dubé, Margaret-Anne Blaney, Mary Schryer, and Marie Claude Blais.

5 The amount of money allotted for the Advisory Council was cut in the March 2011 budget.

6 I am one of the founding members of EVNB and am currently the chair of the EVNB Steering Committee.

References

Bashevkin, Sylvia. 1993. *Toeing the Lines: Women in Party Politics in English Canada.* 2nd ed. Toronto: Oxford University Press.

–. 2009. "'Stage' versus 'Actor' Barriers to Women's Federal Party Leadership." In Sylvia Bashevkin, ed., *Opening Doors Wider: Women's Political Engagement in Canada*, 108-26. Vancouver: UBC Press.

Brodie, Janine. 1985. *Women and Politics in Canada.* Toronto: McGraw-Hill.

Carbert, Louise. 2006. *Rural Women's Leadership in Atlantic Canada.* Toronto: University of Toronto Press.

–. 2010. "Viewing Women's Political Leadership through a Rural Electoral Lens: Canada as a Case Study." In K. O'Connor, ed., *Gender and Women's Leadership: A Reference Handbook*, 137-50. Thousand Oaks: Sage.

Conrad, Margaret. 2003. "Addressing the Democratic Deficit: Women and Political Culture in Atlantic Canada." *Atlantis* 27(2): 82-89.

Cross, William, and Lisa Young. 2007 "Candidate Nomination in New Brunswick Political Parties." In William Cross, ed., *Democratic Reform in New Brunswick*, 102-44. Toronto: Canadian Scholars' Press.

Darcy, R., S. Welch, and J. Clark. 1994. *Women and Elections and Representation.* 2nd ed. Lincoln: University of Nebraska Press.

Desserud, Don. 1997. "Women in New Brunswick Politics: Waiting for the Third Wave." In Jane Arscott and Linda Trimble, eds., *In the Presence of Women: Representation in Canadian Governments*, 254-77. Toronto: Harcourt Brace and Company.

Erickson, Lynda. 1991. "Women and Candidacies for the House of Commons." In Kathy Megyery, ed., *Women in Canadian Politics: Toward Equity in Representation*. Research Studies, Royal Commission on Electoral Reform and Party Financing, vol. 6, 111-37. Toronto: Dundurn Press.

Everitt, Joanna. 2003. "Media in the Maritimes: Do Female Candidates Face a Bias?" *Atlantis* 27(2): 90-98.

Everitt, Joanna, and Michael Camp. 2009a. "One Is Not Like the Others: Allison Brewer's Leadership of the New Brunswick NDP." In Sylvia Bashevkin, ed., *Opening Doors Wider: Women's Political Engagement in Canada*, 127-44. Vancouver: UBC Press.

−. 2009b. "Changing the Game Changes the Frame: The Media's Use of Lesbian Stereotypes in Leadership versus Election Campaigns." *Canadian Political Science Review* 3(3): 24-39.

Everitt, Joanna, and Sonia Pitre. 2007. "Electoral Reform and Issues of Representation." In William Cross, ed., *Democratic Reform in New Brunswick*, 103-21. Toronto: Canadian Scholars' Press.

Gauvreau, Marilyne. 2011. "The Nomination of Women in the 2010 New Brunswick Election." *Canadian Parliamentary Review* 34(2): 43-47.

Gotell, Lise, and Janine Brodie. 1991. "Women and Parties: More than an Issue of Numbers." In Hugh Thorburn, ed., *Party Politics in Canada*, 53-67. 6th ed. Scarborough: Prentice-Hall.

New Brunswick Commission on Legislative Democracy. 2004. *Final Report and Recommendations of the Commission on Legislative Democracy*. Fredericton: Government of New Brunswick.

New Brunswick Advisory Council on the Status of Women. 2004. *Women and Electoral Reform in New Brunswick*. Brief presented by the NBACSW to the New Brunswick Commission on Legislative Democracy. July. Available at http://www.siriussolutions.com/.

O'Neill, Brenda, and Lynda Erickson. 2003. "Evaluating Traditionalism in the Atlantic Provinces: Voting, Public Opinion, and the Electoral Project." *Atlantis* 27(2): 113-22.

Pitre, Sonia. 2003a. "Political Parties and Female Candidates: Is There Resistance in New Brunswick?" In Manon Tremblay and Linda Trimble, eds., *Women and Electoral Politics in Canada*. Don Mills: Oxford University Press.

−. 2003b. "Women's Struggle for Legislative Power: The Role of Political Parties." *Atlantis* 27(2): 102-9.

−. 2004. "Les processus de recrutement et de sélection des candidatures comme obstacles à la représentation politique des femmes: Le cas des élections provinciales de juin 1999 au Nouveau-Brunswick." PhD diss., Université Laval.

Robinson, Gertrude, and Armande Saint-Jean. 1991. "Women Politicians and Their Media Coverage: A Generational Analysis." In Kathy Megyery, ed. *Women in Canadian Politics: Toward Equity in Representation*. Research Studies, Royal Commission on Electoral Reform and Party Financing, vol. 6, 127-69. Toronto: Dundurn Press.

−. 1995. "The Portrayal of Women Politicians in the Media: Political Implications." In François-Pierre Gingras, ed. *Gender and Politics in Contemporary Canada*, 176-90. Toronto: Oxford University Press.

Studlar, Donley T., and Gary F. Moncrief. 1997. "The Recruitment of Women Cabinet Ministers in the Canadian Provinces." *Governance: An International Journal of Policy and Administration* 10(1): 67-81.

Tremblay, Manon, and Réjean Pelletier. 2001. "More Women Constituency Party Presidents: A Strategy for Increasing the Number of Women Candidates in Canada?" *Party Politics* 7: 157-90.

Trimble, Linda, and Jane Arscott. 2003. *Still Counting: Women and Politics across Canada*. Peterborough: Broadview.

Young, Lisa. 2000. *Feminists and Party Politics.* Vancouver: UBC Press.
–. 2002. "Representation of Women in the New Canadian Party System." In William
    Cross, ed., *Political Parties, Representation, and Electoral Democracy in Canada,*
    181-200. Toronto: Oxford University Press.

6

A Laggard No More?

Women in Newfoundland and Labrador Politics

AMANDA BITTNER AND ELIZABETH GOODYEAR-GRANT

The recent electoral history of Canada's easternmost province provides evidence of Bashevkin's (1993) two "rules" of women in politics: first, the higher, the fewer; second, the more competitive, the fewer. This chapter examines the patterns of women's involvement in elite-level politics in Newfoundland and Labrador, relying on comparative literature from other Canadian jurisdictions, the United States, and elsewhere in order to understand the trends in the province over roughly the past decade with regard to women's share of candidacies, legislative seats, cabinet positions, and leadership posts. We also identify and assess explanations for these patterns, finally moving to a discussion of what this all means in relation to prospects for equitable gender representation in the province.

Background

Newfoundland and Labrador has changed over the past few decades. Reliance upon natural resources has continued, but with offshore oil replacing the commercial fishery as a primary economic activity. Employment, education, and income levels have all increased in the province. In broad strokes, unemployment and lack of economic opportunity continue to pose problems for both genders. While women's labour force participation has increased, two patterns have contributed to their political under-representation in the province: (1) occupational segregation that has concentrated women

POLITICAL REPRESENTATION OF WOMEN IN
NEWFOUNDLAND AND LABRADOR

FIRSTS
Right to vote and stand for election
- Most women win right to vote and stand for election   1925

Contesting office
- First women to contest office: (pre-Confederation) Helena Squires   1930 by-election /
  (Liberal) / (post-Confederation) Grace Sparkes (PC)   1949
- First women to win office: (pre-Confederation) Helena Squires   1930-32 /
  (Liberal) / (post-Confederation) Hazel McIsaac (Liberal)   1975-79
- First woman appointed to cabinet: Hazel Newhook (PC), consumer   1979-80
  affairs and environment

CURRENT REPRESENTATION AT A GLANCE

	Date of election	Women elected Number	Women elected Percent
Women in legislature	2011/10/11	8 of 48	17
Women in cabinet	2011/10/11	4 of 16	25

Women political party leaders
- Lorraine Michael (NDP), 2006 to present
- Kathy Dunderdale (PC), 2010 to present

Lieutenant governor
- None at present

Advisory council on the status of women
- The Provincial Advisory Council on the Status of Women (PACSW) was created in
  1980.

disproportionately in lower-status, lower-paying jobs and (2) gender-income gaps, with women generally being paid less than men.

The distribution of the population across the province is concentrated in a few regions. The largest concentration (just over 35 percent of the province's total population) is located in the metropolitan area of the province's capital, St. John's, which includes the largest cities and suburbs. The province's larger urban centres tend to supply the female candidates. This overlays one of the important cleavages in Newfoundland and Labrador: a rural-urban divide and, perhaps more important, a divide between St. John's and the rest of the province. The other important political cleavages, especially historically, have been religious and socio-economic. A Catholic-Protestant cleavage has existed throughout the province's history, though its importance has waned considerably. This cleavage involved ethnicity in that most Catholics were Irish and French, while most Protestants were English. A socio-economic divide also exists, which is, in turn, an important driver of the urban-rural cleavage.

Newfoundland and Labrador is not racially or ethnically diverse, inasmuch as visible minorities make up about 1 percent of the population of half a million (Statistics Canada 2010), which is one reason why few visible minority candidates and members of the House of Assembly (MHAs) exist in Newfoundland and Labrador. The situation is unlikely to change demographically in the future since Newfoundland and Labrador attracts less than 0.2 percent of Canada's immigrants and often has trouble retaining them (Newfoundland and Labrador, Department of Human Resources, Labour and Employment 2007). The recruitment and election of a greater number of candidates from non-majority backgrounds, particularly among Aboriginals in the province, who number over twenty-three thousand, provides one window of opportunity (Statistics Canada 2006). The greater representation of Aboriginal people in the politics of the province would inevitably result in greater integration of Labradorian perspectives with those of the Island and provide greater voice for Labradorians in the province's politics.

Changes have occurred in the legislature since the early 1990s, including increases in the representation of women, despite continued wage gaps and occupational segregation. Structure and culture are largely responsible for the changes in women's political representation. Economic growth should stimulate further improvements in women's representation. Public opinion in the province also supports the increased representation of women; attitudes regarding traditional family values, gender, and women's representation appear to be (for the most part) similar to those in the rest of Canada (see below).

Structure and culture are two sets of factors that condition women's access to political power, and the third is politics. This category encompasses all the institutions that define the political arena, and political parties foremost of all, since they control recruitment and nomination, they structure campaigns, and parties define legislative agendas. Broadly, party politics in Newfoundland and Labrador operate much like they do in other Canadian jurisdictions: they are not particularly proactive on the issue of enhancing women's representation. There is, however, variance across parties: the two mainline parties, the Progressive Conservative Party and Liberal Party, do the least to promote women's representation, while the New Democratic Party (NDP) does the most. For all parties, however, a decentralized structure makes coordinated action on the matter difficult.

Women's Political Representation: The Numbers

While the province has lagged behind the others in the timing of growth in women's representation – an important finding of Arscott's (1997) analysis in *In the Presence of Women* (see also Brodie 1991; Studlar and Matland 1996) – recent increases in the number of women running for and winning office in Newfoundland and Labrador bring it more in line with the federal level as well as with some of the other provinces (such as Quebec and Manitoba, both of which have been at or near 33 percent female representation provincially in recent years, outstripping the other provinces and the national Parliament). At the same time, some of the patterns in women's representation in Newfoundland and Labrador politics are not reflective of trends common elsewhere, a natural consequence of the fact that local conditions and political context are powerful influences on electoral and legislative politics.

Candidates

For most of its electoral history, Newfoundland's performance on women's numerical representation lagged behind that of many other jurisdictions in the country. Over the past half decade, this seems to have changed. In the last two provincial elections, both of which saw the return of a Progressive Conservative government, 27 percent and 24 percent of the candidates running for office in 2007 and 2011, respectively, were women, and 21 percent and 17 percent of MHAs elected in those years were also women (Table 6.1).

Women's success rates – the number of women elected as a proportion of the number of women candidates – are lower than the success rates of male candidates over nearly the entire electoral history of the province. Part of the explanation is the large number of women who have run as NDP candidates. While the NDP has won seats in the province, in the past it has not been electorally competitive, and NDP candidates are historically more likely to lose than are Liberal and PC candidates. In fact, until the most recent election, of the small number of NDP MHAs, only one of these, current party leader Lorraine Michael, has been a woman. In 2011, the NDP won

TABLE 6.1

Women in the Newfoundland and Labrador legislature, by election

Election date	Party elected	Total number of legislators	Women elected	
			Number	%
1928/06/28	Liberal/FPU	40	1	3
1932/06/11	United Newfoundland	27	0	0
1949/05/27	Liberal	28	0	0
1951/11/26	Liberal	28	0	0
1956/10/2	Liberal	36	0	0
1959/08/20	Liberal	36	0	0
1962/11/19	Liberal	42	0	0
1966/09/8	Liberal	42	0	0
1971/10/28	PC	42	0	0
1972/03/24	PC	42	0	0
1975/09/16	PC	51	1	2
1979/06/18	PC	52	2	4
1982/04/06	PC	52	3	6
1985/04/02	PC	52	1	2
1989/04/20	PC	52	3	6
1993/05/03	Liberal	52	2	4
1996/02/22	Liberal	48	7	15
1999/02/09	Liberal	48	8	17
2003/10/21	PC	48	10	21
2007/10/09	PC	48	10	21
2011/10/11	PC	48	8	17

Source: Newfoundland and Labrador, House of Assembly, http:// www.assembly.nl.ca/.

more seats than it had in Newfoundland and Labrador history (winning a total of five seats), and one additional NDP woman was elected: Gerry Rogers, a documentary filmmaker and activist unseated a prominent PC cabinet minister in the City of St. John's. The exception to the general finding of women's lower success rates is the 2003 provincial election, in which women's and men's success rates were 34 percent and 34 percent, respectively. This is important for it shows that men and women had equal chances of winning once they had decided to run, and it may also suggest that women were not disproportionately placed in lost-cause ridings in 2003. In the 2007 provincial election, a ten-point gap re-opened in women's and men's success rates, a development accounted for, in part, by the greater proportion of women on the NDP slate in 2007 compared to their much

TABLE 6.2
Women candidates in Newfoundland and Labrador, by party and election

	Liberal		PC		NDP	
Election date	Number	%	Number	%	Number	%
1982/04/06	2	4	3	6	4	17
1985/04/02	7	13	4	8	8	16
1989/04/20	3	6	3	6	7	19
1993/05/03	6	12	6	12	18	35
1996/02/22	7	15	10	21	3	15
1999/02/09	10	21	7	15	7	20
2003/10/21	9	19	10	21	6	18
2007/10/09	13	28	9	9	14	39
2011/10/11	17	35	6	13	12	25

Source: Newfoundland and Labrador, House of Assembly, http:// www.assembly.nl.ca/.

lower proportions from 1996 to 2003. The gap widened further in 2011, to thirteen points.

There are obviously some interesting idiosyncrasies that deserve exploration regarding the parties' records on women candidates. The first, and striking, observation is the instability in women's share of candidacies across the three major parties (Table 6.2). Both the Liberal and PC parties have had modest increases in their proportions of women candidates over that time, but with variations from one election to the next. In 1993, the NDP had 35 percent women candidates, and in 2007, 39 percent were women. Both of these satisfy the 30 percent critical mass threshold commonly thought to encourage the translation of numerical representation to substantive representation for marginalized groups (Dahlerup 1988). Yet, between 1996 and 2011, the NDP's proportion of women candidates plummeted and was actually below the Progressive Conservative Party's in 1996 and both the Conservatives' and the Liberals' proportions in 2003. While the NDP led the way in nominating women in 1993 and 2007, the other parties nominated more women in the three intervening elections: the PCs nominated the most in 1996, the Liberals in 1999, and the PCs again in 2003. In 2011, the Liberal Party surpassed the others in women nominated, but this did not translate into seats: Yvonne Jones was the only woman to win a seat in the legislature. Looking at parties' averages over the period, however, the typical pattern exists: the NDP leads the way in women candidates with 25 percent, the Liberals follow with 20 percent, and the PCs bring up the rear with 17 percent. This ordering, if not the magnitude of proportions, is common to the parties of the same name at the federal level over the past two decades.

Legislators

Women's share of seats in the legislative assembly has grown substantially since the early 1990s. The legislature has transitioned from a skewed group, in which women comprised less than 15 percent of the total, to a tilted group, in which women MHAs comprise between 15 percent and 40 percent of the total (Kanter 1977). From 1993 to 1996, the number of seats held by women more than tripled, then gradually increased to a high of 21 percent in 2003 and 2007, and fell back to 17 percent in 2011. Women's representation in the province has been similar to their representation in the House of Commons over the last decade, although 2011 has opened up a gap. Representation by women plateaued in the last three elections, a development anticipated by Trimble and Arscott (2003) and confirmed by Bashevkin (2009, 2011). In the longer term, women have moved beyond the token numbers of 1996 (Arscott 1997).

The Liberal caucus had higher proportions of women MHAs than did its PC counterpart in the five elections from 1996 to 2011, the average proportion of which was 20 percent for the Liberal caucus. PC caucuses have consisted on average of about 10 percent women in that period. Similar patterns whereby Liberals outstrip Conservatives on women's representation in caucus have been reported at the federal level as well as in other provinces (e.g., Trimble and Arscott 2003, 59; Young 2002, 186). The gap between the Liberal and PC parties in Newfoundland and Labrador has narrowed in recent years, particularly following the 2003 provincial election. The number of women MHAs in the Progressive Conservative Party only increased by one, from seven to eight members, in 2007. In 2011, the PCs lost seats, some of which were held by women: only five PC women sat in the House of Assembly following that election. Women's presence in the PC caucus has not kept pace with the party's overall growth in seats in recent years.

The NDP presents a different story. The party has not been a major force in provincial elections and, until 2011, had never won more than two seats in a single election. For most of the party's history there has been only one female NDP House member, Lorraine Michael, the party's current leader. Thus, while the party sometimes runs far more women candidates than do the other principal parties in the province, these women are almost universally defeated. And, without members, neither an NDP caucus nor NDP women MHAs exist.

TABLE 6.3
Women party leaders in Newfoundland and Labrador

Name	Political party	Period of service
Lynn Verge	PC	1995-96
Lorraine Michael	NDP	2006 to present
Yvonne Jones	Liberal	2007-11
Kathy Dunderdale	PC	2010 to present

Source: Newfoundland and Labrador, House of Assembly, http:// www.assembly.nl.ca/.

Party Leaders

Four women have been party leaders in Newfoundland and Labrador, two of them current. Lynn Verge was the first woman leader; she led the PCs from 1995 to 1996. Verge was also the Opposition leader during this time. Until recently, all three major parties were led by women, which was a first for a Canadian legislature. This is a major change; prior to 2006 only one woman had led a provincial party. A former teacher and community organizer, NDP leader Lorraine Michael has held the post since 2006. Like Verge, she identifies as a feminist and further describes herself as a "committed activist for gender and racial social and economic justice."[1] Opposition and Liberal leader Yvonne Jones announced her resignation on 9 August 2011. She had led the party since 2007. A former mayor of Mary's Harbour in Labrador, Jones had been in the Newfoundland and Labrador legislature since 1996.

Since 2010, Kathy Dunderdale has been premier and PC leader. Former deputy mayor of Burin and the first woman to be elected president of the Newfoundland and Labrador Federation of Municipalities, she also held various cabinet posts before taking the leadership. At the same time, Danny Williams is regarded as having supported her rise to the top. Williams preceded Dunderdale as premier and PC leader and is generally thought to have selected her as his replacement. Indeed, in the lead-up to her swearing in, news stories refer to the "leadership coronation" (Gatehouse 2011) resulting from her having attained the position uncontested. She has also been characterized as Williams's "hand-picked successor" (Moore 2011). Thus, while Dunderdale does lead a highly competitive and powerful party, her success has been attributed, in part, to the influence of her male sponsor. During the 2011 campaign, Dunderdale made substantial efforts to differentiate herself from her mentor, who has since been critical of her leadership (e.g., CBC 2011). However, Williams's influence contributed to making it "acceptable" for a woman to become premier. He remains a beloved figure

TABLE 6.4
Women premiers in Newfoundland and Labrador

Name	Political party	Period of service
Kathy Dunderdale	PC	2010 to present

in the province, and he enjoyed approval ratings above 80 percent while premier. His appointment of Dunderdale as interim leader contributed to the public's acceptance of her as an individual qualified to lead the party and head the government.

With regard to Jones and Michael, their roles fit the "more competitive, the fewer" pattern identified by Bashevkin (1993). Put simply, the NDP and Liberals are uncompetitive parties. The NDP has never been a major political force in the province, although its performance in the 2011 election raises the possibility that this may change in the future. Though unable to challenge the PCs for control of government the Liberal Party remains politically important. In March 2011, 73 percent of decided voters in the province said that they would vote PC if an election were held the following day (Corporate Research Associates 2011). The outcome of the most recent election reinforced the gap between the governing party and the two opposition parties. While the PCs lost seats, neither of the other two parties were positioned to form a government.

Jones took over the Liberal leadership when the party was financially strapped and had been reduced to three of forty-eight seats in the provincial legislature, a poor showing for a party that had formed government two elections earlier. Jones was acclaimed as party leader in the summer of 2010. It is fairly straightforward, then, to understand why both Michael and Jones would fit Bashevkin's (2009, 44) explanation for the "loser syndrome" that seems to plague so many women politicians.

Cabinet

Women's representation in cabinet has exceeded their legislative representation for more than a decade (see Table 6.5). From 1993 to 2011 women's share of House seats was 15 percent, on average, whereas their share of cabinet seats was nearly 10 percent larger. The largest single increase in women's cabinet representation came after the 1996 provincial election. Following the 1999 provincial election – won again by Brian Tobin's Liberals – women's representation in cabinet increased to 31 percent (five of sixteen), about the critical mass threshold of 30 to 35 percent. This is slightly higher than

TABLE 6.5
Women in cabinet in Newfoundland and Labrador, by election

Election date	Party elected	Total number of cabinet ministers*	Women appointed to to cabinet		Number of women in governing caucus	% of women in governing caucus in cabinet
			Number	%		
1993/05/03	Liberal	14	1	7	3	3
1996/02/22	Liberal	16	4	25	16	11
1999/02/09	Liberal	16	5	31	22	16
2003/10/21	PC	14	4	29	21	12
2007/10/09	PC	18	5	28	18	11
2011/10/11	PC	16	4	25	14	11

* Includes the premier.
Source: Newfoundland and Labrador, House of Assembly, http:// www.assembly.nl.ca/.

women's representation in the federal cabinet formed by Prime Minister Stephen Harper following the 2008 federal election, which was the most gender-equitable in federal history.

Cabinet representation also raises the question of which types of portfolios are assigned to women. First identified by Duverger (1955), an important gender-based pattern has characterized portfolio allotments worldwide, whereby women tend to be assigned disproportionately to "softer socio-cultural ministerial positions rather than ... the harder and politically more prestigious positions ... which are often seen as stepping-stones to national leadership" (Reynolds 1999, 564; see also Bashevkin 1993; Davis 1997; Krook and O'Brien 2010; Moon and Fountain 1997; Studlar and Moncrief 1999). The pattern persists, in part, as the result of stereotypes about women's policy skills, but it may also reflect women legislators' own policy priorities and political experience. Women legislators gravitate more than do their male colleagues towards policy fields such as health, social welfare, education, and women's issues (e.g., Childs and Withey 2004; Little, Dunn, and Deen 2001; Schwindt-Bayer 2006; Skjeie 1991).

However, Studlar and Moncrief's (1999) examination of provincial cabinet allotments suggests that women have had greater success attaining prestigious positions as time progressed (see also Escobar-Lemmon and Taylor-Robinson 2005, 838; Erickson 1997). Is there evidence of this progression in the makeup of cabinet posts in Newfoundland and Labrador?

We use White's (1998) tripartite scheme for classifying portfolios as important, middle-range, and junior (see also Studlar and Moncrief 1999).[2]

TABLE 6.6

Women's distribution across Newfoundland and Labrador cabinet portfolios, 1993-2011

Election	Number of women in cabinet		Number of portfolios held by women		
			Important	Middle-range	Junior
1993	1	(7%)	0	1	1
1996	4	(25%)	0	2	3
1999	5	(31%)	3	2	1
2003	4	(29%)	2	2	2
2007	5	(28%)	1	4	2
2011	4	(25%)	2	1	1
Total	23		8	12	10

Source: Newfoundland and Labrador, House of Assembly, http:// www.assembly.nl.ca/.

Overall, from 1993 to 2011, of the thirty portfolios held by women,[3] eight have been important, twelve middle-range, and ten junior (Table 6.6). Women have been most likely to head middle-range ministries, followed by junior, then important ministries, showing a clear imbalance favouring men in the assignment of portfolios.

A shift seems to have occurred after 1999, whereby the majority of portfolios held by women tend to be important or mid-range (rather than midrange or junior). The evidence is a bit mixed, however. Women's appointment to important portfolios seems to have decreased over the past few election cycles. Moreover, women in the important category have tended to hold the education or health portfolios, often regarded as "soft" or "feminine" in nature. This evidence supports the claim that a gendered pattern exists in cabinet assignments. Other important portfolios assigned to women are industry, trade, rural development/technology, and the premiership (held by Dunderdale since 2010). From 1993 to 2012, no woman held the finance or justice/attorney general portfolios, arguably the most high-status posts in the important category after the premiership, which may point to a lack of progress in women's role in cabinets.

Explanations

The various factors that affect women's representation can be classified into three broad categories: structure, culture, and politics. Together, these categories explain the supply of and demand for women in formal politics.

Structural Explanations

Structural perspectives focus on the effects of social structures, such as family, education, and the workforce, on women's opportunities for entry into the political system. Social structures may or may not be configured in such a way as to enable women to gain the key skills and resources necessary for attaining political office. The evidence is mixed, but it does suggest that women who may otherwise emerge as candidates encounter obstacles. Interestingly, the contemporary gender gap in education levels favours women: increasing numbers of women are educated, and at higher levels than men. In the long run, this has the potential to improve women's presence in the legislature as increased education levels may lead to increased employment in political "pipeline" careers as well as increased interest in and awareness of the importance of women in politics (Burns, Schlozman, and Verba 2001; Lawless and Fox 2005).

The labour market also differs by gender but with fewer positive results for women. Women participate at lower rates (56 percent) than men (64 percent), despite a 50 percent increase in women's participation in the last two decades. In addition, many more employed men work full time (92 percent), and somewhat fewer (79 percent) women (Statistics Canada 2009). Underemployment no doubt contributes greatly to the gender income gap we see in the province but so, too, does occupational segregation.

There are important differences in the types of work that women and men do, resulting in occupational segregation and gender-income gaps that likely decrease women's prospects for political representation. The division of labour is especially clear in industry related to resource extraction, which is dominated by men (and better paid), while services, especially retail, health, and education, tend to be female-concentrated industries that are lower paid (Newfoundland and Labrador 2008).[4] In highly valued industries related to resource extraction and the production of goods, men tend to hold most of the jobs and to earn more money.

Similar patterns emerge with regard to income (Statistics Canada 2007) for part-time or seasonal workers, and a gender income gap favouring men exists, as for full-time workers. Women earn approximately 57 percent of what men earn in the province (Williams 2010), and women in Newfoundland and Labrador have the lowest average incomes across all provinces. Newfoundland women are also more likely to live below low-income thresholds than are Newfoundland men.

Cultural Explanations

Turning to culture, which is related to structure, the combination of an older population, gender-based occupational segregation, and the gender-income gap might lead us to expect that the province holds less progressive attitudes about women's place in society, therefore leading to lower demand for female legislators. However, a comparison of attitudes in the province with those in the rest of Canada does not support this idea. Not only do we observe the lack of discriminatory attitudes towards women writ large in the province, but Newfoundland and Labrador is strikingly similar to the rest of the country on important indicators related to questions about women's equality, feelings about feminist groups, candidate quotas, and the like (see Table 6.7).[5] These data offer no support for the notion that the province offers a less progressive, more socially traditional political environment in relation to the range of issues usually associated with questions about women's political power. Our findings suggest that the environment is no less hospitable to women's political power than that found elsewhere in the country. While challenges still remain, the combination of education, labour force participation, and recent history bodes well for women's representation. An examination of values across jurisdictions may provide valuable insight into the barriers women may face, and it offers one potential direction for future research.

Political Explanations

With this final set of factors, we focus in particular on political parties and the women's movement. Like many parties elsewhere, those in Newfoundland and Labrador are not extraordinarily active in the recruitment and support of women candidates. Their levels of activity vary; however, the two mainline parties – PCs and Liberals – do the least, while the NDP is more active. The decentralized structure of all parties makes coordinated action on the matter difficult. None of the parties has quotas for women candidates, and among the parties the PCs have the fewest measures in place to aid in the identification and recruitment of women. The Liberal Party has a women's commission – much as it does at the national level – and this body performs a recruitment function (Thompson 2011). The Liberals also give money to female candidates to help with campaign expenses, though this support occurs informally. The NDP recruits and supports women the most, providing formal grants to women candidates' campaigns, and it has also incorporated formal affirmative action requirements into its constitution.

TABLE 6.7

Attitudes towards women, gender, and representation: Newfoundland and Labrador and the rest of Canada, 1997-2008

Indicator	Rest of Canada	NL	PR value	Number of respondents (rest of Canada/NL)
Family values				
Society better off if women stay home with children	0.570	*0.616*	0.000	84,011/2,233
Greater emphasis on family values	*0.330*	0.259	0.001	8,633/205
Sex equality only attained when men and women have same government, business, and family roles	0.237	*0.298*	0.038	8,615/205
Abortion position: (1) never permitted, (2) permitted only after need established by a doctor, (3) matter of women's personal choice	*0.663*	0.585	0.000	67,442/1,710
Political values				
How much do you think should be done for women?	0.689	*0.741*	0.000	82,461/2,201
Gone too far in pushing equal rights in this country	0.500	0.500	0.960	27,072/696
Attitude to feminism: very sympathetic to not sympathetic at all	*0.610*	0.579	0.019	16,856/505
Feelings towards feminist groups	0.632	*0.694*	0.000	43,243/1,029
Discrimination makes it difficult for women to get jobs equal to their ability	0.532	0.535	0.389	18,494/491
Workplace quotas are good or hiring based strictly on merit	*0.109*	0.057	0.010	8,626/210
Quotas and Parliament				
Favour or oppose requiring parties to have sex parity in candidacies?	0.403	*0.551*	0.000	8,477/235
Best way to protect women's interests is to have more women in Parliament	0.550	*0.592*	0.000	27,116/690
Many more men than women in the House of Commons – very serious problem to not a problem at all	*0.340*	0.292	0.001	24,669/546
Parties should be required by law to have a *minimum* number of female candidates, or it should be up to each party to decide how many female candidates	*0.616*	0.512	0.000	22,520/561

Note: Variables coded 0-1, where 1 reflects more "progressive" or "pro-woman" attitudes.
Source: Data pooled from 1997-2008 CES; Means reported, results of *t*-tests.

These general findings reflect similar observations of the three main parties' activities at the national level (e.g., Cross 2004), with the PCs, Liberals, and NDP ranked from least to most engaged in efforts to enhance women's access to office.

The fact that the NDP is most active in searching out and supporting women candidates is a familiar pattern, but few NDP candidates are elected. Changes have occurred recently in the province requiring parties to run full slates of candidates in order to qualify for party status. Informal discussions with party insiders suggest that this provides part of the explanation for the swings in women's proportion of NDP candidacies. Indeed, the party is not competitive in large swaths of the province where no constituency associations are maintained. The full-slate rule results in a scramble by the NDP to put a name on the ballot in some ridings. Often, it is a woman who volunteers, resulting in a new breed of sacrificial lambs created as a result of the rule change.

Overall, women's representation in the province has often occurred despite the actions of political parties rather than because of them. This may be partially explained by a very active women's movement in the province. In the early 1970s, the Newfoundland Status of Women Council (NSWC) was formed in St. John's. A women's centre was opened there, as was a rape crisis centre, and in the early 1980s the NSWC was renamed the St. John's Status of Women Council (SJSWC) to reflect the growing number of women's councils that had been created across the province. A website created at Memorial University in 2005 to "teach about women" in the province credits the NSWC and the SJSWC with a number of milestones in women's rights, and women's organizations have had an important influence on policy issues as well as on education and consciousness-raising (Let's Teach About Women 2005b).

Arguably, activities in the 1970s and 1980s paved the way for increases in women's legislative representation in the 1990s and beyond. The older organizations still exist, and newer ones are also emerging on the scene: Equal Voice has recently opened a St. John's chapter. In sum, while the effects of organizational and movement resources on women's representation are difficult to quantify, important advances have certainly been the result. This is because not only does a healthy movement work to identify and encourage women office-seekers, but it also creates social, cultural, and political conditions favourable for growth in women's representation by normalizing women's political activism and providing a network for co-ordinated action.

Conclusion: Prospects for Gender Parity

Bashevkin's (1993) seminal work on women in politics points to two key rules: first, the higher you go up the political food chain, the fewer women you will find; second, increasing levels of political competitiveness have a damaging effect on women's presence. Newfoundland and Labrador provides an interesting backdrop within which to examine these two axioms. For more than a year (2010-11), Newfoundland and Labrador politics were defined by three women party leaders, a phenomenon we suspect is a Canadian first, and all the more surprising given the province's laggard status, which is described by Arscott (1997) in *In the Presence of Women*. Arguably, this flies in the face of at least one of Bashevkin's rules, "the higher, the fewer," as these women held positions at the very top of provincial politics. As for her second rule, her observations stand as two of the three recent women leaders have headed up uncompetitive parties (Michael and Jones). Moreover, even though Danny Williams is no longer premier, his strong influence on voters remains, and Kathy Dunderdale has benefited from his legacy. Even with Dunderdale's success, it does not appear as though women have broken through the glass ceiling in Newfoundland and Labrador.

The work of women such as Kathy Dunderdale, Yvonne Jones, and Lorraine Michael, and the twenty-four other women past and present who have held seats in the legislature, provides grounds for optimism about the future of women's political representation in the province. Added to this, women's presence in cabinet has exceeded their legislative presence for most of the past two decades, ranging from 25 percent to 31 percent. While not a large number of women are in leadership positions (generally, in a twenty-person cabinet about five people are women), there is a large enough number that we would expect to see these women affect the future of women's representation through role model effects. Past research has shown that women legislators have a positive influence on both women and girls, resulting in their greater levels of interest and participation in politics (see Wolbrecht and Campbell 2007). The increase in women's presence over the last twenty years, particularly in powerful leader and cabinet positions, will have significant effects in the years to come. Role model effects should also make it easier to recruit more women in the future as well as to demonstrate to parties and voters that women are viable, highly qualified candidates for office. In sum, recent advances may have positive supply- and demand-side effects that bode well for continued growth in women's numerical representation in future electoral cycles, suggesting that change becomes permanent through reinforcing processes.

Additional groundwork necessary for increases in women's presence has been laid as well: structurally, education levels in the province are such that women are not at a disadvantage; the gender gap in labour force participation rates has decreased over the last twenty years, and, while important workforce-related gaps remain (including the wage gap), improvements have occurred. Culturally, Newfoundlanders and Labradorians' attitudes towards issues related to women's representation are similar to those of other Canadians, and in some cases they are more progressive. Moreover, while the efforts of the political parties in the province could be better, some measures exist to assist women candidates. Combined with a vibrant women's movement in the province, this prospect contributes to an improved political environment from which further advances might yet be made.

Notes

An earlier version of this chapter was presented at the Canadian Political Science Association Annual Meetings, Wilfred Laurier University, Waterloo, Ontario, 16-18 May 2011. The authors would like to thank Susan Piercey and Garikai Chaora for research assistance.

1 NLNDP website, http://www.nl.ndp.ca/.
2 Important portfolios: premiership, attorney general, education, health, industry/ economic development, and finance. And in Newfoundland and Labrador fisheries would be added to this list for a total of seven. Middle-range portfolios are agriculture, environment, forests, housing, intergovernmental relations, labour, municipal affairs, natural resources, provincial secretary, public works, social services, transport, treasury board, and planning and development. All other portfolios are considered junior.
3 There are more portfolios than women cabinet members over the same time period because individual members sometimes hold more than one portfolio. For this portion of the analysis the portfolio is the unit of analysis.
4 Current data are available fromnd Company the Economic Research and Analysis Division   of the Department of Finance for the Government of Newfoundland and Labrador. See http://www.economics.gov.nl.ca/.
5 Pooled data gathered by the authors are from the Canadian Election Studies, 1997 to 2008. The generalizations in this section are drawn from this material, which would add a further dimension to the gender and politics subfield. Space constraints do not permit their development here.

References

Arscott, Jane. 1997. "Between the Rock and a Hard Place: Women Legislators in Newfoundland and Nova Scotia." In Jane Arscott and Linda Trimble, eds., *In the Presence of Women: Representation in Canadian Governments*, 279-308. Toronto: Harcourt Brace.

Bashevkin, Sylvia. 1993. *Toeing the Lines: Women and Party Politics in English Canada.* 2nd ed. Toronto: University of Toronto Press.

—. 2009. *Women, Power, Politics: The Hidden Story of Canada's Unfinished Democracy.* Don Mills: Oxford University Press.

—. 2011. "Women's Representation in the House of Commons: A Stalemate?" *Canadian Parliamentary Review* 34(1): 17-22.

Brodie, Janine, with Celia Chandler. 1991. "Women and the Electoral Process in Canada." In Kathy Megyery, ed., *Women in Canadian Politics: Toward Equity in Representation.* Research Studies, Royal Commission on Electoral Reform and Party Financing, vol. 6, 3-60. Toronto: Dundurn Press.

Burns, Nancy, Kay Lehman Schlozman, and Sidney Verba. 2001. *The Private Roots of Public Action: Gender, Equality, and Political Participation.* Boston: Harvard University Press.

CBC. 2011. "Not Up to Williams to Judge Me: Dunderdale." http://www.cbc.ca/news/.

Childs, Sarah, and Jane Withey. 2004. "Women Representatives Acting for Women: Sex and the Signing of Early Day Motions in the 1997 British Parliament." *Political Studies* 52(3): 552-64.

Corporate Research Associates. 2011. "Support for the NL Progressive Conservative Party Remains High." *Poll Newsroom*, 7 March. Available at http://cra.ca/.

Cross, William. 2004. *Political Parties.* Vancouver: UBC Press.

Dahlerup, Drude. 1988. "From a Small to a Large Minority: Women in Scandinavian Politics." *Scandinavian Political Studies* (4): 275-98.

Davis, Rebecca Howard. 1997. *Women and Power in Parliamentary Democracies: Cabinet Appointments in Western Europe, 1968-1992.* Lincoln: University of Nebraska Press.

Duverger, Maurice. 1955. *The Political Role of Women.* Paris: UNESCO.

Erickson, Lynda. 1997. "Parties, Ideology, and Feminist Action: Women and Political Representation in British Columbia Politics." In Jane Arscott and Linda Trimble, eds., *In the Presence of Women: Representation in Canadian Governments*, 106-27. Toronto: Harcourt Brace and Company.

Escobar-Lemmon, Maria, and Michelle M. Taylor-Robinson. 2005. "Women Ministers in Latin American Government: When, Where, and Why?" *American Journal of Political Science* 49(4): 829-44.

Gatehouse, Jonathon. 2011. "Kathy Dunderdale: The One to Beat." *Maclean's*, 31 March. http://www2.macleans.ca/.

Kanter, Rosabeth Moss. 1977. "Some Effects of Proportions on Group Life: Skewed Sex Ratios and Responses to Token Women." *American Journal of Sociology* 82(5): 965-90.

Krook, Mona Lena, and Diana Z. O'Brien. 2010. "All the President's Men? Numbers and Portfolio Allocations of Female Cabinet Ministers." Paper presented at the

Midwest Political Science Association National Conference, Chicago, 22-25 April. Available at http://krook.wustl.edu/.

Lawless, Jennifer L., and Richard L. Fox. 2005. *It Takes a Candidate: Why Women Don't Run for Office.* Cambridge: Cambridge University Press.

Little, Thomas H., Dana Dunn, and Rebecca E. Deen. 2001. "A View from the Top: Gender Differences in Legislative Priorities among State Legislative Leaders." *Women and Politics* 22(4): 29-49.

Moon, Jeremy, and Imogen Fountain. 1997. "Keeping the Gates? Women and Ministers in Australia, 1970-1996." *Australian Journal of Political Science* 32(3): 455-66.

Moore, Oliver. 2011. "Apparent Rift Exposed as Danny Williams Skips His Tribute Dinner." *Globe and Mail,* 25 March. http://www.theglobeandmail.com/.

Newfoundland and Labrador. 2008. Seasonally Adjusted Average Weekly Earnings (Including Overtime) by Industry Newfoundland and Labrador 2004 to 2008. Available at http://www.gov.nl.ca/.

Newfoundland and Labrador, Department of Human Resources, Labour and Employment. 2007. Diversity, Opportunity and Growth: An Immigration Strategy for Newfoundland and Labrador. http://www.nlimmigration.ca/.

Newfoundland and Labrador, House of Assembly. http://www.assembly.nl.ca

Reynolds, Andrew. 1999. "Women in the Legislatures and Executives of the World: Knocking at the Highest Glass Ceiling." *World Politics* 51(4): 547-72.

Schwindt-Bayer, Leslie A. 2006. "Still Supermadres? Gender and the Policy Priorities of Latin American Legislators." *American Journal of Political Science* 50(3): 570-85.

Skjeie, Hege. 1991. "The Rhetoric of Difference: On Women's Inclusion into Political Elites." *Politics and Society* 19(2): 233-63.

–. 2006. 2006 Aboriginal Population Profile. Available at http://www12.statcan.gc.ca/.

–. 2007. St. John's, Newfoundland and Labrador (Code001) (table). 2006 Community Profiles. 2006 Census. Statistics Canada Catalogue no. 92-591-XWE. Ottawa. Available at http://www12.statcan.ca/.

–. 2009. 2009 Perspectives on Labour and Income. Cat. No. 75-001-X. Ottawa. Available at http://www.gov.nl.ca/.

–. 2010. Projections of the Diversity of the Canadian Population: 2006 to 2031. Cat. No. 91-551-X. Ottawa. Available at http://www.statcan.gc.ca/.

Studlar, Donley T., and Richard E. Matland. 1996. "The Dynamics of Women's Representation in the Canadian Provinces: 1975-1994." *Canadian Journal of Political Science* 29(2): 269-93.

Studlar, Donley T., and Gary F. Moncrief. 1999. "Women's Work? The Distribution and Prestige of Portfolios in the Canadian Provinces." *Governance: An International Journal of Policy and Administration* 12(4): 379-95.

Thompson, Emily C. 2011. "Electoral Institutions and Women's Representation: The Impact of Electoral Systems and Party Nomination Practices in Newfoundland and Labrador and Tasmania." Honour's thesis, Memorial University of Newfoundland.

Trimble, Linda, and Jane Arscott. 2003. *Still Counting: Women in Politics across Canada.* Peterborough: Broadview Press.

White, Graham. 1998. "Shorter Measures: The Changing Ministerial Career in Canada." *Canadian Public Administration* 41(3): 369-94.

Williams, Cara. 2010. *Women in Canada: A Gender-Based Statistical Report (Economic Well-Being)*. Ottawa. Statistics Canada. Available at http://www.statcan.gc.ca/.

Wolbrecht, Christina, and David E. Campbell. 2007. "Leading by Example: Female Members of Parliament as Political Role Models." *American Journal of Political Science* 51(4): 921-39.

Young, Lisa. 2002. "Representation of Women in the New Canadian Party System." In William Cross, ed., *Political Parties, Representation, and Electoral Democracy in Canada*, 181-200. Don Mills: Oxford University Press.

7

Electoral Breakthrough
Women in Nova Scotia Politics
LOUISE CARBERT AND NAOMI BLACK

In 2009, for the first time, the people of Nova Scotia elected a New Democratic government. Apart from the NDP's tenure as the government of Ontario from 1990 to 1995, this was the first NDP government east of Manitoba. The New Democrats steadily increased their vote share and their number of seats in the provincial legislature from 1998 forward and their ascent brought more women into the House with every election. The rise of a woman-friendly leftist party had a decisive impact; as a result, the province has finally caught up to the national average in terms of percentage of women elected. The victory of the NDP in Nova Scotia, with its achievement of a secure majority, is all the more striking because party loyalties run deep and strong in this small province. In a population of fewer than a million, political life is intimate and personal.

In addition to enumerating and discussing women in Nova Scotia's provincial politics, this chapter seeks to understand the NDP's rise to power and the way that it increased the presence of women in the government. Premier Dexter coined the term "conservative progressive" to describe himself (Kimber 2009). We may ask: "Whatever happened to social democracy, let alone socialism, as a defining characteristic of the New Democrats?" The answer is important because the ideology of social democracy has historically driven the long-standing measures to promote the full participation of women inside the party as well as to support of other woman-friendly policies. The experience of the Nova Scotia legislature is

POLITICAL REPRESENTATION OF WOMEN IN
NOVA SCOTIA

FIRSTS
Right to vote and stand for election
- Women win right to vote and stand for election   1918*

Contesting office
- First women to contest office: Grace McLeod Rogers   1920
  (Conservative) and Bertha A. Donaldson (Labour Party)
- First woman to win office: Gladys Porter (PC)   1960-67
- First woman to be elected Chief: Mary Ellen Pierro, Wagmatcook 1962
  First Nation
- First woman to lead a political party: Alexa McDonough (NDP)   1980-94
- First African Nova Scotian woman to contest office: Daurene   1988
  Lewis (Liberal)
- First African Nova Scotian woman to be win office: Yvonne   1998-99
  Atwell (NDP)
- First woman appointed to cabinet: Maxine Cochran (PC): minister 1985-88
  of transportation (1985-87)

CURRENT REPRESENTATION AT A GLANCE

| | | Women elected | |
	Date of election	Number	Percent
Women in legislature	2009/06/09	12 of 52	23
Women in cabinet	2009/06/19	4 of 12	33

Women political party leaders
- None at present

Lieutenant governor
- None at present

Advisory council on the status of women
- The Nova Scotia Advisory Council on the Status of Women, an appointed council to
  advise the minister on the status of women, was created in 1977.

* Women who met the property qualifications voted in elections for Nova Scotia's House of Assembly
from 1758. In 1851, their franchise was revoked – ninety-three years after representative government was
established in Nova Scotia (Cuthbertson 1994, 9, 152, 317).

critical to the country at large: when on the cusp of forming the Official Opposition in Ottawa, Jack Layton looked to the Nova Scotia NDP for guidance on how to win and secure a majority government by offering a more practical, less ideological version of social democracy (Maher 2011). Dexter (2009) described the NDP strategy as the "politics of people," which had "no place for strict party ideology."

Perched on the rocky edge of the North Atlantic, separated by a narrow isthmus from the mainland, Nova Scotia is on the periphery of national affairs, and its provincial government has rarely aspired to innovate. Nevertheless, a surprising dynamism has emerged around the electoral project. The politicization of women in this largely rural and economically dependent region of the country is a crucial part of the overall advancement of Canadian women to political leadership, beginning with elected office. An improved understanding of their political situation may also shed light on the challenges facing women elsewhere in the world, in political settings that are similarly rural and on the economic periphery (Carbert and Black 2003, 78).

Background

Nova Scotia's economy lagged behind the rest of the country for much of the twentieth century, especially after 1970. Resource extraction industries were beset by ecological crises and by declining commodity prices determined by global markets. Old manufacturing industries languished as the added competition brought by expanded free trade agreements exposed the shortcomings of aging facilities. The impact of these economic problems was exacerbated by federal government cuts to provincial transfers in the 1990s. But the painful process of economic restructuring gradually took effect after the turn of the century, bringing lower unemployment levels and expanded urbanization to the province (Bickerton 1994; Savoie 2006).

Geographically, the province is divided into three areas: Halifax Regional Municipality, mainland Nova Scotia, and Cape Breton Island. Halifax Regional Municipality is home to almost half of the province's population, and it is the service centre for the entire Atlantic region. The military, medical, and postsecondary sectors employ many highly educated professionals, and their presence makes Halifax a more cosmopolitan centre than numbers alone warrant. The broad economic prospects are better for Halifax than for the rest of the province, especially since the Irving-owned Halifax shipyard was awarded a $25 billion contract from the Department of National

Defence in 2011 (Moore 2011). By contrast, mainland Nova Scotia continues to decline economically and demographically, apart from the transportation hub running between Halifax and Moncton. The complete dismantling of the state-subsidized coal and steel industry makes economic prospects even dimmer in Cape Breton Island. Public-sector employment continues to be a mainstay of the province's economy. In 2010, roughly one in three of the paid workforce was employed in the broader public sector, including educators and health-care workers (Statistics Canada 2011). Public-sector unions emerged as the "centre of gravity" on the left; the New Democrats expanded out from Halifax, where the public-sector workforce was concentrated (Clancy 2010).

Most Nova Scotians are descended from the original Anglo-Celtic wave of migration. There has been no large-scale immigration to the province since Confederation, and there has been continuing out-migration in search of economic opportunity. First Nations play a less prominent role in the political life of the province than in other provinces; some fifteen thousand individuals have Status under the Indian Act, almost all members of the Mi'kmaq Nation (University of Cape Breton, Mi'kmaq Resource Centre 2011). Many women have been elected as band chief, but not one has been elected to the legislature. The more than thirty thousand Acadians comprise the largest minority group; they are descendants of the original French Roman Catholic population that either escaped the Expulsion of 1758 or returned later from exile. Although Nova Scotia is not officially bilingual, the province provides French-language services to predominantly francophone communities. There is continuing uncertainty as to how many Acadians are also Métis (Association des Acadiens-Métis Souriquois 2011). No woman of Acadian descent has been elected to provincial office. In 1974, Coline Campbell, an Acadian, was the first woman from Nova Scotia to be elected federally.

Most African Nova Scotians descend from the black Loyalists who came to Nova Scotia from the United States between 1783 and 1785; they were joined in the nineteenth century by small numbers of slaves and free blacks and, more recently, by immigrants from the Caribbean and Africa (Pachai and Bishop 2006, 2-4). Numbering about twenty thousand, African Nova Scotians are both culturally and politically significant. The Preston district north of Halifax, where many African Nova Scotians live, had its boundaries deliberately drawn in order to elect a black MLA. Yvonne Atwell, the first – and only – woman of African Nova Scotian heritage to be elected provincially or federally, represented the riding for the NDP from 1998 to

1999. Atwell was deeply ambivalent about the job of an MLA. She went into politics to give voice to African Nova Scotians, but it was the minority of relatively privileged white constituents who demanded most of her attention (Atwell 2003, 110).

This background is essential to understanding the scale of political life in the province. For those people who have stayed in the province, politics operates on a remarkably personal and accessible scale: it sometimes seems that almost everyone has a politician somewhere in the family tree and can claim some sort of lineage. In an interview, MLA (and political scientist) Leonard Preyra draws attention to the intimate nature of Nova Scotia's fifty-two-person legislature:

> There's a difference between small legislatures in small provinces and big legislatures in big provinces. People in Nova Scotia relate on an individual human level. We're connected through families, schools, and community activity. There are lots of links and bonds that unite people right across the political spectrum and that imposes a check on our behaviour.

Women's Political Representation: The Numbers

Women in the Legislature

In 1960, in the eleventh election after women became eligible to stand for office, Gladys Porter, mayor of Kentville, became the first woman elected to the Nova Scotia House of Assembly. She died in office in 1967, and no other woman was elected until 1974. Women's share of the legislative seats increased only slowly. In 1997 the proportion of women elected to the Nova Scotia House of Assembly was still below 10 percent; only Prince Edward Island and Newfoundland and Labrador were as low. However, as Table 7.1 shows, the proportion of women elected in Nova Scotia has now increased to 23 percent.

More than doubling the proportion of women elected over so many years is not, on its own, a particularly impressive feat, considering the low starting point. But the increase is startling in the context of the original reasons that were given to explain the distinct lag in the Atlantic provinces. Jane Arscott proposed in 1997 that a traditionalist political system inhibited women in the region (Arscott 1997, 318). That is, high incumbency rates, a two-party brokerage system, a tendency for sons to inherit seats from their fathers, and patronage practices together served as barriers to women's political participation. Richard Matland and Donley Studlar's (1998) quantitative

TABLE 7.1
Women in the Nova Scotia legislature, by election

Election date	Party elected	Total number of legislators	Women elected	
			Number	%
1960/06/07	PC	43	1	2
1963/10/08	PC	43	1	2
1967/05/30	PC	46	0	0
1970/10/13	Liberal	46	0	0
1974/04/02	Liberal	46	1	2
1978/09/19	PC	52	0	0
1981/10/06	PC	52	1	2
1984/06/05	PC	52	2	4
1984/11/06	PC	52	3	6
1988/09/06	PC	52	3	6
1993/05/25	Liberal	52	5	10
1998/03/24	Liberal	52	6	12
1999/07/27	PC	52	5	10
2003/08/05	PC	52	6	12
2006/06/13	PC	52	9	17
2009/06/09	NDP	52	12	23

Note: The table begins in 1960, when a woman won election for the first time. For information on previous elections, see Elections Nova Scotia.
Source: Elections Nova Scotia (2010).

work found that the predominantly rural character of the Atlantic provinces worked to deter women. In their view, conditions outside of the major urban centres – the absence of an organized women's movement and lower educational levels – might contribute to women's lower rates of participation.

Louise Carbert's subsequent interview series with rural women leaders across Atlantic Canada sheds new light on the causes of the rural deficit of elected women. Despite an abundance of qualified potential candidates, the number of actual women candidates was severely limited by a strong reluctance on the part of the women themselves, intense opposition by notably eager male competitors, and resistance by local elites to any sort of change, including nominating more women. The interviews tied these impediments to rural expectations for a political representative to act like a traditional patron. While this role is considered archaic in metropolitan settings, it persisted in much of rural Atlantic Canada not because of traditionalist attitudes but, rather, due to rational calculations of collective self-interest in a fragile, undiversified economic setting (Carbert 2006, 154).

Even so, there does not seem to be any fundamental obstacle in the political culture of the province. Brenda O'Neill and Lynda Erickson's (2003, 117) analysis of public opinion concludes that Nova Scotians are not distinctly traditional or uniquely hostile either to women or to feminists. In this sense, public opinion confirms the judgment of historian Margaret Conrad (2010, 59), who observes that social-democratic leanings in the Atlantic provinces have often been expressed in terms of left Liberalism and "progressive" Conservatism (or "red" Toryism) rather than CCF/NDP support. Finally, Joanna Everitt's (2003, 95) study of media coverage of Maritime elections finds that, if anything, women candidates receive *more* and usually friendlier coverage as a result of their novelty value. In this context of a small, relatively homogeneous population operating in a relatively compressed ideological spectrum, the personal characteristics of individual party leaders and individual candidates become crucial to the outcome of elections.

The numbers of women elected plodded along at a low rate from 1960. The 1998 election was significant: it marked a turning point from the old two-party system to a new system in which the NDP was visibly established on a path to forming a government. The core class of 1998 now forms the inner circle of government. The greater number of NDP members elected brought more women into office. In the 2006 election, the proportion of women elected rose to a potentially significant 17 percent. In that 2006 election, the governing Progressive Conservatives had their minority government reduced to twenty-three seats, just three more than the opposition New Democrats who won twenty seats. Nine women were elected: one Liberal incumbent, two Progressive Conservatives (one incumbent), and one new NDP to join the five NDP women incumbents. For the next three years of minority PC government, the NDP waited and consolidated its plans to assume power after the next election.

When the 2009 election was called, an NDP majority government was a foregone conclusion (Turnbull 2009). During the previous three years in Opposition, the NDP share of decided voters had never fallen below 34 percent. The NDP crafted a cautious and modest platform to assume power, campaigning on the leader's personal credibility as an incrementalist. Because it could foresee certain victory, the NDP's ascent to government in Nova Scotia is more like Roy Romanow's 1991 comeback in Saskatchewan (Carbert 1997) than Bob Rae's surprise 1990 breakthrough in Ontario (Burt and Lorenzin 1997).

The NDP elected nine women in 2009, five of whom were incumbents and four of whom were new MLAs. The defeat of Rodney MacDonald's

Progressive Conservative government took down two incumbent women cabinet ministers (Carolyn Bolivar-Getson and Judy Streatch). Karen Casey, also a minister, was one of the few PCs to keep a seat; she became interim leader of the party. On the Liberal side of the House, one re-elected incumbent woman was joined by one newcomer.

We have met and interviewed all the women MLAs, and though we do not know them well, we would describe them as extraordinary people from ordinary lives. They are outstanding in their charm, their dedication to the public good, their intelligent grasp of complex public policy issues, and their tenacious drive to achieve. Yet these traits could not have been predicted from their previous lives. These were the occupations of the women backbenchers in 2009: management consultant, school administrator, community volunteer, market gardener, potter and small business-owner, broadcaster, and actor. Their electoral success should be read as a cautionary tale against adopting all of the findings in the political-science research coming from the United States, where the scale of political life is so much larger and more expensive. American-dominated research on women and electoral politics posits that there is an "occupational pipeline" that women candidates need to pass through (Lawless and Fox 2005, 26-28). No such senior professional status is required in Nova Scotia. On the contrary, elected office is remarkably democratic in Canadian legislatures (Bashevkin 2009, 117). It is useful to be reminded that the former premiers of New Brunswick and Nova Scotia were both teachers prior to entering politics. Nor should the crucial nominating function of Canadian political parties be overlooked (Goodyear-Grant and Crosskill 2011, 247).

Women Candidates

Women comprised 44 percent of NDP candidates in 1988 and 36 percent in 1998. An occasional brave soul broke with traditional family allegiances by standing for the NDP. Indeed, one NDP candidate recalled being told: "Your grandfathers would be rolling over in their graves." Another woman reported that the NDP riding association revoked her candidacy because her sudden divorce constituted a threat to the party's reputation for conventional respectability, which was ironic because she had sought out the NDP precisely for its progressive values (Carbert 2006, 87).

As the NDP came closer to challenging the two-party system, and formerly lost-cause races became seriously competitive for the first time, the party nominated fewer women candidates. In 2003, 25 percent of the party's candidates were women; in 2006, that had dropped to 23 percent. The Nova

TABLE 7.2

Women candidates in Nova Scotia, by party and election

	Liberal		PC		NDP	
Election date	Number	%	Number	%	Number	%
1981/10/06	9	17	0	0	12	23
1984/11/06	3	6	4	8	14	27
1988/09/06	8	15	3	6	23	44
1993/05/25	8	15	6	12	17	33
1998/03/24	7	13	3	6	19	36
1999/07/27	11	21	7	13	18	35
2003/08/05	9	17	8	15	13	25
2006/06/13	11*	22	7	13	12	23
2009/06/09	10	19	7	13	17	33

* The Liberals ran 51 candidates in this election.
Source: Elections Nova Scotia (2010).

Scotia NDP now has elaborate provisions for gender parity and women's rights representatives in the decision-making affairs of the extra-parliamentary wing of the party, but no formal rules exist to require gender parity in the nomination of candidates for provincial election (Nova Scotia NDP Constitution, section 29). Nevertheless, in 2009, when the NDP was preparing to form the next government, 33 percent of NDP candidates were women, and women subsequently made up 29 percent of the NDP caucus. For the Liberals and the Progressive Conservatives, the proportion of women candidates remained considerably lower (see Table 7.2). A slight "contagion from the left" may have occurred as the two traditional parties picked up the pace to avoid lagging too far behind the NDP. More important, the rising numbers of women running for the NDP generated the increase in the number of women elected since the mid-1990s.

Women Party Leaders

Of the women who have led political parties in Nova Scotia, only one has had a substantial impact on her party and province: Alexa McDonough. The Nova Scotia CCF began contesting elections in 1933, but the current New Democratic Party, in its organization, base of support, and policy orientation, was born in 1980 when McDonough was elected leader. She led the NDP through four elections over fourteen years, and it was under her leadership that the NDP repositioned itself as a social reform movement. McDonough expanded the party from its traditional CCF base with

TABLE 7.3
Women party leaders in Nova Scotia

Name	Political party	Period of service
Alexa McDonough	NDP	1980-94
Helen MacDonald	NDP	2000-1

industrial trade unions in Cape Breton and made the NDP more broadly appealing to the growing population of public-sector workers and professionals in the metropolitan Halifax area (Clancy 2010). She left provincial office to become leader of the national NDP in 1995 and sat as the MP for Halifax from 1997 to 2008. Almost everyone who is active in public affairs in Nova Scotia knows our "Alexa" personally, and she continues to be a respected and admired figure, even after her retirement from elected office. She has been especially effective at recruiting and mentoring women to stand as candidates.

Helen MacDonald was a Cape Breton teacher who led the NDP for only nine months, from July 2000 to April 2001. She had won a 1997 by-election but was defeated in the 1999 election. After a second defeat, in a 2000 by-election, she resigned as leader of the party. According to a local journalist, the reasons for her resignation were apparent in her parting words: "I belong to the NDP because we are a party of ideas and ideals, not personalities and power. Whether we are first, second, or third, we keep working to make life better for Nova Scotians." By 2001, that idealistic and abstract version of the NDP was a thing of the past as the party looked ahead to forming the government (Donham 2001).

After Premier Rodney MacDonald was defeated by the NDP in 2009, he resigned as leader of the Progressive Conservative Party and Karen Casey was appointed interim leader. She is an assertive and capable woman who might have had leadership ambitions herself. Instead, in a surprise move, she crossed the floor to join the Liberal Party in 2011. According to local gossip, there had been substantial criticism of her by "a silent faction of the party": "One party insider employed the term 'diva'; another describes an ego that became 'too big'" (Walsh 2011, 5). This sort of hostile and demeaning assessment of a strong woman leader is all too familiar (Bashevkin 2009).

Casey's move speaks to the structure of partisan politics in Nova Scotia, in particular to where the provincial Liberals stand ideologically. Her praise for the Liberal Party's defence of small business and rural communities – "where the economy is everything" – confirms Lori Turnbull's (2009, 73) observation that Nova Scotia Liberals are further to the right than Liberals elsewhere in Canada. They thus open up a space for the NDP on the centre-left of the ideological spectrum.

Women in the Cabinet

The numbers relating to women cabinet ministers are a bit deceptive: since there was always a minister responsible for the status of women in this period, it was pretty well guaranteed that at least one portfolio went to a woman. In fact, most of these governments appointed all the women in caucus to cabinet positions. The PC government even appointed two non-elected women to cabinet during its final days in office. Neither of them won seats in the subsequent 1993 election (Arscott 1997, 334)

The PC government elected in 2006 appointed all three PC women MLAs to major portfolios. The NDP government elected in 2009 appointed four women to major portfolios. Maureen MacDonald (initially appointed to health, then to finance) is the most senior female minister. A former professor of social work, she was first elected in 1998, when the NDP broke through weaknesses in the old parties with a popular vote of 35 percent.

TABLE 7.4
Women in cabinet in Nova Scotia, by election

Election date	Party elected	Total number of cabinet ministers*	Women appointed to to cabinet		Number of women in governing caucus	% of women in governing caucus in cabinet*
			Number	%		
1981/10/06	PC	21	0	0	0 of 37	0
1984/11/06	PC	22	1	0	2 of 42	50
1988/09/06	PC	17	0	0	1 of 28	0
1993/05/25	Liberal	17	2	12	4 of 40	50
1998/03/24	Liberal	12	1	8	1 of 19	100
1999/07/27	PC	11	1	9	3 of 30	33
2003/08/05	PC	15	1	7	1 of 25	100
2006/06/13	PC	18	3	11	3 of 23	100
2009/06/09	NDP	12	4	33	9 of 31	44

* Includes the premier.
Source: Nova Scotia Executive Council (1968-2011).

At 33 percent of cabinet, women might be expected to form a "critical mass" able to be influential as a group. At 23 percent, women in the House have not even reached the notional crucial percentage of thirty. However, Drude Dahlerup suggests that the notion of "critical acts" to empower women should replace that of any direct impact of increased numbers. Such a formulation may be more appropriate for Nova Scotia's legislature as, in her words, women there move "from a small to a large minority" (Dahlerup 1988, 296).

Moreover, power may not reside in those formal bodies alone. In interviews we were told that there are circles within circles and that even some ministers feel excluded from the centre of decision making around the premier. There may well be even more exclusive circles of power to which only the premier or a party leader is privy. Perhaps the next generation of research on women and politics will look past the external, public face of elected office to consider more personalized forms of power. As Donald Savoie (2010, 200-2) observes, the informal conventions of parliamentary governance make political power ever more slippery and difficult to pin down.

Female Representatives of the Crown

Nova Scotia has had two women serve in succession as lieutenant governor. Both appointments were innovative and intended to highlight "diversity." Myra Freeman, a Liberal Party appointment, was a teacher, active in the Liberal Party, and Jewish. The Progressive Conservatives appointed Mayann Francis, a senior public servant working in the field of human rights administration. She was the first African Nova Scotian lieutenant governor; her parents had emigrated from the Caribbean to head the African Orthodox Church in Sydney (Lieutenant Governor of Nova Scotia 2011).

Explanations

The election of an NDP government in 2009 was hugely significant. The emergence, consolidation, and victory of a third party broke the traditional system of two-party competition between Liberals and Conservatives. It

TABLE 7.5
Female representatives of the Crown in Nova Scotia

Name	Period of service
Myra Freeman	2000-6
Mayann E. Francis	2006-12

seemed to mark the end of the old Maritime way of doing politics. The election of Lenore Zann is a case in point. She is a successful actor who returned to make Truro her home base, and the riding association was thrilled when she volunteered to stand. During the election campaign, in an attempt to discredit her, the Liberals released a topless photo of her from a scene in the TV series *The L Word,* but the stunt backfired as public outrage turned on the Liberals (Patten 2009). As Zann told us:

> For many years, it felt like Truro was owned by a few small families, who had the power and owned the factories. As I've been told, people were afraid to have any kind of signs on their lawn that were anything but Tory for fear of losing their job. So everything revolved around that factory town mentality, but that has been changing.

"For years," she said, "my mom and dad were the only ones to have an NDP sign on their lawns":

> Toward the end of the election campaign, when the orange signs had grown and grown, I was standing at Tim's when this big truckful of big construction guys pulled up and recognized me: "Hey Zann, you Zann! You kick out that old boys club; you get rid of those old boys for us."

Even allowing for Zann's theatrical zest, this episode captures some of the sense of a new day dawning for the province. There would be new sorts of candidates, including those from families who had earned their wealth from elsewhere in the world. Such changes seem to promise advantages for women.

Until the past few elections, the scarcity of women standing for the Liberals and the Progressive Conservatives explained the small number of women elected to the Nova Scotia House of Assembly. So long as the traditional two-party system of competition between the two old brokerage parties was intact, the majority of women nominated by the NDP were running as lost-cause candidates. This was especially true in rural Nova Scotia, beyond the beachhead established in Halifax Regional Municipality. When we seek lessons for similar provincial environments in which the representation of women in elected office still lags – as, for instance, in Newfoundland and Labrador or New Brunswick – we look for increase in female candidacy for parties with a chance of forming the government. The conditions that enabled the NDP to break through in Nova Scotia – first the historical legacy of trade unionism from industrial Cape Breton and, more recently, the geographical concentration of a relatively affluent population of highly educated public-sector professionals – may not be so easy to reproduce elsewhere in the Maritimes. In Nova Scotia, it was to be expected that a relatively centrist NDP government would bring more women to the House of Assembly, even apart from Alexa McDonough's recruitment of generations of women into the party. In any case, a viable three-way competition seems necessary to avoid a plethora of lost-cause ridings identified with a single party.

In addition, there were other contributions to the increased number of women MLAs. Long before other Canadian jurisdictions began to experiment with campaign schools and recruitment campaigns, there was a surge of government and government-funded activity in Nova Scotia to promote women's political leadership, with particular attention to rural women. In 1977, the Government of Nova Scotia established the Nova Scotia Advisory Council on the Status of Women (NSACSW) to address the provincial implications of the recommendations made by the national Royal Commission on the Status of Women in 1970. Thanks to exceptionally able administrators, it has maintained good relations with successive governments of various political stripes. Perhaps as a result, unlike other provincial and national councils, this one has survived its initial mandate to continue as an appointed body that advises the minister responsible for the status of women (Guildford 2005).

The NSACSW organized the Winning Women Political Skills Forum in 1991. Soon after, the council published *Votes for Women: A Political Guidebook for Nova Scotia Women,* which eventually went to three printings. In 2003, Carolyn Bolivar-Getson, the minister responsible for the status of women, mounted political participation workshops across the province, featuring panels of prominent women speaking about their experience of running for elected office. Then, in 2004, the NSACSW began the Nova Scotia Campaign School, the first and, to date, the only campaign school to be mounted by a Canadian government. By 2011, there had been six campaign schools (Carbert 2011, 79).

At the same time as the Advisory Council embarked on its women and leadership agenda, a parallel municipal route to elected office was in the works. In her capacity as president of the Federation of Canadian Municipalities (2004-5), Ann Maclean, long-time mayor of New Glasgow, launched a multifaceted initiative to elect more women to municipal governments. She worked closely with Anna Allen, mayor of Windsor, who embarked on a parallel set of initiatives at the provincial level with the Union of Nova Scotia Municipalities (UNSM). The UNSM conducted research, published a report, and established a standing committee for women in local government. In 2008, the UNSM mounted a series of four municipal campaign schools (Carbert 2011, 81). Overall, Nova Scotia achieved some success in enabling the increased engagement of women in politics, if measured only in terms of programming designed and implemented. But there is no quick and easy payoff for the campaign schools, and much work remains to be done.

Some of this work will have to be done by non-governmental activists. In 2007 a Nova Scotia branch of Equal Voice (EVNS) was established – on the third try. EVNS mounts events related to women in electoral politics, and its circulation list constitutes an extensive network that includes the elected women in Nova Scotia.

Conclusion: Prospects for Gender Equality

The NDP government in Nova Scotia differs from the one in Ontario in one way that is particularly relevant here: the role of the women's movement. In Ontario, there were strong ties between the provincial NDP and activists who, after 1990, expected the Rae government to implement the feminist policy agenda that the party had formally endorsed. And they expected to be consulted on the process (Burt and Lorenzin 1997, 224; Byrne 2009, 98). The 1990 recession put paid to such expectations immediately, and women in cabinet bore the brunt of recriminations from the women's movement (Byrne 2009, 100).

Unlike Ontario, the Nova Scotia NDP has enjoyed sedate relations with the women's movement. It is not that there is no women's movement in the province: the women's movement is historic, multifaceted, and very much alive (Black 2006). Our impression is that, for those women who are feminist and on the left, their first priority is still to safeguard the NDP. Furthermore, even the most radical activists in a small province that has experienced over a century of economic decline are convinced of the virtue of balanced budgets. Therefore, female cabinet ministers seem to enjoy immunity from pressure from the women's movement.

In addition, many women politicians know and work with the numerous volunteer-based non-governmental women's organizations such as the YWCA and the women's centres located throughout rural Nova Scotia. In 2011, however, some social activists were dissatisfied with the pace of change. WAC-NS (Women's Action Alliance for Change Nova Scotia) was attempting to organize a revival of its 1990s activities as lobbyist for social programs supportive of women (Women's Action Alliance for Change Nova Scotia 2011).

As more women are elected, their situation becomes increasingly normalized, in the sense that their careers are subject to standard political influences. Some people are more effective politicians than others, so it becomes increasingly difficult to tease out what is a gendered factor in political careers. For example, opposition member Diana Whalen, who contested the Liberal Party leadership in 2007, was defeated by a mere sixty-eight votes. Was she defeated because she was a woman, because she could not be expected to carry rural Nova Scotia from her suburban Halifax seat, or because she just failed to sign up enough supporters? Entirely apart from the leadership race, Whalen told us of her initial disappointment at there being less "team" in caucus than she expected. Apparently, when the House is sitting, out-of-town members from all three parties go to dinner together and talk late into the evening. But was she excluded from the "session" after the Session because she was a woman or because she returned to her family in the suburbs? The rural members have their own sort of cohesion, and the Cape Bretoners are particularly close, in part because they sometimes share long trips back and forth to the Island with each other.

All the same, it does seem that women MLAs have different perceptions of life in the House than do their male colleagues. The conditions of legislative life are significant. An NDP backbencher told us of a gendered component in what she experienced as the surprising physicality of the job: "Most MLAs are large men who have a history in sports and it's how they use their body language. There's a lot of locker room stuff." A tiny woman, she felt overwhelmed by the bodily presence of so many large men as everyone squeezed in together. Another woman MLA expressed a similar sentiment, reminding us just how much time caucus spent with each other in and out of the House. She agreed that caucus was more like a group marriage than anything else. This is not a likely reaction from the men in the House.

Numbers do not tell the whole story, as we were reminded when we interviewed the current MLA backbenchers. Admittedly, Nova Scotia's eight female backbenchers − five NDPers, three Liberals, and no Conservatives − comprise a small group. Yet their lives and experiences speak to many of the generalizations current in the literature about women in electoral politics − and in some cases cast doubt on them. For example, though these women know and respect each other, they do not collaborate across party lines as an earlier generation did. A female MLA who attempted to organize some sociability among women of the different parties found her efforts unwelcome. Even within the NDP, we were told by a female MLA, the women do not work together in any special way. Nor do they all object, as women, to the conditions of work. These are women who have long led active and demanding lives. While several expressed dissatisfaction with the House organization, especially its evening meeting hours, others felt they were no more demanding than shift work or participation in volunteer organizations. Another objected to evenings in the House not because they interfered with her family responsibilities but because they made it difficult to attend community events in the evening.

It is too early to tell if the NDP women will have an impact on the government's public policy record or even on the possible changes in processes and procedures. It is not yet clear whether some form of "critical mass" is emerging or even if women find the political environment more comfortable now that they are more numerous. Dahlerup's reflections on "politics as a workplace" are relevant. She suggests that the presence of a larger proportion of women in elected office will, most importantly, enable those women to pursue their political goals, whatever they are (Dahlerup 2006, 19).

Further investigation of the current NDP government in Nova Scotia will make it possible to ask whether, now that the proportion of women elected to the Nova Scotia House of Assembly has increased, there has been a corresponding increase in the quantity and quality of public policy initiatives directed towards women. That is, has the descriptive representation of women in strictly numerical terms led to substantive representation of women-specific interests? Our discussion of the women who are currently MLAs shows that this question is not as easily answered as we often assume.

Note

The authors thank Brigitte Neumann for advice and Michelle Coffin for compiling the tables. MLA interviews were conducted by Louise Carbert in May 2011.

References

Arscott, Jane 1997. "Between a Rock and a Hard Place: Women Legislators in Newfoundland and Nova Scotia." In Jane Arscott and Linda Trimble, eds., *In the Presence of Women: Representation in Canadian Governments*, 307-37. Toronto: Harcourt Brace and Company.

Association des Acadiens-Métis Souriquois. 2011. Information available at http://www.acadiens-metis-souriquois.ca/.

Atwell, Yvonne 2003. "Commentary." *Atlantis* 27(2): 110-12.

Bashevkin, Sylvia. 2009. "'Stage' versus 'Actor': Barriers to Women's Leadership." In Sylvia Bashevkin, ed., *Opening Doors Wider: Women's Political Engagement in Canada*, 108-26. Vancouver: UBC Press.

Bickerton, James. 1998. "Atlantic Canada: Regime Change in a Dependent Region." In James Bickerton and Alain Gagnon, eds., *Canadian Politics*, 426-49. Peterborough: Broadview Press.

Black, N. 2006. "Feminism in Nova Scotia: Women's Groups, 1990-2004." *Atlantis* 31(1): 64-75.

Burt, Sandra, and Elizabeth Lorenzin. 1997. "Taking the Women's Movement to Queen's Park: Women's Interests and the New Democratic Party Government of Ontario." In Jane Arscott and Linda Trimble, eds., *In the Presence of Women: Representation in Canadian Governments*, 202-27. Toronto: Harcourt Brace and Company.

Byrne, Lesley. 2009. "Making a Difference when the Doors Are Open: Women in the Ontario NDP Cabinet, 1990-95." In Sylvia Bashevkin, ed., *Opening Doors Wider: Women's Political Engagement in Canada*, 93-107. Vancouver: UBC Press.

Carbert, Louise. 1997. "Governing on the Correct, the Compassionate, the Saskatchewan Side of the Border." In Jane Arscott and Linda Trimble, eds., *In the Presence of Women: Representation in Canadian Governments*, 154-79, Toronto: Harcourt Brace and Company.

– 2006. *Rural Women's Leadership in Atlantic Canada: First-Hand Perspectives on Local Public Life and Participation in Electoral Politics*. Toronto: University of Toronto Press.

–. 2011 "Making It Happen in Practice: Organized Efforts to Recruit Rural Women for Local Government Leadership." In Barbara Pini, ed., *Women and Representation in Local Government: International Case Studies*, 76-94. London: Routledge.

Carbert, Louise, and Naomi Black. 2003. "Building Women's Leadership in Atlantic Canada." *Atlantis* 27(2): 72-78.

Clancy, Peter. 2010. "Bluenose Socialism: The Nova Scotia NDP in Year One." Paper presented at the Annual Meeting of the Atlantic Provinces Political Science Association, Dalhousie University, October.

Conrad, Margaret. 2010. "Remembering Firsts: Female Politicians in the Atlantic Provinces in the 20th Century." In Janet Guildford and Suzanne Morton, eds., *Making up the State: Women in 20th-Century Atlantic Canada*, 57-77. Fredericton, NB: Acadiensis Press.

Cuthbertson, Brian. 1994. *Johnny Bluenose at the Polls: Epic Nova Scotian Election Battles, 1758-1848*. Halifax: Formac.

Dahlerup, Drude. 1988. "From a Small to a Large Minority: Women in Scandinavian Politics." *Scandinavian Political Studies* 11(4): 275-98.

–. 2006. "The Story of the Theory of Critical Mass." *Politics and Gender* 2(4): 511-22.

Dexter, Darrell. 2009. Keynote address to the national New Democratic Party Convention. Halifax, Nova Scotia, 18 August.

Donham, Parker Barss. 2001. "Exit Helen MacDonald." *Daily News*, 25 April. Available at http://rabble.ca/.

Elections Nova Scotia. 2010. *Summary Results 1867-2010*. Available at http://electionsnovascotia.ns.ca/.

Everitt, Joanna. 2003. "Media in the Maritimes: Do Female Candidates Face a Bias?" *Atlantis* 27(2): 90-98.

Goodyear-Grant, Elizabeth, and Julie Croskill. 2011. "Gender Affinity Effects in Vote Choice in Westminster Systems: Assessing 'Flexible' Voters in Canada." *Politics and Gender* 7(2): 223-50.

Guildford, Janet. 2005. "A Fragile Independence: The Nova Scotia Advisory Council on the Status of Women." In Judith Fingard and Janet Guildford, eds., *Mothers of the Municipality: Women, Work, and Social Policy in Post-1945 Halifax*, 281-304. Toronto: University of Toronto Press.

Kimber, Stephen. 2009. "Who Is Premier Darrell Dexter?" *The Coast*, 9 June. Available at http://www.thecoast.ca/.

Lawless, Jennifer, and Richard Fox. 2005. *It Takes a Candidate: Why Women Don't Run for Office*. New York: Cambridge University Press.

Lieutenant Governor of Nova Scotia. 2011. Information available at http://lt.gov. ns.ca/.

Maher, Stephen. 2011. "Layton Took Page from Dexter's Book, Federal NDP Made Retirement Security a Key Issue." *Halifax Chronicle Herald*, 2 May.

Matland, Richard E., and Donley T. Studlar. 1998. "Gender and the Electoral Opportunity Structure in the Canadian Provinces." *Political Research Quarterly* 51(1): 117-40.

Moore, Oliver. 2011. "Shipbuilding Contract Will Bring Nova Scotians Home." *Globe and Mail*, 19 October. Available at http://www.theglobeandmail.com/.

Nova Scotia Executive Council. 1968-2011. *Province of Nova Scotia Members of the Government*. Papers located at Legislative Library, Nova Scotia House of Assembly.

O'Neill, Brenda, and Lynda Erickson. 2003. "Evaluating Traditionalism in the Atlantic Provinces: Voting, Public Opinion and the Electoral Project." *Atlantis* 27(2): 113-22.

Pachai, Bridglal, and Henry Bishop. 2006. *Historic Black Nova Scotia*. Halifax: Nimbus Publishing.

Patten, Melanie. 2009. "Grits Sorry for Leaking Topless Pic of Candidate." *Halifax Chronicle Herald*, 10 April.

Savoie. Donald. 2006. *Visiting Grandchildren: Economic Development in the Maritimes*. Toronto: University of Toronto Press.

–. 2010. *Power: Where Is It?* Montreal and Kingston: McGill-Queen's University Press.

Statistics Canada. 2011. Summary Tables, Labour Force Characteristics: Public Sector Employment, Seasonally Adjusted, by Province. Available at http://cansim2.statcan.gc.ca/.

Turnbull, Lori. 2009. "The Nova Scotia Provincial Election of 2009." *Canadian Political Science Review* 3(3): 69-76.

University of Cape Breton, Mi'kmaq Resource Centre. 2011. Information available at http://www.cbu.ca/mrc/.

Walsh, Dan. 2011. "Karen and Stephen, Blow by Blow." *Atlantic Canada Frank* 603: 5-7.

Women's Action Alliance for Change Nova Scotia. 2011. Information available at http://womenandgirlstakeaction.blogspot.com/.

8

Breaking the Holding Pattern?
Women in Ontario Politics

TRACEY RANEY

On 6 October 2011, the Province of Ontario made history by sending its largest cohort of women to its legislature: thirty female MPPs won their constituencies, constituting 28 percent of the seats in Queen's Park. While this record high is cause for excitement, the fact remains that this percentage is far below that of gender parity in Ontario politics. To put this election in historical context, while gains have been made for women the last twenty years have produced a holding pattern for women elected to provincial politics, with the percentage of seats held by female MPPs unable to breach the 30 percent threshold. In the aftermath of the 2011 election, questions remain: Will women in Ontario continue to climb towards the goal of gender parity in provincial politics or will their numbers remain in this holding pattern that has characterized much of the last few decades? What changes, if any, are required to ensure that Ontario women are able to achieve gender parity in the foreseeable future?

My main objective in this chapter is to explain women's pathways to gender parity in the legislature of Ontario. I explore three sets of explanations for the incremental advancements of women in the province: (1) the role of political parties in recruiting and nominating women, (2) the nature of the electoral and party system competition in the province, and (3) the presence of the women's movement in electoral campaigns. I argue that women's slow ascension towards public office in Ontario is due in large part to a lack of formal rules governing nomination processes within provincial political

POLITICAL REPRESENTATION OF WOMEN IN
ONTARIO

FIRSTS
Right to vote and stand for election
- Most women win right to vote / right to stand for election — 1917 / 1919
- Aboriginal women win right to vote — 1954

Contesting office
- First women to contest office: Henrietta Bundy (Liberal) and Justerna Sears (Independent) — 1919
- First women to win office: Agnes Macphail (CCF) / Rae Luckock (CCF) — 1943-45, 1948-51 / 1943-45
- First black female MPP and cabinet minister: Zanana Akande (NDP) — 1990-94
- First publicly identified lesbian cabinet minister: Kathleen Wynne (Liberal) — 2006 to present
- First South Asian female to win office: Amrit Mangat (Liberal) — 2007 to present
- First woman appointed to cabinet: Margaret Birch (PC) — 1972-83
- First woman premier: Kathleen Wynne (Liberal) — 2013 to present

CURRENT REPRESENTATION AT A GLANCE

	Date of election	Women elected Number	Percent
Women in legislature	2011/10/06	30 of 107	28
Women in cabinet	2011/10/06	6 of 22	27

Women political party leaders
- Andrea Horwath (NDP): 2009 to present
- Kathleen Wynne (Liberal): 2013 to present

Lieutenant governor
- None at present

Advisory council on the status of women
- The Ontario Advisory Council on the Status of Women was created in 1973 and disbanded in 1996.

parties, to an incumbency rate that makes the competitive field more challenging for female candidates compared to male incumbents, and to the absence of the women's movement in electoral politics until, in recent elections, the emergence of Equal Voice. Set within this broader context, women's gains in political representation in 2011 must be viewed with continued concern about what the future might bring for the goal of gender parity in the Province of Ontario.

Background

Women in Ontario have made important strides towards gender equality over the last half century. Since the first two CCF women – Agnes Macphail and Rae Luckock – took their seats at Queen's Park in 1943, women have experienced improvements in education, employment, and income levels. Ontario women achieve higher rates of education today than did women of previous generations, and they are more likely to have a university degree than are women in other provinces (Statistics Canada 2006, 90). The employment gap between women and men is also narrowing in the province: while in 1976, 46 percent of women aged fifteen and over were employed (compared to 75 percent of men over fifteen), by 2009, 58 percent of women were employed (compared to 64 percent of men) (Statistics Canada 2010). Ontario women also have the second highest average income of women in the country, behind only Alberta women (ibid.). At the same time, women have yet to achieve economic, social, and political equality in the province. After two decades of pay equity legislation, Ontario women earn 29 percent less than their male counterparts in the workforce, two-thirds of minimum wage workers are women, and female university graduates earn 16 percent less than their male counterparts (Equal Pay Coalition 2008).

Ontario women are not a homogeneous group. In 2006, over half of Canada's visible minority population lived in the province (Statistics Canada 2006, 25), almost one-third of all females living in Ontario were born outside of Canada, and 21 percent of all Aboriginal women in Canada live in Ontario (Statistics Canada 2010). Many of these women are disproportionately poorer than other women in the province: Aboriginal, visible minority, immigrant, and non-unionized women earn significantly less than non-Aboriginal, non-visible minority, Canadian born, and unionized women (Equal Pay Coalition 2008). Recent changes in Ontario's economy will also have gendered and racialized effects as the global economic downturn in 2008 hit the province especially hard, and, for the first time in its history, Ontario now receives equalization payments as a "have-not" province in the country.

Against this cultural and economic backdrop, gender and racial inequities in political representation persist in Ontario. Although the presence of women and visible minorities is clearly not enough to solve these inequities, their lack of representation in provincial politics – where crucial decisions are made about issues that affect women's daily lives, such as health, day care, and social spending – is troubling. I now turn to an examination of women's political representation in the Ontario legislature and look at why women continue to have limited access to the levers of political power and decision making made available through provincial public office.

Women's Political Representation: The Numbers

Over the last century, women's political representation in the province has increased substantially. Table 8.1 shows the number and percentage of women elected in each provincial general election since 1919, the year most women had the right to stand for office in the province. Between 1943 and 1971, women never constituted more than 5 percent of the provincial representatives in Ontario. In 1981, only 5 percent of Ontario's legislative seats were held by women, and by 2011 the percentage had risen to 28 percent, an increase of twenty-three percentage points. Despite constituting 23 percent of the Ontario population, visible minorities are also under-represented at Queen's Park. In the 2011 election, only thirteen visible minorities were elected (12 percent of all MPPs) (Siemiatycki 2011).

Table 8.2 shows the percentage of female candidates for each of the three main political parties since 1981. [1] Overall, the picture is positive: in the last two decades all three parties have increased their numbers of female candidacies. Between 1981 and 2007, the left-leaning Ontario New Democratic Party ran the highest percentage of female candidates in every election since 1981, followed by the centre-right Ontario Liberal Party, and the right-leaning Progressive Conservative Party of Ontario trails behind. In the 2011 provincial election, the Liberal Party ran its highest percentage of female candidates: 42 women (39 percent of their total candidates), while the Progressive Conservative Party ran the same number (24 or 22 percent of its candidates) of women as it did in the previous election. In contrast, the NDP ran fewer women in 2011 (39 or 36 percent of its candidates) than it did in 2007 (42 or 40 percent). Interestingly, for the first time in the province's history, the Liberals fielded more female candidates than did the NDP in 2011 (42 to 39). In 2011, a total of 57 candidates were visible minorities, constituting 18 percent of the total candidate pool for the three main parties (Siemiatycki 2011). Overall, in 2011 women and visible minorities were under-represented as candidates relative to their populations in the province.

Tracey Raney

TABLE 8.1
Women in the Ontario legislature, by election

Election date	Party elected	Total number of legislators	Women elected	
			Number	%
1919/10/20	United Farmers of Ontario	111	0	0
1923/06/25	Conservative	111	0	0
1926/12/01	Conservative	112	0	0
1929/10/30	Conservative	112	0	0
1934/06/19	Liberal	90	0	0
1937/10/06	Liberal	90	0	0
1943/08/04	PC	90	2	2
1945/06/04	PC	90	0	0
1948/06/07	PC	90	1	1
1951/11/22	PC	90	0	0
1955/06/09	PC	98	0	0
1959/06/11	PC	98	0	0
1963/09/25	PC	108	1	1
1967/10/17	PC	117	2	2
1971/10/21	PC	117	2	2
1975/09/18	PC (minority)	125	7	6
1977/06/09	PC (minority)	125	6	5
1981/03/19	PC	125	6	5
1985/05/02	Liberal (minority)	125	9	7
1987/09/10	Liberal	130	20	15
1990/09/06	NDP	130	28	22
1995/06/08	PC	130	19	15
1999/06/03	PC	103	18	17
2003/10/02	Liberal	103	22	21
2007/10/10	Liberal	107	29	27
2011/10/06	Liberal (minority)	107	30	28

Sources: Elections Ontario, various years, http://www.elections.on.ca/; Legislative Assembly of Ontario, http://www.ontla.on.ca/.

In 1993, Bashevkin (1993, 89) noted that the higher, more powerful, and more competitive political positions remain in the hands of men. At the highest levels of Ontario public office, this still holds true. Table 8.3 shows that only three women (neither of whom was a visible minority) have been leaders of their parties. Lyn McLeod, Ontario's first female party leader (Liberal, 1992-96), took over the helm of her party after Liberal premier

TABLE 8.2

Women candidates in Ontario, by party and election

	NDP		Liberal		PC	
Election date	Number	%	Number	%	Number	%
1981/03/19	24	19	9	7	12	10
1985/05/02	28	22	14	11	17	14
1987/09/10	46	35	27	21	23	18
1990/09/06	40	31	27	21	19	15
1995/06/08	38	29	31	24	20	15
1999/06/03	31	30	20	19	18	18
2003/10/02	33	32	23	22	21	20
2007/10/10	43	40	38	36	24	22
2011/10/06	39	36	42	39	24	22

Sources: Elections Ontario, Province of Ontario Election Statistics on Female Candidatures, 1919-2010, http://www.elections.on.ca/.

TABLE 8.3

Women party leaders in Ontario

Name	Political party	Period of service
Lyn McLeod	Liberal	1992-96
Andrea Horwath	NDP	2009 to present
Kathleen Wynne	Liberal	2013 to present

David Peterson was punished by voters for calling a snap election in 1990. Charged with the responsibility of re-energizing the defeated Liberals, McLeod's leadership arc follows that of several other Canadian female party leaders. After losing to Mike Harris's Progressive Conservatives in the 1995 election in what many felt was a "sure bet" win for the Liberals, McLeod stepped down as leader. Her political fate was unlike that of the next Liberal leader, Dalton McGuinty, who survived a failed election bid in 1999 to go on to win back-to-back elections in 2003 and 2007 (Trimble and Arscott 2003).

The 2011 election was unique in that one of the leaders of a main party (the NDP) was female, the province's second female leader of a main political party. Elected as the leader of the NDP in 2009, Andrea Horwath fought her first electoral campaign in 2011 and performed well by delivering seventeen seats for her party (up from ten in 2007). Horwath's campaign is noteworthy not only because she was the first female party leader in the province in fifteen years but also because of the style of her campaign. Rather than downplay her sex, Horwath played to her gender as a way to differentiate her campaign from those of her two male opponents. In a televised ad entitled "Shoes," which aired for the NDP during the campaign, a woman is filmed from the waist down standing in a pencil skirt and a pair of orange high-heeled shoes positioned between two men dressed in red and blue trousers. As the woman coyly turns her high heel outward towards the camera the announcer comments: "This election, there's another choice." When asked about her leadership skills, Horwath stated: "A lot of my political experience has been positive because I don't leave my gender at home, I actually work the way I would work in politics, I work the way I would work in anything else. Bringing my experience, bringing my perspective and my way of doing things as a woman" (Metro Canada 2011). Horwath's use of her gender as a campaign strength is unusual as, often, female politicians and candidates will downplay their sex in order to be perceived as "fitting in" in the world of politics, a world that has been and continues to be dominated largely by men. Horwath's 2011 campaign raises important questions about the extent to which she was able to make her gender more visible during the campaign because she was leader of the third-place party and, therefore, not a serious contender in the fight to form the government.

The third woman party leader, Kathleen Wynne, is the first woman premier of Ontario and the first openly gay premier in Canada. Wynne was among seven candidates who competed for the Liberal Party leadership when Dalton McGuinty resigned in October 2012. Acknowledged as a frontrunner in the leadership contest, Wynne prevailed over Sandra Pupatello on the third ballot at the convention vote held 26 January 2013. Up-front about her sexual orientation, Wynne declared in her speech to convention delegates, "I don't believe the people of Ontario judge their leaders on the basis of race, colour, or sexual orientation" (Morrow and Howlett 2013). Whether or not Wynne will be able to last in the top job remains to be seen, as the Liberals were reduced to a minority in the 2011 election and, after McGuinty's resignation, trailed the New Democrats and Conservatives in the opinion polls.

Table 8.4 shows the number and percentage of women occupying cabinet positions since 1981. The highest percentage of female cabinet ministers occurred in the NDP government of 1990 (42 percent). The last column in Table 8.4 shows the percentage of women in the governing caucus who secured a cabinet position, with the highest percentages in the Liberal

TABLE 8.4

Women in cabinet in Ontario, by election

Election date	Party elected	Total number of cabinet ministers*	Women appointed to cabinet		% of women in governing caucus in cabinet
			Number	%	
1981/03/19	PC	27	2	7	50
1985/05/02	Liberal (minority)	23	2	9	67
1987/09/10	Liberal	30	6	20	6
1990/09/06	NDP	26	11	42	58
1995/06/08	PC	19	4	21	36
1999/06/03	PC	25	5	20	56
2003/10/02	Liberal	23	5	22	29
2007/10/10	Liberal	28	9	32	47
2011/10/06	Liberal (minority)	22	6	27	40

* Includes the premier.

minority cabinet in 1985 (67 percent) and the NDP government in 1990 (58 percent).

While the appointment of women and visible minorities to positions of high political power is sometimes perceived as politically "risky," firmly ensconced in his second majority mandate Premier McGuinty took the issues of inclusion and diversity more seriously in his cabinet shuffles before the 2011 election. In early 2010, he increased his complement of female cabinet ministers to eleven (42 percent), tying the record set by the NDP cabinet in 1990. As a result, women were proportionally better represented in cabinet than in the legislature at that time. After the 2011 election, however, the premier's commitment to diversity faded. In his 2011 "leaner" cabinet of twenty-two, he appointed only six women and three visible minorities. The percentage of women in this cabinet constitutes a lower percentage than was found in the previous cabinet and than was elected in 2011 (27 percent compared to 28 percent), and a higher percentage of visible minorities than is found in the legislature as a whole (14 percent compared to 12 percent).

Finally, Table 8.5 shows the two women who have held the position of lieutenant governor of Ontario: the Honourable Hilary M. Weston (1997-2002) and, earlier, the Honourable Pauline McGibbon (1974-80), who was the province's first female lieutenant governor and the first woman to hold a vice-regal position in the Commonwealth.

TABLE 8.5
Female representatives of the Crown in Ontario

Name	Period of service
Pauline M. McGibbon	1974-80
Hilary M. Weston	1997-2002

Explanations

Why are there so few women in Ontario politics? Below are some explanations.

Party Paths: Recruiting and Nominating Women

Research indicates that key determinants of women's political representation are political parties, which act as "gatekeepers," regulating the flow of candidates into legislatures (Brodie 1985, 98). Examination of the organizational structure and, particularly, the nomination processes of political parties reveals varying levels of commitment to increasing the number of women and visible minorities in Ontario. Not surprisingly, the New Democrats remain the most open to nominating persons from marginalized groups. In 1982, the Ontario NDP adopted affirmative action guidelines, which state that 50 percent of all ridings should have women candidates and that 75 percent of the non-incumbent "targeted" seats should have candidates from affirmative action target groups, including: "women, visible minorities, youth, people living with disabilities, aboriginal people, gays, lesbians, bisexual and transgender individuals and francophones" (ONDP 2011). According to one party official, although the central party monitors and ensures that the guidelines are followed, the "buy-in" from activists on the ground ensures that the party is able to achieve its targets in almost all cases. The NDP also provides funds for female candidates to finance expenses such as childcare throughout a campaign.

For the Liberal Party, nomination processes are somewhat more integrated, with the central party working with the local levels to find suitable candidates. Although the party does not have firm targets, a central Candidate Search Committee provides oversight in virtually every riding, paying particular attention to the recruitment of women and persons from "cultural communities," especially in ridings the party considers most "winnable."[2] The strongest authority is exercised in the five candidate appointments made available to the leader, and it has occasionally been used to nominate women and/or members of "cultural communities." The discretionary power of the leader to appoint candidates illustrates the considerable power of party leaders and first ministers to recruit and appoint women to higher positions of political power in Canadian politics. In terms of financial assistance for female candidates, in the 2007 election, through the Margaret Campbell Fund (established in 1984), the Liberal Party provided funds to all its female candidates, giving one thousand dollars to those who had not previously won a seat and three hundred dollars to incumbents.

In contrast, the PCs do not establish targets for women candidates, and the party's nomination processes remain the most decentralized of the main political parties. In 1987 the party established the Women in Nomination Program (WIN) to help run training programs for women and to help female candidates set up campaign teams and organize fund raising (Bird 2003). After the 2007 election the WIN program was disbanded due to inertia within the party as no one within the party organization pursued the program further.

Overall, the lack of formal party rules relating to female candidacies helps explain why women's political representation is so low in the province historically. Recent successes in the 2007 and 2011 elections, therefore, are not attributed to the emergence of new internal structures or formalized rules relating to women but, rather, at least in part, to the responsiveness of each party (particularly within the leaders' offices) to an extra-party actor: Equal Voice (discussed later).

The Field of Competition: Party System and Type of Seats Available

Research indicates that parliamentary turnover matters to the election of women, providing legislative space for women and visible minorities to compete (Young 1991; Tremblay 2009). After the end of the long-standing PC dynasty in 1985, Ontario's electorate has been quite volatile, and, in its last six provincial elections, three separate parties have formed majority governments: the NDP in 1990, the PCs in 1995 and 1999, and the Liberals in 2003 and 2007. In 2011, another change occurred with the re-election of the Liberals with just a minority of seats. Despite the magnitude of electoral change in the province over the last two decades, women's political representation has not increased with each subsequent change of government.

The Ontario case demonstrates that parliamentary turnover matters only insofar as the parties that do well electorally take seriously the issue of gender representation. Collier (1997, 268) observes that, throughout the 1990s, the social-democratic New Democratic and the neoconservative Progressive Conservative parties that formed governments throughout the

1990s each had very different approaches to the nominations of women. Not surprisingly, women fared much better in politics under the left-wing NDP government than under the right-wing PC government. Adding the more recent elections into the mix, while the Liberal Party ran only 22 percent in the 2003 election, it increased its percentage of female candidates to 35 percent in 2007. Significantly, this increase of female candidates within the winning party was converted into clear victories for women: of the twenty-nine women elected that year nineteen were Liberal (or 66 percent of the total intake of women elected to Queen's Park). However, despite fielding its highest percentage of women ever (39 percent) this increase was not as easily converted into clear victories for women in 2011: of the thirty women who were elected in this election just fifteen (or 50 percent) were Liberals. These instances demonstrate how Ontario's competitive party system influences gender representation in politics as different types of electoral outcomes produce different outcomes for women. When the Ontario electorate provides a majority mandate, the party that forms government must be committed to gender equality, while in minority situations more than just the party that forms government matters: all the major parties must be committed to the goal of ensuring that the legislature adequately represents women.

In order to understand women's pathways to power in Ontario, it is important to also consider where women are placed on the ballot and to look, for example, at the types of seats they contest (Tremblay 2010, 89). As candidate recruitment and nomination remain the responsibilities of political parties in Ontario, parties play a crucial role in framing the competitive field for their candidates. While some seats may be held by the same politician (an incumbent) or party over a long period of time (safe seats), other seats may become more winnable when an incumbent steps down (open seats) or through redistricting. The type of seats made available to women therefore influences their prospects for legislative success.

Following the work of Tremblay (2009), the candidates of the three main political parties over the last five provincial general elections were divided into four types: challengers (the candidate ran against an incumbent), dissidents (the candidate ran against someone who inherited the seat from their party), inheritors (the candidate inherited an open seat from their party that won it in the previous election), and incumbents (the candidate won the seat in the previous election).[3] These five elections resulted in two consecutive Ontario PC majority governments (1995 and 1999), two consecutive

Liberal majority governments (2003 and 2007), and a Liberal minority government.[4] The analyses do not go beyond the last five general elections as the 1990 election was an outlier in that it produced the province's first and as yet only NDP government.

In total, over the last five elections there were 445 female and 1,205 male candidates. Looking at the most difficult candidacies – the challengers who ran against an incumbent – we see a disproportionate percentage of women: 63 percent of female candidates (281 of 445), compared to 56 percent of male candidates (671 of 1,205), were challengers. Roughly the same proportion of female and male candidates ran as dissidents (7 percent, or 32 of 445 women, and 8 percent, or 95 of 1,205 male candidates). Among those who inherited a seat from their party, women actually fared better than men, although the total percentages are low: 7 percent of female candidates (29 of 445) ran as an inheritor, compared to 3 percent of male candidates (40 of 1,205).

Research indicates that incumbency poses an especially formidable barrier to women's entry into politics because women are less likely than men to have already won a seat. Further, the advantages given to incumbents (e.g., established networks and campaign teams, financing, electoral support) may put female candidates at a disadvantage (Schwindt-Bayer 2005). In Ontario, examination of incumbency by the sex of candidates reveals stark differences between women and men: over five elections there was a total of 502 incumbents, only 21 percent (103) of whom were women compared to 79 percent (399) who were men. Interestingly, rather than increase over time, the total proportion of female incumbents compared to female non-incumbents has remained somewhat steady over the last five elections: while 28 percent of female candidates were incumbents in 1995, the percentage slides to 25 percent in 1999 and 20 percent in each of the 2003 and 2007 elections. In 2011, there was a slight increase of 24 percent of all female candidates who were incumbents. Incumbency clearly remains a significant hurdle for Ontario women seeking public office today.

There is another dimension to incumbency that may also play a role in keeping gender parity at bay in Ontario. Given the advantages accrued by incumbency, female incumbents might also be more susceptible to defeat than male incumbents. Research suggests that female incumbents may be perceived as more electorally vulnerable than their male counterparts, and this vulnerability may be linked to gender stereotypes held by voters and opposing parties and perpetuated by the media (Palmer and Simon 2005).

As Palmer and Simon note, although female and male candidates may be equally likely to win elected office, female incumbents may be perceived as easier to defeat and may face a more competitive environment than male incumbents (47).

Examination of electoral results from the last five Ontario elections confirms that, overall, female incumbents have had more difficulty being re-elected than have male incumbents. As Table 8.6 shows, 68 percent (70 of 103) of female incumbents compared to 75 percent (301 of 400) of male incumbents were successfully re-elected – a difference of seven percentage points below men. Female incumbents have also experienced drastic swings of success from election to election: in the 1995 election only 36 percent were successful in retaining their seat, while the percentage more than doubles to 76 percent in 1999. This upswing, however, was followed by a rapid drop in 2003, when the percentage of victorious female incumbents dove to 53 percent, only to rise again to an impressive 95 percent success rate in the 2007 election.[5] In 2011, this "see-saw" pattern continued as the success rate for female incumbents dropped down to 80 percent.

A comparison of female and male incumbent success per election is of even further interest: in 1995, male incumbents were far more successful than female incumbents as half of them managed to hold on to their seat – a difference of 14 percent. In the 1999 election the male incumbency edge narrowed considerably, as 81 percent of male incumbents were successful, a difference of just 5 percent between them and their female counterparts. In the 2003 election, the male incumbency advantage reappears as 69 percent of male incumbents retained their seats, a difference of 16 percent in relation to women. In the 2007 election the women come out ahead as female incumbents edged out their male counterparts by a margin of 95 to 93 percent. In the 2011 election, we observe another change as the male incumbency edge reappears, with 92 percent of male incumbents compared to just 80 percent of female incumbents reclaiming their seat.

Three observations follow from the data in Table 8.6. First, it is clear that one of the reasons women have not achieved gender parity at Queen's Park concerns the competitive nature of seats women must vie for compared to those for which men are vying. Rather than see the proportion of female incumbents relative to female non-incumbents grow from election to election, the volatility of Ontario's party system has prevented some female incumbents (and, to a lesser extent, male incumbents) from securing

TABLE 8.6

Incumbency success rate in Ontario, by sex of candidate, 1995-2011

Election year	Male winners		Female winners		% difference between females and males
	Number	%	Number	%	
1995	47 of 94	50	9 of 25	36	−14
1999	75 of 93	81	13 of 17	76	−5
2003	54 of 78	69	8 of 15	53	−16
2007	70 of 75	93	20 of 21	95	+2
2011	55 of 60	92	20 of 25	80	−12
Total	301 of 399	75	70 of 103	68	−7

consecutive victories from one election to the next. Generally, Ontario's highly competitive party system appears to have cycled some female politicians out of politics to a greater extent than it has male politicians.

The second observation is that the different success rates between male and female incumbents is most pronounced in the "change" elections, or elections that were particularly volatile, irrespective of the party that formed government. These elections include those that resulted in a new party forming the government (1995 and 2003) and the downgrading of the governing party from majority to minority status (2011). Comparatively, when the electorate is seeking the status quo, female incumbency appears safer, as was the case in 1999 and 2007, when the incumbency advantage men had over women narrowed considerably or disappeared. In the 1990s, Collier (1997) argues that most women were swept into office in Ontario when an unexpected wave in voter support brought in a new party with ridings previously considered "unwinnable," such as the 1990 NDP victory – a phenomenon referred to as the "landslide factor" for women (Murray 2010). A consequence of these landslide victories appears to cut both ways for women in Ontario: while the number of female politicians has increased in a single election cycle, the incumbencies of these women appear more vulnerable than those of their male counterparts in the next election cycle *when and if* the electorate has an appetite for electoral change.

The third and final observation involves the reappearance of the male incumbency edge in the most recent election, an election that resulted in a Liberal government one seat short of a majority. In 2011 twenty of twenty-five female incumbents were able to secure their seat. Interestingly, all five losses were female MPPs from the governing Liberals, and three of them were former Liberal cabinet ministers (Sophia Aggelonitis, Hamilton Mountain; Leona Dombrowsky, Prince Edward-Hastings; and Carol Mitchell, Huron-Bruce). Put more bluntly, all the female incumbents who lost their seat were members of the governing party, the Liberals, which had been punished by the voters by reducing their standing to minority government status. The case of Ontario demonstrates that incumbency matters to the election of women. Future research on how incumbency shapes women's political participation in Ontario would be beneficial. Particularly, questions of how and whether female incumbents are disproportionately disadvantaged or "punished" by voters seeking electoral change in party systems that are competitive would be worthwhile.

Other Players on the Field: Equal Voice and Women's Activism

In 2006, a new player emerged on the provincial electoral field: Equal Voice, a multi-partisan, non-profit organization. Leading up to the 2007 campaign and election, Equal Voice provided information to the media and public that tracked the number of female candidates and women elected, something absent from the Ontario electoral scene until then. Since 2007, Equal Voice has become one of the media's key sources of information on gender representation in the province.

In 2006, in addition to its tracking role, Equal Voice issued its first "Ontario Challenge" to the leaders of all three main political parties, asking them to commit jointly to the goal of nominating more women candidates in Ontario elections. All three main party leaders responded favourably to the 2007 Ontario Challenge, with the Liberals pledging to run women in 50 percent of their unheld ridings, the NDP committing to having 50 percent of their candidates be women, and the PCs promising 33 percent (Wilson 2007). Although the NDP came close, only the Liberal Party met its target. Additionally, Equal Voice ran female candidate "bootcamps" for municipal candidates in the 2010 elections.

Equal Voice and other women's groups, like the Disabled Women's Network Ontario (DAWN) were also active in pushing for electoral reform in the province in 2007. The failure of the provincewide referendum on electoral reform in October 2007 was a significant setback for the political representation of women and visible minorities in Ontario as literature suggests that, in addition to other factors, barriers to women's political representation included first-past-the-post systems with low district magnitudes and without party lists (Norris 2006).[6]

Another barrier to women's political representation is the lack of afford-able childcare in the province. In 2007, PC MPP Lisa MacLeod (Nepean-Carleton, also the mother of a small child) tabled a resolution to create an all-party committee to investigate ways in which the Ontario legislature could make a more "family-friendly" environment, including providing day care, limiting evening debates, and creating a spousal association. Although a resolution was passed making the legislature more family-friendly in some respects (such as fewer night sittings), other changes have had the reverse effect. Sitting hours were moved to Monday mornings from after-noons, making it more difficult for MPPs who live outside the Greater Toronto Area to spend time with their families on Sunday evenings as they must now travel to Queen's Park (Ferguson 2011).

Conclusion: Prospects for Gender Parity

Based on these results several conclusions can be drawn about the pros-pects for – and barriers to – women's political representation in Ontario. First, none of the main political parties in the province has adopted formal-ized procedures for the nomination of female candidates. Thus, while the 2011 election saw an increase in the number of female candidates, this up-tick could be short lived and is vulnerable on a number of fronts, including the lack of formal rules governing nominations in both the Liberal and PC parties, the continued low percentage of female incumbents from election to election, and voter volatility. More positively, in February 2011 Equal Voice launched its second Ontario Challenge and announced that all three party leaders had pledged to run more female candidates in the fall 2011 Ontario election than they did in 2007 (Equal Voice 2011). Equal Voice seems poised to remain an important part of the electoral scene in the prov-ince for some time. That said, given that control over candidate recruitment and nominations remains under the exclusive purview of the parties, achiev-ing gender parity at Queen's Park in subsequent elections will likely require the coalescence of both external (e.g., women's movement actors and media) and internal (party leaders, rules, and ideologies) factors around issues of gender equality in politics.

A second area of concern has to do with the future governing party in a province with a strongly competitive party system. The results here indicate that the party that wins matters to women's political representation and that, when the Ontario electorate has an appetite for electoral change, female incumbents are potentially at greater risk of losing their seat than are male incumbents. The Liberal minority win in 2011 reaffirms the competitive nature of the Ontario party system. Compared to people in other provinces, Ontarians have a habit of ousting political parties after only one or two mandates, and the 2011 election is rare in that it produced the third consecutive mandate for a party since the 1970s. Given the Progressive Conservative Party's track record as the party that has historically nominated the fewest women and visible minorities, provided the least amount of funding to candidates, and appointed the fewest women to cabinet positions, a 2015 PC government (or sooner should the Liberal minority government fall) may return the province to percentages of elected women circling around the high teens and low twenties.

Looking forward, an area of continued concern is the under-representation of visible minorities in Ontario politics. Historically, the Liberal Party has been more successful than the other parties in nominating and electing visible minority candidates who are women. A future PC victory may also adversely affect the percentage of visible minorities in the Ontario legislature, making the prospects of more equitable gender and racial representation in politics even less certain in the province. Further work needs to be conducted on the candidacies of visible minorities provincially, as it has been at the federal level (see Black and Hicks 2006).[7]

Ontario's legislature does not adequately reflect the diversity of its population, and members of several marginalized communities remain seriously under-represented today. In this chapter, I have identified three barriers to political representation for women in Ontario: the reluctance of parties to adopt formalized rules and procedures to recruit and nominate more women and visible minorities; the volatility of the Ontario electorate, which makes female incumbents more vulnerable than male incumbents; and, until only recently, the absence of a strong presence on the electoral field by the women's movement. On balance, while more women were elected than ever before in 2011, significant barriers continue to keep women from full and active involvement in the traditional political process. It would seem that, into the foreseeable future, women's political representation in the Province of Ontario will likely remain in a holding pattern that hovers far below gender parity.

Notes

I am thankful for the research assistance provided by Ryerson University students Gillian Hards and Margarita Kalika, made possible by a grant from the dean of arts. I would also like to thank Bryan Evans, Graham Murray, and Loleen Berdahl for their assistance as well as the party officials who provided me with their valuable insights.

1   Analyses include the three main political parties only: the Ontario Liberal Party, the Ontario New Democratic Party, and the Progressive Conservative Party of Ontario.

2   For instance, in 2007 Premier McGuinty appointed Amrit Mangat as the Liberal candidate in the riding of Mississauga-Brampton South, a new riding without an incumbent. She was elected and became the first female MPP of South Asian descent.

3   Open seats include those where an incumbent did not run again or where a new seat was created due to redistricting. Data made available from Elections Ontario. Further analyses are available from the author upon request.

4   Due to redistricting the number of seats dropped from 130 to 103 in 1999, forcing thirty-four incumbents to square off against one another in seventeen ridings. Female incumbents were not disadvantaged by this (only two female incumbents ran against one another). Inherited seats in 1999 were calculated by giving the seat to any party if it had won all of the 1995 districts that had been merged into a single riding in 1999. In the case of three districts (London-Fanshawe, Ottawa-Orleans, and Toronto Centre-Rosedale), more than one party was successful in one or more of the 1995 districts. In each of these three districts, two parties were given "inherit-or" status. Transposition of the 2003 votes onto the 2007 districts was provided by Elections Ontario.

5   In the only riding (Don Valley West) in which an incumbent faced off against another incumbent in 2007, Kathleen Wynne (Liberal), an out lesbian, defeated the leader of the PCs, John Tory, by winning 50.4 percent of the popular vote.

6   The fact that the Liberal government set an extremely high threshold for the "yes" side cannot go without mention: it required 60 percent of the overall popular vote plus at least 50 percent in sixty-four ridings to win. Ontarians rejected reform 63 percent to 37 percent (results from Elections Ontario).

7   At the municipal level, see Bird (2008).

References

Bashevkin, Sylvia. 1993. *Toeing the Lines: Women and Party Politics in English Canada*. 2nd ed. Don Mills: Oxford University Press.

Bird, Karen. 2003. "The Political Representation of Women and Ethnic Minorities in Established Democracies: A Framework for Comparative Research." Working paper presented for the Academy of Migration Studies in Denmark (AMID), Aalborg University, 11 November, 1-32. Available at http://www.hks.harvard.edu/.

–. 2008. "Many Faces, Few Places: The Politics of Under-Representation of Ethnic Minorities and Women in the City of Hamilton." In Caroline Andrew, John Biles, Myer Siemiatycki, and Erin Tolley, eds., *Electing a Diverse Canada: The Representation of Immigrants, Minorities, and Women*, 136-55. Vancouver: UBC Press.

Black, Jerome H., and Bruce M. Hicks. 2006. "Visible Minority Candidates in the 2004 Federal Election." *Canadian Parliamentary Review* 29(2): 26-31.

Brodie, Janine. 1985. *Women and Politics in Canada*. Toronto: McGraw-Hill Ryerson.

Collier, Cheryl. 1997. "Judging Women's Political Success in the 1990s." In Graham White, ed., *Government and Politics of Ontario*. 5th ed., 268-83. Toronto: University of Toronto Press.

Elections Ontario. Province of Ontario: Election Statistics on Female Candidatures 1919-2010. Available upon request from http://www.elections.on.ca/.

Equal Pay Coalition. 2008. Information available at http://www.equalpaycoalition. org/.

Equal Voice. 2011. "Parties Accept Equal Voice's Second Ontario Challenge." Available at http://equalvoice.ca/.

Ferguson, Rob. 2011. "Help Wanted: More Female MPPs encouraged." *Toronto Star*, 23 February. Available at http://www.thestar.com/.

Metro Canada. 2011. "Decision Ontario: Metro speaks with NDP's Andrea Horwath." 2 October. Available at http://www.metronews.ca/.

Morrow, Adrian, and Karen Howlett. 2013. "Wynne Makes History as First Openly Gay Premier in Canada." *Globe and Mail*, 26 January. Available at http://www.theglobeandmail.com/.

Murray, Graham. 2010. "Women MPPs at Queen's Park, 1981 through 2010 (4)." Working Paper provided by G.P Murray Research Limited. Toronto.

Norris, Pippa. 2006. "The Impact of Electoral Reform on Women's Representation." *Acta Politica* 41: 197-13.

Ontario NDP. 2011. Affirmative Action Guidelines. Candidate Search and Nomination Guidelines. Approved by Provincial Council, 9-10 December 1989, current as of January 2011.

Palmer, Barbara, and Dennis M. Simon. 2005. "When Women Run against Women: The Hidden Influence of Female Incumbents in Elections to the US House of Representatives, 1956-2002." *Politics and Gender* 1: 39-63.

Schwindt-Bayer, Leslie A. 2005. "The Incumbency Disadvantage and Women's Election to Legislative Office." *Electoral Studies* 24: 227-44.

Siemiatycki, Myer. 2011. "The Diversity Gap: The Electoral Under-Representation of Visible Minorities." DiverseCity – The Greater Toronto Leadership Project. Diversity Counts Series. Available at http://diversecitytoronto.ca/.

Statistics Canada. 2006. *Women in Canada: A Gender-Based Statistical Analysis.* 5th ed. Ottawa: Statistics Canada.

–. 2010. Women in Canada: *A Gender-Based Statistical Analysis.* 6th ed. Available at http://www.statcan.gc.ca/.

Tremblay, Manon, with Stephanie Mullen. 2009. "Women in the Québec National Assembly: Why So Many?" In Sylvia Bashevkin, ed., *Opening Doors Wider: Women's Political Engagement in Canada*, 51-69. Vancouver: UBC Press.

Tremblay, Manon. 2010. *Québec Women and Legislative Representation.* Vancouver: UBC Press.

Trimble, Linda, and Jane Arscott. 2003. *Still Counting: Women in Politics across Canada.* Peterborough: Broadview Press.

Wilson, Jennifer. 2007. "Reaching Critical Mass: Women in the Ontario Legislature." Equal Voice. Available at http://www.equalvoice.ca/pdf/.

Young, Lisa. 1991. "Legislative Turnover and the Election of Women to the Canadian House of Commons." In Kathy Megyery, ed., W*omen in Canadian Politics: Toward Equity in Representation.* Research Studies, Royal Commission on Electoral Reform and Party Financing, vol. 6, 81-99. Toronto: Dundurn Press.

9

Getting Women's Names on the Ballot

Women in Prince Edward Island Politics

JOHN CROSSLEY

This chapter examines the pattern of participation by women in Prince Edward Island legislative politics. It discusses both the growth in participation in the late 1980s and the plateauing of women's participation as candidates, MLAs, and cabinet ministers after 1989. I argue that the levelling-off of representation of women in the Legislative Assembly after 1989 is a result of the reluctance of the two major political parties to nominate more than a relative handful of female candidates for election to the legislature. The facts and analysis lead me to conclude that the prospect of increasing the presence of women in the Legislative Assembly beyond the level that has prevailed since 1989 is bleak.

Background

Access to participation in electoral and legislative politics in Prince Edward Island is controlled primarily by a traditional two-party system dominated by the Liberal Party and the Progressive Conservative Party. Only those two parties have ever formed government, and the two parties take turns governing. Both parties are traditional brokerage parties, downplaying ideology and presenting voters with similar platforms, differentiated primarily by claims to be the most effective team to govern. Between them, these two parties routinely win well over 90 percent of the popular vote in general elections; in the last five elections the combined share of popular vote ranged from a low of 91 percent in the 1996 and 2011 elections to a high of

POLITICAL REPRESENTATION OF WOMEN IN
PRINCE EDWARD ISLAND

FIRSTS
Right to vote and stand for election
- Most women win right to vote / stand for election   1921
- Aboriginal women (status Indian) receive full franchise   1963[1]

Contesting office
- First woman to contest office: Hilda Ramsay (CCF)   1951
- First woman to win office: Jean Canfield (Liberal)   1970-79
- First woman appointed to cabinet: Jean Canfield (Liberal),   1972-74
  minister without portfolio (responsible for housing)

CURRENT REPRESENTATION AT A GLANCE

	Date of election	Women elected Number	Percent
Women in legislature	2011/10/03	6 of 27	22
Women in cabinet	2011/10/03	2 of 11	18

Women political party leaders
- Olive Crane (PC), 2007 to present (appointed interim leader in 2007 and elected leader at convention in 2010)
- Sharon Labchuk (founding leader of Green Party), 2007-12

Lieutenant governor
- None at present

Advisory council on the status of women
- The PEI Advisory Council on the Status of Women was established by order-in-council in 1975; the Advisory Council on the Status of Women Act was passed in 1988. The Council is advisory to the minister responsible for the status of women and is funded by the Interministerial Women's Secretariat.

97 percent in 2003. Typically, the party that forms the government has been supported by over 50 percent of the voters.

Third parties have experienced insignificant electoral success and rarely affect the outcome of elections in Prince Edward Island. Since 1974, the New Democratic Party of PEI has competed in every provincial election but has nominated a full slate of candidates only in 1996 and 2000.[2] The Green Party of PEI nominated eighteen candidates in 2007 and twenty-two candidates in 2011. However, third parties have paid more attention to electoral participation by women than have the two dominant parties. The first woman ever nominated in a provincial election was Hilda Ramsay, who was nominated by the CCF in 1951. Slates of candidates for the NDP have always included women, often in significant numbers. In the 2011 election, for example, 43 percent of the NDP candidates (six of fourteen) were women. Similarly, thirteen (59 percent) of the twenty-two candidates nominated by the Green Party of Prince Edward Island in 2011 were women.

The dominance of the two traditional parties in Prince Edward Island is heightened by an electoral system that tends to produce enormous majorities for the party that wins. Support for the two major parties is fairly evenly spread across the province, and, as a result, when flexibly partisan or nonpartisan voters switch allegiance from one party to another, they tend to do so across all constituencies. Thus, 50 percent of the popular vote easily becomes 80 percent or 90 percent of the seats in the Legislative Assembly. In the early years of the twenty-first century, a group of Islanders became convinced that the electoral system was damaging representative democracy and parliamentary government in PEI. They were concerned about the tendency for the electoral system to produce assemblies with numerically strong governing caucuses and tiny oppositions and also about the under-representation of certain groups of Islanders, including women. In response to these arguments, the government appointed a royal commission on electoral reform. In October 2005, Islanders were asked in a provincewide plebiscite whether they favoured changing the Island's election system to the mixed-member proportional representation system proposed by the royal commission. The proposal was soundly rejected by 64 percent of the voters. The position of the Liberal Party and the Progressive Conservative Party as gatekeepers to electoral and legislative participation by women was solidified.

Women's Political Representation: The Numbers

Women in the Legislature

The first woman elected to the Legislative Assembly of Prince Edward Island was Jean Canfield, Liberal, elected at the general election of 1 May 1970. Canfield had run unsuccessfully for election in 1966 but was re-elected in 1974 and 1978 before losing in the 1979 election, an election that ended twelve years of Liberal government. In the nineteen years and five general elections following Canfield's first election to the Legislative Assembly, only four other women sat in the assembly: Catherine Callbeck (Lib.), Leone Bagnall (PC), Marion Reid (PC), and Betty Jean Brown (Lib.).[3] These women were pioneers, recruited by the men who controlled the parties because they were outstanding individuals with a history of volunteer activism within their parties. Leone Bagnall, for example, worked within the party for several years, "nominating candidates, working with Angus MacLean's federal campaign, and serving as a provincial vice-president" (Drake 1992). Each of the other pioneers had a similar history of party work before she was nominated. In addition, each of these pioneers was well known in her community and was thought likely to win election. Given that the temper of the time required that political parties be seen to include women, the men who controlled the two major parties looked within their organizations and found a few exceptional women who were willing and able to run and serve.

The climate in which these pioneers served in the Legislative Assembly was distinctly chilly. The Island's political culture and the attitudes and traditions of the Legislative Assembly created, at best, suspicion about, and, at worst, hostility towards, women as elected representatives. However, by the mid-1980s the temper of electoral politics in Prince Edward Island had changed to the extent that it was no longer thought to be sufficient for the Legislative Assembly to include only token numbers of women. Both major political parties set out to increase the number of women in their caucuses.

Societal changes and the politicization of women motivated leaders of the two major parties to seek more female candidates after the 1986 general election. For the 1989 election, the leaders of both parties actively sought women to stand as candidates. Interviews I conducted in the mid-1990s (Crossley 1997) suggest that Liberal Party polls conducted in preparation for the 1989 election showed that women candidates would be an electoral asset for the party. Furthermore, party insiders reported that the leader of the Liberal Party, Joe Ghiz, was personally committed to the cause of women's equality. The leaders of the Progressive Conservative Party were reported by interviewees to have been profoundly affected by the adverse reaction of women following party leader Jim Lee's dismissal of employment and pay equity as passing fads during the party leaders' televised debate in the 1986 election campaign. In interviews with female MLAs from both parties, I was told repeatedly that the party had sought them out and asked them to run.

Because the two major political parties deliberately and prudentially increased the number of women nominated in the 1989 provincial general election, the number of women members of the Legislative Assembly increased from two after the 1986 election (three with the 1987 by-election victory of Nancy Guptill) to seven. The proportion of women MLAs increased from 9 percent to 22 percent, a dramatic change by any standards but not, it turns out, the beginning of a trend towards equality of representation of women in the Legislative Assembly.

In the six elections after 1989, the number of women elected to the Legislative Assembly remained relatively unchanged (see Table 9.1). In fact, the largest number of women MLAs ever elected was in 1993, when eight of the thirty-two MLAs were women. In the 1996 election, only five (19 percent) of the twenty-seven winning candidates were women. Each subsequent election has returned six or seven female MLAs, 22 percent or 26 percent of the total.

The lives of the women who have served in the PEI Legislative Assembly do not appear to be very different from the lives of other middle-class Island women or from the lives of their male colleagues in the assembly (Crossley 1997). Female MLAs tend to be highly educated, with almost all holding one or more university degrees. Their careers, outside the home, have tended to be in the professions, particularly education and business. Like all members of the assembly, they are not demographically representative of the general population but, rather, of middle-class Islanders. As MLAs, they struggle to maintain a balance between their personal and work lives and report slightly less success at maintaining a healthy balance than do their male colleagues (Coalition for Women in Government 2009b, 4). They spend, on average, at least eleven hours each week meeting or communicating with individual constituents, which is more than is spent on this function by male MLAs; however, they spend less time than male MLAs attending meetings and functions in their constituencies (Coalition for Women in Government 2009b, 7). Like working women everywhere, they spend considerable time on home management. In 2008, 41 percent of the female MLAs reported spending six to ten hours each week on home management and another 47 percent reported spending one to five hours on this function. Women tend to be older than men when they enter electoral politics and to have already raised a family, which probably accounts for why 47 percent of the female MLAs surveyed in 2008 reported that caring for family members is not an activity that is applicable to them, whereas only 25 percent of the male

TABLE 9.1
Women in the PEI legislature, by election

Election date	Party elected	Total number of legislators	Women elected	
			Number	%
1923/07/24	Conservative	30	0	0
1927/06/25	Liberal	30	0	0
1931/08/06	Conservative	30	0	0
1935/07/23	Liberal	30	0	0
1939/05/18	Liberal	30	0	0
1943/09/15	Liberal	30	0	0
1947/12/11	Liberal	30	0	0
1951/04/26	Liberal	30	0	0
1955/06/25	Liberal	30	0	0
1959/09/01	PC	30	0	0
1962/10/10	PC	30	0	0
1966/05/30	Liberal	32	0	0
1970/05/11	Liberal	32	1	3
1974/04/29	Liberal	32	2	6
1978/04/24	Liberal	32	1	3
1979/04/43	PC	32	2	6
1982/09/27	PC	32	2	6
1986/04/21	Liberal	32	3	9
1989/05/29	Liberal	32	7	22
1993/03/29	Liberal	32	8	25
1996/11/18	PC	27	5	19
2000/04/17	PC	27	6	22
2003/09/29	PC	27	6	22
2007/05/28	Liberal	27	7	26
2011/10/03	Liberal	27	6	22

Sources: Canadian Parliamentary Guide (various years); Report of the Chief Electoral Officer of Prince Edward Island (various elections); Elections Prince Edward Island (n.d. [b]).

MLAs said this (Coalition for Women in Government 2009b, 8). They are, in sum, an extraordinary group of ordinary middle-class women.

Women Candidates
As the PEI Coalition for Women in Government (2009a) has pointed out, the problem at the heart of increasing the representation of women in the Legislative Assembly "does not lie with electing women, it lies with getting women's names on the ballot." Since 1970, the success rate for female

TABLE 9.2

Women candidates in PEI, by party and election

Election date	Liberal		PC		NDP	
	Number	%	Number	%	Number	%
1982/09/27	3	9	2	6	0	0
1986/04/21	2	6	3	9	3	19
1989/05/29	7	22	10	31	5	29
1993/03/29	8	25	5	16	7	30
1996/11/18	5	19	4	15	11	41
2000/04/17	3	11	7	26	10	37
2003/09/29	5	19	6	22	10	42
2007/05/28	6	22	4	15	6	40
2011/10/03	6	22	7	26	6	43

Sources: *Report of the Chief Electoral Officer of Prince Edward Island* (various elections); Elections Prince Edward Island (n.d.[a]).

candidates in provincial elections has been similar to, and often better than, the success rate for male candidates (Crossley 1997, 292). In fact, in the four elections between 1993 and 2003, women candidates ran against male candidates in thirty constituency races; women won eighteen (60 percent) of those races (Coalition for Women in Government 2009a).

The problem actually lies, of course, in getting women's names on the ballot as candidates for either the Liberal Party or the Progressive Conservative Party (see Table 9.2). Before 1966, neither the Liberals nor the Progressive Conservatives had ever nominated a woman as a candidate for election to the provincial legislature. Between 1966 and 1986, neither party nominated more than three women as candidates in any particular election. For reasons explored below, both parties decided in 1989 to significantly increase the number of female candidates; the Progressive Conservatives nominated ten women, up from three in the 1986 election, and the Liberals nominated seven, up from two in 1986.

Since 1989, the two major parties have continued to nominate women but not in numbers greater than those in 1989. In fact, the ten female candidates nominated by the Progressive Conservative Party in 1989 was the largest number of female candidates that party has ever fielded in a provincial election. The Liberal Party has only once nominated more than the seven female candidates it ran in 1989; it nominated eight in 1993, a number it has never again matched. Both the Advisory Council on the Status of Women and the Coalition for Women in Government have urged the two major

TABLE 9.3
Women party leaders in PEI

Name	Political party	Period of service
Catherine Callbeck	Liberal	1993-96
Pat Mella	PC	1990-96
Olive Crane	PC	2010 to present

parties to modify their nomination processes to increase the likelihood that women will be nominated, but neither party has done so.

Women Party Leaders
Every woman who has sought the leadership of one of the two major parties in Prince Edward Island has won the leadership. Since 1961, the Liberal Party has held eight leadership conventions. Only the 1993 convention included a female candidate, Catherine Callbeck, who at that time was the sitting federal member for the Malpeque constituency. Callbeck was clearly the candidate of the party establishment, and many party insiders expected her to be acclaimed. However, two party outsiders, Larry Creed and Bill Campbell, contested the leadership. Creed, an unemployed labourer, used the leadership campaign to highlight the concerns of the poor and marginalized, running what he called a "beans and bologna" campaign. Callbeck won on the first ballot, with 79 percent of the 1,566 votes cast (Crossley 1993).

The Progressive Conservative Party has conducted ten leadership conventions, the first in 1950. In two of these races there were women candidates: both won.[4] In 1990, Patricia (Pat) Mella, a long-time party worker, contested the leadership against another party insider and former provincial cabinet minister, Barry Clark. Roger Whittaker, a businessman who was not part of the PC establishment, also ran. Mella won on the first ballot with 53 percent of the 887 votes cast (Crossley 1990). Because she was not a member of the Legislative Assembly, she led the party from outside the assembly until the 1993 general election.

In 2010, the Progressive Conservative Party leadership convention selected Olive Crane as its leader. Crane had been elected to the assembly in a by-election in 2006 and was re-elected in the general election of 2007. The Conservatives, who had won three consecutive elections, lost the 2007 election, and its leader, Pat Binns, resigned. The party called on Crane, one of only four PC MLAs, to serve as the interim leader, which she did for over three years while the party prepared for a leadership convention that was timed so it could be used to launch its bid for government in 2011. The convention was scheduled for 2 October 2010. Candidates included four well known men: a former provincial cabinet minister, a former MLA, a former mayor of Georgetown, and a former police chief. All were party insiders, but of these four the establishment candidate was Jamie Ballem, who had served as minister of the environment in Binns's government. Crane resigned the interim leadership of the party so she could seek the leadership at the convention and brought with her significant support from the party establishment. Crane led on the first ballot and defeated Ballem on the second.

It is too early to tell how successful Olive Crane will be as leader of the Progressive Conservative Party. In the 2011 general election, the party's share of the popular vote was 40 percent, similar to the 41 percent share it won in 2007; but it won five seats in 2011 compared to four in 2007. Pat Mella did not lead the party to electoral victory, but she successfully rebuilt the party organization and positioned it well for success under Pat Binns's leadership. She served as treasurer in Binns's government. Catherine Callbeck led the Liberal Party to victory in the 1993 general election, but her government quickly became unpopular when it almost simultaneously reduced public-sector wages and salaries, amalgamated municipalities, and struggled with reductions in federal transfer payments for health and education. Having lost the confidence of the voters and Liberal Party insiders, Callbeck resigned from electoral politics before the 1996 election. Sharon Labchuk is a final woman party leader; founder of the Green Party, she led the party from 2007 to 2011.

Women in Cabinet

In total, fourteen women have been appointed to the cabinet in Prince Edward Island. Among them, they have held at least sixteen portfolios, including premier, treasurer, and attorney general. Three served as ministers of education. Health and social services, tourism and parks, and labour have each been led twice by female ministers.

TABLE 9.4
Women premiers in PEI

Name	Political party	Period of service
Catherine Callbeck	Liberal	1993-96

Before 1989, premiers appear to have been weakly committed to the idea that the executive council (i.e., cabinet), if it is to be representative of significant sectors of the electorate, should, when possible, include women. Jean Canfield was the sole female MLA elected in 1970, but she wasn't included in the cabinet until 1972, when she was appointed minister without portfolio, responsible for housing. Following the 1974 election, there were two female members on the government benches, and Catherine Callbeck was appointed minister of health and social services, a position she held throughout her four years in the assembly. The 1978 election left Jean Canfield, once again, the sole female on the government benches, but she was not appointed to cabinet. Following the 1979 election, the PC government had two female members in caucus but neither was appointed to the executive council. After the 1982 election, however, one of the two, Leone Bagnall, was appointed minister of education and the other, Marion Reid, while not appointed to the executive council, became speaker of the Legislative Assembly. In 1986, when the Liberals returned to government with only a single female member of caucus, that member became minister of education.

Since 1989, a pattern of representative cabinet making that includes the representation of women has emerged. In the seven elections since 1989,

TABLE 9.5
Women in cabinet in PEI, by election

Election date	Party elected	Total number of cabinet ministers*	Women appointed to to cabinet		Number of women in governing caucus	% of women in governing caucus in cabinet*
			Number	%		
1982/09/27	PC	10	1	10	2	50
1986/04/21	Liberal	11	1	9	1	100
1989/05/29	Liberal	11	2	18	6	33
1993/03/29	Liberal	10	2	20	7	29
1996/11/18	PC	9	2	22	3	67
2000/04/17	PC	10	2	20	6	33
2003/09/29	PC	10	2	20	5	40
2007/05/28	Liberal	11	2	18	6	33
2011/10/03	Liberal	11	2	18	5	40

* Includes the premier.
Sources: *Canadian Parliamentary Guide* (various years); *Report of the Chief Electoral Officer of Prince Edward Island* (various elections); Prince Edward Island, Executive Council Office (2011).

government caucuses have included between three (1996) and seven (1993) women, with five or six being the apparently normal level of female representation on the government benches (see Table 9.5). Premiers from both political parties, however, have not defined a "fair share" of cabinet seats as a proportion of the women available for appointment to cabinet but, rather, as a fixed number – two. Thus, when building cabinets designed to appropriately represent the demographics of the province, premiers are careful to appoint a certain number of MLAs from each of the major urban centres, plus others from the various rural districts, as well as an Acadian. Evidently, including two women – a fraction of the total number of cabinet members – is considered "good enough" representation for a group constituting half of the province's population.

Women Representatives of the Crown

Two women have served as vice-regal representative in Prince Edward Island. Marion Reid was appointed in August 1990. This was, in effect, her fourth career. By the time she became lieutenant governor, she had raised eight children, taught school for twenty-one years, and served ten years as a member of the Legislative Assembly. With Leone Bagnall, she was one of the first two female members of the Progressive Conservative Party of Prince Edward Island to serve in the assembly. In 1983, she became the first women to hold the office of speaker of the Legislative Assembly, and in 1990 she became the first female lieutenant governor. Her appointment was solidly in the tradition of vice-regal appointments as rewards for partisan service and recognition of widespread public respect.

The appointment of Barbara Hagerman as lieutenant governor in July 2006 reflected the other, much less frequently observed, tradition of vice-regal appointments – that of recognition of a lifetime of leadership in, and making contributions to, the community. Hagerman is a musician and a teacher with an outstanding record of community service in Prince Edward Island and nationally – service that did not include candidacy for elected office.[5]

TABLE 9.6
Female representatives of the Crown in PEI

Name	Period of service
Marion Loretta Reid	1990-95
Barbara A. Hagerman	2006-11

Explanations

Neither the party system nor the electoral system has made it easy for women to enter the Legislative Assembly. The major parties and, therefore, access to membership in the Legislative Assembly were, and to a large extent continue to be, controlled by an elite made up of male partisan activists. Nor, for most of the Island's political history, did the social and political culture of the province encourage women to seek elected office. Until the 1970s, government was thought to be a male domain. The province did not have a historical suffragist movement (Stetson 1977, 3; Stetson n.d., 5) and few women challenged the status quo.

The rapid increase in the number and proportion of women members of the Legislative Assembly after the 1989 general election was a belated reflection of societal changes that had nurtured political activism by women outside the confines of the two major parties and the Legislative Assembly. During the 1970s and 1980s, many societal barriers to participation by women began to lower. Island society urbanized and modernized; rural schools were closed and regionally consolidated schools opened; a modern postsecondary education system was put in place; the economy diversified; government expanded and intervened to restructure the economy; and participation by women in the labour force increased dramatically (Dasgupta 1982; Prince Edward Island, Department of the Provincial Treasury, Economics, Statistics and Federal Fiscal Relations 1994; Prince Edward Island, Department of Finance, Economics, Statistics, and Fiscal Analysis 1990a, 1990b; Smitheram 1982.) In short, many of the traditional social, economic, and political norms changed, and with these changes came a new generation of women with an expectation of equality, awareness of issues of particular importance to women, and a growing understanding of the political technology required to effect change (Crossley 1997, 287).

The societal changes of the 1970s and early 1980s were reflected in new types and levels of political activism by Island women. In the 1970s, a number of equality-seeking organizations and agencies were begun, including the Advisory Council on the Status of Women, Women's Network, and Women in Support of Agriculture (Whittaker 1992, 8). These organizations marshalled evidence showing the unequal treatment of women in the economy, government, legal system, and schools (Prince Edward Island Advisory Council on the Status of Women 1982; Provincial Advisory Committee on the Status of Women 1973). It became evident to many Island women that under-representation of women in government and the public service contributed to the broader inequality of women (Outcalt 1976; Dunn 1979). Some of these women turned to the New Democratic Party of Prince Edward Island as a means of promoting equality. Others chose to work for change within the major parties. Many, perhaps most, have worked outside the party system to increase the proportion of women in the Prince Edward Island Legislative Assembly.

Four major non-partisan organizations and agencies work to promote equality of women in Prince Edward Island. The Women's Network was formed in 1981 to apply feminist analysis and practice to issues affecting the status of women in the province. For several years, the Women's Network published a magazine entitled *Common Ground*. The Women's Network continues to conduct research on matters affecting social justice and women. The Interministerial Women's Secretariat is a government agency that supports the minister responsible for the status of women, coordinates the activities of various departments and agencies of governments as they relate to the status of women, and funds community projects that promote the status of women. While both of these organizations help create a social and policy environment that supports electoral participation by women, neither has directly engaged the issue of increasing that participation. The other two organizations, the PEI Advisory Council on the Status of Women and the Coalition for Women in Government, have actively worked to increase the number of women in the Legislative Assembly.

The Advisory Council on the Status of Women, created by order-in-council in 1975 and mandated by statute since 1988, is an arm's-length advisor to government whose nine members are appointed by the government.[6] It has a broad mandate to work for the equality of, and full participation by, women in all aspects of provincial life, including electoral politics. The council has explicitly called for increased representation of women in the Legislative Assembly, and it regularly emphasizes the importance of all types of political participation by women. During elections, the council typically encourages all political parties and candidates to address issues relating to gender equality and urges all voters to ask candidates about such issues. Thus, during the fall 2011 election campaign, the council published and distributed a pamphlet entitled *PEI Election 2011: Equality Matters*, which identified a number of issues of particular importance to women: training and economic development, increasing the number of women in decision-making positions, domestic violence, health and wellness, and social assistance and housing.

During the campaign leading to the 2005 provincial plebiscite on electoral reform, the Advisory Council published a number of policy guides, recommendations, fact sheets, and other background documents highlighting the importance of electoral reform to women's equality. In its *Policy Guide: Women and Electoral Reform* the council emphasizes that a key consideration in reforming the electoral system has to be women's underrepresentation in the Legislative Assembly: "More than fifty percent of voters never see themselves fairly or adequately reflected in the faces of elected officials ... Women need the system to change and to include them" (PEI Advisory Council on the Status of Women 2005, 1). If the plebiscite supported reform, then the council favoured the recommended mixed-member proportional system, applied in a way to increase representation by women in the Legislative Assembly; if the plebiscite rejected the proposed system, then the council recommended an extensive list of reforms to the existing electoral system to provide incentives for, and remove barriers to, women's participation.

In addition to its activities during elections and plebiscites, the Advisory Council on the Status of Women has, since 2008, published an annual equality report card, which includes a report on "women in decision-making." Measuring against the goal of "increasing women's participation in the highest levels of decision-making," the 2011 report card gives the provincial government a grade of C. Significantly, the grade on this section is based on three subgoals. With respect to increasing women's leadership roles within the provincial civil services, the government was given a grade of B+; with respect to appointments to agencies, boards, and commissions, the grade was C; and with respect to examining and reducing barriers to women in elected office, the grade was D (PEI Advisory Council on the Status of Women 2011).

The Coalition for Women in Government was formed in February 2004 in direct response to the stagnation of progress towards female equality of representation in the Legislative Assembly and cabinet.[7] The coalition is both multi- and non-partisan. Its founding members included a former Liberal MLA and cabinet minister, a former NDP candidate for the provincial legislature, and women prominent in the broader provincial women's movement, including a senior public servant, the executive director of the Women's Network of PEI, and a legal and rights activist. The primary source of funding for the coalition is Status of Women Canada, which, on 15 March 2010, renewed the coalition's grant for three years.[8]

The Coalition for Women in Government seeks to increase women's participation and representation at all levels of government and has been particularly active in encouraging women to run for municipal and provincial offices. The main focus of the coalition, however, is the provincial Legislative Assembly. On its website, the coalition identifies its long-term goal as being a Legislative Assembly comprising 50 percent female members by 2015 (and 33 percent in 2011.) The coalition has identified the party-controlled candidate nomination process as the major barrier to achieving this goal. Many of the coalition's activities, then, have focused on understanding the factors that prevent or disincline women from seeking or winning nominations.

The coalition has held focus groups, conducted research, and promoted the cause of equality of representation. It has attempted to demystify the nomination and election processes and to emphasize the importance of women's participation in government. In 2005, it sought and received commitments from each political party to nominate at least nine women (one-third of the total) in the next provincial election (Prince Edward Island Advisory Council on the Status of Women 2005, 2). While the NDP and Green parties met this commitment, neither of the two major parties did so. Finally, before each of the last two general elections, the coalition organized and ran two-day "campaign" (2007) or "leadership" (2011) schools for women. Approximately fifty women attended each of the May 2006 and April 2011 schools, where a veritable who's who of successful Island and national female politicians shared their experiences and wisdom with regard to the decision to run, the nomination process, campaigning, and media and public relations (Coalition for Women in Government 2006; Callbeck 2011).

Conclusion: Prospects for Gender Parity

In spite of the efforts of the Advisory Council on the Status of Women and the Coalition for Women in Government, the number and proportion of women candidates (at least for the major parties), legislators, and cabinet ministers in Prince Edward Island have changed little over the seven general elections since 1989. Women either do not seek nomination for election or are simply not nominated in sufficiently large numbers by the two parties that elect members to the Legislative Assembly. The prospects of increasing the presence of women in the Legislative Assembly, then, are closely connected to the prospects of increasing the number of women nominated as candidates by the two major parties.

There are, no doubt, a number of factors that limit the willingness or ability of women to seek nomination for election to the provincial legislature. As the PEI Advisory Council on the Status of Women has pointed out, overcoming these factors will require attention and effort from the major parties and government in addition to the women's movement (Prince Edward Island Advisory Council on the Status of Women 2005). The parties need to review their formal and informal processes and rules for nominating candidates for election and systematically recruit and develop a pool of partisan female activists. Until a critical mass of female party members is achieved, party leaders will have to consciously and deliberately act to make their parties welcoming for women. The advisory council recommends that the government encourage the political parties to nominate more women by providing larger subsidies and other financial incentives for female candidates. It also recommends that government provide care-giving subsidies to women to encourage them to become active in electoral politics earlier in their lives, and it advises the Department of Education to introduce a curriculum into the public school system that would educate young women about the political process and the importance of participation by women in electoral politics and parliamentary government.

Without concerted effort by the government and the major political parties, the prospects for further improvement in the representation of women in the Legislative Assembly of Prince Edward Island seem bleak. It has been over twenty years since the major parties used the nomination process to increase the number of women running for election, but the presence of women in the Legislative Assembly and the cabinet has changed not at all since 1989. In the same period, the presence of women in public service, education, and business has increased dramatically, but these improvements in the status of women in other parts of Island life have not provided a demonstration effect that has influenced the major political parties to nominate women as candidates for elected office. In addition, the efforts of the Coalition for Women in Government over two electoral and legislative cycles have not had the desired effects of encouraging more women to run for office and encouraging party elites to actively recruit more female candidates. Furthermore, the prospect of introducing an electoral system based on principles of proportional representation, a system that would very likely lead to more equal representation of women and other underrepresented groups, was soundly rejected by Islanders in October 2005. The initiative for change, then, rests with the two major parties that, between them, control the nomination process and, thus, membership in the assembly and cabinet. Unfortunately, it is not clear that those who control these parties see electoral advantage in taking the steps necessary to increase the presence of women in the Legislative Assembly of Prince Edward Island.

Notes

1 Before 1963, Aboriginal people living off reserves could vote for assemblymen and for councillors if they had the property qualification. After the First World War, status Indians living on reserves could vote in provincial elections if they had served in a theatre of war. In 1963 the property qualification and the disenfranchisement of status Indians living on reserves were ended.

2 In the 1996 election, one NDP candidate won election, the only MLA in the history of the province not to belong to one of the two major parties. Dr. Herb Dickieson was elected in a Prince County constituency, where the election was shaped by local issues revolving around the proposed closing of a regional hospital. In a close three-person race, he won with 38 percent of the vote.

3 A fifth woman, Nancy Guptill (Lib.), was elected in a by-election on 14 September 1987.

4 Leone Bagnall served as interim leader of the Progressive Conservative Party in 1987-88 following the resignation of James Lee. She did not seek the leadership at the 1988 convention.

5 Only two other lieutenant governors appear to have been appointed primarily because of their community service: W.J. MacDonald, 1963-69, and J.A. Doiron, 1980-85. MacDonald was a hero of both world wars, while Doiron was a leader within the Island Acadian community. See biographies of lieutenant governors of Prince Edward Island at http://www.gov.pe.ca/.

6 Funding for the Advisory Council on the Status of Women is provided by the Interministerial Women's Secretariat.

7 The coalition's coordinator, Kirstin Lund, said in a letter to the editor of the Charlottetown *Guardian* that the founders of what became the coalition began working in 2003 by holding focus groups to find out why women were not running for elected office (Lund 2011).

8 The coalition was awarded $197,960 for thirty-six months (Canada, Status of Women Canada, 2011).

References

Callbeck, Hon. Catherine. 2011. "PEI Coalition for Women in Government – Women in Leadership School." Statement made on 8 June 2011 in the Senate of Canada. Downloaded from the Liberal Senate Forum. Available at http://www.liberalsenateforum.ca/.

Canada. Status of Women Canada. 2011. Disclosure of Grant and Contribution Awards. Available at http://www.swc-cfc.gc.ca/.

Canadian Parliamentary Guide. Various years. Toronto: Grey Publishing.

Coalition for Women in Government. 2004. "Coalition Forms to Elect More Women in PEI." Charlottetown, 15 March, press release. Available at http://www. womeningovernmentpei.ca/.

—. 2006. *PEI Women's Campaign School, May 4-6, 2006, Evaluation Report.* Available at http://www.womeningovernmentpei.ca/.

—. 2009a. *It's about Time: Research Findings and Conclusions, Summary.* Available at http://www.womeningovernmentpei.ca/.

—. 2009b. *Whose Job Is It Anyway? The Life and Work of an MLA.* Charlottetown. Available at http://www.womeningovernmentpei.ca/.

Crossley, John. 1990. "Prince Edward Island." In *Canadian Annual Review of Politics and Public Policy, 1990,* 219-27. Toronto: University of Toronto Press.

—. 1993. "Prince Edward Island." In *Canadian Annual Review of Politics and Public Policy, 1993.* Toronto: University of Toronto Press.

—. 1997. "Picture This: Women Politicians Hold Key Posts in Prince Edward Island." In Jane Arscott and Linda Trimble, eds., *In the Presence of Women: Representation in Canadian Governments,* 278-307. Toronto: Harcourt Brace Canada.

Dasgupta, Satadal. 1982. "The Island in Transition: A Statistical Overview." In Verner Smitheram, David Milne, and Satadal Dasgupta, eds., *The Garden Transformed: Prince Edward Island, 1945-1980,* 243-68. Charlottetown: Ragweed Press.

Drake, Carolyn. 1992. "Profile: Teacher, Housewife, Politician ... Leone Bagnall Takes on Many Roles." *The Islander* (supplement to *Guardian* [Charlottetown]), 19 September.

Dunn, Kate. 1979. "Women, Civil Service Mixture Not Always Right." *Guardian* (Charlottetown), 24 March.

Elections Prince Edward Island. N.d.(a). "Provincial Election Results." Available at http://www.electionspei.ca/.

—. N.d.(b) "Women in Prince Edward Island Politics." Available at http:www. electionspei.ca/.

—. Various elections. *Report of the Chief Electoral Officer of Prince Edward Island.* Available at http://www.electionspei.ca/.

Lund, Kirstin. 2011. "Partisan Politics Turns People Off." Op-ed., *Guardian* (Charlottetown), 11 October. Available at http://www.theguardian.pe.ca/.

Outcalt, Janice. 1976. "PEI Seen Ripe for Women Candidates." *Guardian* (Charlottetown), 5 August.

Prince Edward Island Advisory Council on the Status of Women. 1982. *One Yardstick: A Progress Report on the Implementation of the Recommendations Made by the Provincial Advisory Committee on the Status of Women.* Charlottetown: Queen's Printer.

—. 2005. *Policy Guide: Women and Electoral Reform.* Available at http://www. gov.pe.ca/.

—. 2011. *PEI Equality Report Card, 2011.* Available at http://www.gov.pe.ca/.

Prince Edward Island. 2011. Office of the Lieutenant Governor. Lieutenant Governors Gallery. Available at http://www.gov.pe.ca/.

Prince Edward Island. Executive Council Office. 2011. Members of Executive Council as of 18 October. Available at http://www.gov.pe.ca/.

Prince Edward Island. Department of Finance, Economics, Statistics, and Fiscal Analysis. 1990a. *Economic Overview of Prince Edward Island.* Charlottetown: Queen's Printer.

—. 1990b. *Prince Edward Island Statistics: Past and Present.* Charlottetown: Queen's Printer.

Prince Edward Island. Department of the Provincial Treasury, Economics, Statistics and Federal Fiscal Relations Division. 1994. *Twentieth Annual Statistical Review, 1993.* Charlottetown: Queen's Printer.

Provincial Advisory Committee on the Status of Women. 1973. *Report.* Charlottetown: Queen's Printer.

Smitheram, Verner. 1982. "Development and the Debate over School Consolidation." In Verner Smitheram, David Milne, and Satadal Dasgupta, eds., *The Garden Transformed: Prince Edward Island, 1945-1980,* 177-202. Charlottetown: Ragweed Press.

Stetson, Beverly Mills. 1977. "Island Women and the Vote." In Mari Basiletti, Donna Greenwood, and Beverly Mills, eds., *Changing Times: Essays by Island Women,* 1-8. Charlottetown: Women's Legal Project of PEI.

—. N.d. "Times They're Sure A-Changing." *Common Ground* 8(3): 5.

Whittaker, Sally. 1992. "Some Important Dates in PEI Women's History." *Guardian* (Charlottetown), 7 March.

10

Hitting a Glass Ceiling?

Women in Quebec Politics

MANON TREMBLAY

Those working in the field of women and politics say that elected women so often hit their heads against a glass ceiling that occupational health and safety codes should be introduced to prevent injuries in the workplace. This characterization is rarely applied to women's electoral presence in Quebec; however, representation by women in the Assemblée nationale du Québec hit a glass ceiling in the early twenty-first century. This is not to say that an invisible hand is orchestrating a plot against women's access to political spaces (Tremblay 2008, 130-31); rather, it emphasizes that women's presence on the terrain of parliamentary representation does not follow a linear and upward progression according to which a larger number of women would enter the Assemblée nationale. Gender parity seems unlikely in the near future, or even over the long term, unless certain features of Quebec political society change significantly.

In this chapter, I present some of the factors that structure women's participation in Quebec political life. Then, I describe the evolution of the proportion of women in the Quebec parliament[1] and cabinet, and advance some explanations for the imbalance of representation by women and men in the Assemblée nationale. Finally, I suggest some further avenues for research.

Background

Anyone who wants to be involved in electoral politics, including sitting in the Assemblée nationale du Québec, must negotiate a number of hurdles:

POLITICAL REPRESENTATION OF WOMEN IN
QUEBEC

FIRSTS

Right to vote and stand for election

▪ Most women win right to vote and stand for election	1940
▪ Aboriginal women win right to vote	1969

Contesting office

▪ First women to contest office: Gisèle Bergeron (CCF), Marie-Thérèse Forget-Casgrain (CCF), Ange Paradis (Independant), and Jeannette Pratte-Walsh (Ouvrier progressiste) – none elected	1952
▪ First woman to win office: Marie-Claire Kirkland (Liberal)	1961-73
▪ First Muslim woman to win office: Fatima Houda-Pépin (Liberal), elected to the National Assembly	1994 to present
▪ First publicly identified lesbian to win office: Agnès Maltais (PQ), elected to National Assembly	1998 to present
▪ First black woman to win office: Yolande James (Liberal), elected to the National Assembly	2004 to present
▪ First woman appointed to cabinet: Marie-Claire Kirkland (Liberal), minister without portfolio	1962-64
▪ First woman premier: Pauline Marois (PQ)	2012 to present

CURRENT REPRESENTATION AT A GLANCE

		Women elected	
	Date of election	Number	Percent
Women in legislature	2012/12/08	41 of 125	33
Women in cabinet	As of September 2012	8 of 24	33

Women political party leaders

▪ Françoise David, co-leader of Québec Solidaire, 2011 to present
▪ Pauline Marois, leader of the PQ, 2011 to present

Lieutenant governor

▪ Lise Thibault, 1997-2007

Advisory council on the status of women

▪ The Conseil du statut de la femme was created in 1973.

eligibility, recruitment, selection, and election. Each of these hurdles is composed of cultural, socio-economic, and political factors that interfere with the capacity of women to win a mandate for parliamentary representation (Tremblay 2012). Eligibility corresponds to the legal capacity to run for office. Recruitment "consists of identifying from the total population the persons interested in political activity and having the resources available to undertake this activity; it involves building a pool of candidates likely to become involved, to various degrees, in political governance" (Tremblay and Pelletier 1995, 13 [my translation]). Selection is the process through which political parties choose their candidates. Election is the procedure used by voters to select the individuals who will represent them in the legislature. In short, a collection of cultural, socio-economic, and political factors structure the path towards legislative representation, from eligibility through recruitment (or supply of candidates) and selection (or demand for candidates) to election. Considering the under-representation of women in the Quebec parliament, these factors are very real, although they tend to operate informally. The image of a glass ceiling manipulated by an invisible hand captures the subtle nature of these barriers.

Women's Political Representation: The Numbers
This section paints a statistical portrait of the presence of women in the Assemblée nationale and the cabinet of the Quebec government for the period 1976 to 2010. As I show below, women are certainly under-represented in the legislative and executive branches of the Quebec government in comparison to their demographic weight, although some data hold out hope for the future.

Women in the Assemblée nationale du Québec
Although a number of political parties have presented female candidates in the nineteen general elections held since 1940 (when women obtained the rights to vote and run for office in provincial elections), the more than one hundred women elected to the Assemblée nationale have belonged to five parties: the Parti libéral du Québec (PLQ), the Parti québécois (PQ), the Action démocratique du Québec (ADQ, which merged with Coalition Avenir Québec [CAQ] at the beginning of 2012), and Québec Solidaire (QS). Only two women from ethno-racial minorities are among these women members of the Assemblée nationale (MANs): Fatima Houda-Pépin and Yolande James.

TABLE 10.1

Women in the Assemblée nationale du Québec, by election

Election date	Party elected	Total number of legislators	Women elected	
			Number	%
1944/08/08	Union nationale	91	0	0
1948/07/28	Union nationale	92	0	0
1952/07/16	Union nationale	92	0	0
1956/06/20	Union nationale	93	0	0
1960/06/22	Parti libéral	95	0	0
1962/11/14	Parti libéral	95	1	1
1966/06/05	Union nationale	108	1	1
1970/04/29	Parti libéral	108	1	1
1973/10/29	Parti libéral	110	1	1
1976/11/16	Parti québécois	110	5	5
1981/04/13	Parti québécois	122	8	7
1985/12/02	Parti libéral	122	18	15
1989/09/25	Parti libéral	125	23	18
1994/09/12	Parti québécois	125	23	18
1998/11/30	Parti québécois	125	29	23
2003/04/14	Parti libéral	125	38	30
2007/03/26	Parti libéral	125	32	26
2008/12/08	Parti libéral	125	37	30
2012/09/04	Parti québécois	125	41	33

Table 10.1 shows the changes in the proportion of women among MANs from 1944 (the first provincial general election in which women voted) to 2012. During this period, 120 women were elected (data not shown), including 57 (48 percent) for the PLQ, 49 (41 percent) for the PQ, 13 (11 percent) for the ADQ/CAQ, and 1 (1 percent) for QS. Altogether, these representatives assumed 258 mandates, or 12 percent (258/2,113) of all mandates contested in the nineteen provincial general elections from 1944 to 2012 inclusive. Of these 258 mandates, 133 (52 percent) were won by Liberal members, 110 (43 percent) by PQ members, 14 (5 percent) by ADQ/CAQ members, and 1 (.004 percent) by Québec Solidaire.

The rate of feminization of the Assemblée nationale du Québec has been rising steadily. More precisely, the overall period can be broken down into three subperiods: first, up to the 1981 election, when the proportion of female representatives was under 10 percent; second, from 1985 to 1994

TABLE 10.2
Women candidates in Quebec, by party and election

Election date	Parti libéral du Québec		Parti québécois		Action démocratique du Québec/ Coalition Avenir Québec (from 2012)		Québec Solidaire	
	Number	%	Number	%	Number	%	Number	%
1976/11/16	3	3	7	6	–	–	–	–
1981/04/13	13	11	16	13	–	–	–	–
1985/12/02	17	14	20	16	–	–	–	–
1989/09/25	21	17	32	26	–	–	–	–
1994/09/12	28	22	28	22	12	15	–	–
1998/11/30	30	24	31	25	21	17	–	–
2003/04/14	35	28	43	34	32	26	–	–
2007/03/26	44	35	41	33	26	21	65	0
2008/12/08	41	33	39	31	25	20	65	0
2012/09/04	48	38	34	27	27	22	62	50

inclusive, with feminization rates varying from 10 percent to 20 percent; and third, starting with the election of 1998, when the proportion of female representatives was above 20 percent. That said, the results of the 1994 and 2007 elections indicate that successive elections do not necessarily increase the number of women elected. The 1994 election initiated a stagnation in the overall proportion of female MANs, which did not rise above the 1989 rate, and the 2007 election resulted in a drop in the feminization rate from the peak of 30 percent reached in the previous general election. This is explained in good part by the success in the 2007 elections of the ADQ, a party with only 21 percent women candidates (compared to 33 percent for the PQ and 35 percent for the PLQ; see Table 10.2), whose parliamentary caucus was even less feminized after the vote (19 percent, compared to 25 percent for the PQ and 33 percent for the PLQ; see Table 10.3). Thus, the glass ceiling that stopped the increase in the proportion of female MANs is due, at least in part, to the electoral success of a right-wing party for which political representation by women is a less important issue. The 2012 election confirmed the weak enthusiasm that right-wing parties had for women: the Coalition Avenir Québec, the most right-wing party on the Québec political chessboard (which had swallowed Action démocratique du Québec earlier that year) ran a slate of candidates that was only 22 percent female, compared to 27 and 38 percent for the PQ and the PLQ, respectively. By contrast, Québec Solidaire, the most left-wing party, but also the one having the lowest chances of electoral success, ran a gender-balanced slate of candidates.

Table 10.2 presents an overall picture of female candidates (numbers and proportions) by political party in Quebec general elections from 1976 to 2012, while Table 10.3 takes a closer look at the political parties that have elected at least one female candidate to the Assemblée nationale du Québec since 1976. It appears that the two major parties, the PLQ and the PQ, have performed differently with regard to the proportion of women among total candidates, the degree of feminization of their parliamentary wing, and the success rate of their female candidates. As Table 10.3 shows, whereas the proportions of women running for office and elected are almost identical in the PLQ (23 percent versus 22 percent), the proportion of women elected is slightly lower than that of candidates in the PQ (20 percent versus 24 percent). Moreover, not only is the success rate of PLQ female candidates higher than that of PQ female candidates (46 percent versus 38 percent), but it is almost identical to that of male Liberal candidates (49 percent; data not shown for male candidates), whereas in the PQ the success rate of female candidates trails that of their male counterparts by more than 8 percent (38 percent versus 46 percent; data not shown for male candidates). For the ADQ/CAQ, the proportion of women running and elected was relatively balanced (20 percent compared to 21 percent), as was the success rate of ADQ/CAQ female and male candidates (10 percent versus 9 percent). The success rate of female and male QS candidates is the same – 1 percent. Finally, during the three aforementioned subperiods, the proportion of women within the parliamentary caucuses of the PLQ and the PQ also grew (except in 1994 and 2007 for the latter); the proportion of female representatives in the ADQ, however, rose above 20 percent only in the 2003 election (and dropped below this threshold in the 2007 and 2008 elections). However, although the rate of feminization of the PLQ and PQ caucuses increased overall during the three periods mentioned above, the pattern of increase varies by party. Feminization of the Liberal parliamentary caucus rose steadily from 1976 to 2012, while it followed a saw-tooth pattern for the PQ. On the other hand, in each general election since 2003, the proportion of female representatives in the ADQ has dropped, although a quarter of the CAQ caucus is composed of women following the 2012 election.

TABLE 10.3

Women candidates for the Assemblée nationale du Québec, by election and party, 1976-2012

Year	Parti libéral du Québec			Parti québécois			Action démocratique du Québec/ Coalition Avenir Québec (from 2012)*			Québec Solidaire		
	Women candidates	Women elected	Success rate	Women candidates	Women elected	Success rate	Women candidates	Women elected	Success rate	Women candidates	Women elected	Success rate
1976	3 of 110	1 of 26	1 of 3	7 of 110	4 of 71	4 of 7	–	–	–	–	–	–
%	3	4	33	6	6	57						
1981	13 of 122	3 of 42	3 of 13	16 of 122	5 of 80	5 of 16	–	–	–	–	–	–
%	11	7	23	13	6	31						
1985	17 of 122	14 of 99	14 of 17	20 of 122	4 of 23	4 of 20	–	–	–	–	–	–
%	14	14	82	16	17	20						
1989	21 of 125	15 of 92	15 of 21	32 of 125	8 of 29	8 of 32	–	–	–	–	–	–
%	17	16	71	26	28	25						
1994	28 of 125	8 of 47	8 of 28	28 of 125	15 of 77	15 of 28	12 of 80	0 of 1	0 of 12	–	–	–
%	22	17	29	22	19	54	15	0	0			
1998	30 of 125	10 of 48	10 of 30	31 of 124	19 of 75	19 of 31	21 of 125	0 of 1	0 of 21	–	–	–
%	24	21	33	25	25	61	17	0	0			

2003	35 of 125	22 of 76	22 of 35	43 of 125	15 of 45	15 of 43	32 of 125	1 of 4	1 of 32	–	–	–
%	28	29	63	34	33	35	26	25	3	–	–	–
2007	44 of 125	16 of 48	16 of 44	41 of 125	9 of 36	9 of 41	26 of 125	7 of 36	7 of 26	65 of 123	0 of 0	0 of 65
%	35	33	36	33	25	22	21	19	27	53	0	0
2008	41 of 125	22 of 66	22 of 41	39 of 125	14 of 51	14 of 39	25 of 125	1 of 7	1 of 25	65 of 122	0 of 1	0 of 65
%	33	33	54	31	27	36	20	14	4	53	0	0
2012	48 of 125	18 of 50	18 of 48	34 of 125	17 of 54	17 of 34	27 of 125	5 of 19	5 of 27	62 of 124	1 of 2	1 of 62
%	38	36	38	27	31	50	22	26	19	50	50	2
TOTAL	280 of 1,229	129 of 594	129 of 280	291 of 1,228	110 of 541	110 of 291	143 of 705	14 of 68	14 of 143	192 of 369	1 of 3	1 of 192
%	23	22	46	24	20	38	20	21	10	52	33	1

Note: Parties that have never elected women, such as the Union nationale, are excluded.

* The ADQ ran candidates starting only in the 1994 election, and Québec Solidaire in the 2007 election.

Sources: Table taken from Tremblay (2010, 87) and adapted for the 2007, 2008, and 2012 provincial general elections using data from Québec, Directeur général des élections (2007, 2008, 2012).

Overall, the feminization rate in the Assemblée nationale du Québec has grown steadily since 1976, although there have been occasional halts, and even retreats, as demonstrated by the 1994 and 2007 elections. The chances that women candidates will win vary depending on the party, with the PLQ offering the best prospects for success. This is also the case with regard to appointments to the cabinet of the Government of Quebec.

Women in the Cabinet

The PQ victory in the 2012 election made Pauline Marois the first woman premier of Quebec. That said, even before Pauline Marois reached the pinnacle of power, women had been well represented in the cabinet. From the first cabinet formed following the PQ victory in 1976 to the cabinet formed by Pauline Marois after the 2012 election, forty-seven women were appointed ministers, twenty-two of them (47 percent) in a PLQ government and twenty-five (53 percent) in a PQ government.

Tables 10.5 and 10.6 show the proportion of women in the cabinet of the Quebec government. More specifically, Table 10.5 reveals the progressive increase, from 7 percent to 48 percent, of Quebec cabinets since the beginning of the 1980s. However, it is quite ironic that women comprise only one-third of the cabinet of the first woman premier of Quebec,[2] while Jean Charest's cabinets following the 2007 and 2008 elections almost achieved gender parity. Table 10.6 explores in detail three more indicators of the feminization of Quebec politics since the Parti québécois took power in 1976: the overall percentage of female representatives, the percentage of women in the government caucus, and the rate of female ministers among female representatives of the government caucus. Between 1976 and 2012 (including the Marois government here), about 24 percent of ministers were women, a higher proportion than that of all women in the Assemblée nationale (20 percent) and of women in the government caucus (19 percent). Essentially, the premier decides who will be in the cabinet, and the appointment of women to ministerial positions depends no doubt in part on the premier's convictions with regard to equality between women and men. In

TABLE 10.4
Female representatives of the Crown in Quebec

Name	Period of service
Lise Thibault	1997-2007

TABLE 10.5
Women in cabinet in Quebec, by election

Election date	Party elected	Total number of cabinet ministers*	Women elected	
			Number	%
1981/04/13	Parti québécois	28	2	7
1985/12/02	Parti libéral	28	4	14
1989/09/25	Parti libéral	30	6	20
1994/09/12	Parti québécois	20	6	30
1998/11/30	Parti québécois	27	8	30
2003/04/14	Parti libéral	25	8	32
2007/03/26	Parti libéral	19	9	47
2008/12/08	Parti libéral	27	13	48
2012/09/04	Parti québécois	24	8	33

* Includes the premier.

this respect, the performance of former premier Charest is remarkable since the cabinets that he appointed following the elections of 2007 and 2008 almost reached gender parity.

The proportion of women in the cabinet of the Government of Quebec, like their proportion in the Assemblée nationale, has been increasing steadily since 1976, although there was a pullback with the 1996 Bouchard and 2012 Marois governments. In fact, the proportion of women in the Quebec cabinet can be defined by three periods: from 1976 to the second Lévesque cabinet inclusive, when the rate of feminization remained below 10 percent; from Pierre-Marc Johnson's 1985 cabinet to Lucien Bouchard's first cabinet in 1996 inclusive, when the proportion of female ministers varied between 14 percent and 23 percent (except for the Parizeau cabinet, in which the feminization rate was 30 percent); and, finally, from Bouchard's second cabinet in 1998 to Jean Charest's third cabinet in 2008, when the percentage of women on the ministerial team varied between 29 percent and parity. Whereas it seems that a glass ceiling is blocking a rise in the feminization rate in the Assemblée nationale, there appears to be no glass ceiling in the Quebec cabinet. In fact, the disappointing percentage of women in the Marois cabinet could be temporary. Premier Marois leads a minority government and an election will likely be held in 2014, which may provide more opportunities for her to appoint women cabinet ministers provided that she can count on a pool of PQ female MANs qualified for ministerial appointments.

TABLE 10.6

Women in cabinet and governing caucus in Quebec, by party and election, 1976-2012

Year	Premier	Party	Women ministers[1]		Women representatives[2]		Women in governing caucus[3]		Women ministers among women representatives in governing caucus[4]	
			Number	%	Number	%	Number	%	Number	%
1976	Lévesque	PQ	1 of 24	4	5 of 110	5	4 of 71	6	1 of 4	25
1981	Lévesque	PQ	2 of 28	7	8 of 122	7	5 of 80	6	2 of 5	40
1985	P.-M. Johnson	PQ	4 of 29	14	10 of 120[5]	8	5 of 80	6	4 of 5	80
1985	Bourassa	PLQ	4 of 28	14	18 of 122	15	14 of 99	14	4 of 14	29
1989	Bourassa	PLQ	6 of 30	20	23 of 125	18	15 of 92	16	6 of 15	40
1994	D. Johnson Jr.	PLQ	4 of 21	19	22 of 118[6]	19	15 of 92	16	4 of 15	27
1994	Parizeau	PQ	6 of 20	30	23 of 125	18	15 of 77	19	6 of 15	40
1996	Bouchard	PQ	5 of 22	23	23 of 125	18	15 of 77	19	5 of 15	33
1998	Bouchard	PQ	8 of 27	30	29 of 125	23	19 of 76	25	8 of 19	42
2001	Landry	PQ	7 of 24	29	29 of 121[7]	24	19 of 76	25	7 of 19	37
2003	Charest	PLQ	8 of 25	32	38 of 125	30	22 of 76	29	8 of 22	36
2007	Charest	PLQ	9 of 19	47	32 of 125	26	16 of 48	33	9 of 16	56
2008	Charest	PLQ	13 of 27	48	37 of 125	30	22 of 66	33	13 of 22	59
2012	Marois	PQ	8 of 24[8]	33	41 of 125	33	17 of 54	31	8 of 17[8]	47
Total			85 of 348	24	338 of 1,713	20	203 of 1,064	19	85 of 203	42

1 Establishing the proportion of women in the cabinet is not easy, simply because there are a number of ways of doing so. It would have been possible to consider the feminization rate of the first cabinet formed following a general election. However, this formula would have left out many women. For example, P.-M. Johnson formed his cabinet on 3 October 1985, incorporating only one woman (Pauline Marois). A few days later, however, on 16 October, he added three women: Louise Beaudoin, Rollande Cloutier, and Lise Denis. Thus, the figures are those recorded by the Assemblée nationale at the following source: Québec, Assemblée nationale (1962).

2 The proportions corresponding to the presence of women in the Assemblée nationale after a general election do not take account of the variations due to by-elections (Québec, Assemblée nationale [n.d.-a]). With regard to the cabinets of Pierre-Marc Johnson (1985), Daniel Johnson Jr. (1994), Lucien Bouchard (1996), and Bernard Landry (2001), the proportions of female representatives reflect the presence of women in the Assemblée nationale at the time these premiers formed their initial cabinets.

3 These data are based on the following sources: Québec, Assemblée nationale (1961, n.d.[b]).

4 These data are based on the following sources: Québec, Assemblée nationale (1961, 1962).

5 At the time when P.-M. Johnson became premier, in October 1985, two seats were vacant in the Assemblée nationale.

6 At the time when Daniel Johnson Jr. became premier, in January 1994, seven seats were vacant in the Assemblée nationale.

7 At the time when Bernard Landry became premier, in March 2001, four seats were vacant in the Assemblée nationale.

8 Including Pauline Marois as premier but not as minister.

Sources: Table taken from Tremblay (2010, 87) and adapted for the 2007, 2008, and 2012 provincial general elections using data from Québec, Directeur général des élections (2007, 2008, 2012).

A comparison between the parliament and the cabinet reveals that, although increasing numbers of Quebec women have filled representative and ministerial roles since 1976, they gained more ground, and more quickly, at the executive than at the legislative level. The proportion of women in both bodies remained below 10 percent until the first half of the 1980s. However, while the feminization rate in the cabinet reached 20 percent by the end of the 1980s, the equivalent occurred in the Assemblée nationale only a decade later, in 1998. Since the turn of the millennium, the proportion of women MANs has stagnated at about 30 percent, but in the cabinet female/male parity was almost attained in 2007. What is more, since 1981 the proportion of female ministers has been equal to or higher than the proportion of women in the government caucus, underlining the premier's power to promote the presence of women at the heart of executive power. That being said, given that the premier's wishes are essential to the presence of women in cabinet, light remains to be shed on why the premier would decide to choose women to be ministers. No doubt, it is possible that the premier's convictions with regard to equality of the sexes will lead her or him to appoint women to the cabinet. It is also true that today the presence of women in the cabinet is imperative in terms of representativeness (Massicotte 2009; White 2005, 35-36).

One last observation regarding Table 10.6 concerns the (excellent) chances that female MANs in the government caucus will become ministers: 42 percent of female representatives belonging to the party in power served as ministers in one (or more) of the fourteen cabinets formed in Quebec from 1976 to 2012. In a study concerning the careers of federal ministers from 1935 to 2008, Kerby (2009) shows that women had a 50 percent greater chance than men of being appointed to the cabinet.

A key idea for work on participation by women in politics is that their inclusion at the executive level is differentiated along two dividing lines – one horizontal and the other vertical. In the first case, women are chosen to head "pink" ministries associated with their conventional roles in the private life and the family. They thus are given portfolios such as health and welfare, education, childhood and old age, employment and human resources, and municipal affairs. In the second case, women are at the bottom of the ministerial hierarchy, in junior rather than in senior positions. However, such a gendered reading must be nuanced.

As Table 10.7 shows, the idea that women assume ministerial responsibilities associated mainly with their conventional roles according to the sexual

TABLE 10.7

Number and percentage of portfolios held by women in Quebec governments, by ministerial mission and political party, 1976-2012

Mission*	All parties		PLQ		PQ	
	Number	%	Number	%	Number	%
1976-2010						
Royal prerogative	11	5	5	5	6	6
Economic	37	18	16	14	21	22
Socio-economic	68	33	39	35	29	30
Social and cultural	85	41	45	41	40	41
Without portfolio	6	3	5	5	1	1
Total	207	100	110	100	97	100
1976-85 (R. Lévesque's second cabinet included)						
Royal prerogative	0	0	0	0	0	0
Economic	2	17	0	0	2	17
Socio-economic	2	17	0	0	2	17
Social and cultural	8	67	0	0	8	67
Without portfolio	0	0	0	0	0	0
Total	12	101	0	0	12	101
1985 (P.-M. Johnson's cabinet) to 1996 (L. Bouchard's first cabinet included)						
Royal prerogative	2	3	0	0	2	5
Economic	12	18	4	14	8	22
Socio-economic	18	27	5	17	13	35
Social and cultural	32	49	18	62	14	38
Without portfolio	2	3	2	7	0	0
Total	66	100	29	100	37	100
1998 (L. Bouchard's second cabinet) to 2012 (P. Marois's cabinet included)						
Royal prerogative	9	7	5	6	4	8
Economic	23	18	12	15	11	23
Socio-economic	48	37	34	42	14	29
Social and cultural	45	35	27	33	18	38
Without portfolio	4	3	3	4	1	2
Total	129	100	81	100	48	100

* The composition of missions by portfolio is the following: royal prerogative: intergovernmental affairs, justice, international relations, public security; economic missions: Treasury Board, economy, finance, industry and commerce, infrastructure, natural resources, revenue, transportation, public works; socio-economic: education, employment, municipal and regional affairs, environment, tourism, recreation and sports; social and cultural: health, family, status of women, cultural and identity, immigration, administration, public service and government services, social affairs in general.

Sources: Québec, Assemblée nationale (1961, 1962).

division of labour proves to be well founded: from 1976 to 2012, almost three-quarters of portfolios assigned to women were of a cultural, social, or socio-economic nature. This proportion has tended to drop over time, from 83 percent during the period from 1976 to 1985, to 76 percent from 1985 to 1996, then to 72 percent since 1998 – a decrease attributable mainly to the PQ. Over time, PQ premiers have entrusted to women a growing proportion of royal prerogative (i.e., responsibilities related to intergovernmental affairs, justice, international relations, and public security) and economic ministerial portfolios, and in greater proportions than have their Liberal counterparts.

The idea of a vertical dividing line through which women take on less important ministerial responsibilities does not convey the reality in Quebec. As the figures presented in Table 10.8 show, a fairly balanced number of senior and junior ministerial responsibilities were entrusted to women from 1976 to 2012. On the other hand, Liberal women were much more likely to hold senior portfolios, while PQ women held portfolios of lesser importance – a difference that is statistically significant at an observed threshold of 99 percent. The gap between the PLQ and the PQ is particularly pronounced for the period from 1985 to 1996: whereas almost three-quarters of ministerial responsibilities assumed by Liberal women were at a senior level during this period, 62 percent of the ministerial portfolios held by PQ women were at a junior level. It would be important to shed light on the poor performance by the PQ, but this finding is quite surprising for a party that claims to have formed the "first feminist government in the history of Quebec" (Gagné and Langlois 2002, 85 [my translation]).

There is no question that more than seven decades after having gained the rights to vote and run for election in the Province of Quebec, women are still under-represented on the Quebec electoral scene (in comparison to their demographic weight) as candidates, representatives, and ministers. How then can this overall imbalance be explained?

Explanations

As mentioned above, the path to a seat in the Assemblée nationale du Québec is marked by four stages: eligibility, recruitment, selection, and election. These obligatory milestones offer both advantages and difficulties to candidates, and so this is where we must seek explanations for the under-representation of women in Quebec politics. Likely, the explanations are to be found not in the eligibility and election stages but in the recruitment and selection stages.

TABLE 10.8

Number and percentage of portfolios held by women in Quebec governments, by ministerial status and political party, 1976-2012

Mission[1]	All parties		PLQ		PQ	
	Number	%	Number	%	Number	%
1976-2010[2]						
Junior	107	52	47	43	60	62
Senior	100	48	63	57	37	38
Total	207	100	110	100	97	100
1976-85 (R. Lévesque's second cabinet included)						
Junior	7	58	0	0	7	58
Senior	5	42	0	0	5	42
Total	12	100	0	0	12	100
1985 (P.-M. Johnson's cabinet) to 1996 (L. Bouchard's first cabinet included)[2]						
Junior	31	47	8	28	23	62
Senior	35	53	21	72	14	38
Total	66	100	29	100	37	100
1998 (L. Bouchard's second cabinet) to 2012 (P. Marois's cabinet included)[3]						
Junior	69	53	39	48	30	63
Senior	60	47	42	52	18	38
Total	129	100	81	100	48	101

1 The number of portfolios held by women refers to the total duration of a premier's cabinet, for example, from 12 December 1985 to 11 October 1989 for the Bourassa cabinet and from 8 March 2001 to 29 April 2003 for the Landry cabinet.

2 Significant at $p \le .01$.

3 Significant at $p \le .10$.

Sources: Québec, Assemblée nationale (1961, 1962).

Formally, eligibility no longer poses an obstacle to women, who have been able to run in provincial elections since 1940. Nor is it certain that election still poses serious difficulties to women, although this final step on the path towards exercise of legislative power has several dimensions. Here, two of these dimensions receive a closer look: the electorate and the voting system. As many studies on women's representation in other countries (notably, Inglehart and Norris 2003, 127-46) have shown, an egalitarian concept of gender roles has contributed to higher proportions of women in parliaments. In other words, the electorate does not discriminate against women candidates by not voting for them (see Hunter and Denton 1984). In Quebec, a recent study shows that the electorate is indifferent to the sex of

TABLE 10.9
Women party leaders in Quebec

Name	Political party	Period of service
Thérèse Casgrain	Parti social-démocratique du Québec	1951-57
Françoise David (co-leader)	Québec Solidaire	2006 to present
Pauline Marois	Parti québécois	2007 to present

candidates for election to the Assemblée nationale (Bélanger and Nadeau 2009, 69, 110; see also Pelletier and Tremblay 1992). However, this indifference has the consequence that the two parties with a female leader, the PQ (with leader Pauline Marois, premier of Quebec since September 2012) and the Québec Solidaire party (with co-leader Françoise David), do not benefit from greater support by women voters than men voters (Bélanger and Nadeau 2009, 110, 156).

A few words should be written about Françoise David and Pauline Marois, who, in 2013, were heads of Quebec political parties (see Table 10.9). A long-time activist in Quebec's women's movement and president of the Fédération des femmes du Québec from 1994 to 2001, Françoise David is co-leader and spokesperson for Québec Solidaire. Founded in 2006, QS defines itself as a left-wing, ecological, alter-globalist, sovereignist, and feminist party. However, David's failure to be elected to the Assemblée nationale du Québec in the 2008 election placed her in the shadow of Amir Khadir, the other co-leader of QS and its only representative in the Assemblée nationale. Events sometimes put feminist principles, notably that of equality of women and men, to a tough test, even in left-wing parties. That said, David was elected in the 2012 Quebec election, and a preliminary analysis suggests that she is no longer in the shadow of Khadir – now, the opposite may be true.

Pauline Marois is a pillar of parliamentary life in Quebec. A long-time activist in the Parti québécois, she was elected to the Assemblée nationale du Québec for the first time in 1981. Repeatedly appointed to PQ cabinets, Marois ran for leader of the sovereignist party in 1985 and 2005. Her defeat in 2005 to a much younger adversary with a more modest legislative and ministerial career than hers led many to believe that Quebec politics is not yet fully free from sexist attitudes towards women. And yet, following the crushing defeat of the PQ in the 2007 election, which forced the leader elected in 2005 to resign, Marois was asked to lead the party, confirming Trimble and Arscott's (2003, 76) observation: "Governing parties whose popularity is plummeting sometimes see a woman leader as their last hope." Now that Pauline Marois has returned the PQ to power, her challenge will be to win a majority government in the next election.

A key idea emerging from studies is that proportional voting systems would create a situation more favourable to the election of female candidates than do first-past-the-post systems (among others, MacIvor 2003; Matland 2005; Norris 2004, 179-208; Rule 1994). More and more researchers, however, contest the sometimes overblown impact attributed to proportional voting systems on the feminization of parliaments (Inglehart and Norris 2003, 141; Salmond 2006; Schmidt 2008; Tremblay 2012). Furthermore, the results of some studies challenge the idea that the first-past-the-post systems necessarily work against women candidates. In fact, a number of studies have shown that, as a general rule, female candidates for the PLQ and the PQ do not run in ridings in which their chances of victory are statistically different from those of male candidates (Pelletier and Tremblay 1992; Studlar and Matland 1996; Tremblay 2009). Nevertheless, when parties select the person who will represent their party in the riding on election day, activists are guided by an idealized concept of the "winning candidate," whose traits may correspond more to masculine gender roles than to women's experiences. An investigation of this possibility remains to be conducted in Quebec.

It seems that research has neglected the recruitment aspect – or candidate supply – as an explanatory factor for the low number of women in the Assemblée nationale du Québec. This factor is much more sensitive since it attributes part of the responsibility for their exclusion from political representation to women themselves. Although distressing, this possibility cannot be ignored. Of course, it is no longer realistic or credible to maintain that Quebec has a lack of women with the cultural, socio-economic, and political resources necessary for their nomination to be considered by parties. Today, women are in the majority among college and university student populations in Quebec, and more women than men earn a college diploma, bachelor's degree, or master's degree. What is more, greater numbers of women are in professional fields traditionally associated with a parliamentary career – particularly law, but also, in general, as members of regulated professions such as engineering, nursing, and social work (Québec, Conseil du statut de la femme 2010, 3, 7).

On the other hand, an explanation widely put forward – and apparently blindly endorsed – is that women tend not to enter politics because of their family responsibilities. Family may pose an obstacle to the political ambitions of *some* women, especially those who have young children at home. But the "family" argument cannot explain why more women without family responsibilities are not trying their hand at running for office. Here, the intention is not to deny the limiting role that the family may play in the political ambitions of *some* women but, rather, to question the explanatory power of the "family" argument – the contention that "family" regulates the lives of all women and all women are subject to "family" constraints (see also Fox and Lawless 2010). Brodie (1985, 79) argues that family is discursively constructed as an obstacle to women who seek political roles. In other words, it is the societal expectations of women as wives and mothers rather than the actual day-to-day performance of these roles that is the barrier. The "family responsibilities explanation" has become virtually hegemonic for explaining the low proportion of women in politics; it needs to be qualified and examined critically.

Similarly, recruitment, or the supply of female candidates, as an explanation of the low numbers of women in the Quebec parliament needs to be subjected to critical examination and further research. In a study conducted from 2000 to 2005 among a sample of American and Canadian women, Gidengil, Giles, and Thomas (2008) observed that college-educated women did not manifest as much confidence in their capacity to understand politics as did college-educated men. There is no doubt that one must feel strongly that one has political skills in order to aspire to legislative representation. Although this study was conducted on a nation-wide scale (Canada and the United States), there is no reason to think that women in Quebec are any different in this respect.

Conclusion: Prospects for Gender Equality

The premise of this chapter is that representation by women in the Assemblée nationale du Québec is hitting a glass ceiling. In fact, since the beginning of the 2000s, the proportion of female representatives has stagnated at about 30 percent. On the other hand, parity in the cabinet has been close to a reality since 2007, although this target has slipped with the Marois government. This gap between the legislative and executive branches (albeit reduced by the 2012 election results) compels a reconsideration of the indictment of political parties as responsible for the low numbers of women in politics. In fact, the parties are not monolithic entities, and the gap in feminization rates between the legislature and the cabinet, particularly starting in the mid-1990s, might evoke the thought that the leadership is more forward-thinking than the activist base. Put simply, a premier who wants women in the cabinet has the power to appoint them, but a leader can neither select the female candidates for her or his party nor cause them to be elected to the Assemblée nationale du Québec.

As a consequence, parity between women and men in the Assemblée nationale du Québec seems to be only on the distant horizon. Up to now, researchers have apparently neglected to explore seriously how recruitment (or supply of candidates) may contribute to this situation. A better understanding of why there are fewer female than male candidates, and of the expectations of activists when they select the person who will run for election for their party in their riding, invites future inquiry. It would be useful to identify the resistance, by the state and by parties, to adoption of measures to encourage women to run in elections. A new research avenue would be to explore the reasons that women who present all the assets for entering politics are simply not interested in the electoral and parliamentary adventure. Could it be that politics is an arena for male performativity (that is to say, a space created by and for men, whose discourses and practices re/produce male identity) that, in turn, reinforces male dominance of that space? Perhaps. If so, women are unsurprisingly less likely to be interested in, and to identify themselves with, politics than are men.

Notes

1 The term "Quebec parliament" is used synonymously with "Assemblée nationale du Québec."
2 That is, eight women ministers out of twenty-three ministers (35 percent).

References

Bélanger, Éric, and Richard Nadeau. 2009. *Le comportement électoral des Québécois.* Montreal: Presses de l'Université de Montréal.

Brodie, Janine. 1985. *Women and Politics in Canada.* Toronto: McGraw-Hill Ryerson.

Fox, Richard L., and Jennifer L. Lawless. 2010. "If Only They'd Ask: Gender, Recruitment, and Political Ambition." *Journal of Politics* 72(2): 310-26.

Gagné, Gilles, and Simon Langlois. 2002. *Les raisons fortes: Nature et signification de l'appui à la souveraineté du Québec.* Montreal: Presses de l'Université de Montréal.

Gidengil, Elisabeth, Janine Giles, and Melanee Thomas. 2008. "The Gender Gap in Self-Perceived Understanding of Politics in Canada and the United States." *Politics and Gender* 4(4): 535-61.

Hunter, Alfred A., and Margaret A. Denton. 1984. "Do Female Candidates 'Lose Votes'? The Experience of Female Candidates in the 1979 and 1980 Canadian General Elections." *Canadian Review of Sociology and Anthropology* 21(4): 395-406.

Inglehart, Ronald, and Pippa Norris. 2003. *Rising Tide: Gender Equality and Cultural Change around the World.* Cambridge: Cambridge University Press.

Kerby, Matthew. 2009. "Worth the Wait: Determinants of Ministerial Appointment in Canada, 1935-2008." *Canadian Journal of Political Science* 42(3): 593-611.

MacIvor, Heather. 2003. "Women and the Canadian Electoral System." In Manon Tremblay and Linda Trimble, eds., *Women and Electoral Politics in Canada,* 22-36. Don Mills: Oxford University Press.

Massicotte, Louis. 2009. "Le pouvoir exécutif: La monarchie, le premier ministre et les ministres." In Réjean Pelletier and Manon Tremblay, eds., *Le parlementarisme canadien,* 4th rev. and expanded ed., 379-415. Quebec City: Presses de l'Université Laval.

Matland, Richard E. 2005. "Enhancing Women's Political Participation: Legislative Recruitment and Electoral Systems." In Julie Ballington and Azza Karam, eds., *Women in Parliament: Beyond Numbers,* rev. ed., 93-111. Stockholm: International IDEA.

Norris, Pippa. 2004. *Electoral Engineering. Voting Rules and Political Behavior.* Cambridge: Cambridge University Press.

Pelletier, Réjean, and Manon Tremblay. 1992. "Les femmes sont-elles candidates dans des circonscriptions perdues d'avance? De l'examen d'une croyance." *Canadian Journal of Political Science* 25(2): 249-67.

Québec, Assemblée nationale. N.d.(a). *La présence féminine.* Available at http://www.assnat.qc.ca/.

—. N.d.(b). *La répartition des sièges aux élections générales.* Available at http://www.assnat.qc.ca/.

—. 1961. *Les femmes parlementaires depuis 1961.* Available at http://www.assnat.qc.ca/.

—. 1962. *Nombre de ministres dans les cabinets et la représentation féminine depuis 1962.* Available at http://www.assnat.qc.ca/.

Québec, Conseil du statut de la femme. 2010. *Portrait des Québécoises en 8 temps.* Québec: CSF. Available at http://www.csf.gouv.qc.ca/.

Québec, Directeur général des élections. 2007. *Candidatures féminines lors des élections générales du 26 mars 2007.* Available at http://www.electionsquebec.qc.ca/.

—. 2008. *Candidatures féminines lors des élections générales du 8 décembre 2008.* Available at http://www.electionsquebec.qc.ca/.

—. 2012. *Candidatures féminines lors des élections générales du 4 septembre 2012.* Available at http://www.electionsquebec.qc.ca/.

Rule, Wilma. 1994. "Parliaments of, by, and for the People: Except for Women?" In Wilma Rule and Joseph F. Zimmerman, eds., *Electoral Systems in Comparative Perspective: Their Impact on Women and Minorities,* 15-30. Westport: Greenwood Press.

Salmond, Rob. 2006. "Proportional Representation and Female Parliamentarians." *Legislative Studies Quarterly* 31(2): 175-204.

Schmidt, Gregory D. 2008. "The Election of Women in List PR Systems: Testing the Conventional Wisdom." *Electoral Studies* 28(2): 190-203.

Studlar, Donley T., and Richard E. Matland. 1996. "The Dynamics of Women's Representation in the Canadian Provinces: 1975-1994." *Canadian Journal of Political Science* 29(2): 269-93.

Tremblay, Manon. 2008. *100 questions sur les femmes et la politique*. Montreal: Remue-ménage.

–. 2009. "Women in the Quebec Assemblée nationale: Why So Many?" In Sylvia Bashevkin, ed., *Opening Doors Wider: Women's Political Engagement in Canada*, 51-69. Vancouver: UBC Press.

–. 2010. *Quebec Women and Legislative Representation*. Vancouver: UBC Press.

–. 2012. Introduction. In Manon Tremblay, ed., *Women and Legislative Representation: Electoral Systems, Political Parties, and Sex Quotas*, 1-22. Revised and updated. New York: Palgrave Macmillan.

Tremblay, Manon, and Réjean Pelletier. 1995. *Que font-elles en politique?* Ste-Foy: Presses de l'Université Laval.

Trimble, Linda, and Jane Arscott. 2003. *Still Counting: Women in Politics across Canada*, Peterborough: Broadview Press.

White, Graham. 2005. *Cabinets and First Ministers*. Vancouver: UBC Press.

11

A Prairie Plateau
Women in Saskatchewan Politics

LOLEEN BERDAHL

Saskatchewan has a long history of progressive social policy and socialism. In addition to pioneering universal health care in Canada (1946), Saskatchewan was the first Canadian government to pass human rights legislation (1947), was the first province to adopt multiculturalism legislation (1974), and was among the first provinces to establish an office for the advancement of women (1964; Braun and Quinney 2006). The Co-operative Commonwealth Federation (CCF) achieved some its greatest electoral successes in Saskatchewan, and between 1944 and 2010, the CCF and its successor, the New Democratic Party, held power for forty-seven years – or 70 percent of the time. It is no wonder that Saskatchewan "is widely viewed as the cradle of Canadian social democracy" (Wesley 2011, 1).

However, decades of social democratic governments have not resulted in above-average numerical representation for women. As of the 2011 election, women hold fewer than one-fifth of Saskatchewan's legislative seats and cabinet positions, and both of the major party leaders are male. Although Saskatchewan has boasted a number of women's "political firsts," including Canada's first female president of a Canadian political party (Gladys Strum, president of the CCF in 1944), Canada's first female finance minister (Janice MacKinnon, NDP, 1993-97), and Canada's first female Aboriginal cabinet minister (Joan Beatty, NDP, 2003-7), the province has never had a female premier. Furthermore, while women's legislative and cabinet representation grew in the early 1980s and then again in the early 1990s, since then women's

POLITICAL REPRESENTATION OF WOMEN IN
SASKATCHEWAN

FIRSTS

Right to vote and stand for election

- Most women win the right to vote and stand for election — 1916
- Aboriginal women win the right to vote and stand for election — 1960

Contesting office

- First woman to contest office: Zoa Haight (Non-Partisan League) — 1917
- First woman to win office: Sarah Ramsland (Liberal) — 1919-25
- First Aboriginal woman to win office: Joan Beatty (NDP) — 2003-8
- First women appointed to cabinet: Joan Duncan (PC), minister of government services and revenue, minister of supply and services; Patricia Smith (PC), minister of social services — 1982-89 / 1982-83

CURRENT REPRESENTATION AT A GLANCE

		Women elected	
	Date of election	Number	Percent
Women in legislature	2011/11/07	11 of 58	19
Women in cabinet	2011/11/07	3 of 18	17

Women political party leaders

- None at present

Lieutenant governor

- Vaughn Solomon Schofield, 2012 to present

Advisory council on the status of women

- Status of Women Office, 2002 to present
- Women's Secretariat, 1984-2002

representation has plateaued below the one-quarter mark. This plateau is puzzling, as research in other jurisdictions finds that women's legislative representation typically increases with the success of social democratic parties (McGrane 2008). Why has this not been the case in Saskatchewan?

This chapter argues that the numerical under-representation of women in the Saskatchewan legislature has three causes: the reluctance of Saskatchewan women to enter electoral politics, political parties' inattention (or inconsistent attention) to increasing the number of female candidates, and the weakness of organized feminism in the province in recent decades. I begin by examining the history of women's legislative representation and then explain the persistent under-representation of women in the Saskatchewan legislature. I conclude by considering the short-term prospects for change.

Background

To understand women's electoral representation in Saskatchewan, it is critical to first understand the provincial context. Until the election of the CCF in 1944, the centrist Liberal Party dominated Saskatchewan provincial politics (Smith 1975, 324). After 1944, Saskatchewan had a classic two-party system, with the CCF/NDP opposed by the Liberal Party until the late 1970s and by the Progressive Conservative Party until the early 1990s. The party system went through a period of adjustment in the 1990s: after the defeat of Grant Devine's Progressive Conservatives, the PCs had very limited electoral viability. The Liberal Party struggled to rebuild, and although the Liberals formed the Official Opposition after the 1995 election, internal conflicts limited the party's prospects. Overall, then, neither the Liberals nor the PCs presented a viable alternative to the governing NDP in the early- to mid-1990s. The electoral landscape changed in 1997, when former PC and Liberal party members united to create the Saskatchewan Party. This new party was quickly recognized as the Official Opposition and presented a true electoral challenge to the NDP; indeed, after the 1999 election, the NDP required the support of the three Liberal MLAs to retain power. Since this time, Saskatchewan has had a two-party system; while the Progressive Conservative and Liberal parties continue to exist, neither has elected representatives since the turn of the century.

Broadly speaking, in the decades since 1944, the CCF/NDP were more often than not the electoral victors: together, the CCF/NDP have been referred to as "North America's most successful socialist parties," and the NDP has been labelled Saskatchewan's "natural governing party" (Wesley 2011, 115, 173). The CCF/NDP's electoral dominance, combined with the changes in opposition parties over the years, has meant that the CCF/NDP has been critical in setting the tone for women's electoral representation in Saskatchewan. Further, the fact that Saskatchewan typically has had a two-party system may have limited the opportunities for women's candidacy and election.

Saskatchewan's history as an agricultural economy is also relevant to provincial politics. Although Saskatchewan currently has a more diversified economy, with strong mining (potash and uranium) and energy (oil and gas) sectors, agriculture was the core of the Saskatchewan economy for much of the province's history. Women were integral to agrarian labour and entered the paid labour force more slowly than women in many other provinces (McGrane 2008), a fact that may have shaped the emergence and tone of organized feminism in the province. The agricultural economy also meant that the province urbanized at a slower rate than did many other Canadian provinces, and Saskatchewan remains less urbanized than many other provinces in Canada. As of the 2011 census, only 46 percent of Saskatchewan residents lived in one of Saskatchewan's two Census Metropolitan Areas (CMAs) – Regina (pop. 210,556) and Saskatoon (pop. 260,600) – while 33 percent (343,398) of the Saskatchewan population was classified as rural (Saskatchewan Bureau of Statistics 2012). This less urbanized provincial makeup is reflected in the legislature, although it should be noted that Saskatchewan electoral law places strict limits on deviations from provincial electoral quotients in the construction of electoral boundaries (Blake 2001, 10) and that, as a result, rural areas are not over-represented in the provincial legislature (Blake 2006).

Women's Political Representation: The Numbers

It has taken Saskatchewan women a long time to establish their presence in the provincial legislature. Indeed, in the first six and a half decades after women received the right to stand for office, only ten women *in total* were elected as members of the Legislative Assembly (see Table 11.1). Sarah Katherine Ramsland, Saskatchewan's first female MLA, was elected in a by-election in 1919, replacing her deceased husband; she retained her seat in the 1921 election. After the election of Ramsland, the province experienced a drought in female representation: between 1925 and 1952, there was only one female MLA, and she served only one term (Beatrice Janet Trew, 1944-48). Women's representation improved somewhat after 1952, and the Legislative Assembly had at least one female member at all times between 1952 and 1967 (reaching a high of three MLAs, or 5 percent of the legislature, in the 1960 election). However, these gains were short-lived: there were no female MLAs between 1967 and 1975, and while two women were elected in 1975, there was only one female MLA after the 1978 election. Thus, although the CCF/NDP ruled for over thirty years between 1944 and

TABLE 11.1

Women in the Saskatchewan legislature, by election

Election date	Party elected	Total number of legislators	Women elected	
			Number	%
1917/06/26	Liberal	59	0	0
1921/06/09	Liberal	63	1	2
1925/06/02	Liberal	63	0	0
1929/06/06	Conservative-Progressive alliance	63	0	0
1934/06/19	Liberal	55	0	0
1938/06/08	Liberal	52	0	0
1944/06/15	CCF	52	1	2
1948/06/24	CCF	52	0	0
1952/06/11	CCF	53	1	2
1956/06/20	CCF	53	2	4
1960/06/06	CCF	55	3	6
1964/04/22	Liberal	59	2	3
1967/10/11	Liberal	59	0	0
1971/06/23	NDP	60	0	0
1975/06/11	NDP	61	2	3
1978/10/18	NDP	61	1	2
1982/04/26	PC	64	5	8
1986/10/20	PC	64	5	8
1991/10/21	NDP	66	12	18
1995/06/21	NDP	58	13	22
1999/09/16	NDP	58	13	22
2003/11/05	NDP	58	11	19
2007/11/07	Saskatchewan Party	58	13	22
2011/11/07	Saskatchewan Party	58	11	19

Source: Legislative Assembly of Saskatchewan (2009).

1982, the presence of social democratic politics was not accompanied by a strong political role for women – a fact that was not altered by the emergence of the women's movement in the 1960s and 1970s.

After this very slow start, women's presence in the legislature began to build in the 1980s. It took the election of a new PC government to usher in a new era for women in politics: PC women won five seats in the 1982 election, raising the proportion of women in the legislature to 8 percent. (The NDP did not elect a single female MLA in this election.) Further, Grant Devine's

PC government included the province's first female cabinet ministers. The increased political presence of women, it must be noted, did not reflect a new feminist politics in the province: McGrane (2008, 192) specifies a number of cuts to "women's issues" by the Devine government, including cuts to daycare, women's shelters, and rape crisis centres; further, "the Conservative female MLAs were publicly anti-feminist, and several were members of a conservative women's group called REAL Women."

The second large advance in women's numerical representation occurred almost a decade later. In 1991, the NDP returned to power, and again a change in government resulted in a dramatic increase in women's legislative presence. In 1991, the number of female MLAs more than doubled to twelve (18 percent of the seats), and, just as in 1982, all of the elected women were in the new governing party. The number of female representatives increased by one, to thirteen, in the 1995 election; this, combined with a reduction in the number of total seats in the legislature, increased the proportion of women to 22 percent. The 1995 result set the high-water mark, and Saskatchewan has yet to exceed thirteen women in the legislature; indeed, numbers dropped in 2003 (eleven women elected, or 19 percent), rebounded in the 2007 election, and then dropped again in 2011. At present, women's legislative representation in Saskatchewan remains below 20 percent. Simply put, after two decades, the numerical representation of women in the Saskatchewan legislature remains largely unchanged.

The proportion of women in the governing caucus has also not changed dramatically in the past decades. In 1982, when the Progressive Conservatives swept to power, the five PC women comprised 9 percent of the governing caucus. The proportion of women in the governing caucus jumped to 20 percent with the 1991 NDP watershed. In 1999, women made up 28 percent of the governing caucus, but it should be noted that this growth reflects a reduction in the total number of NDP MLAs elected rather than an increased number of female government members. After the election of the Saskatchewan Party in 2007, the proportion of women in the governing caucus echoed 1991 levels: 21 percent of Saskatchewan Party MLAs were women. Following the 2011 election, only 18 percent of the Saskatchewan Party MLAs are women, and this change reflects a significant increase in the size of the governing caucus.

The pattern in women's legislative representation roughly parallels women's candidacies for the major political parties. In 1982, 8 percent of candidates for electorally viable parties and 8 percent of the elected MLAs

TABLE 11.2
Women candidates in Saskatchewan, by party and election

Election date	PC		NDP		Saskatchewan Party		Liberal	
	Number	%	Number	%	Number	%	Number	%
1982/04/26	5 of 64	8	5 of 64	8	–		–	
1986/10/20	4 of 64	6	11 of 64	17	–		15 of 64	23
1991/10/21	9 of 66	14	14 of 66	21	–		13 of 66	20
1995/06/21	9 of 58	16	13 of 58	22	–		12 of 58	21
1999/09/16	–		14 of 58	24	14 of 58	24	7 of 58	12
2003/11/05	–		10 of 58	17	11 of 58	19	–	
2007/11/07	–		13 of 58	22	13 of 57	23	–	
2011/11/07	–		13 of 58	22	10 of 58	17	–	

Note: Table includes only those parties that elected at least one member to the legislature.

were female. Although there were more female candidates (16 percent) in the 1986 election, the proportion of female MLAs did not rise until the 1991 election, in which 18 percent of candidates for electorally viable parties were female; it was the combination of increased female candidacies and the change in government that resulted in the jump in the number of women MLAs at this time. Since 1991, the proportion of female candidates has ranged from a low of 18 percent (2003 election) to a high of 22 percent (2007 election).

The NDP has not significantly increased its number of female candidates over the 1991 levels; indeed, women continue to account for less than one-quarter of NDP candidates. One might expect the NDP's centre (Liberal) and centre-right (Saskatchewan Party) opponents to be less likely to prioritize women's legislative representation. However, it is interesting to note that the NDP's opponents generally matched the party's female candidate levels in the 1990s and 2000s: in the 1990s, the Liberal Party had the same number of female candidates as did the NDP (although the struggling right-of-centre Progressive Conservative Party did not), and from its first election in 1999 until the 2007 election, the Saskatchewan Party has had a similar number of female candidates as the NDP. As a result, the removal of the NDP from office in 2007 did not result in lower levels of legislative representation for women.[1]

Women have also had a limited role in Saskatchewan political leadership, and women's leadership trajectories in Saskatchewan reflect the "no one else

TABLE 11.3

Women party leaders in Saskatchewan political parties with legislative representation during tenure as leader

Name	Political party	Period of service
Lynda Haverstock	Saskatchewan Liberal Party	1989-95
Iris Dennis	PC	1997-2006

Source: Personal communication with Saskatchewan Legislative Library, 13 December 2010.

wants the job" pattern seen in many other provinces (Trimble and Arscott 2008). Five women have served as party leaders for Saskatchewan provincial parties, and in each case the woman assumed the leadership of a political party with highly limited electoral prospects (see Table 11.3). Lynda Haverstock, the first female party leader in Saskatchewan, revived the nearly defunct Liberal Party, taking it from zero seats when she assumed the leadership to eleven seats by 1995; further, by the 1995 election she had helped to increase the party's share of the popular vote to its highest levels since 1971 (Haverstock 2001, 235). Yet, despite bringing her party to Official Opposition status, in November 1995 – just five months after the 1995 election – Haverstock faced considerable caucus dissension and resigned from leadership, spending the remainder of her term as an "Independent Liberal" (238). According to Trimble and Arscott (2008, 78), Haverstock implied that "gender-differentiated expectations for politicians ... had a good deal to do with her decision to resign."

Haverstock is the only woman to have led a party with representation in the Saskatchewan legislature. The other four female party leaders have had considerably less success. Iris Dennis served as the leader of the electorally marginal Progressive Conservative Party for almost ten years, and the Green Party of Saskatchewan, which has yet to elect an MLA, has had three different female leaders since 2006: Sandra Finley, Amber Jones, and Larissa Shasko. It should be noted that the NDP's Janice MacKinnon was considered a potential party leader contender when Premier Roy Romanow stepped down. MacKinnon was Canada's first female minister of finance, a top minister in the Romanow cabinet, and remains the only woman to serve as government house leader in Saskatchewan. MacKinnon chose not to run for the party leadership;[2] had she successfully contested the leadership, she would have been the first Saskatchewan woman to assume the leadership of an electorally viable party and would have been Saskatchewan's first female premier. To date, these "firsts" have not been realized in the province.

TABLE 11.4
Women in cabinet in Saskatchewan, by election

Election date	Party elected	Total number of cabinet ministers*	Women appointed to to cabinet		% of women in governing caucus in cabinet
			Number	%	
1982/04/26	PC	17	2	12	40
1986/10/20	PC	16	2	13	100
1991/10/21	NDP	11	4	36	36
1995/06/21	NDP	15	2	13	20
1999/09/16	NDP	19	5	26	63
2003/11/05	NDP	17	4	24	57
2007/11/07	Saskatchewan Party	18	4	22	50
2011/11/07	Saskatchewan Party	18	3	17	33

* Includes the premier.
Source: Legislative Assembly of Saskatchewan (2010).

Just as women's legislative numbers and candidacy rates have stagnated, so too has the growth in the number of women in cabinet (see Table 11.4). As noted earlier, the 1982 election resulted not only in the election of a record number of women (five) but also in the appointment of Saskatchewan's first female cabinet ministers. Progressive Conservative premier Grant Devine appointed two women to his cabinet after both the 1982 and 1986 elections. Women's cabinet representation doubled to four after the election of Roy Romanow's NDP government in 1991. Due to the small size of the cabinet, women held over one-third of the cabinet seats – a proportion that has not been seen since. The gains in cabinet representation were short-lived, however, as only two women were given positions in the NDP cabinet immediately after the 1995 election. Since the 1999 election, women have accounted for roughly one-quarter of cabinet seats; this proportion did not change with the election of the Saskatchewan Party government in 2007 but did decline with the re-election of the Saskatchewan Party in 2011. Overall, for the past decade, women's representation in cabinet has been relatively proportionate to women's representation in the legislature and in the governing caucus. Indeed, after the 2011 election, 18 percent of the governing caucus, 19 percent of the legislature, and 17 percent of the cabinet were women.

Finally, it should be noted that three women have been appointed as lieutenant governor in Saskatchewan. Prior to being appointed by Prime

TABLE 11.5

Female representatives of the Crown in Saskatchewan

Name	Period of service
Sylvia O. Fedoruk	1988-94
Lynda M. Haverstock	2000-6
Vaughn Solomon Schofield	2012 to present

Source: Lieutenant Governor of Saskatchewan (2006).

Minister Brian Mulroney in 1988, physicist Sylvia Fedoruk was the first fe-male chancellor of the University of Saskatchewan. In 2000, Prime Minister Jean Chrétien appointed former Saskatchewan Liberal Party leader Lynda Haverstock as Saskatchewan's second female lieutenant governor, and in 2012 Prime Minister Stephen Harper appointed Vaughn Solomon Schofield, an active community leader, as Saskatchewan's third woman in the post.

To summarize, women's numerical representation in Saskatchewan pol-itics increased in the 1980s and then again in the 1990s but has been at a relative standstill for the past two decades.

Explanations

In Saskatchewan, the proportion of female candidates for the electorally vi-able parties has translated closely into the proportion of women in the legis-lature, which in turn has translated into the proportion of women in cabinet. Thus, in order to understand the plateau in the women's legislative and cab-inet representation, we must ask why the number of female candidates has remained largely unchanged since 1991. Three factors seem most relevant: a low supply of female candidates, the lack of aggressive political party efforts to recruit women candidates, and the lack of external pressures on political parties for increased women's representation.

Low Supply of Female Candidates

As Carbert (2006, 9) explains: "An absence is never easy to investigate. Asking why a riding association did *not* choose a woman as its candidate is not really about the closed-door vote that completed the nomination pro-cess. In many cases there simply was no woman to vote for at that meeting." Thus, it may be "that some women might be excluding themselves" (10). This appears to be an important factor in Saskatchewan. Former premier Roy Romanow reports that the NDP faced numerous challenges in recruiting fe-male candidates in the 1990s. In particular, family and personal obligations, as well as the often combative nature of political debate, prevented women from running for office (Roy Romanow, personal interview, 15 March 2011). The problems persist: in 2010, Premier Brad Wall was quoted as saying that attracting female candidates "has always been a problem"; similarly, the NDP reported that potential female candidates cite numerous obstacles that deter them from running (Hall and Wood 2010).

Why are Saskatchewan women less likely to enter electoral politics? There are a number of socio-demographic barriers that must be acknowledged. Although the province's agricultural economy initially limited women's labour market participation, Saskatchewan women now enjoy a high level of labour market integration: Saskatchewan women have employment rates that are higher than the national average (61.8 percent in 2009, compared to the national average of 58.3 percent) (Ferrao 2010, 6). Yet, despite strong employment rates, Saskatchewan women's total income as a percentage of men's was 62 percent in 2008 (Williams 2010, 7, as calculated by author), and women's average employment income (before taxes) as a percentage of men's was 59 percent in 2006 (Sask Trends Monitor 2010b).

Gender segregation in education and employment may also present a barrier to women's electoral participation. Although Saskatchewan women were more likely than men to be postsecondary graduates in 2006, men and women differed strongly in their fields of study, with 72 percent of female and 25 percent of male postsecondary graduates holding degrees, diplomas, or certificates in fields such as education, health, public administration, and management, and 4 percent of female and 51 percent of male postsecondary graduates holding degrees, diplomas, and certificates in fields such as engineering, agriculture, and natural resources (Sask Trends Monitor 2010a). The differences continue into careers: women are more likely than men to work in the public sector, and they strongly dominate the health and social assistance sectors (Sask Trends Monitor 2010d). Research suggests that women, even those with a high level of professional accomplishment, are less likely than men to consider themselves qualified for public office (Fox and Lawless 2004). It is possible that public service career paths, which may be perceived as less aggressive and competitive than private-sector careers, contribute to women's underestimating their qualifications for public office.

Research also suggests that family structures and personal responsibilities can be important barriers to some women who attempt to enter politics. As in many other jurisdictions, Saskatchewan women report more hours than do men performing unpaid tasks such as caring for children and seniors and performing house work, and they also report more volunteer hours (Sask Trends Monitor 2010d). Women are also more likely than men to be lone parents, with four out of five Saskatchewan lone-parent families being headed by women in 2006 (Sask Trends Monitor 2010c). Interviews with female MLAs from both the Saskatchewan Party and the New Democratic Party reveal that many potential female candidates cite family considerations as a key barrier to entering political life. In the words of one interviewee (7 January 2011): "For women, entering politics is a family decision, not just a personal decision." Elected political life, it is suggested, is not compatible with the raising of minor children, which may deter some women.

Aboriginal women in particular face considerable personal challenges in entering politics. Compared to non-Aboriginal women, Aboriginal women in Saskatchewan are younger, less educated, more mobile, less likely to participate in the labour force, more likely to be unemployed, more likely to have incomes below the low income cut-off level, and more likely to be lone parents (Saskatchewan Status of Women Office 2009). Further, Aboriginal women may face additional barriers to achieving electoral candidacy. As Tremblay (2003, 35) writes: "It is possible to argue – with little risk of being wrong – that Aboriginal women have more trouble getting through the selection process to become a political party's official candidate than women from the non-Aboriginal majority, because of the combined weight of racism and sexism." Almost 15 percent of the Saskatchewan population is Aboriginal, and the under-representation of women as candidates in Canada is greater for the Aboriginal population than for the general population (Smith 2005). However, as 47 percent of the Aboriginal population is aged nineteen or younger (2006 Census data; Saskatchewan Bureau of Statistics n.d.), the influence of the Aboriginal population on women's overall candidacy levels in Saskatchewan should not be overstated.

An additional barrier for women may be the province's lower rate of urbanization. Carbert argues that the numerical under-representation of women in Canadian politics can be linked to the fact that women are less likely to run for office in rural areas. As she observes: "The dearth of female candidates is much more extreme in rural areas" (Carbert 2006, 9). The 2007 provincial election suggests support for this. In the 2007 provincial election, 14 percent of major party candidates in Saskatchewan's twenty-one rural ridings and 35 percent of major party candidates in the province's thirty-four urban and urban-rural hybrid ridings were female. While rural areas are not over-represented in the Saskatchewan legislature, the fact that Saskatchewan is less urbanized than some other provinces makes the low proportion of female candidates in rural areas a relevant factor.

Overall, socio-demographic barriers may help to explain why so few Saskatchewan women enter provincial politics. An additional factor to consider is the province's political culture. McGrane (2008, 181) argues that Saskatchewan has a persistent "patriarchal political culture that sees women as subjects occupying traditional roles of mother and wife and that discourages women's participation in the political sphere." And Michael Adams (2003, 85) finds that Saskatchewan (as well as Alberta and Manitoba) residents hold more traditional family and gender role beliefs than do residents of other provinces. While such a political culture is likely not unique to Saskatchewan (see, for example, O'Neill and Erickson 2003) the province's more traditional political culture might contribute to the low number of Saskatchewan women entering provincial politics. It must be noted that the interview respondents stated that Saskatchewan women cite the combative tone of political life and the lack of privacy due to media attention directed at political candidates as additional reasons for not entering political life.

Political Parties

Saskatchewan's political parties have not aggressively sought to increase the number of women candidates. One might expect that the NDP, as a social democratic party, would lead in promoting women's legislative representation. However, Hayford (2006) writes that, in the 1970s and 1980s, "the NDP leadership was not supportive of women who stepped outside auxiliary roles and [was] ambivalent about such important issues as access to abortion and support for daycare." This ambivalence demonstrates that, although left-of-centre parties are typically viewed as being more favourable to feminism and women in politics, it is important to consider individual parties within their historical and political context. In the Saskatchewan case, McGrane (2008, 181) reports that NDP members, including the Saskatchewan New Democratic Women (SNDW), have emphasized a more limited liberal feminism over socialist or radical feminism. This more cautious feminism prevented the party from taking stronger positions on women's representation and other feminist issues. This approach changed in 1991, when the NDP placed emphasis on increasing the number of female candidates. According to former premier Roy Romanow (personal interview, 15 March 2011), the party sought to increase the diversity of its candidates more broadly and deliberately recruited women and other less represented groups to run for office. These efforts were rewarded with a doubling of the number of female MLAs. However, Romanow reports that the party had trouble attracting new candidates (male and female) for the 1995 election, and the government's workload, particularly with respect to fiscal restructuring, resulted in less attention to gender parity issues after the 1995 election. It should also be noted that some have accused the NDP of being hostile to feminists within the party during the 1990s and 2000s (Smart 1992; Ruddy 2007, 148; Wagner 2009).[3]

In recent years, both the Saskatchewan Party and NDP leaders have asserted that increasing women's legislative representation is a priority for their party. Premier Brad Wall has stated: "We work at it, I work at it, almost every day to recruit women to run in seats where we're very competitive" (Hall and Wood 2010). And during his successful NDP leadership campaign, Dwain Lingenfelter (2009) proclaimed that the under-representation of women as candidates "is unacceptable in the 21st century" and that ensuring gender parity "is critical to the New Democratic Party's chances of defeating the right-wing Wall Government."

The two parties have adopted different approaches to increase the number of female candidates. The Saskatchewan Party does not have targets or quotas for the number of female candidates, and it does not have funds available to potential female candidates; instead, it places emphasis on individual candidate recruitment on a case-by-case basis as well as on informal mentoring.[4] The NDP does not have gender quotas for candidates but recently established a target: the party passed a resolution put forward by the SNDW at its March 2008 convention to "work toward the goal of nominating women in 50 percent of the constituencies for the 2011 provincial election" (McIntyre 2008). Further, the SNDW has made a number of efforts to engage or assist potential women candidates, including creating a database of potential female candidates, drafting a nomination manual, providing modest ($400) funding support to women seeking nominations through the Bessie Ellis Fund, establishing a mentorship program and hosting an "election school." Neither the Saskatchewan Party's nor the New Democratic Party's approach has worked to date: the NDP did not increase its number of female candidates in the 2011 election, while the Saskatchewan Party had fewer female candidates than it did in 2007.

Research in the United States demonstrates that women are less likely than men to be recruited to run for political office (Fox and Lawless 2010).

The fact that Saskatchewan political parties have not to date aggressively sought to increase the number of female candidates plays a significant role in explaining the low numerical representation of women in the Saskatchewan legislature.

External Pressures

The relatively low priority that Saskatchewan political parties place on women's legislative representation may reflect a lack of external pressures to do things differently. Relative to some other provinces, organized feminism is weak in Saskatchewan. Hayford (2006) reports that Saskatchewan feminism has faced a number of challenges over the years: in the 1970s, feminists were indecisive about the need for organization; in the 1980s, feminism and women's issues were under attack by the Progressive Conservative government; and by the 1990s, after the re-election of the NDP, "feminism [had] little public presence [in Saskatchewan]." Similarly, Leger-Anderson (2006) writes:

> As for women's organizations, once a source of women's influence (albeit limited), they have been overshadowed by complex economic, social, and cultural transformation. Membership fell in established organizations, urban and rural, as women took jobs, developed new interests and needs, or simply aged. Emergent organizations were likely to focus primarily upon interests of identifiable segments of women, for example: Aboriginal women's groups, Immigrant, Refugee, and Visible Minority Women of Saskatchewan, Elizabeth Fry Society, or Women Entrepreneurs of Saskatchewan.

The limited feminist movement in the province has resulted in less pressure on the political parties to promote women's political representation (McGrane 2008) and less public attention to the issue.

Feminist organizing is re-emerging in the province: in 2008, the Prairie Lily Feminist Society (2009, 6) was established to create a new voice for Saskatchewan feminists, and the organization hosted workshops on women and politics in 2009 and in 2010. In addition, Equal Voice, the multi-partisan non-profit group that promotes women in Canadian electoral politics, launched its Saskatchewan chapter in summer 2011; and University of Saskatchewan students launched a student initiative, Women in the Legislature, in fall 2011. Given these developments, the external pressures on the political parties to increase the number of female candidates will likely increase in the years ahead.

Conclusion: Prospects for Gender Parity

The Saskatchewan experience demonstrates that the presence of strong social democratic parties and long periods of social democratic governments do not necessarily translate into gender equity in political representation. Despite decades of CCF/NDP governments, women remain numerically under-represented in the Saskatchewan legislature. Indeed, women's representation in the Saskatchewan legislature has changed significantly only twice: with the election of the Progressive Conservatives in 1982 and the election of the NDP in 1991. In both cases, the new governing party won a landslide victory and set a new "plateau" level for women's legislative representation.

What can explain the puzzle of low female representation in the Saskatchewan legislature? This chapter suggests three causes: (1) Saskatchewan women may be excluding themselves from electoral politics due to socio-demographic barriers and the province's more traditional political culture; (2) political parties have not prioritized women's electoral representation; and (2) until recently there has been limited feminist pressure on the political parties to increase the numerical representation of women.

Given these realities, will the Saskatchewan legislature achieve "critical mass" (over 30 percent of legislative seats held by women) in the near future? Prospects for this are dim. As noted earlier, in the November 2011 election the Saskatchewan Party failed to match its number of female candidates for the 2007 election, and despite its 2008 resolution and the SNDW's efforts, the NDP not only failed to meet its goal of 50 percent female candidates for the 2011 election but also failed in its efforts to increase its number of female candidates above the 2007 election level. Given the importance of candidate numbers to women's representation in Saskatchewan, it is not surprising that the number of female MLAs decreased. That being said, given that significant changes in women's legislative representation have occurred in "watershed" changes of government, if the NDP is able to realize success in its goal for gender parity in candidacies, the party has the potential to change the gender composition of the legislature in the future.

Experience demonstrates that Saskatchewan is unlikely to achieve legislative gender parity through incremental change. Given the low priority placed on the issue in the province, the prairie plateau in women's legislative representation is likely to persist for some time to come.

Notes

I would like to thank David McGrane for his comments on an earlier draft of this chapter, Kelton Doraty and Tara Longmire for their research assistance, Elections Saskatchewan and the Saskatchewan Legislative Library for providing the necessary data, and the current and past elected officials who spoke with me.

1 It is possible that the number of Saskatchewan Party female candidates is an example of a "contagion effect." Contagion theory asserts that if parties of the left nominate more women, other parties will feel pressure to respond in kind (Matland and Studlar 1996). At the same time, the fact that the NDP has not significantly increased the proportion of female candidates over time has limited the extent to which "contagion" has increased women's electoral representation in Saskatchewan.

2 On her decision to leave electoral politics and not to pursue the party leadership, MacKinnon (2003, 280-81) writes: "Both Lingenfelter and I embraced the changers of the 1990's – strategic government, the reality of the market economy, and the virtues of mutual responsibility. Either of us would have had a shot at successfully leading the Saskatchewan people. But neither of us could lead the NDP ... I stayed, even after Romanow left in the fall of 2000, because I had unfinished business and it was difficult for another senior minister to leave so soon after Lingenfelter and Romanow. I found humour in the comments of people willing to accept that it was okay for the two men to leave, but somehow it was my duty to hold the fort."

3 Smart (1992, 61) reports that supporters of her 1991 nomination race opponent "were telling people that 'women are getting too much power' and that it was time to 'stop the women.'" Ruddy (2007, 119-21) writes that the NDP attempted to discredit the SNDW through rumours and ridicule.

4 The political left's failure to prioritize women's political representation may help to explain the low priority of the issue for Saskatchewan's political right. As a centre-right party, the Saskatchewan Party might be expected to only prioritize women's numerical representation if its opponents (the NDP) do so.

References

Adams, Michael. 2003. *Fire and Ice: The United States, Canada and the Myth of Converging Values.* Toronto: Penguin Canada.

Blake, Donald. 2001. *Electoral Democracy in the Provinces.* Montreal: Institute for Research on Public Policy.

–. 2006. "Electoral Democracy in the Provinces and Territories." In Christopher Dunn, ed., *Provinces: Canadian Provincial Politics.* 2nd ed., 115-44. Peterborough: Broadview Press.

Braun, Donna, and Gail Quinney. 2006. "Status of Women Office." *Encyclopedia of Saskatchewan.* Regina: Canadian Plains Research Center. Available at http://esask.uregina.ca/.

Carbert, Louise. 2006. *Rural Women's Leadership in Atlantic Canada: First-Hand Perspectives on Public Life and Participation in Electoral Politics.* Toronto: University of Toronto Press.

Ferrao, Vincent. 2010. *Paid Work: Women in Canada – a Gender-Based Statistical Report.* Ottawa: Statistics Canada. Available at http://www.statcan.gc.ca/.

Fox, Richard L., and Jennifer L. Lawless. 2004. "Entering the Arena? Gender and the Decision to Run for Office." *American Journal of Political Science* 48(2): 264-80.

—. 2010. "If Only They'd Ask: Gender, Recruitment, and Political Ambition." *Journal of Politics* 72(2): 310-26.

Hall, Angela, and James Wood. "Saskatchewan Legislature Remaining a Boys' Club." *Regina Leader Post*, 20 December. Available at http://www2.canada.com/.

Haverstock, Lynda. 2001. "The Saskatchewan Liberal Party." In Howard Leeson, ed., *Saskatchewan Politics: Into the Twenty-First Century*, 199-250. Regina: Canadian Plains Research Center, University of Regina.

Hayford, Alison. 2006. "Feminism: Consciousness and Activism Since the 1960s." *Encyclopedia of Saskatchewan*. Regina: Canadian Plains Research Center, University of Regina. http://esask.uregina.ca/.

Leger-Anderson, Ann. 2006. "Women of Saskatchewan: Historical Overview." *Encyclopedia of Saskatchewan*. Regina: Canadian Plains Research Center, University of Regina. Available at http://esask.uregina.ca/.

Legislative Assembly of Saskatchewan. 2009. Saskatchewan Women in Politics: Representation in the Provincial Legislature. Available at http://www.legassembly.sk.ca/.

—. 2010. Saskatchewan Women Cabinet Ministers. Available at http://www.legassembly.sk.ca/.

Lieutenant Governor of Saskatchewan. 2006. History of the Office of the Lieutenant Governor of Saskatchewan: Government House. Available at http://www.ltgov.sk.ca/.

Lingenfelter, Dwain. 2009. "Gender Parity within the Saskatchewan New Democratic Party: Lingenfelter Policy Statement." Saskatchewan New Democrat Leadership Campaign. Available at http://ndpleadership.blogspot.com/.

MacKinnon, Janice. 2003. *Minding the Public Purse: The Fiscal Crisis, Political Trade-Offs, and Canada's Future*. Montreal and Kingston: McGill-Queen's University Press.

Matland, Richard E., and Donley T. Studlar. 1996. "The Contagion of Women Candidates in Single-Member District and Proportional Representation Electoral Systems: Canada and Norway." *Journal of Politics* 58(3): 707-33.

McGrane, David. 2008. "A Mixed Record: Gender and Saskatchewan Social Democracy." *Journal of Canadian Studies* 42(1): 179-203.

McIntyre, Heather. 2008. "SNDW Resolution Passed 2008." Saskatchewan New Democrats. Available at http://heathermcintyre.ca/.

O'Neill, Brenda, and Lynda Erickson. 2003. "Evaluating Traditionalism in the Atlantic Provinces: Voting, Public Opinion and the Electoral Project." *Atlantis* 27(2): 113-22.

Prairie Lily Feminist Society. 2009. *Prairie Lily Feminist Society Newsletter*. Regina: Prairie Lily Feminist Society. Available at http://prairielilies.wordpress.com/.

Ruddy, Jennifer. 2007. "From Policy Advisors to the Enemies Within: Feminist Activism in the Saskatchewan New Democratic Party, 1982-2006." MA thesis, University of Regina.

Sask Trends Monitor. 2010a. *Sex and Gender Equality in Saskatchewan: Education.* A report prepared for the Status of Women Office, Saskatchewan Ministry of Social Services. Available at http://www.socialservices.gov.sk.ca/.

—. 2010b. *Sex and Gender Equality in Saskatchewan: Income and Wealth.* A report prepared for the Status of Women Office, Saskatchewan Ministry of Social Services. Available at http://www.socialservices.gov.sk.ca/.

—. 2010c. *Sex and Gender Equality in Saskatchewan: Living Arrangements.* A report prepared for the Status of Women Office, Saskatchewan Ministry of Social Services. Available at http://www.socialservices.gov.sk.ca/.

—. 2010d. *Sex and Gender Equality in Saskatchewan: Paid and Unpaid Employment.* A report prepared for the Status of Women Office, Saskatchewan Ministry of Social Services. Available at http://www.socialservices.gov.sk.ca/.

Saskatchewan Bureau of Statistics. N.d. *Saskatchewan Aboriginal Peoples: 2006 Census of Canada.* Regina: Saskatchewan Bureau of Statistics. Available at http://www.stats.gov.sk.ca/.

—. 2012. *Saskatchewan Population Report: 2011 Census of Canada.* Regina: Saskatchewan Bureau of Statistics. Available at http://www.stats.gov.sk.ca/.

Saskatchewan Status of Women Office. 2009. *Socio-Demographic Profiles of Saskatchewan Women: Aboriginal Women.* Regina: Saskatchewan Ministry of Advanced Education, Employment and Labour. Available at http://www.socialservices.gov.sk.ca/.

Smart, Anne. 1992. "Introducing the Feminine into the Body Politics – and Experiencing Its Allergic Reaction." *Canadian Woman Studies* 12(3): 59-63.

Smith, David. 1975. *Prairie Liberalism: The Liberal Party in Saskatchewan, 1905-71.* Toronto: University of Toronto Press.

Smith, Loretta. 2005. "Aboriginal Candidates in the 2004 General Election." *Electoral Insight* 7(1). Available at http://www.elections.ca/.

Tremblay, Manon. 2003. "The Participation of Aboriginal Women in Canadian Electoral Democracy." *Electoral Insight* 5(3): 34-38. Available at http://www.elections.ca/.

Trimble, Linda, and Jane Arscott. 2008. *Still Counting: Women in Politics across Canada.* Toronto: University of Toronto Press.

Wagner, Bernadette L. 2009. "Happy Birthday, Prairie Lilies!" *Canadian Dimension* 43(2). Available at http://thereginamom.wordpress.com/.

Wesley, Jared J. 2011. *Code Politics: Campaigns and Cultures on the Canadian Prairies.* Vancouver: UBC Press.

Williams, Cara. 2010. *Economic Well-Being: Women in Canada – a Gender-Based Statistical Report.* Ottawa: Statistics Canada. Available at http://www.statcan.gc.ca/.

12

In the Presence of Northern Aboriginal Women?

Women in Territorial Politics

GRAHAM WHITE

A glance at the Canada's three northern territories suggests that women – especially Aboriginal women – figure prominently in Northern politics. Women have served as premier in all three territories: Pat Duncan in Yukon, Nellie Cournoyea in the Northwest Territories (NWT), and Eva Aariak (the current premier) in Nunavut. The first woman national leader of a major political party, Audrey McLaughlin, represented Yukon in the House of Commons. Of the five Aboriginal MPs who have served in the federal cabinet, two (Ethel Blondin-Andrew and Leona Aglukkaq) have been women who represented ridings in the territorial North. During the negotiations leading up to the Charlottetown Accord, three northern Aboriginal women – Nellie Cournoyea, Mary Simon, and Rosemary Kuptana – played such a prominent role that they were labelled "the Mothers of Confederation." Several of the powerful Aboriginal organizations in the territories have been or are currently led by women. The commission that designed the Nunavut government in the 1990s recommended that its legislature be structured so as to guarantee the election of an equal number of men and women; the proposal was taken sufficiently seriously that it went to a territory-wide vote. Little wonder that a northern journalist recently wrote gushingly about "a budding estrogen wave" that could transform territorial politics (Gregoire 2011, 36).

On closer inspection, however, this apparently rosy picture gives way to a far less encouraging – indeed, in some ways, quite dismal – assessment of

POLITICAL REPRESENTATION OF WOMEN IN
THE TERRITORIES

FIRSTS
Right to vote and stand for election

- Most women win right to vote and stand for election — YK – 1919 / NWT – 1951 / NT – 1999

- Aboriginal women win right to vote and stand for election — YK – 1960 / NWT – 1960 / NT – 1999

Contesting office

- First women to contest office: YK – Jean Gordon / NWT – Lena Pederson / NT – eleven women — 1967 / 1967 / 1999

- First women to win office: YK – Jean Gordon / NWT – Lena Pederson / NT – Manitok Thompson — 1967-70 / 1970-75 / 1999-2003

- First Aboriginal women to win office: YK – Margaret Commodore / NWT – Lena Pederson / NT – Manitok Thompson — 1982-96 / 1970-75 / 1999-2004

- First visible minority women to win office: YK – none / NWT – Sandy Lee / NT – none — NWT – 1999-2011

- First women appointed to cabinet: YK – Meg McCall / NWT – Nellie Cournoyea / NT – Manitok Thompson — 1978-82 / 1984-85 / 1999-2004

- First Aboriginal women appointed to cabinet: YK – Margaret Commodore / NWT – Nellie Cournoyea / NT – Manitok Thompson — 1985-92 / 1984-85 / 1999-2004

- First women premiers: YK – Pat Duncan / NWT – Nellie Cournoyea (Aboriginal) / NT – Eva Aariak (Aboriginal) — 2000-2 / 1991-95 / 2008 to present

- First visible minority women appointed to cabinet: YK – none / NWT – Sandy Lee / NT – none — NWT – 2007-11

CURRENT REPRESENTATION AT A GLANCE

Women in legislature/cabinet	Date of election	Women elected Number	Percent
Yukon			
Legislature	2011/10/11	6 of 19	32
Cabinet	2011/10/11	1 of 8	13
NWT			
Legislature	2011/10/03	2 of 19	11
Cabinet	2011/10/03	0 of 7	0
Nunavut			
Legislature	2008/10/27	1 of 19	5
Cabinet	2008/10/27	1 of 8	13

the place of women in territorial politics. For example, in the three elections held in Nunavut since its creation in 1999, only four of the fifty-seven members of the Legislative Assembly (MLAs) elected (7 percent) have been women. The record in the other territories has been little better: only twice have more than three women ever served simultaneously in a territorial assembly. Similarly, while women have headed territorial Aboriginal organizations, overall, the elected positions in these organizations have been overwhelmingly held by men. And the proposal for a "gender-equal" legislature was decisively rejected in a May 1997 plebiscite.

This chapter examines the participation of women in the politics of the northern territories. Given the high proportion of northern residents who are Aboriginal – roughly 25 percent in Yukon, 50 percent in the NWT, and over 80 percent in Nunavut – special attention is devoted to the role played by Aboriginal women in territorial politics.[1] Before proceeding to the numbers and the analysis, however, because territorial politics are in important respects substantially different from politics "south of 60," a brief account of the nature and recent history of territorial politics is in order.

Background[2]

The territories are best thought of as "proto-provinces." Although their constitutional status is inferior to that of the provinces (in theory, Ottawa could fundamentally alter, even abolish, a territory, though this is politically inconceivable), they exercise almost all province-like powers, including health, education, welfare, civil law and municipal government, renewable resources, and so on. The only major exception is ownership of Crown land and, thus, control of non-renewable resources.[3] The territorial governments enjoy the same taxing powers as the provinces, but their tax bases are limited.

In the NWT and Nunavut, what has been termed "consensus government" holds sway. Political parties are absent and all candidates, including incumbent MLAs and ministers, run as independents; the premier is chosen by secret ballot of all MLAs, as are cabinet ministers. Until quite recently, "government" in the territories effectively amounted to being administered by federal bureaucrats.

The three territorial governments are, by a wide margin, the largest, most powerful, and best-resourced political institutions in the North (at least in terms of territorial organizations – the federal government remains exceptionally powerful). However, largely by virtue of the finalized comprehensive land claim agreements – which are in effect modern-day treaties, enjoying constitutional protection under section 35 of the Constitution Act,

1982 – Aboriginal organizations and governments exercise very substantial political influence and in some areas wield considerable governmental authority. To southern Canadians, the Aboriginal organizations may look like interest groups but they are hugely more important in territorial politics than such a conception might suggest. Accordingly, I look briefly at the involvement of women in organizations such as Nunavut Tunngavik Incorporated and the Tlicho Government.

Women's Political Representation: The Numbers

Women in Territorial Legislatures

Data on women's participation in territorial elections are presented in Table 12.1. The table only contains data from 1978 in Yukon and 1979 in the NWT. Prior to these dates, women were exceedingly scarce in the territorial councils, though as indicated in the "Firsts for Women," a few individual women had won elected office.

Currently, the territorial assemblies consist of only nineteen members each. Thus, more than is usually the case, percentages must be assessed in concert with actual numbers. By way of illustration, even when a territorial legislature reaches or slightly exceeds 20 percent women – as only rarely happens – this means only four women MLAs. Reaching the 20 percent mark in Yukon (four women) is qualitatively different from reaching 20 percent in the House of Commons (sixty-two women) or in the Quebec National Assembly (twenty-five women).

The overall pattern is familiar. Women typically represent a higher proportion of candidates than of elected MLAs: 24 percent of all candidates (20 percent successful) in Yukon since 1978; 16 percent of candidates and 11 percent of elected MLAs in the NWT since 1979; and 15 percent of candidates and 7 percent of elected MLAs in Nunavut since 1999. Unlike elsewhere in Canada, however, this discrepancy cannot be attributed to the tendency of political parties to relegate women, as "sacrificial lambs," to unwinnable ridings. Parties do not contest elections in Nunavut and the NWT;[4] in Yukon, where parties are as dominant as in the South, riding populations are so small and winning margins so narrow that few ridings can be characterized as lost causes for specific parties.

Rather more important than the gap between proportions of women who run and are successful is the elemental fact that women continue to be badly under-represented both on the ballot and, once the ballots are counted, in office. The record in Yukon is substantially better than in the other territories,

TABLE 12.1

Women candidates and members in the territories, by election

Election date	Party elected	Number of legislators	Candidates		Elected		Aboriginal	Non-Aboriginal
			Number	%	Number	%		
A – Yukon								
1978/11/20	Conservative	16	8 of 52	15	2	13	0	2
1982/06/07	Conservative	16	11 of 51	22	3	19	1	2
1985/05/13	NDP	16	8 of 44	18	3	19	2	1
1989/02/20	NDP	16	10 of 47	21	4	25	2	2
1992/10/19	Yukon Party	17	12 of 52	23	3	18	1	2
1996/09/30	NDP	17	11 of 54	20	3	18	0	3
2000/04/17	Liberal	17	17 of 49	35	5	29	1	4
2002/11/04	Yukon Party	18	16 of 60	27	3	17	1	1
2006/10/10	Yukon Party	18	16 of 58	28	2	11	1	1
2011/10/11	Yukon Party	19	16 of 62	26	6	32	1	5
B – Northwest Territories								
1979/10/01		22	8 of 66	12	2	9	1	1
1983/11/21		24	6 of 64	9	3	13	2	1
1987/10/05		24	7 of 64	11	2	8	2	0
1991/10/15		24	15 of 84	18	3	13	3	0
1995/10/16		24	12 of 93	13	2	8	1	1
1999/02/15		19	15 of 64	23	2	11	0	2
2003/11/24		19	12 of 58	21	2	11	0	2
2007/10/01		19	11 of 55	20	3	16	0	3
2011/10/03		19	9 of 47	19	2	11	0	2
C – Nunavut								
1999/02/15		19	11 of 71	16	1	5	1	0
2004/02/16		19	9 of 82	11	2	11	2	0
2008/10/27		19*	10 of 50	20	1	5	1	0

* A bizarre set of circumstances resulted in election postponements in two ridings; the subsequent by-elections are treated as part of the general election.

Sources: Data for tables in this chapter were taken from official reports on territorial elections, media accounts of territorial elections, and personal knowledge.

but even there only once has more than one candidate in three been a woman and only three times has as many as one MLA in four been a woman. Over the past three decades barely one NWT MLA in ten has been a woman. In Nunavut, three elections have produced but four women MLAs – a truly dismal 7 percent. Thus Nunavut experienced the paradox of Eva Aariak's being elected as premier following the 2008 election and being the only woman in the legislature.[5] Aariak's emergence as premier should not be interpreted as a gesture to compensate for the paucity of women in the assembly; rather, it is better seen as the victory of a moderate, competent candidate who, at a time when public opinion seemed to favour a change in Nunavut's political direction, did not carry the political baggage of her male opponents.

Slight upward trends may be discerned in the proportions of women candidates in Yukon and in the post-division NWT; in Nunavut, which has had only three elections (and a sharp decline in the total number of candidates in the most recent election), it is not possible to discern any trend. In terms of women actually elected, the numbers are so minuscule that the addition or loss of one or two women MLAs produces a large difference in the female/male ratio, so that it makes little sense to attempt to discern trends. The primal reality is clear: very few women win election to the territorial assemblies.

Table 12.1 presents data on the number of women MLAs in the three territories who were Aboriginal and non-Aboriginal. While many issues of concern to women transcend cultural divisions, few would disagree that, in important respects, the situation of Aboriginal women in the territories differs markedly from that of non-Aboriginal women, so that the participation – or lack of it – of Aboriginal women in the territorial assemblies is a matter of great importance. Non-Aboriginal women MLAs have outnumbered their Aboriginal counterparts in the Yukon Legislative Assembly, but the ratio (2.7:1) has been slightly lower than in the population (roughly 3:1). As well, while there have never been more than two Aboriginal women in the Yukon House, in only two elections – including the most recent one – were no Aboriginal women elected. In Nunavut, all women MLAs have been Aboriginal (including women elected in by-elections, whose presence is not reflected in the table). This is not surprising given the overwhelming numerical dominance of Inuit; few non-Inuit, male or female, contest Nunavut elections.

In the NWT, an intriguing pattern is evident in terms of the presence of Aboriginal women MLAs. Prior to division in 1999, three-quarters of the dozen women elected to the legislature were Aboriginal, but in the four elections since Nunavut split away, no Aboriginal women have been elected to the NWT House. The departure of Nunavut, with its predominantly Inuit population, doubtless explains some of this remarkable reversal. How to explain the complete absence of Aboriginal women MLAs, given that effect- ively half the residents of the current NWT are Aboriginal, remains a puz- zle. Although precise figures are not available, it is clear that a substantial proportion of the women candidates in each election were Aboriginal. One potential explanation can be dismissed immediately: as is evident from a later discussion, it is clearly not the case that the lack of Aboriginal women in the House reflects a surfeit of women leaders of Aboriginal governments and organizations.

Although it never came to be, the proposal for a gender-equal legislature in Nunavut deserves brief mention. The Nunavut Implementation Commis- sion (NIC), the organization that advised the three "parties" to the Nunavut land claim (the federal and territorial governments and Nunavut Tunngavik Incorporated (NTI), the principal Inuit land claim organization) on the de- sign of the Nunavut government, issued a discussion paper proposing a path-breaking innovation for the Nunavut Assembly. Each constituency would return two members: one chosen from a list of male candidates and one from a list of female candidates (Nunavut Implementation Commission 1994, 1995). If adopted, this proposal would have produced the world's first legislature mandated to be "gender-equal."

This approach to encouraging the participation of women in Nunavut's political life generated much discussion across Nunavut as well as extensive national and international interest. Two widely held misconceptions pre- vailed. First, some believed that it would restrict men to voting for men and women to voting for women, whereas the proposal was that each voter would cast two votes, one for a man and one for a woman. Second, some believed that creating a gender-equal assembly would inflate its size and increase costs accordingly, whereas the proposal was to establish ten or eleven two- member districts rather than twenty or twenty-two single-member ridings.

The Status of Women Council of the Northwest Territories (1997) strong- ly endorsed the proposal. Others, however, were either unconvinced or were adamantly opposed. Most members of the Nunavut Caucus, the MLAs elected from the area that would become Nunavut, opposed the notion of a gender-equal legislature. A particularly vociferous opponent was Manitok Thompson, the only Inuk woman in the NWT Assembly and minister re- sponsible for the status of women. Where supporters saw a unique oppor- tunity to implement a vision of a more balanced political system, opponents saw a plan that insulted women's ability to get elected if they chose to run. Where supporters saw a gender-equal legislature as a return to the values of traditional Inuit society, in which families were built on an equal division of labour between men and women, opponents dismissed this view as a romanticized retelling of history. Where supporters saw the proposal as reflecting the "creative but within Canadian political norms" tone of the Nunavut project as a whole, opponents saw it as an unwelcome, unnecessary, and unworkable scheme that the Nunavut leadership was trying to impose on an unsuspecting electorate. A vocal minority of fundamentalist Christians attacked the proposal, sometimes on biblical grounds.

At the insistence of the Government of the Northwest Territories, Ron Irwin, the minister of Indian affairs and northern development and the key Ottawa figure on the Nunavut file called a plebiscite to decide the issue; NIC, NTI, and Pauktuutit, the national Inuit women's organization, campaigned in favour. Opposition, less well organized, was led by Manitok Thompson. In a recent memoir, Thompson explains that her opposition to gender parity reflects her view that policies designed to assist women are wrong-headed in that they divide rather than support the family. "I see feminists," she wrote, "as the same type of people who protest against the seal hunt" – a severe condemnation in Inuit society (Thompson 2010, 153). Only 39 percent of those eligible actually cast ballots, possibly because many families would have been out on the land at that time, possibly because, beyond the vocal and active camps of supporters and opponents, gender parity in the legislature was not a centrally important issue.

In the plebiscite, held in May 1997, the proposal was defeated 57 percent to 43 percent.[6] Many voters were simply unconvinced of the merits of a gender-equal legislature. Some, doubtless, were misinformed about what the proposal entailed. Others may have voted "no" less because they opposed the idea of gender parity than because they opposed dual-member ridings; many in Nunavut prefer that each electoral district encompass only a single community, whereas the gender-equal proposal would have produced many ridings with two or more communities. Finally, the general disdain for elite-driven constitutional change prominent across Canada in the late 1990s may also have played a role in the voting. Ironically, when the first Nunavut election was held in early 1999, only one woman was elected: Manitok Thompson.

Women in Territorial Cabinets
Since only sitting MLAs are eligible for appointment to cabinet, it is hardly surprising that the numbers and the proportions of women in territorial cabinets are low. With the remarkable exception of Yukon during the Liberal government headed by Pat Duncan (2000-2), in which four of the seven

TABLE 12.2

Women in cabinet in the territories, by election

Election date	Party elected	Women in governing caucus	Women in cabinet		Aboriginal women	Non-Aboriginal women
			Number	%		
A – Yukon						
1978/11/20	Conservative	1 of 11	0 of 5	0	0	0
1982/06/07	Conservative	3 of 9	1 of 6	17	1	0
1985/05/13	NDP	2 of 8	1 of 5	20	1	0
1989/02/20	NDP	3 of 9	1 of 5	20	1	0
1992/10/19	Yukon Party	0 of 7	0 of 6	0	0	0
1996/09/30	NDP	1 of 11	1 of 6	17	0	1
2000/04/17	Liberal	4 of 10	3 of 6	50	0	3
2002/11/04	Yukon Party	1 of 12	1 of 7	14	0	0
2006/10/10	Yukon Party	2 of 10	2 of 8	25	1	1
2011/10/11	Yukon Party	2 of 11	1 of 8	13	0	1
B – Northwest Territories						
1979/10/01			0 of 5	0	0	0
1983/11/21			1 of 8	13	1	0
1987/10/05			2 of 8	25	2	0
1991/10/15			1 of 8	13	1	0
1995/10/16			1 of 8	13	1	0
1999/02/15			1 of 7	14	0	1
2003/11/24			0 of 7	0	0	0
2007/10/01			1 of 7	14	0	1
2011/10/03			0 of 7	0	0	0
C – Nunavut						
1999/02/15			1 of 8	13	1	0
2004/02/16			2 of 8	25	2	0
2008/10/27			1 of 8	13	1	0

cabinet posts were at one point held by women – a female cabinet majority, surely a Canadian first – territorial cabinets, as Table 12.2 shows, typically have one or two women ministers. Occasionally women are shut out completely, as happened in the NWT following the 2003 election and in 2011 when Sandy Lee, the sole woman minister, resigned to run in the federal election. Following the selection of the cabinet in 2003, Lee spoke up in the House on the lack of female representation:

We are now the owner of the only Cabinet in Canada without women representation ... it should also be strongly noted that we have no aboriginal
women representation in the House ... I call upon this legislature, this
Cabinet, and all aboriginal governments to step up to the plate and take
strong measures to improve this situation. (Legislative Assembly of the
NWT 2003, 15)

No measures – strong or otherwise – have been taken by the assembly or
the cabinet in the NWT or by its Aboriginal governments to enhance the
position of women in government, though Lee was elected to cabinet following the 2007 election, becoming the only woman minister. Following the
2011 election, no women were voted into cabinet.

Women in the North, as elsewhere, tend to be appointed to "female portfolios" such as health or social services. Responsibility for the status of
women is typically assigned to a woman minister in addition to her depart-
mental tasks.

Table 12.3 lists the three women who have served as party leaders in
Yukon. As noted earlier, Pat Duncan won the premiership in 2000; she resigned as party leader shortly after the disastrous 2002 election in which not
only was her government soundly defeated but she was the lone Liberal
MLA returned to office. Elizabeth Hanson, the current NDP leader, is of
course in line to become premier should her party emerge victorious in the
next election. Although Hilda Watson served only briefly as leader of the

TABLE 12.3
Women party leaders in Yukon

Name	Political party	Period of service
Hilda Watson	PC	09/1978 to 11/1978
Pat Duncan	Liberal	1998-2005
Elizabeth Hanson	NDP	2009 to present

TABLE 12.4
Women premiers in the territories

Name	Political party	Period of service
Nellie Cournoyea (NWT)	–	1991-95
Pat Duncan (Yukon)	Liberal	2000-2
Eva Aariak (Nunavut)	–	2008 to present

Yukon Progressive Conservative Party (now known as the Yukon Party), she became the first woman in Canada to lead her party to electoral victory. The Conservatives won the 1978 Yukon election, the first to be contested on a party basis, but Watson did not win her own seat and gave up the leadership of the party to a man immediately after the election and thus did not become premier.

The women who have become premier in the territories, and their time in office, are listed in Table 12.4. The numbers, though small, are remarkable. Only six Canadian women have led their parties to victory in elections and two – Hilda Watson and Pat Duncan – are from the territories (and were two of the first three). Only ten women in Canada have served as first minister, but a third have been from the territories. And yet these notable successes at the highest level of territorial politics stand in sharp contrast to the low overall rate of women holding elected office in the territories.

This situation was earlier described as a paradox, implying the need for explanation. Might it be that what has been called "the Queen Bee Syndrome" is at work here? This interpretation sees some women who "make it" to the top of male-dominated professions, such as politics, as at best indifferent if not outright hostile to feminist analyses of systemic discrimination against women who require concerted action. Such women – former British prime minister Margaret Thatcher is a prime example – tend to view society in terms of individuals rather than of collectivities and believe that if they can make it, any woman can. They may also have self-interested reasons for wanting to remain the only prominent woman in their organizations (Staines, Travis, and Jayaratne 1974). In effect, they become defenders of the status quo, at least as far as women's lack of representation is concerned.

Little, if any, evidence of the queen bee syndrome exists in territorial politics. Aariak became premier only *after* an election in which she was the only woman elected. Moreover, like most northern Aboriginal women who rise to leadership positions, both Aariak and Nellie Cournoyea before her worked extensively at supporting and encouraging young people, women as well as men, who showed promise as potential leaders, and they are certainly not defenders of the status quo.[7]

A number of women, mostly Aboriginal, have served as territorial commissioners, the territorial equivalents of lieutenant governors. In Yukon, three modern-era commissioners have been women: Ione Christensen (1979), Judy Gingell (1995-2000), and Geraldine Van Bibber (2005-10); the latter two are Aboriginal (Gingell was also the grand chief of the Council of Yukon Indians [now the Council of Yukon First Nations] from 1989 to 1995).

In the NWT, two Aboriginal women, Helen Maksagak (1995-99) and Glenna Hansen (2000-5), have served as commissioners. Maksagak was Nunavut's first commissioner (1999-2000); two other Inuit women, Ann Meekitjuk Hanson (2005-10) and Edna Elias (2010-), have also held the post.

Women in Aboriginal Governments and Organizations

Many of the Aboriginal governments and organizations in the territorial North are powerful political bodies whose leadership is elected (sometimes directly, sometimes indirectly) by their members. As important representative institutions, any analysis of women's participation in territorial politics must include them. Their nature, size, and perspective vary a good deal, as do their resources, their capacity, and, indeed, their effectiveness and importance. On one dimension, however, broad similarity is evident: the lack of women in elected leadership roles.

A key element in all finalized comprehensive land claim settlements is the establishment of an Aboriginal organization (usually a successor to the organization that negotiated the claim). These land claim organizations represent the interests of the affected Aboriginal people in dealings with the federal and territorial governments, exercise a range of governmental powers, own and control the extensive lands conveyed to the claimant groups, and manage the substantial monies that comprehensive land claim settlements involve ($1.14 billion in the case of the Nunavut claim). They engage in wide-ranging commercial activities carried out through wholly owned arm's-length economic development agencies. In short, these are substantial and powerful entities. The organizations arising from the finalized claims in the territorial North are Nunavut Tunngavik Incorporated (NTI), the Council of Yukon First Nations (CYFN), and the four regional NWT organizations: the Tlicho Government, the Sahtu Dene Council/Sahtu Secretariat Incorporated (SSI), the Gwich'in Tribal Council (GTC), and the Inuvialuit Regional Corporation (IRC). In the southern NWT, where no claims have been settled, the umbrella Aboriginal organizations are the Deh Cho First Nations and the Akaitcho Territory Government. Two other organizations are included in the analysis: the Dene Nation, a territory-wide entity including all NWT First Nations, and the NWT Métis Nation. Both are noteworthy but lack the political and economic significance of the land claims bodies. The Dene Nation lacks the resources and the formal authority of regional organizations and governments, while the NWT Métis Nation and its predecessors have been beset by serious divisions within the Métis community and by other political problems.

At the time of writing, several of these organizations – NTI, IRC, CYFN, SSI, and the NWT Métis Nation – were headed by women. (All positions mentioned in this paragraph are filled by election.) However, this apparently high level of women's representation turns out to be misleading. Some organizations – the Tlicho Government and the Gwich'in Tribal Council, for example – have never had a woman as leader, and only one of the others has had a woman at the helm for an extended period (Nellie Cournoyea, who has been chair and CEO of the IRC since 1996). Beyond the impressive proportion of major Aboriginal governments/organizations led by women – five of the ten – the number and percentage of women holding elected office drops off dramatically. By way of illustration, aside from President Cathy Towtongie, only one of the other seven elected NTI board members is a woman, and on several occasions the entire board has been male. At the IRC, Cournoyea is the only woman among the seven-member elected Board of Directors. Aside from her, women have only rarely been elected to the board. Similar examples could be cited from the other main Aboriginal governments and organizations.

Comprehensive data are not available on numbers and proportions of women holding elected office in local and regional political Aboriginal governments and organizations such as band councils, Métis locals, self-governing Yukon First Nations, local hunters and trappers organizations (HTOs), and regional Inuit associations. A study conducted in 2006 by Pauktuutit concluded that only 9 percent of Nunavut HTO members were women (CBC North 2006). An impressionistic overview suggests that the findings of the Pauktuutit study would be replicated for other local and regional Aboriginal political organizations, which is to say that, as in the larger, more prominent Aboriginal political institutions, women are poorly represented.

Overall, the pattern is clear: below the level of top leadership, where women have been reasonably well represented, few women have held elected office in the Aboriginal governments and organizations that play such an influential role in northern governance. As with public governments, the pattern appears to hold across the three territories.

Status of Women Councils

Each territory has a government-mandated status of women council, which engages in research and advocacy on behalf of women. They publish important reports on family violence, homelessness, childcare, and the like, and they draw public and state attention to issues of importance to Northern women. The NWT Native Women's Association and the Yukon Aboriginal Women's Council also represent important political voices for northern women. Without detailed research, however, it is not possible to gauge these organizations' influence and effectiveness.

In Nunavut recent incidents suggest a troubling hostility towards women's advocacy groups. In 2008, for example, the government-appointed president of the Nunavut Status of Women Council, who worked full-time for the Government of Nunavut, resigned following a phone call from a superior warning her about speaking out publicly (in a radio interview she had been critical of the election of an Inuit politician who was serving a suspended sentence for an assault conviction). Two years later, another president was forced to quit her job with NTI in order to accept an appointment to the council (a part-time position compensated only with a small honorarium), supposedly on the grounds that serving on the council would constitute a conflict of interest. The council's executive director said at the time that council members felt intimidated and unable to perform their duties for fear of reprisals by their employers, the Government of Nunavut and the Inuit organizations (Bell 2010). A valuable research project would entail determining the pervasiveness of such attitudes in Nunavut.

Explanations

In important respects, explanations for the persistent under-representation of women in territorial politics match those that apply throughout Canada and elsewhere. Structural barriers – formal and informal – as well as cultural dispositions work against women's participation in politics. Most are well covered in the literature and need not be repeated here. Of greater interest are distinctive northern explanations.

In one sense, structural barriers would seem to play a far lesser role in the North than they do in the South. In the "consensus government" model of politics in Nunavut and the NWT, the baneful influence of political parties, which frequently operate as "old boys' clubs," relegating women to unwinnable ridings, is simply not a factor. Moreover, since ridings typically have small, geographically concentrated populations,[8] costs – financial and non-monetary – of campaigning are low. To run, a candidate needs only to pay a small fee or deposit (currently two hundred dollars in each territory) and have as few as fifteen eligible voters sign a nomination form. Without parties, and therefore without nomination campaigns and meetings, any eligible resident can run for territorial office. While some candidates, usually those in Yellowknife or Iqaluit, do spend substantial amounts (spending ceilings are currently thirty thousand dollars), it is very possible to run a credible, winning campaign with very little money, especially in the smaller communities.

In the literature on women's political representation in Canada and elsewhere, it is commonly argued that political parties constitute significant barriers to increasing the numbers of women in legislative institutions. Certainly the literature identifies several aspects of parties, especially candidate selection processes, that could pose challenges for women seeking elected office (Fox and Lawless 2010; Lovenduski 2005, 45-82; Opello 2006, 21-23; Young 2002, 413-25; Young 2005, 76-90). However, that women make up a somewhat higher proportion of candidates in Yukon, where parties dominate, than in the NWT or Nunavut, which lack parties, suggests that the parties-as-structural-barriers argument is not much help in explaining the under-representation of women in territorial electoral politics.

Indeed, although the numbers are small, the territorial experience suggests that the *absence* of parties may play a role in women's under-representation. Parties can and do recruit, encourage, train, and support candidates. A party committed to – or even open to – having women as its standard-bearers can thus be a structural support rather than a structural barrier to women's participation. A substantial number of parties in Canada and elsewhere, particularly in Scandinavia (Dahlerup 1988, 297), have established meaningful quotas for women not only in important internal party councils but also in legislative candidacies. Tremblay and Mévellec (Chapter 1, this volume) cite evidence from Canadian municipal politics – which, like politics in Nunavut and the NWT, are typically not structured along party lines – that raises questions as to the effects of political parties on women's representation. At the least, the data presented above underscore the need for further research on the role of Canadian political parties in hindering or promoting women's efforts to win elected office.

What of culture? In particular, what of Aboriginal culture? These questions raise exceedingly complex issues, rendered all the more complex because, although important communalities exist across various northern Aboriginal peoples, significant cultural and ideological differences are also evident between and among (for instance) Inuit and First Nations. In the North, as in Canada generally, both Aboriginal women activists and academics have been critical of male-dominated political institutions as disrespectful and hostile to women. Some see this downgrading of women as a perversion of the traditional equality that reigned between men and women in precontact times – a downgrading caused by colonialism and its institutional manifestations, such as the Indian Act, with its long-standing discrimination against women (Green 2001; Royal Commission on Aboriginal Peoples 1996, 4:7-106). As emerged in the debate over the proposal for a gender-equal legislature in Nunavut, however, not everyone agrees that precontact Aboriginal societies were as egalitarian as this view suggests.[9] A proper evaluation of the nature of Aboriginal culture and its significance for women's political participation would require far deeper and extensive analysis than is possible here.[10]

A quick look at women in the senior ranks of the territorial bureaucracies is revealing. Women fare rather better in the upper reaches of the territorial bureaucracies than in electoral politics. Table 12.5 presents data on numbers and proportions of women holding posts at the apex of the territorial public services – deputy ministers (DMs) and assistant deputy ministers (ADMs).[11] Across the three territories, women hold 41 percent of the top bureaucratic positions in government, ranging from 35 percent in the NWT to 48 percent in Nunavut. Aboriginal women are not so strongly in evidence, though half of the senior female administrators in the Nunavut public service are Inuit. The substantially higher proportion of women mandarins than elected politicians in the northern territories is in line with overall Canadian trends: a 2006 survey of DMs and ADMs across the federal, provincial, and territorial governments found that 34 percent of them were women (Evans, Lum, and Shields 2007, 614). With the appointment of a woman Aboriginal lawyer to the Supreme Court of the Northwest Territories in December 2011, all four justices on the court were women.

The contrast between the territorial public services (which have policies designed to seek out, nurture, and promote talented women) and the

TABLE 12.5
Women and men holding deputy and assistant deputy minister positions in the territories

| | Men | | Women | | Aboriginal |
	Number	%	Number	%	Number
Yukon	21	60	14	40	0
NWT	17	65	9	35	2
Nunavut	13	52	12	48	6

electoral arena (in which women are accepted but lack anything like the encouragement and support available in the bureaucracy) is instructive. The obvious lesson to be drawn from the contrast is that positive, targeted measures to assist women could substantially boost the numbers of elected officials – in both public and Aboriginal governments – who are women.

Conclusion: Prospects for Gender Parity

Three conclusions emerge from the foregoing analysis. First and foremost, women have been and continue to be woefully under-represented in elected office in governments – public and Aboriginal – across the three territories. Some progress can be detected since the late 1970s when the territorial governments became wholly elected, and powerful Aboriginal organizations began to emerge, but change has been painfully slow.

Second, a paradox is evident in the representation of women in the politics of the northern territories. Women have been prominent in top elected leadership positions, though hardly in overwhelming or indeed representative numbers, but below the very top, women are few and far between. This is somewhat surprising and anomalous in that women have moved into top bureaucratic positions (at least in the territorial governments [data on senior administrators of Aboriginal governments and organizations are not readily available]), in no small measure reflecting the growing gap in educational achievement between Aboriginal women and men across the North. By every indicator, Aboriginal women in the territories stay in school longer, have higher graduation rates, and move on in larger numbers to postsecondary education than do their male counterparts. A particularly telling illustration: of the eleven graduates of the path-breaking Akitsiraq Law School in Nunavut, all but one were women.[12] Why the systematically higher education levels of Aboriginal women has yet to translate into greater numbers in elected positions is unclear.

The third principal conclusion is that the need for further research into women's political participation in the North is great, as are the opportunities for intellectually stimulating research projects carrying significant practical applications. Further research on women's political under-representation in the territories could lead to a deeper, nuanced understanding of various structural and cultural factors and, thus, assist in substantially increasing the numbers and proportions of women in both the public and Aboriginal governments of the North.

Notes

1 The generic term "Aboriginal" is used throughout the chapter in recognition of the substantial diversity of indigenous peoples in the three territories. In Yukon, almost all Aboriginal people belong to First Nations; in Nunavut, almost all are Inuit; the NWT is home to First Nations, Métis, and Inuit (the Inuvialuit).

2 On society and politics in the northern territories, see Abele et al. (2009); Brownsey and Howlett (2001); Dahl, Hicks, and Jull (2001); Evans and Smith (forthcoming); Henderson (2009); and Irlbacher-Fox (2009).

3 Through a "devolution" arrangement in 2003, Yukon controls its natural resources, though actual ownership of Crown land still rests with Ottawa. The NWT's long pursuit of devolution may be approaching its final stages; Nunavut has expressed interest, but at the time of writing, little progress had been registered.

4 The NDP has occasionally run candidates under its party banner in the NWT, though never anything like a full slate. None of its candidates has been elected.

5 Subsequent by-elections brought a second and a third woman into the Nunavut Assembly, one of whom became a minister.

6 On the proposal and the plebiscite on it, see Gombay (2000); Hicks and White (2000, 70-74); Minor (2002, 82-84); Tremblay and Steele (2006); Williamson (2006); Young (1997).

7 See the life stories and philosophies of the women profiled in McComber and Partridge (2010) as well as Aariak's foreword to the book, along with Gregoire (2011).

8 Ridings outside the urban centres encompass vast areas, but all, or virtually all, people live in one or two small communities.

9 For example, the dozen Inuit women leaders who contributed to a recent volume on leadership expressed widely divergent views on the roles of men and women in traditional Inuit society. See McComber and Partridge (2010).

10 The literature on Aboriginal culture in Canada is extensive. On Aboriginal culture(s) and governance in the territories, see Henderson (2009); Irlbacher-Fox (2009); Kulchyski (2005); Nadasdy (2003); Royal Commission on Aboriginal Peoples (1996, 6:387-517). Minor (2002) offers an analysis of Inuit women's political participation in Nunavut based on a categorization of different periods of interaction between Inuit and Western societies.

11 Data were gathered from territorial government websites in mid-2011. Classification of DMs/ADMs by gender and Aboriginal status was conducted on the basis of personal knowledge, supplemented by information supplied by knowledgable local observers.

12 The Akitsiraq Law School was a one-time project of the University of Victoria Law School in which promising young residents of Nunavut (primarily Inuit) earned law degrees that featured both standard Canadian and traditional Inuit approaches to law.

References

Abele, Frances, Thomas J. Courchene, F. Leslie Seidle, and France St-Hilaire, eds. 2009. *Northern Exposure: Peoples, Powers and Prospects in Canada's North.* Montreal: Institute for Research on Public Policy.

Bell, Jim. 2010. "Paranoid Chill Still Afflicts Nunavut Women's Council." *Nunatsiaq News,* 17 February.

Brownsey, Keith, and Michael Howlett, eds. 2001. *The Provincial State in Canada: Politics in the Provinces and Territories.* Peterborough: Broadview Press.

CBC North. 2006. "Women Have Little Say on Wildlife Boards, Inuit Group Finds." 2 August. Available at http://www.cbc.ca/canada/north/.

Dahl, Jens, Jack Hicks, and Peter Jull, eds. 2001. *Nunavut: Inuit Regain Control of Their Lands and Their Lives.* Copenhagen: International Work Group for Indigenous Affairs.

Dahlerup, Drude. 1988. "From a Small to a Large Minority: Women in Scandinavian Politics." *Scandinavian Political Studies* 11(4): 275-98.

Evans, Bryan, Janet Lum, and John Shields. 2007. "Profiling of the Public Service Elite: A Demographic and Career Trajectory Survey of Deputy and Assistant Deputy Ministers in Canada." *Canadian Public Administration* 50(4): 609-34.

Evans, Bryan, and Charles Smith, eds. Forthcoming. *Neoliberalism and the Provincial State.* Toronto: University of Toronto Press.

Fox, Richard, and Jennifer L. Lawless. 2010. "If Only They'd Ask: Gender, Recruitment, and Political Ambition." *Journal of Politics* 72(2): 310-26.

Gombay, Nicole. 2000. "The Politics of Culture: Gender Parity in the Legislative Assembly of Nunavut." *Études/Inuit/Studies* 24(1): 125-48.

Green, Joyce. 2001. "Canaries in the Mines of Citizenship: Indian Women in Canada." *Canadian Journal of Political Science* 34(4): 715-38.

Gregoire, Lisa. 2011. "Madam Premier: How Eva Aariak is Reinventing the Politics of the North." *The Walrus,* January-February, 32-37.

Henderson, Ailsa. 2007. *Nunavut: Rethinking Political Culture.* Vancouver: UBC Press.

Hicks, Jack, and Graham White. 2000. "Nunavut: Inuit Self-determination through a Land Claim and Public Government?" In Jens Dahl, Jack Hicks, and Peter Jull, eds., *Nunavut: Inuit Regain Control of Their Lands and Their Lives,* 46-51. Copenhagen: International Work Group for Indigenous Affairs.

Irlbacher-Fox. Stephanie. 2009. *Finding Dashaa: Self-Government, Social Suffering, and Aboriginal Policy in Canada.* Vancouver: UBC Press.

Kulchyski, Peter. 2005. *Like the Sound of a Drum: Aboriginal Cultural Politics in Denendeh and Nunavut.* Winnipeg: University of Manitoba Press.

Legislative Assembly of the Northwest Territories. 2003. *Hansard,* 13 December.

Lovenduski, Joni. 2005. *Feminizing Politics.* Cambridge: Cambridge University Press.

McComber, Louis, and Shannon Partridge, eds. 2010. *Arnait Nipingit: Voices of Inuit Women in Leadership and Governance.* Iqaluit: Nunavut Arctic College.

Minor, Tina. 2002. "Political Participation of Inuit Women in the Government of Nunavut." *Wicazo Sa Review* 17(1): 65-90.

Nadasdy, Paul. 2003. *Hunters and Bureaucrats: Power, Knowledge and Aboriginal-State Relations in the Southwest Yukon.* Vancouver: UBC Press.

Nunavut Implementation Commission. 1994. "Two-Member Constituencies and Gender Equality: A 'Made in Nunavut' Solution for an Effective and Representative

Legislature." Iqaluit: NIC. (A slightly revised version was included as Appendix A-8 of NIC [1995].)

—. 1995. *Footprints in New Snow: A Comprehensive Report from the Nunavut Implementation Commission to the Department of Indian Affairs and Northern Development, Government of the Northwest Territories and Nunavut Tunngavik Incorporated Concerning the Establishment of the Nunavut Government.* Iqaluit: NIC.

Opello, Katherine A.R. 2006. *Gender Quotas, Parity Reform, and Political Parties in France.* Lanham: Lexington Books.

Royal Commission on Aboriginal Peoples. 1996. *Report.* Ottawa: Supply and Services Canada.

Staines, Graham, Carol Travis, and Toby Epstein Jayaratne. 1974. "The Queen Bee Syndrome." *Psychology Today,* January, 55-60.

Status of Women Council of the Northwest Territories. 1997. Press release. 25 February.

Thompson, Manitok. 2010. "Don't Just Think about It, Do It!" In Louis McComber and Shannon Partridge, eds., *Arnait Nipingit: Voices of Inuit Women in Leadership and Governance,* 138-55. Iqaluit: Nunavut Arctic College.

Tremblay, Manon, and Jackie F. Steele. 2006. "Paradise Lost? Gender Parity and the Nunavut Experience." In Marian Sawer, Manon Tremblay, and Linda Trimble, eds., *Representing Women in Parliament,* 221-35. London: Routledge.

Williamson, Laakkuluk Jessen. 2006. "Inuit Gender Parity and Why It Was Not Accepted in the Nunavut Legislature." *Études/Inuit/Studies* 30(1): 51-68.

Young, Lisa. 1997. "Gender Equal Legislatures: Evaluating the Proposed Nunavut Electoral System." *Canadian Public Policy* 23(3): 306-15.

—. 2002. "Going Mainstream? The Women's Movement and Political Parties in Canada and the US." In Joanna Everitt and Brenda O'Neill, eds., *Citizen Politics: Research and Theory in Canadian Political Behaviour.* Don Mills: Oxford University Press.

—. 2005. "Can Feminists Transform Party Politics? The Canadian Experience." In Manon Tremblay and Linda Trimble, eds., *Women and Electoral Politics in Canada,* 76-90. Don Mills: Oxford University Press.

13

Slow to Change

Women in the House of Commons

LISA YOUNG

From the 1970s on, the role of women in Canadian society and politics gradually began to change, and the number of women elected increased. Under-
representation of women in Canadian legislatures was identified as a
concern by the Royal Commission on the Status of Women in its 1970 report, and women's groups within political parties and outside them began to
mobilize to increase the number of women running for office and to address
barriers to their selection as candidates or election as legislators (Young
2000, 58).

Examined in comparative context, it is clear that Canada performs much
better on measures of gender equality in law, public policy, and quality of life
than it does on measures of women's political representation (UNDP 2010;
Hausman, Tyson, and Zahidi 2010). This should not be taken to imply that
the women's equality "is complete" as the minister for the Status of Women
declared in 2006 (Brodie 2008); rather, it reminds us that the number of
women in the national legislature is not the sole determinant of policy and
other outcomes for women. Public attitudes, institutional arrangements,
and constitutional guarantees, among other factors, all contribute to these
outcomes. Even with Canada's enviable international record, complete
gender equality remains an elusive goal. Canadian women continue to earn
less, overall, than men, and they are more likely to live in poverty, to be victims of most forms of violence, and to take on care-giving responsibilities,

WOMEN IN
THE HOUSE OF COMMONS

FIRSTS
Right to vote and stand for election
- Most women win the right to vote / stand for election — 1918[1] / 1919
- Chinese and East Indian Canadians win right to vote — 1947
- Japanese Canadians win right to vote — 1948
- Inuit win right to vote — 1950
- Status Indians win right to vote — 1960

Contesting office
- First women to contest office: Rose Mary Louise Henderson — 1921
  (Labour), Elizabeth Bethune Kiely (Liberal), Agnes Macphail
  (Progressive), Harriet Dunlop Prenter (Labour), and Harriet
  S. Dick (Independent, Winnipeg Centre)[2]
- First woman to win office: Agnes Macphail (Progressive Party — 1921-40
  of Canada, United Farmers of Ontario–Labour; later CCF)
- First First Nations woman to win office: Ethel Blondin-Andrew — 1988-2006
  (Liberal)
- First Inuit woman to win office: Nancy Karetak-Lindell (Liberal) — 1997-2008
- First black women to win office: Jean Augustine (Liberal) / — 1993-2005 /
  Hedy Fry (Liberal) — 1993 to present
- First Indian women to win office: Nina Grewal (Conservative) / — 2004 to present /
  Ruby Dhalla (Liberal) — 2004 to present
- First Muslim woman to win office: Yasmin Ratansi (Liberal) — 2004 to present
- First Japanese woman to win office: Bev Oda (Conservative) — 2004 to present
- First Chinese woman to win office: Sophia Leung (Liberal) — 1997-2004
- First Vietnamese woman to win office: Ève-Mary Thaï — 2007 to present
  Thi-Lac (Bloc)
- First lesbian woman to win office: Libby Davies (NDP) — 1997 to present
- First woman appointed to cabinet: Ellen Fairclough (PC), — 1957-63
  secretary of state of Canada

CURRENT REPRESENTATION AT A GLANCE

	Date of election	Women elected Number	Women elected Percent
Women in legislature	2011/05/02	76 of 308	25
Women in cabinet	2011/05/08	10 of 39	26

Women political party leaders
- Elizabeth May, Green Party, 2006 to present

Advisory council on the status of women
- The Canadian Advisory Council on the Status of Women was created in 1973 and disbanded in 1995. The independent body, funded by the federal government, was mandated to advise the government and inform the public on issues of concern to women. It reported to the minister responsible for the status of women, and its members were appointed by an order-in-council.

---

either at the expense of or in addition to paid work (Statistics Canada 2006, 7, 13; Statistics Canada 2010, 6, 20).

Women's Political Representation: The Numbers

The proportion of women in the House of Commons climbed through the 1970s and 1980s but then remained steady from 1993 to 2008. The 2011 election saw the first increase in over a decade as the NDP's surprise wins in Quebec swept many newly elected women into the Commons (see Table 13.1).

Since 1980, women have come to play a more prominent role in Canada's national politics. A woman has served as prime minister, albeit briefly; women have led the Progressive Conservative, New Democratic, and Green parties; a woman has served as the chief justice of the Supreme Court of Canada; and the office of the governor general has been filled by women – including two women from minority ethnic groups – for the majority of the period (see Table 13.2). Despite all these significant "firsts," the representation of women in the national legislature has increased only very slowly. The goal of equal representation in the House of Commons remains elusive.

In 2010, Canada ranked eighth in the world on the United Nations Development Programme's Gender Equality Index (UNDP 2010) and twentieth (of 134 countries) on the World Economic Forum's Global Gender Gap Report (Hausmann, Tyson, and Zahidi 2010, 8-9). Canadian women enjoy constitutionally entrenched equality rights, have access to education at all levels (and in fact comprise a majority of undergraduate students in Canadian universities), and participate in paid employment on almost an equal footing with men. Given the generally equal status of Canadian women, one might expect to find Canada among the international leaders in women's political representation.

TABLE 13.1

Women in the House of Commons, by election

Election date	Party elected	Total number of legislators	Women elected Number	Women elected %
1917/12/17	Conservative	235	0	0
1921/12/06	Liberal	235	1	< 1
1925/10/29	Conservative	245	1	< 1
1926/09/14	Liberal	245	1	< 1
1930/07/28	Conservative	245	1	< 1
1935/10/14	Liberal	245	2	1
1940/03/26	Liberal	245	1	< 1
1945/06/11	Liberal	245	1	< 1
1949/06/27	Liberal	262	0	0
1953/08/10	Liberal	265	4	2
1957/06/10	PC	265	2	1
1958/03/31	PC	265	2	1
1962/06/18	PC	265	5	2
1963/04/08	Liberal	265	4	2
1965/11/08	Liberal	265	4	2
1968/06/25	Liberal	264	1	< 1
1972/10/30	Liberal	264	5	2
1974/07/08	Liberal	264	9	3
1979/05/22	PC	282	10	4
1980/02/18	Liberal	282	14	5
1984/09/04	PC	282	27	10
1988/11/21	PC	295	39	13
1993/10/25	Liberal	295	53	18
1997/06/02	Liberal	301	62	21
2000/11/27	Liberal	301	62	21
2004/06/28	Liberal	308	65	21
2006/01/23	Conservative	308	64	21
2008/10/14	Conservative	308	69	22
2011/05/02	Conservative	308	76	25

Source: "Women in the Senate and the House of Commons," Parliament of Canada website, http://www.parl.gc.ca/.

Canada can, however, be portrayed as a relative "laggard" in the representation of women in its national House of Commons. As of 2011, with one-quarter of the seats in the Canadian House of Commons held by women, Canada ranks thirty-eighth on the Inter-Parliamentary Union's ranking of women in national legislatures (IPU 2011). This places Canada

TABLE 13.2

Female representatives of the Crown: Governors General

Name	Period of service
Jeanne Sauvé	1984-90
Adrienne Clarkson	1999-2005
Michaëlle Jean	2005-10

well behind not only the Scandinavian and Western European countries often associated with gender equality in their politics but also such countries as Rwanda (56 percent), South Africa (45 percent), Costa Rica (39 percent), and Nepal (33 percent). When compared to other countries that share similar political institutions and histories, the Canadian record on women's representation looks somewhat better: Canada is now on par with Australia's lower house (25 percent) and surpasses the UK (22 percent), France (19 percent), and the United States (17 percent).

Women's representation in the House of Commons also lags behind that in many Canadian provinces. As shown in Table 13.3, in 2011 the legislatures of five Canadian provinces – that is, British Columbia with 29 percent of women MLAs, Manitoba (28 percent), Ontario (29 percent), Quebec (33 percent), and Yukon (32 percent) – perform better in terms of women's representation than does the national House of Commons, with eight provinces and territories reporting lower rates of women's representation. Since the mid-1980s there have been significant gains in women's representation in British Columbia, Manitoba, Ontario, Quebec, and, to a lesser extent, in Yukon, with the percentage of women fluctuating between one-quarter and one-third of the legislators in those provinces. The positive rate of change in several provinces is a relatively new phenomenon. When the earlier volume of this book was published in 1997, the federal House lagged substantially behind British Columbia and Prince Edward Island, and slightly behind Alberta and Quebec. Now the gains in women's representation in several provinces are firmly established.

The parties represented in the House of Commons over this period have varied considerably in their approaches to the representation of women. These variations are reflected to a degree in the representation of women in their caucuses, shown in Table 13.4 and Table 13.5. In many countries, parties on the left have led the way on women's representation; often, these are the parties with the closest ties to organized feminism, and quotas or other mechanisms for guaranteeing women's representation are consistent with

TABLE 13.3

Representation of women in legislatures in the 1980s, 1990s, and 2000s, by province and election

Legislature	1980s		1990s		2000s	
	Year	%	Year	%	Year	%
Canada – House of Commons	1984	10	1997	21	2011	25
Canada – Senate	1980-84	11	1994-97	22	2011-	36
Alberta	1982	8	1993	19	2008	21
British Columbia	1983	11	1996	27	2009	29
Manitoba	1981	12	1995	19	2011	28
New Brunswick	1982	7	1995	16	2010	15
Newfoundland and Labrador	1982	6	1993	4	2011	17
Northwest Territories	1983	13	1995	8	2011	11
Nova Scotia	1981	2	1993	10	2009	23
Nunavut	–	–	1999	5	2008	5
Ontario	1981	5	1995	18	2011	29
Prince Edward Island	1982	6	1996	19	2011	22
Quebec	1981	7	1994	18	2008	30
Saskatchewan	1982	8	1995	22	2011	19
Yukon	1982	19	1996	18	2011	32

party ideology (Caul 1999). Canada is no exception in this regard. In almost every election since 1980, the left-of-center New Democratic Party has run more female candidates than any other party. This has not always translated into a large proportion of women in the NDP caucus as the party has had relatively few winnable seats, particularly through the period from 1993 to 2008. In 2011, when the party unexpectedly swept Quebec, forty of the 102 NDP MPs were women, driving the overall representation of women in the House from 22 to 25 percent.

The left-of-centre sovereignist Bloc Québécois and the centrist Liberal Party have lagged somewhat behind the NDP in the nomination of female candidates, although the Liberal Party surpassed the NDP in 2008. Parties on the right – the Progressive Conservatives, the Reform Party/Canadian Alliance, and the merged Conservative Party of Canada – have tended to lag behind the centre-left parties in the nomination of women candidates.

Party leaders are of great importance in the Canadian political system as they form the public "face" of their party. In fact, voters' evaluations of the party's leader can be an important determinant of vote choice in general elections (Gidengil and Blais 2007). Many of the major Canadian parties

TABLE 13.4

Women candidates in federal elections, by party and election

Election date	Liberal		Conservative		PC		Alliance		Reform		Bloc		NDP	
	N	%	N	%	N	%	N	%	N	%	N	%	N	%
1980/02/18	23	8	–		14	5	–		–		–		33	12
1984/09/04	44	16	–		23	8	–		–		–		64	23
1988/11/21	53	18	–		37	13	–		8	11	–		84	28
1993/10/25	64	22	–		67	23	–		23	11	10	13	113	38
1997/06/02	84	28	–		56	19	–		23	10	16	21	107	36
2000/11/27	65	22	–		39	13	32	11	–		18	24	88	30
2004/06/28	75	24	36	12	–		–		–		18	24	96	31
2006/01/23	79	26	38	12	–		–		–		23	31	108	35
2008/10/14	113	37	63	21	–		–		–		20	27	104	34
2011/05/02	90	29	68	22	–		–		–		24	32	124	40

* No female Independents or non-major party candidates have won an election since 1980. In 2011, Elizabeth May was the first MP elected for the Green Party.

TABLE 13.5
Women in party caucuses at the federal level

Election date	Liberal		Conservative		PC		Alliance		Reform		Bloc		NDP	
	N	%	N	%	N	%	N	%	N	%	N	%	N	%
1980/02/18	10 of 147	7	–	–	2 of 103	2	–	–	–	–	–	–	2 of 32	6
1984/09/04	5 of 40	13	–	–	19 of 211	9	–	–	–	–	–	–	3 of 30	10
1988/11/21	13 of 83	16	–	–	21 of 169	12	–	–	0*	–	–	–	5 of 43	12
1993/10/25	36 of 177	20	–	–	1 of 2	50	–	–	7 of 52	13	8 of 54	15	1 of 9	11
1997/06/02	37 of 155	24	–	–	2 of 20	10	–	–	4 of 60	7	11 of 44	25	8 of 21	38
2000/11/27	39 of 172	23	–	–	1 of 12	8	7 of 66	11	–	–	10 of 38	26	5 of 13	38
2004/06/28	34 of 135	25	12 of 99	12	–		–	–	–	–	14 of 54	26	5 of 19	26
2006/01/23	21 of 103	20	14 of 124	11	–		–	–	–	–	17 of 51	33	12 of 29	41
2008/10/14	19 of 77	25	23 of 143	16	–		–	–	–	–	15 of 49	31	12 of 37	32
2011/05/02	6 of 34	18	28 of 167	17	–		–	–	–	–	1 of 4	25	40 of 102	39

* A Reform MP, Deborah Grey, was elected in a by-election shortly after the 1988 election.

TABLE 13.6

Women party leaders at the federal level

Name	Political party	Period of service
Kim Campbell	PC	06/1993 to 12/1993
Audrey McLaughlin	NDP	1989-95
Alexa McDonough	NDP	1995-2002
Elizabeth May	Green	2006 to present

TABLE 13.7

Women government leaders at the federal level

Name	Political party	Period of service
Kim Campbell	PC	06/1993 to 11/1993

have been led at some time by a female leader (see Table 13.6 and Table 13.7). Kim Campbell led the Progressive Conservative Party in 1993 and was briefly prime minister, until her party lost the 1993 election. Two women have led the New Democratic Party, and one now leads the Green Party. Neither the Liberal Party nor the new Conservative Party of Canada has been led by a woman. In a systematic examination of female candidacies for party leaderships between 1975 and 2009, Bashevkin (2010, 72) concludes that women were able to win federal party leaderships when the parties were electorally weak and positioned in the centre or to the left on the ideological spectrum.

Inclusion in the federal cabinet is arguably very significant for women's representation, both for symbolic and for substantive reasons. Cabinet plays a key role in determining the government's policy direction, and individual cabinet ministers have considerable discretion over policy and administration within their area of jurisdiction. Representation of women in cabinet may affect policy outcomes. For instance, Atchison and Down (2007) examine the impact of women's cabinet representation on family leave policy in several established democracies and find evidence of a connection. Women have been represented as well, or better, in the federal cabinet than in the House of Commons since 1980. Table 13.8 shows that the proportion of women in cabinet was quite similar to the proportion of women in the governing party's caucus. The first two Harper cabinets (following the 2006 and 2008 elections) represent the most significant over-representation relative to the proportion of women in the governing party's caucus. Although

TABLE 13.8
Women in the federal cabinet, by election

Election date	Party elected	Total number of cabinet ministers[1]	Women appointed to cabinet	
			Number	%
1980/02/18	Liberal	33	2	6
1984/09/04	PC	40	6	15
1988/11/21	PC	39	6	15
1993/10/25	Liberal	29[2]	7	24
1997/06/02	Liberal	37[3]	8	22
2000/11/27	Liberal	37[4]	10	27
2004/06/28	Liberal	39	9	23
2006/01/23	Conservative	27	6	22
2008/10/14	Conservative	38	11	29
2011/05/02	Conservative	38	11	29

1 Includes the prime minister.
2 Chrétien included secretaries of state in his cabinet. In 1993, three of the seven female cabinet
   members were secretaries of state.
3 In 1997, two of the eight cabinet members were secretaries of state.
4 In 2000, two of the ten female cabinet members were secretaries of state.

women made up only 11 and 16 percent of the Conservative caucus after those elections, they comprised 22 and 29 percent of the Conservative cabinets. Each woman in the Conservative caucus had more than a 40 percent probability of being appointed to cabinet in 2006 and 2008. In the 2011 election, the proportion of women in the Conservative caucus increased to 22 percent, but the representation of women in the cabinet did not increase. Although women have comprised between one-quarter and one-third of the members of recent cabinets, and have held a variety of prestigious portfolios, including national defence and international affairs, no woman has ever held the influential post of minister of finance.

The ethno-cultural diversity of the Canadian electorate is only partially reflected by the women elected to the House of Commons. Several of the "firsts" – women from various ethnic groups – are listed in the information box. Although minority women remain under-represented in the House of Commons, they have made significant strides in recent years. Black (2008, 236) observes that there is a persistent under-representation of ethno-cultural minorities in the Canadian House of Commons; although the numbers of minority MPs have increased over the past fifteen years, so too has the proportion of the Canadian population considered to be minorities. Within this context of broader under-representation, minority women have fared somewhat better than have minority men. Minority women's representation doubled between 1993 and 2004, from under 4 percent of the members of the Commons up to over 8 percent in 2004. In 2004, minority women comprised 40 percent of all minority MPs, a better rate than we find for non-minority women.

Explanations

Before beginning an examination of the explanations for the relatively slow rate of increase in women's representation in the Canadian House of Commons, it is important to rule out potential explanations that have no empirical support. There is no compelling evidence that Canadian voters discriminate against female candidates (Black and Erickson 2003). The relatively high rate of turnover in Canadian elections means that incumbency does not unduly slow the rate of change in the composition of Parliament (Coletto 2010, 61; Docherty 1998, 31-59). Similarly, there is no evidence that female candidates are less able to raise money than their male counterparts (Coletto 2010, 60).

Any explanation for the rates of women's representation in the House of Commons must begin with an examination of the practices of political parties around nomination of candidates. Traditionally, the selection of the party's candidate is a decision made by the local electoral district association of each party, with minimal interference from the national party organization. In practice, however, national party organizations are involved in these decisions in a variety of ways. During the string of minority governments from 2004 to 2011, several parties guaranteed re-selection for MPs or even for candidates who had run in the prior election in order to ensure election readiness. The national parties also impose rules governing the selection process, may set the date of the meeting (in some instances to protect an incumbent), pre-screen potential candidates, and step in to recruit "star" candidates or "stopgap" candidates in areas where the party is weak (Sayers 1999, 44-46; Cross, 2004, 53-54). In some instances, national parties also involve themselves in the selection of candidates by the local party in order to increase the demographic representativeness of their party's slate of candidates.

In the absence of some involvement by the national party, local selection of candidates is best understood as a series of 308 unrelated decisions by loosely connected groups. The party members in each electoral district select the candidate they believe is best equipped to contest the election, with the overall composition of the candidate pool not considered relevant. Thus, any effort by the national party to ensure some degree of representativeness among candidates has the potential to be seen as an unwelcome national intrusion into local party affairs.

In the earliest political science literature examining women's numerical under-representation, parties were seen as gatekeepers to political office and the role of parties was characterized as negative: in this account, parties were worried about the electability of female candidates and were therefore unlikely to nominate women in winnable seats. Compelling empirical evidence supported this interpretation until the mid-1980s, but most analysts concluded that the practice ended at that time (Studlar and Matland 1994). Noting that between 2004 and 2008 women's candidacies as a proportion of all candidacies rose substantially while the proportion of women in the House did not, Louise Carbert (2011) undertook a sophisticated analysis to determine whether parties were nominating women disproportionately in electoral districts in which the party was less likely to win. She concludes that there is no difference between male and female candidates in the likelihood of winning the race. While there is little evidence that parties stand in the way of female candidates, as suggested by the gatekeeper model, there are significant variations in the level of effort they devote to encouraging women's candidacies.

The party that has implemented the most successful and sustained plan to ensure that its candidate pool is representative, both in terms of gender and other socio-demographic characteristics, is the NDP. The NDP's nomination and affirmative action policy states that 60 percent of winnable ridings should have women running as candidates and that 15 percent of these ridings should be contested by candidates who reflect the diversity of Canada. In addition, search committees in local ridings are required to actively seek out visible minority and female candidates, and they are responsible for satisfying party officials that substantial search efforts were made if no such candidate is found (Cross 2004, 70).

The Liberal Party has also periodically adopted measures designed to increase the number of women running under the party's banner. These efforts have been less consistent than those of the NDP, and they have tended to vary depending on the leader and the political conditions of the day. In 1993, then party leader Jean Chrétien made use of a recent change to the party's Constitution, allowing him to appoint candidates in order to meet an expressed target of 25 percent women candidates. He appointed nine women, mainly in ridings in which the group Liberals for Life was trying to run anti-choice candidates (Koop and Bittner 2010). When he was running for the leadership of the Liberal Party, Stéphane Dion promised that, as leader, he would ensure that one-third of the party's candidates in the next election would be women. In order to reach this target in the 2008 election, local riding associations were encouraged to seek out women candidates, and provincial party committees were empowered to approve or reject nomination papers, in some cases rejecting outright the nomination papers of male candidates (Bryden, 2007). The Liberal Party has since continued the policy of striving to field 33 percent female candidates.

Although the now-defunct Progressive Conservative Party did undertake some systematic efforts to promote women's candidacies, the Reform Party/Canadian Alliance made no such efforts. The product of the PC/CA merger, the Conservative Party, has no internal women's organization and has no formal program for encouraging women to run. Its leader, Stephen Harper, has made comments indicating opposition to any such efforts (Young 2006, 62). Despite this formal stance, the number of women running as Conservative candidates and being elected as Conservative MPs has increased markedly over the past three elections, from 12 percent to 17 percent. It is possible that the party has made some behind-the-scenes efforts to encourage this trend in order to address a potentially embarrassing absence of women from its caucus.

Regardless of whether there is an affirmative action plan in place, parties play a very significant role in recruiting candidates to run, as illustrated by the proportion of women in party caucuses. A study of Liberal and NDP candidates in the 2008 federal election found that parties, and particularly local party executives, continue to play a prominent role in encouraging candidates to run for office. Female candidates were much more likely to report having been recruited, either by the local party organization or by representatives of the national party and/or a party women's organization (Cross and Young 2013). Until the 1990s, local parties' recruitment function tended to be performed informally, but concerns about women's representation (among other issues) has led to a greater degree of formalization of the candidate search (Patten 2010, 141). Erickson and Carty's (1991) study finds that a female candidate is more likely to be selected when a formal candidate search committee is in place, suggesting that this trend towards formalization may be advantageous for female candidates. The informal aspect of the recruitment process remains significant. Both Tremblay and Pelletier

(2001) and Cheng and Tavits (2009) find that female candidates are more likely to be nominated in constituencies in which the local party president is female. These findings highlight the complex character of local recruitment efforts and serve as a reminder that when a party's leadership in a constituency is largely male, informal recruitment efforts may not yield potential female candidacies.

Because there is such variation among parties in the proportion of women nominated as candidates, vote swings can have a direct impact on the number of women elected. Carbert (2011) notes that the shift of seats away from the Liberals towards the Conservatives in 2004 reduced the number of women elected, but only by about five. Similarly, the 2011 election saw a shift of seats away from the Liberal Party in favour of the Conservatives, again reducing the number of women elected by a small number. The unanticipated surge of support for the NDP in 2011 more than offset this loss (this "landslide factor" is discussed briefly in Chapter 8, this volume). It must also be noted that, in 2008, the Conservative Party ran considerably more female candidates than it had in the past, increasing the proportion of its women candidates from 12 percent in 2004 to 21 percent in 2008. As the Conservatives have narrowed the gap between themselves and other parties in terms of women's candidacies, the impact of swings on the overall number of women in the House has been less.

Some research has also noted that women are more likely to run and win urban rather than rural electoral districts (Carbert 2009, 70-77). Regional variations in the rates of women's election (see Table 13.9) also occur, with women faring above the national average in Quebec and British Columbia, and below the national average in other regions, most notably in Atlantic Canada. These regional patterns are not random. Quebec and

TABLE 13.9

Women members of Parliament by region, 2008 and 2011

Region	2008		2011	
	Number	%	Number	%
Atlantic	5	16	4	13
Quebec	21	28	28	37
Ontario	21	20	20	19
Prairies	11	20	11	20
BC	10	28	12	33

British Columbia are notable among the provinces in which women's rates of representation are the highest in the provincial legislatures. The question of whether this should be seen as a product of provincial political culture, the extent of feminist activism in the province, or development of a pipeline of female candidates from provincial to federal politics has not been investigated thoroughly and requires further research.

While it is difficult to draw concrete connections between women's movement activism and the number of female candidates parties nominate, a revival of activism around women's representation at the national level over the past decade is noteworthy, and is discussed in Chapter 8 (this volume). Equal Voice, a multi-partisan, non-governmental non-profit organization that has become an advocate for women's political representation at both the national and provincial levels in English Canada, has pushed the parties to examine their internal practices around nominating women. This may have encouraged the Liberals and NDP to consider their practices related to the nomination of women. The Conservative Party has not been publicly receptive to Equal Voice's message. The increase in women's representation among Conservative candidates more likely has been driven by the party's desire to reduce the gender gap among voters, in which men have tended to be more likely than women to vote for the party.

One persistent issue relating to women's representation in the House of Commons is women's apparent unwillingness to run for political office. There is considerable evidence that women are less likely than men to express political ambitions. Lawless and Fox (2005, 2-12) surveyed men and women in professions that were likely to lead to political careers and found ample evidence that men were more likely than were women to consider, and to aspire to, holding elected office. Supporting this, Cross and Young (2013) analyzed the recruitment of Liberal and NDP candidates in 2008 and found that women were significantly less likely to be among those "self-selected" candidates who ran without being recruited by their party. There are many potential obstacles to women's developing political ambitions: they range from gender roles that perceive politics to be a hostile or distasteful environment to a preference for informal political action (in an interest group or social movement). Clearly, extensive recruitment efforts would be needed to overcome such considerations.

What, then, can be concluded about why women remain numerically under-represented in the Canadian House of Commons? There is evidence supporting both "supply" and "demand" explanations. In this context, "supply" refers to the number of women willing to run for public office. Supporting the supply explanation is research (discussed above) that demonstrates that women are less likely than men to express ambition for a political career and are more likely to need to be invited to run rather than initiating their candidacies independently. We also know that once women are nominated, they are as likely as similarly situated men to win their seat (Carbert 2011). Little evidence exists to suggest that parties are systematically turning away promising female candidates, and this lends credibility to the idea that the supply of potential female candidates is low. Nevertheless, it is overly simplistic to say that we would have more women in the House of Commons if only more women were to offer themselves as candidates.

The "demand" for female candidates is also a critically important factor. Canadian political parties have not undertaken the kinds of systematic recruitment efforts that would yield significant increases in women's representation. The exception to this generalization is the NDP, which has demonstrated that it is entirely possible to find well over one hundred women willing to run for office in any given election year if they are recruited, encouraged, and supported by their party. If women's representation were a high priority for the other parties (i.e., if demand increased), they would likely be able to replicate this accomplishment. That they do not do so tells us that the demand for women in politics at the national level in Canada is, at best, weak. It should also be noted that supply and demand are not independent of one another in this regard: when parties increase the demand for female candidates (as the NDP has done over the course of several elections), the supply increases to meet the demand.

Beyond these supply and demand explanations, it is useful to place Canada in comparative context. Canada's single-member-plurality electoral system is less amenable to efforts to improve the representation of women than proportional representation electoral systems (MacIvor 2003), though, as discussed in Chapter 9 (this volume) the electorate may reject a change when it is offered. Generally, single-member systems are less amenable to parties' efforts to increase the number of women elected because the selection of each candidate is constructed as a choice of the one "best-qualified" candidate. In a system in which parties nominate several candidates to run in a multi-member seat, the decision to nominate five men and no women (for example) lays bare the inequities in representation. Moreover, multi-member systems (including proportional representation) lend themselves more readily to parties' efforts to require the nomination of women or members of other under-represented groups.

Similarly, comparative analysis demonstrates that legislated quotas for women's representation, when enforced effectively, improve women's representation substantially (Tripp and Kang 2008; Krook 2009, 37-56). Notably, Canada is not a laggard among the Anglo-American democracies that share its single-member electoral system and liberal political culture; rather, Canada lags behind the countries that have electoral systems that lend themselves to more inclusive candidate pools as well as behind countries that have parties or legislatures that have implemented gender quotas. The idea that political parties be required to run a certain proportion of women as candidates runs up against two deeply ingrained elements of Canadian political culture. First, we have inherited the British notion that political parties are private entities that should not be subject to extensive state regulation (Gauja 2010, 2), and we have maintained this conception even when our parties have become largely state-supported entities. The idea that parties should not be subject to extensive regulation makes the notion that the state would dictate the composition of the candidate pool highly problematic in the eyes of many Canadians. Although a majority of Canadians surveyed in 2001 indicated that they believed that parties should be required to choose more female candidates (Howe and Northrup 2001, 17-22), such views tend to get drowned out by criticisms of the importance of "merit" in the candidate selection process, particularly among politicians and commentators on the right. Second, even though the Canadian Charter of Rights and Freedoms explicitly allows for positive discrimination, affirmative action measures tend to collide with a deeply held belief that merit should trump all other considerations in the hiring of employees, including politicians. In a comparative analysis of the relationship between models of political citizenship and propensity to adopt gender quotas, Krook, Lovenduski, and Squires (2009, 792) characterize Canada as having a predominantly "liberal" citizenship model, which is not amenable to the development of legislated quotas. Taken together, these elements of Canadian (or at least English-Canadian) political culture stand in the way of most of the bold measures that might be taken to increase women's representation in the House of Commons. In this respect, Canada appears destined to lag far behind Rwanda, Costa Rica, and the other countries that have adopted effective quotas for gender equality in political representation.

Conclusion: Prospects for Gender Parity

Issues of gender equality have, to a remarkable extent, fallen off the agenda of the federal government over the past decade (Bakker and Brodie 2008).

There are several plausible explanations for this. The absence of a vociferous and influential national feminist movement has certainly contributed to this decline, as has the election of three successive Conservative governments. The contrast between the Mulroney Progressive Conservative governments and the Harper Conservative governments is striking: more has been lost than the adjective "Progressive." While the Mulroney PCs tried to appeal to female voters by promoting women as candidates and in caucus, and in taking relatively progressive stances on non-economic issues (Young 2000, 132-82), the Harper Conservatives have made no formal efforts to promote women within the party and have espoused policies such as the Universal Child Benefit and income splitting, both of which reward families with two parents and one income.

In the heyday of the Canadian women's movement, the federal government was the focus of feminist lobbying, and provincial governments were peripheral. Since that time, Canadian federalism has evolved to make the federal government a less significant player in some policy areas of particular importance to women. The federal government's sole jurisdiction over criminal law and its pre-eminent position in fiscal and tax policy mean that it will continue to be relevant to matters of women's equality. Nevertheless, much of the action has shifted to the provinces, heightening the importance of women's representation in those venues.

Over the past thirty years, women have achieved many "firsts" in Canadian political life: they have served as party leaders, prime minister, Supreme Court chief justice, and governor general. Despite this, the number of women in the House of Commons increases slowly. The kinds of reform that would alter this pattern – electoral system change or introduction of representational quotas – are quite unlikely, so the focus of activists interested in women's representation will continue to be on increasing the supply of women interested in pursuing a political career and on encouraging political parties to heighten their efforts to recruit more female candidates.

Notes

Thanks to Julie Croskill and Kelly Pasolli for research assistance.

1   Women who had served in the military or who were closely related to servicemen could vote in 1917.

2   The Parliament of Canada website does not include Dick in its list of female candidates in federal elections. She is, however, listed as a candidate in the account of the 1921 federal election.

References

Atchison, Amy, and Ian Down. 2009. "Women Cabinet Ministers and Female-Friendly Social Policy." *Poverty and Public Policy* 1(2), Article 3.

Bakker, Isabella, and Janine Brodie. 2008. *Where Are the Women? Gender Equality, Budgets and Canadian Public Policy.* Ottawa: Canadian Centre for Policy Alternatives.

Bashevkin, Sylvia. 2010. "When Do Outsiders Break In? Institutional Circumstances of Party Leadership Victories by Women in Canada." *Commonwealth and Comparative Politics* 48(1): 72-90.

Black, Jerome H. 2008. "Ethnoracial Minorities in the 38th Parliament: Patterns of Change and Continuity." In Caroline Andrew, John Biles, Myer Siemiatycki, and Erin Tolley, eds., *Electing a Diverse Canada: The Representation of Immigrants, Minorities, and Women,* 229-54. Vancouver: UBC Press.

Black, Jerome H., and Lynda Erickson. 2003. "Women Candidates and Voter Bias: Do Women Politicians Need to Be Better?" *Electoral Studies* 22(1): 81-100.

Brodie, Janine. 2008. "We Are All Equal Now: Contemporary Gender Politics in Canada." *Feminist Theory* 9(2): 145-64.

Bryden, Joan. 2007. "Liberals Set to Bar Men in Some Ridings in Bid to Boost Female Candidates." *New Brunswick Telegraph Journal* (St. John), 9 February.

Carbert, Louise. 2009. "Are Cities More Congenial? Tracking the Rural Deficit of Women in the House of Commons." In Sylvia Bashevkin, ed., *Opening Doors Wider: Women's Political Engagement in Canada,* 70-92. Vancouver: UBC Press.

–. 2011. "The Hidden Rise of New Women Candidates Seeking Election to the House of Commons, 2000-2008." Unpublished manuscript.

Caul, Miki. 1999. "Women's Representation in Parliament: The Role of Political Parties." *Party Politics* 55(1): 79-98.

Cheng, Christine, and Margit Tavits. 2009. "Informal Influences in Selecting Female Political Candidates." *Political Research Quarterly* 64(2): 460-71.

Coletto, David. 2010. "A Matter of Quality? Candidates in Canadian Constituency Elections." PhD diss., University of Calgary.

Cross, William. 2004. *Political Parties.* Vancouver: UBC Press.

Cross, William, and Lisa Young. 2013. "Candidate Recruitment in Canada: The Role of Political Parties." In Amanda Bittner and Royce Koop, eds., *Parties, Elections, and the Future of Canadian Politics,* 24-45. Vancouver: UBC Press.

Docherty, David. 1998. *Mr. Smith Goes to Ottawa: Life in the House of Commons.* Vancouver: UBC Press.

Erickson, Lynda, and R.K. Carty. 1991. "Parties and Candidate Selection in the 1988 Canadian General Election." *Canadian Journal of Political Science* 24(2): 331-49.

Gauja, Anika. 2010. *Political Parties and Elections: Legislating for Representative Democracy.* Surrey: Ashgate Publishing.

Gidengil, Elisabeth, and André Blais. 2007. "Are Party Leaders Becoming More Important to Vote Choice in Canada?" In Hans J. Michelmann, Donald C. Story, and Jeffrey S. Steeves, eds., *Political Leadership and Representation in Canada: Essays in Honour of John C. Courtney,* 39-59. Toronto: University of Toronto Press.

Hausmann, Ricardo, Laura D. Tyson, and Saadia Zahidi. 2010. *The Global Gender Gap Report*. World Economic Forum. Available at http://www3.weforum.org/.

Howe, Paul, and David Northrup. 2000. "Strengthening Canadian Democracy: The Views of Canadians." *Policy Matters* 1(5). Institute for Research on Public Policy. Available at http://www.irpp.org/.

Inter-Parliamentary Union. 2011. Information available at http://www.ipu.org/.

Koop, Royce, and Amanda Bittner. 2010. "Candidate Nomination, 'Parachuted Candidates,' and Legislative Roles in Canada." Paper presented at the annual meeting of the Canadian Political Science Association, Montreal, 1-3 June.

Krook, Mona Lena. 2009. *Quotas for Women in Politics: Gender and Candidate Selection Reform Worldwide*. New York: Oxford University Press.

Krook, Mona Lena, Joni Lovenduski, and Judith Squires. 2009. "Gender Quotas and Models of Political Citizenship." *British Journal of Political Science* 39(4): 781-803.

Lawless, Jennifer L., and Richard L. Fox. 2005. *It Takes a Candidate: Why Women Don't Run for Office*. New York: Cambridge University Press.

MacIvor, Heather. 2003. "Women and the Canadian Electoral System." In Manon Tremblay and Linda Trimble, eds., *Women and Electoral Politics in Canada*, 22-36. Don Mills: Oxford University Press.

Patten, Steve. 2010. "Democracy and the Candidate Selection Process in Canadian Elections." In Heather MacIvor, ed., *Election*, 135-54. Toronto: Emond Montgomery Publications.

Sayers, Anthony 1999. *Parties, Candidates, and Constituency Campaigns in Canadian Elections*. Vancouver: UBC Press.

Statistics Canada. 2006. "Measuring Violence Against Women: Statistical Trends 2006." Minister of Industry. Available at http://www.statcan.gc.ca/.

–. 2010. "Economic Well-Being." In *Women in Canada: A Gender-Based Statistical Report*. Minister of Industry. Available at http://www.statcan.gc.ca/.

Studlar, Donley T., and Richard E. Matland. 1994. "The Growth of Women's Representation in the Canadian House of Commons and the Election of 1984: A Reappraisal." *Canadian Journal of Political Science* 27(1): 53-79.

Tremblay, Manon, and Réjean Pelletier. 2001. "More Women Constituency Party Presidents: A Strategy for Increasing the Number of Women Candidates in Canada?" *Party Politics* 7(2): 157-90.

Tripp, Aili Mari, and Alice Kang. 2008. "The Global Impact of Quotas: On the Fast Track to Increased Female Legislative Representation." *Comparative Political Studies* 41(3): 338-61.

United Nations Development Programme (UNDP). 2010. *Gender Equality Index*. Available at http://hdr.undp.org/.

Young, Lisa. 2000. *Feminists and Party Politics*. Vancouver: UBC Press.

–. 2006. "Women's Representation in the Canadian House of Commons." In Marian Sawer, Manon Tremblay, and Linda Trimble, eds., *Representing Women in Parliament: A Comparative Study*, 47-66. New York: Routledge.

14

"Way Past That Era Now?"

Women in the Canadian Senate

STEPHANIE MULLEN, WITH THE COLLABORATION
OF MANON TREMBLAY AND LINDA TRIMBLE

A life-size sculpture of five women wearing hats and taking tea entices visitors to Canada's Parliament Buildings. Who are these women and why are they given such prominence on Parliament Hill? As a plaque explains, these Alberta women are now famous because they mounted a successful legal challenge to secure women's right to be considered persons under the law and, thereby, to be seen to be eligible for appointment to the Senate. Thanks to the persistence of the so-called "Famous Five," the first female senator was appointed in 1930. In 2011, at the beginning of the 41st Parliament, women held 38 of the 105 Senate seats, 36 percent of the total.

This chapter addresses the following questions: How did the number of female senators grow to the extent that they now exceed the proportion of women elected to the House of Commons? Who are these women and what are their contributions? It begins with an examination of the "Persons" case, which is the starting point for Canadian women's entry into the Senate. The next section explains the key institutional differences between the Senate and the House of Commons. Following this discussion, we examine the number of women appointed to the Senate and the explanations for changes over time. Finally, we offer a discussion of the prospects for gender parity in the Senate and make an appeal for more research on this important but often overlooked legislative body.

THE SENATE OF CANADA

FIRSTS

Women obtain the right to be appointed to the Senate	1930
First woman appointed to the Senate: Cairine Wilson	1930
First woman appointed to the Senate from British Columbia: Nancy Hodges	1953
First woman appointed to the Senate from Alberta: Martha Bielish	1979
First woman appointed to the Senate from Saskatchewan: Raynell Andreychuk	1993
First woman appointed to the Senate from Manitoba: Olive Irvine	1960
First woman appointed to the Senate from Ontario: Cairine Wilson	1930
First woman appointed to the Senate from Quebec: Mariana Beauchamp-Jodoin	1953
First woman appointed to the Senate from New Brunswick: Muriel McQueen Fergusson	1953
First woman appointed to the Senate from PEI: Florence Inman	1955
First woman appointed to the Senate from Nova Scotia: Margaret Norrie	1972
First woman appointed to the Senate from Newfoundland and Labrador: Ethel Cochrane	1986
First Aboriginal woman appointed to the Senate: Thelma Chalifoux	1997
First First Nations woman appointed to the Senate: Lillian Eva Dyck	2005
First Métis woman appointed to the Senate: Thelma Chalifoux	1997
First Inuit woman appointed to the Senate	None
First visible minority woman appointed to the Senate: Anne Cools	1984
First francophone woman appointed to the Senate: Marianna Beauchamp-Jodoin	1953
First female speaker of the Senate: Muriel McQueen Fergusson	1972
First female government leader in the Senate: Joyce Fairbairn	1993
First woman to chair a Senate standing committee: Cairine Wilson (Senate Standing Committee on Immigration and Labour)	1948
First woman of Pakistani origin appointed to the Senate: Salma Ataullahjan	2010
First woman of Korean origin appointed to the Senate: Yonah Martin	2009

Source: Parliament of Canada (2011b)

Background

The "Persons" Case

The "Persons" case is a logical place to begin any discussion of women in the Canadian Senate because it represents the end of a struggle and the formal removal of a legal barrier to women's entry to the Second Chamber. When an Alberta woman named Emily Murphy put her name forward to the prime minister for appointment to the Senate in 1917, she was rejected on the grounds that she was not considered a "person" under the Constitution for this purpose and, thus, was not eligible to serve in the Upper House. While the Alberta government recognized women as persons, this decision only applied to women in that province. The prime minister at the time, Robert Borden, said he was not against the idea of a woman's being appointed to the Senate but was constrained by the British North America Act, which stated that only "qualified persons" could be appointed to the Upper House. It was argued that, when the British North America Act was written, the term "persons" only referred to men and so only men could be appointed to the Senate.

This reasoning was challenged in 1927 when five women from Alberta, today known collectively as the "Famous Five" – Emily Murphy, Henrietta Muir Edwards, Irene Parlby, Louise McKinney, and Nellie McClung – contested the legal interpretation of the word "persons" before the Supreme Court of Canada. The Supreme Court heard the case on 14 March 1928 and rendered its decision on 24 April 1928. The Court essentially supported Prime Minister Borden's view, holding that women were not included in section 24 because, when the British North America Act was signed, women were not included in the legal definition of "persons" (*Edwards v. Canada* [1928] S.C.R. 276). At this point in Canadian history, the Supreme Court of Canada was not the highest legal authority as it is today, and its decisions could be appealed to the Judicial Committee of the Privy Council (JCPC) of England, which is exactly the course the Famous Five took. In October 1929, the JCPC overturned the decision of the Supreme Court, stating: "The exclusion of women from all public offices is a relic of days more barbarous than ours ... and to those who ask why the word should include females the obvious answer is why should it not?" (*Edwards v. A.G. of Canada* [1930] A.C. 124). Specifically, the JCPC decision took the opposite stance to that of Prime Minister Borden and the Supreme Court of Canada and held that the term "person" was ambiguous and that if Parliament had wanted to exclude women from the term "person," it needed to explicitly state this intention. As Lord Sankey wrote: "Their Lordships have come to the conclusion that the word "persons" in sec. 24 includes members both of the male and female sex and that, therefore, the question propounded by the Governor-General must be answered in the affirmative and that women are eligible to be summoned to and become members of the Senate of Canada" (*Edwards v. A.G. of Canada* [1930] A.C. 124). The JCPC decision thereby established that Canadian women were eligible to be appointed to the Senate.

TABLE 14.1
Number of women appointed to the Senate, by parliament

Parliament	Total number of legislators	Women appointed	
		Number	%
32nd (1980-84)	126	14	11
33rd (1984-88)	118	16	14
34th (1988-93)	138	21	15
35th (1994-97)	124	27	22
36th (1997-2000)	136	39	29
37th (2001-4)	120	42	35
38th (2004-5)	113	40	35
39th (2006-8)	102	36	35
40th (2008-11)	125	42	34
41st (2011-)	105	38	36

Source: Parliament of Canada (2011c).

Following the JCPC decision, Prime Minister Mackenzie King appointed Canada's first female senator, Cairine Wilson, in 1930. It is ironic that the woman who actually began the struggle, Emily Murphy, never actually served in the Senate, but all women senators owe her a tremendous debt, and recent efforts of the Famous Five Foundation will ensure that the history of her struggle will not be forgotten. Indeed, the representation of women in the Senate has since grown from one in 1930 to thirty-eight in 2011 (the 41st Parliament), constituting 36 percent of the Senate's membership (see Table 14.1). In total, eighty-five women have sat in the Senate since 1930 (Parliament of Canada 2011c).

The increase in the number of women appointed to the Senate parallels the history of women's election to the House of Commons until quite recently. The appointments of women have now outpaced the number of women elected due to the gradual recognition that equality requires women to figure prominently in national public life. Historically women were appointed at the rate that they were elected federally (Arscott 1998); so, for example, it was only in the 32nd Parliament from 1980 to 1984, when women achieved 10 percent of the seats in the House of Commons, that they broke into the double digits (11 percent) in the Senate as well. A slow but steady climb continued with each succeeding Parliament until women exceeded the 20 percent level in the 35th Parliament (1994-97). In just two more parliaments, the representation of women in the Senate jumped from

22 percent to 35 percent, and the percentage has remained around this level since the 37th Parliament (2001-4). The reasons for the increases, and the recent plateau, are discussed in detail below. First, however, it is important to answer the "why-should-we-care" question. Many Canadians see the Senate as a mere "rubber stamp," lacking the legitimacy and inclination to challenge (never mind change) legislation proposed by the main decision-making body, the House of Commons. So why does it matter that women have equal representation in the Senate?

The Legislative Context of Analysis

The Senate's role in the legislative process cannot be examined without analyzing the legislative process as a whole. The main tasks of the House of Commons are to: support a government that retains the confidence of elected representatives; criticize government legislation; offer the electorate a viable alternative to the current government; hold the political executive (the prime minister and the cabinet) to account; educate the public on government legislation and inform cabinet of public opinion; and conduct investigative review and approval of legislation (Franks 1987, 4-5). Some scholars feel the House does not do a particularly diligent job of legislative review and that the Senate is better suited to this crucial task. In fact, the main functions of the Senate are to serve as a house of legislative review and to represent regional interests in the national policy process (Watts 2003). According to Thomas (2003, 190-91), the House of Commons has become overly focused on criticizing the government and is often ineffective in its review of legislation because, among other things, it is overtly partisan and party discipline is too rigid. This conjuncture may result in unwillingness to compromise between parties, committee deadlock, and overtly partisan posturing in debates. Senators can be partisan at times; however, they are also more likely to work together and propose solutions to difficult policy problems that are of interest to Canadians. Franks (1987, 190) sums up the strengths of the Senate: "Competence, freedom from competing demands on energy, low partisanship, and an absence of pressures of time and fears about re-election, are the keys to successful Senate investigations" (see also Smith 2003, 110-30).

Since Confederation, the Senate has added other functions that help differentiate it from the House of Commons: public policy analysis and the representation and protection of minorities (Franks 1987, 188-94). Therefore, the contemporary Canadian Senate blends two traditional functions, that of legislative review and regional representation, with two modern ones, that of investigation of public policy through its committee system and the protection of minorities.

Legislative Review

Discussions related to the Senate's legislative review function usually focus on the Senate as a legislative body of sober second thought and on the technical revisions to government bills that take up most of the senators' legislative time. However, constitutionally the Senate has a veto on all legislation passed in the lower house. When the UK Parliament passed the British North America Act, which brought the Senate into existence, the intention was to mirror the British House of Lords, where the power to review or revise and ultimately reject government bills was considered a necessary check on the "democratic excesses" of the lower house. In fact, the power to veto is used rarely because of its perceived illegitimacy. Even during the Senate's infamous filibuster on the goods and services tax, a policy initiative most Canadians firmly opposed, many observed that appointed senators should not be able to overturn the decisions of democratically elected representatives. However, some scholars see the Senate's veto as an important constitutional protection against undemocratic behaviour by governments, suggesting that it would be legitimate for the Senate to employ the veto over "highly controversial bills for which the governments lack an electoral mandate; dangerous bills that could do unpredictable and irreparable damage to the national interest; bills that violate the *Constitution*, including the *Charter of Rights and Freedoms*; [and] bills that violate the fundamental rights of linguistic and other minorities" (Thomas 2003, 198 [emphasis in original]).

Many women's organizations felt that Bill C-43, An Act Respecting Abortion, represented one of those rare pieces of controversial legislation for which a Senate veto was appropriate and indeed legitimate. Bill C-43 was designed to replace the criminal code provisions restricting the provision of abortion service, which were struck down by the Supreme Court of Canada in 1988 (Dunsmuir 1998, 3). Specifically, the Supreme Court found that the law was unconstitutional because it violated section 7 of the Charter of Rights and Freedoms by infringing upon a woman's right to "life, liberty and security of the person." Unhappy with a legislative void, in 1990 the federal Progressive Conservative government, led by Prime Minister Brian Mulroney, introduced Bill C-43, which re-criminalized abortion under certain circumstances. Despite concern about the new abortion legislation, Bill C-43 passed third reading in the House of Commons in May

1990 and was sent to the Senate for committee hearings and a final vote. On 31 January 1991, Bill C-43 was defeated by a tie vote in the Senate, and, as a result, abortion was not re-criminalized.

As expected, partisanship shaped the outcome. But gender may have trumped party affiliation in this instance as three women senators from the Tory party and all of the Liberal women senators voted against the bill. Interestingly, no women senators were absent from this vote, which perhaps indicates the seriousness with which female senators approached this issue. The House of Commons debates following the Supreme Court ruling in *Morgentaler v. the Queen* offer an example of gender superseding party: free from party discipline – and thus in a legislative context closely resembling that in the Senate – no woman MP spoke in favour of the "anti-choice" option regarding abortion but all united behind either the "pro-choice" or the "compromise" position (Tremblay and Boivin 1990-91). In both the Commons and the Senate, female legislators shaped the outcome of an issue central to women's rights and bodily autonomy.

Senators do not tend to challenge legislation by voting against it or vetoing it. But when it does occur, it should not be considered an affront to democracy since the Senate's function is legislative review. As a complement to the House of Commons, better legislative review will theoretically result in better legislation, and women need to be present in the Senate to help perform this function. While vetoes are rare, the Senate performs a great deal of unseen and largely unsung legislative oversight, correcting errors in legislation and suggesting vital amendments. As such, it is critical that women are appointed to the Senate and represented equally on its committees.

Women's Political Representation: The Numbers

After the first appointment of a woman to the Senate under Prime Minister King, women were not appointed in any significant numbers until the Trudeau era. As Table 14.2 illustrates, this was the first time a prime minister's appointment of women climbed into the double digits (15 percent). Of Trudeau's eighty-one appointments to the Senate, twelve were women. The next significant increase occurred under the leadership of Prime Minister Mulroney, as 23 percent of his fifty-seven appointments were women (thirteen women). However, the largest jump thus far was initiated by Prime Minister Chrétien, who appointed thirty-three women (44 percent). Under Chrétien's watch, a critical mass of women in the Senate was achieved as women made up 35 percent of the Senate during the 37th Parliament's 3rd

TABLE 14.2
Senate appointments, by prime minister and gender

Prime minister (years)	Party	Female N	Female %	Male N	Male %	Total N
By Royal Proclamation*	–	0	0	72	100	72
John A. Macdonald (1867-73, 1878-91)	Conservative	0	0	91	100	91
Alexander Mackenzie (1873-78)	Liberal	0	0	16	100	16
John Abbott (1891-92)	Conservative	0	0	6	100	6
John Thompson (1892-94)	Conservative	0	0	5	100	5
Mackenzie Bowell (1894-96)	Conservative	0	0	13	100	13
Charles Tupper (1896)	Conservative	0	0	1	100	1
Wilfrid Laurier (1896-1911)	Liberal	0	0	81	100	81
Robert Borden (1911-17, 1917-20)	Conservative	0	0	62	100	62
Arthur Meighen (1920-21, 1926)	Conservative	0	0	15	100	15
Mackenzie King (1921-26, 1926-30, 1935-48)	Liberal	1	1	102	99	103
Richard Bennett (1930-35)	Conservative	1	3	32	97	33
Louis Saint-Laurent (1948-57)	Liberal	4	7	51	93	55
John Diefenbaker (1957-63)	Conservative	2	5	35	95	37
Lester Pearson (1963-68)	Liberal	1	3	38	97	39
Pierre Trudeau (1968-79, 1980-84)	Liberal	12	15	69	85	81
Joe Clark (1979-80)	PC	1	10	10	90	11
John Turner (1984)	Liberal	0	0	3	100	3
Brian Mulroney (1984-93)	PC	13	23	44	77	57
Kim Campbell (1993)	PC	n/a	–	n/a	–	n/a
Jean Chrétien (1993-2003)	Liberal	33	44	42	56	75
Paul Martin (2003-6)	Liberal	6	35	11	65	17
Stephen Harper (2006 to May 2012)	Conservative	15	31	33	69	48
Totals	–	89	9.7	832	90.3	921

* Royal Proclamation means that the Crown appointed these senators. All were appointed on 7 October 1867.
Source: Parliament of Canada (2011c).

Session. This critical mass level has been maintained since then. Thirty-five percent of Prime Minister Martin's appointees were women, but women have constituted only 31 percent of Prime Minister Harper's nominees.

Scholarship on representation asserts the importance of "ethnic and racial designations ... in shaping women's identities, social locations, and access to power" (Ship 1988, 311; see also Andrew et al. 2008). Increasing the diversity of an institution is an important step towards enhancing the substantial representation of issues important to a diversity of women. But senators are no more representative of the general population than their counterparts in the House of Commons. Visible minorities make up approximately 13 percent of Canada's population but constitute only 6 percent of the members of both houses (Black 2003; see also Mullen 2006, 80). This situation has not gone unnoticed by senators themselves; in fact, one senator asked Prime Minister Martin to consider filling the vacancies in the Senate at that time with visible minorities (Mullen 2006, 81). Another senator noted that more work needs to be done, observing that the Senate is "not an ethnically diverse institution" (Mullen 2006, 81).

The situation is no better for First Nations. In the history of appointments to the Senate, there have been fifteen First Nations, Métis, or Inuit senators and only three were women – senators Dyck, Lovelace Nicholas, and Chalifoux. Although women constitute 36 percent of the current Senate, Aboriginal women make up 2 percent of all senators. Turpel-Lafond (1997, 66) states that First Nations people are culturally distinct and linguistically diverse and should not be viewed as a homogeneous group.

Since 2006, Stephen Harper has appointed to the Senate three foreign-born women: Salma Ataullahjan (born in Pakistan), Yonah Martin (South Korea), and Asha Seth (India). The fact that so few women from ethno-cultural communities have been appointed to the Senate means that a representational gap (or deficit) exists within Canada's political institutions.

Explanations

The Senate of Canada is an appointed body, which makes the political opportunity structures clear, though not always accessible by actors outside the top echelons of the governing party. The political opportunity structure is defined as the "forces, structures and ideas that characterize official political systems and enhance or deter women's political participation" (Trimble and Arscott 2003, 142). Since the prime minister appoints senators, the main factor shaping the number of women in the Red Chamber is the willingness of the governing party to nominate them. The prime minister's director of appointments is in charge of putting lists of names together for government appointments.

Marjory LeBreton, who now sits in the Senate, was the director of appointments under Prime Minister Mulroney. During her tenure, there was an explicit outreach program to recruit more women to government appointments. "The prime minister gave specific directives that we were going to get these numbers up, and if we didn't have a significant number of women, he would simply reject all of these appointments until we did" (LeBreton, quoted in McKie 2011). As illustrated in Table 14.2, this strategy was successful, and Prime Minister Mulroney improved upon his predecessor's record of appointing women. That political will is an important component for the increase in the number of women appointed to the Senate is further demonstrated by examining the number of women appointed during the Chrétien era. Penny Collenette served as the director of appointments under Prime Minister Chrétien, who was responsible for the largest increase in women in the Senate to date. During her four years as director of appointments, there was a major increase over the previous government's statistics related to women, which declined after she left the post. Beyond the appointments to the Senate, she was involved with other ground-breaking appointments – the first woman appointed to be the head of CBC, the first woman appointed Usher of the Black Rod, several women appointed to the Supreme Court, as well as women appointed to numerous government boards and commissions that were traditionally male-dominated. Again, this was accomplished through a specific policy put in place by Prime Minister Chrétien, who worked closely with his director of appointments: "We read trade magazines ... We looked for women who won awards. If I found a really good one, I would call a minister and ask, 'Did you know this person?'" (Collenette, quoted in McKie 2011).

Since Prime Minister Stephen Harper took office, the number of women appointed to the Senate has dropped. Ironically, the party official defending the prime minister's track record on appointments is not his current director of appointments, Derek Vanstone, but the leader of the government in the Senate, Marjory LeBreton, the woman responsible for the Mulroney government's positive track record for placing women in top posts, and she has changed her tune. LeBreton asserts that the decrease in the number of women appointed to the Senate is not due to a lack of commitment to gender parity. In fact, in a recent interview, LeBreton states: "The prime minister doesn't have to go out [and talk about the need for more women to apply for positions]. None of us has to go out and say that. It's a given. We're way past that era now. Way past" (LeBreton, quoted in McKie 2011). Accordingly, it is difficult to determine what measures LeBreton or Vanstone are taking, if any, to increase the number of women appointed to the Senate. Although increasing the representation of women in the Senate may be easier than bumping up the numbers of women elected to the House of

Commons, a prime minister's (or indeed a government's) resistance to gender-equity policies and initiatives can put the brakes on progress. With a Conservative majority government, women are unlikely to exceed the 40 percent mark in the foreseeable future.

Regional Representation

Thomas (2003, 206) argues that the Senate plays an important role in expressing regional interests (see also Smith 2003, 70-77). Are female senators equally distributed across the country? That regional political cultures and interests seek expression in national institutions is illustrated by demands for a so-called "Triple E" Senate, with equal, effective, and elected representation from each province. Do women have equal representation as senators in each province? Table 14.3 shows that gender parity does exist in all but a few jurisdictions. The largest regions are provinces that fall well short of gender parity: eight (33 percent) in Ontario and six (26 percent) in Quebec are women. These provinces hold the largest number of total seats in the Senate (24 seats each). If a prime minister wanted to increase the number of women in the Senate, she or he could implement a policy of gender balance within each region since this is how seats in the Senate are

TABLE 14.3

Representation in the Senate by sex and region, 40th Parliament (2008-11)

Jurisdiction	Female		Male		Total
	Number	%	Number	%	
British Columbia	3	50	3	50	6
Alberta	3	50	3	50	6
Saskatchewan	4	67	2	33	6
Manitoba	3	50	3	50	6
Ontario	8	33	16	67	24
Quebec	6	26	17	74	23
New Brunswick	5	50	5	50	10
Prince Edward Island	2	50	2	50	4
Nova Scotia	1	10	9	90	10
Newfoundland	2	40	3	60	5
Yukon	0	0	1	100	1
Northwest Territories	0	0	1	100	1
Nunavut	0	0	1	100	1
Total	37	36	66	64	103

Source: Parliament of Canada (2011d)

distributed. Therefore, these two regions provide readily available mechanisms for further change in the composition of the Senate.

Senate Standing Committees

Since MPs divide their attention between constituency work, critic responsibilities, House duties, and party work, in-depth research on legislation is
sometimes impossible to achieve. The situation is quite the opposite in the
Senate. Senators have more time to conduct research in the Senate for several reasons. First, they have very little constituency work, and, since most
do not have official ridings,[1] they do not have the same level of demand
from constituents as do MPs. Second, their legislative work is heavily focused on committee duties. Third, Senate committees focus more on research and investigations rather than on other legislative tasks such as crafting
legislation.

The Senate standing committees constitute an area in which the increased presence of women could have an influential effect since committee
work has the potential to shape the legislative process and policy outcomes.
Thus it is of particular importance that the perspective of women be present
here. However, in many ways women are under-represented on Senate
standing committees. Three observations can be drawn from Table 14.4.
First, only five of the eighteen (28 percent) committees are chaired, and four
(22 percent) are co-chaired by a woman. Also, women were the chair and
co-chair of two committees: human rights and official languages. Second,
even with the increased level of women's representation in the Senate (36
percent), women were not proportionately represented on the Senate standing committees of the 40th Parliament. More specifically, a majority of the
committees (that is, eleven out of eighteen) had less than 36 percent of
women in their membership, and half (nine out of eighteen) had less than
the commonly fixed critical mass threshold of 30 percent. Only seven committees exceed the 36 percent level of women's representation in the Senate.
Third, of those seven committees with a minimum of 36 percent women as
committee members, four include topics traditionally associated with
women (notably, social affairs, science and technology, with 67 percent of
women members; official languages, 63 percent; the Selection Committee,
56 percent; and human rights, 56 percent). In contrast, in the Fisheries
and Oceans Committee, a traditionally male-defined portfolio, women held
58 percent of the memberships. One can argue that a critical mass of women
in the Senate may help women to branch out into areas traditionally dominated by male legislators. Yet, with women's presence reduced to 17 percent

TABLE 14.4

Women's representation on Senate standing committees, 40th Parliament (2008-11)

Senate standing committee	Female		Male		Total
	N	%	N	%	
Aboriginal Peoples†	5	42	7	58	12
Agriculture and Forestry	3	25	9	75	12
Anti-terrorism (special)	3	33	6	67	9
Banking, Trade and Commerce†	2	18	9	82	11
Conflict of Interest for Senators	2	40	3	60	5
Energy, the Environment and Natural Resources	2	17	10	83	12
Fisheries and Oceans	7	58	5	42	12
Foreign Affairs and International Trade*	3	25	9	75	12
Human Rights*†	5	56	4	44	9
Internal Economy, Budgets and Administration	5	33	10	67	15
Legal and Constitutional Affairs*	2	17	10	83	12
National Finance	3	25	9	75	12
National Security and Defence*	2	22	7	78	9
Official Languages*†	5	63	3	37	8
Rules, Procedures and the Rights of Parliament	4	27	11	73	15
Selection Committee‡	5	56	4	44	9
Social Affairs, Science and Technology	8	67	4	33	12
Transport and Communications	3	25	9	75	12

* Chair of the committee is a woman.
† Deputy chair of the committee is a woman.
‡ This committee officially selects the speaker of the Senate and all members of Senate committees.
Source: Parliament of Canada (2011a).

on the Energy, Environment and Natural Resources Committee as well as on the Legal and Constitutional Affairs Committee; to 18 percent on the Banking, Trade and Commerce Committee; and to 22 percent on the National Security and Defence Committee, all fields traditionally considered as male preserves, it is difficult for female senators to represent women's perspectives on these important issues. Solutions to women's continued under-representation on traditionally male-dominated committees include party procedures to prioritize the appointment of women to under-represented committees (Mullen 2006, 147-48).

Substantive Representation

Has women's greater level of descriptive representation in the Senate translated into more substantive representation? It is difficult to say as few studies have examined the impact of female senators' legislative participation on policy outcomes. The same factors constraining women MPs' ability to perform for women in the House of Commons, notably party discipline, exist in the Senate. The areas in which women senators have made substantive progress are areas that are difficult to quantitatively measure, specifically work within the committee system as well as extra-parliamentary activities. Mullen (2006, 167-72) found that women senators worked on issues related to women or general social issues more than did their male colleagues. Furthermore, they acted as bridges for women to enter into the parliamentary institutions, which was particularly important for groups that did not already have an access point in Parliament.

It is possible that female senators are helping to protect the interests of women and under-represented groups through legislative activities. Thomas (2003, 211) found that, "back in the 1960s, it was a Senate committee that investigated serious poverty ... and ... its report led to a series of new social policies ... During the 1980s, Senate committees did important work on retirement age policies and on children in conflict with the law." All of these issues are of great importance in women's lives. Other groups have benefited from the Senate's function of protecting minorities. From 1990 to 1997, "five bills providing for protection against discrimination based upon sexual orientation were brought before Parliament" (Thomas 2003, 211). After four failed attempts, one did have an effect on legislation. Eventually, Parliament passed a gay rights amendment to the Canadian Human Rights Act. Interestingly, "a result of a late Senate amendment that slipped through the Commons unnoticed, the version of the Bill adopted in 1997 provided for the extension of affirmative action programs to victims of sexual discrimination, even though this feature had been deliberately omitted from the Government bill" (ibid.). Given that women suffer sexual/gender discrimination, this Senate amendment contributed to their substantive representation. More research should explore the Senate's function of protecting minorities and assess its impact on women. Since female senators are no more demographically and ethnically diverse than their counterparts in the Lower House, they face equally daunting challenges in substantively representing women's diversity.

Conclusion: Prospects for Gender Parity

As demonstrated in this chapter, while women are better represented in the Senate than in the House of Commons, and while women senators now make up the highest proportion of women in any legislature in Canada, they are far from achieving gender parity. Although the Senate is more diverse than the House of Commons, both houses still lag behind proportionality in Canadian society. Visible minority and Aboriginal groups in particular continue to be under-represented. While gender parity in the Senate does exist in six of the thirteen provincial jurisdictions, unfortunately, this proportion does not translate into the representation of women on the Senate standing committees. Despite modest gains, women remain excluded from some important Senate standing committees in which power is wielded over public policy. In addition, the downward turn in prime ministerial appointments of women to the Senate since the 1990s should flag a concern about the trend towards lower levels of representation in the Upper House.

This trend is not likely to be reversed by the Harper government's approach to Senate reform. Bill C-7, the Senate Reform Act, is now slowly making its way through the legislative process, but if passed it will impose non-renewable, nine-year term limits for senators, and it will allow provinces to elect Senate nominees, who would then be appointed by the governor general on the advice of the prime minister.[2] Harper has appointed "elected" Senate nominees from Alberta and declares he will continue to do so (CBC 2012). Due in part to opposition to the bill from several provinces, the Government of Canada asked the Supreme Court to rule on its constitutionality, thus the fate of the Harper government's approach to Senate reform is uncertain. Even if Bill C-7 is passed into law and survives a constitutional challenge, it will likely result in fewer women in the Senate. Although the term limits would open up more Senate positions to be filled by women, Alberta's experience with Senate "elections" indicates that few women will contest these positions. Under the auspices of its 1987 Senatorial Selection Act, Alberta has had four Senate nominee elections, held in 1989, 1998, 2004, and 2012, respectively. A total of thirty-three candidates were on these ballots, and only two of them were women (6 percent). The political parties that present the highest number of female candidates in Alberta provincial elections, the Liberals and the New Democrats, have boycotted the Senate election process on the grounds that it is an ineffective mechanism for Senate reform. As a result, only conservative parties actively participate in Senate elections, and, as the Alberta chapter illustrates, these parties have made few efforts to recruit women. This pattern is likely to be replicated in other provinces that agree to hold Senate elections as the NDP favours abolition of the Senate and the Liberal Party of Canada opposes Bill C-7 on constitutional and practical grounds. As a result, Senate candidate slates will continue to be dominated by men. As well, the financial and resource barriers to election that have been highlighted in this volume will likely deter women from seeking election as Senate nominees.

This chapter also highlights the contributions that can be made by women in the Senate, where careful legislative oversight can correct errors in government legislation and can even change the course of government policy. The specific nature of women's contributions is largely unexplored at this point. One of the reasons for this is that research on women in the Senate lags far behind the vast volume of academic works on women in the House of Commons and in provincial legislatures. Nevertheless, this chapter provides a firm foundation for future work, and it is hoped that interested academics will respond to this research challenge by generating a body of writings that will complement what is known about women legislators in the House of Commons.

Notes

Stephanie Mullen would like to thank research assistant Beverly Zawada for her assistance with this chapter.

1 Section 22 of the Constitution Act, 1867, provides that the twenty-four senators representing the province are specifically nominated to one of the twenty-four electoral divisions of Lower Canada.

2 See http://www.parl.gc.ca/.

References

Andrew, Caroline, John Biles, Myer Siemiatycki, and Erin Tolley, eds. 2008. *Electing a Diverse Canada: The Representation of Immigrants, Minorities, and Women.* Vancouver: UBC Press.

Arscott, Jane. 1998. "'More Women': The RCSW and Political Representation, 1970." In Manon Tremblay and Caroline Andrew, eds., *Women and Political Representation in Canada*, 145-69. Ottawa: University of Ottawa Press.

Black, Jerome. 2003. "Differences that Matter: Minority Women MPs 1993-2000." In Manon Tremblay and Linda Trimble, eds., *Women and Electoral Politics in Canada*, 59-73. Don Mills: Oxford.

CBC. 2012. "Quebec Asks Court to Block Harper's Senate Reform Plans." CBC, 1 May. Available at http://www.cbc.ca/.

Dunsmuir, Mollie. 1998. "Abortion: Constitutional and Legal Developments." Ottawa: Library of Parliament, Parliamentary Research Branch, 1998, 3. Available at http://dsp-psd.pwgsc.gc.ca/.

Edwards v. Canada (Attorney General) [1928] S.C.R. 276.

Edwards v. A.G. of Canada [1930] A.C. 124. Available at http://www.chrc-ccdp.ca/.

Franks, C.E.S. 1987. *The Parliament of Canada.* Toronto: University of Toronto Press.

McKie, David. 2011. "Female Appointments dip under Tories Last." CBC News, 8 January. Available at http://www.cbc.ca/.

Mullen, Stephanie. 2006. "The Substantive Representational Effects of Women Legislators in Presence, Legislative Outputs, and Extra-Parliamentary Activity." PhD diss., Carleton University.

Parliament of Canada. 2011a. List of Standing and Special Committees. Available at http://www.parl.gc.ca/.

–. 2011b. Senate Fact Sheet: Women in the Senate. Available at http://www.parl.gc.ca/.

–. 2011c. Senators. Available at http://www.parl.gc.ca/.

–. 2011d. Senators Average Age. Available at http://www.parl.gc.ca/.

Ship, Susan Judith. 1998. "Problematizing Ethnicity and 'Race' in Feminist Scholarship on Women and Politics." In Manon Tremblay and Caroline Andrew, eds., *Women and Political Representation in Canada*, 311-40. Ottawa: University of Ottawa Press.

Smith, David E. 2003. *The Canadian Senate in Bicameral Perspective*. Toronto: University of Toronto Press.

Thomas, Paul. 2003. "Comparing the Lawmaking Roles of the Senate and the House of Commons." In Serge Joyal, ed., *Protecting Canadian Democracy: The Senate You Never Knew*, 189-228. Montreal and Kingston: McGill-Queen's University Press.

Tremblay, Manon, and Guylaine Boivin. 1990-91. "La question de l'avortement au Parlement canadien: De l'importance du genre dans l'orientation des débats." *Canadian Journal of Women and the Law* 4(2): 459-76.

Trimble, Linda, and Jane Arscott. 2003. *Still Counting: Women in Politics across Canada*. Peterborough: Broadview Press.

Turpel-Lafond, Mary Ellen. 1997. "Patriarchy and Paternalism: The Legacy of the Canadian State for First Nations Women." In Caroline Andrew and Sandra Rodgers, eds. *Women and the Canadian State*, 64-78. Montreal and Kingston: McGill-Queen's University Press.

Watts, Ronald L. 2003. "Bicameralism in Federal Parliamentary Systems." In Serge Joyal, ed., *Protecting Canadian Democracy: The Senate You Never Knew*, 67-104. Montreal and Kingston: McGill-Queen's University Press.

Conclusion

A Few More Women

LINDA TRIMBLE, MANON TREMBLAY, AND JANE ARSCOTT

There are only a few more women in Canada's Parliament and legislatures now than there were a decade ago. Since November 2002, forty-four federal, provincial, and territorial elections have been held, but women's share of the legislative seats has increased by a mere five percentage points, that is, from 20 percent to 25 percent. At this rate of increase it will take at least another fifty years to achieve gender parity in electoral politics. When the numbers grew from 2 percent in 1970, to 12 percent in 1988, to 18 percent in 1995, and to 22 percent in 2000, it seemed that steady and continuous progress was possible, even likely (Arscott and Trimble 1997, 2; Trimble and Arscott 2003, 40). But since the turn of the century the pace of change has been glacial. Moreover, as the chapters in this volume demonstrate, women remain markedly under-represented in municipal councils and party leadership positions. A mere handful of women have led governments, as premier or prime minister. While the level of representation is somewhat better in appointed positions, such as senator and cabinet minister, and all but one of Canada's jurisdictions has had at least one female representative of the Crown, women are far from achieving equality in representation in any site of formal political power. The evidence shows, at best, incremental increases over long periods, making gender parity an elusive goal.

This concluding chapter draws the evidence provided in the individual chapters together to identify trends and to explain both commonalities and differences. Our observations are presented in three sections, mirroring the structure of the chapters. First, we examine the numbers, beginning with longitudinal data on women's representation in Canada's legislatures. This section also summarizes trends with respect to women's presence as candidates, party leaders, cabinet ministers, first ministers, and representatives of the Crown. The second section turns to explanations for the overall lack of progress as well as for differences among and between jurisdictions. Finally, the prospects for gender parity in political representation across Canada are assessed. Will the electoral glass ceiling for women remain at 25 percent (or lower) for the foreseeable future?

Women's Political Representation: The Numbers

Women Legislators

Women now hold 25 percent of all legislative positions across Canada and have reached or exceeded the 25 percent mark in the House of Commons and the Senate as well as in five provinces and one territory. Table C.1 shows leaders and laggards in Canada's legislatures. Among the provinces and

TABLE C.1

Women elected in most recent elections (as of March 2013), by jurisdiction

Jurisdiction	Party elected	Year of election	Number of members	Women elected N	Women elected %*
Quebec	PQ	2012	125	41	33
Yukon	Yukon	2011	19	6	32
British Columbia	Liberal	2009	85	25	29
Manitoba	NDP	2011	57	16	28
Ontario	Liberal	2011	107	30	28
Alberta	PC	2012	83	23	26
House of Commons	Conservative	2011	308	76	25
Nova Scotia	NDP	2009	52	12	23
Prince Edward Island	Liberal	2011	27	6	22
Saskatchewan	Saskatchewan	2011	58	11	19
Newfoundland and Labrador	PC	2011	48	8	17
New Brunswick	PC	2010	55	8	15
Northwest Territories	–	2007	19	2	11
Nunavut	–	2008	19	1	5
Total			1,062	265	25

* Percentages of women elected are listed in descending order. Percentages are rounded to the nearest whole number.

territories, only Quebec and Yukon are presently at or exceeding the "critical mass" threshold of 30 percent, though several provinces are close to this level (British Columbia, Manitoba, and Ontario). Two provinces (Nova Scotia and Prince Edward Island) are hovering between 20 and 25 percent, and women hold a quarter of the seats in the federal House of Commons. However, women hold fewer than 20 percent of the legislative positions in many jurisdictions: Saskatchewan, Newfoundland and Labrador, New Brunswick, Nunavut, and the Northwest Territories.

While successive prime ministers have used the power of appointment to boost the representation of women in the Upper House from 15 percent in the 34th Parliament (1988-93) to 35 percent in the 37th Parliament (2001-4), political will to increase the proportion of women in the Senate has stalled in the mid-30 percent range. At the municipal level, the most recent data indicate that women held 26 percent of council seats across Canada in 2009. While received wisdom is that women fare better in winning elections at the municipal level than at higher levels of elected political office, the evidence provided in Chapter 1 (this volume) suggests that the city, local, and municipal levels of politics are no more women-friendly than other electoral levels.

Reaching the halfway point to gender parity has taken decades in Canada (Dahlerup and Freidenvall 2005, 27). As the individual chapters show, very few women were elected anywhere in Canada until the early to mid-1980s, and in some provinces it took until the 1990s for women to exceed 10 percent of the legislators. Also, in each jurisdiction or institution the numbers for women have stalled or even dropped at least once in the last thirty years. Overall, it seems that progress is neither steady nor inevitable. To test this assumption, and to identify longitudinal patterns, we analyzed changes in the percentage of women elected by jurisdiction at five-year intervals, from 1980 to September 2012. This way of looking at the numbers illustrates three distinct patterns.

The first pattern is one of overall progression (see Figure C.1). In six legislatures the long-term trend is of a zigzag-like increase in the number of women legislators. Only Manitoba has produced a relatively steady increase when the percentages are averaged; however, Manitoba's most recent election saw women's share of the seats drop slightly, from 32 to 28 percent. It is too soon to tell whether or not this pattern will continue. In the other five jurisdictions in this category, there have been modest setbacks along the way. Periods of stagnation marred women's progress in the House of Commons, Nova Scotia, and Yukon. For instance, women's share of the seats in

FIGURE C.1
The "overall progression" pattern

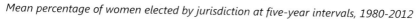

Mean percentage of women elected by jurisdiction at five-year intervals, 1980-2012

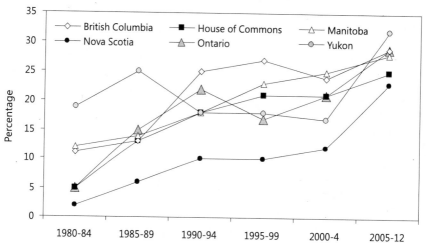

the House of Commons stalled at just over 20 percent for fourteen years before reaching 25 percent in the 2011 election. In Nova Scotia, a small decrease occurred in 1999 but the numbers subsequently climbed, with large increases in recent elections. In British Columbia, Ontario, and Yukon, women's legislative representation recovered from a drop of over five percentage points. For instance, women won 22 percent of the seats in the Ontario legislature in 1990, fell to 18 percent for two elections, then rose to a record 29 percent in 2011. Women's share of the seats in British Columbia plummeted from a high of almost 27 percent in 1996 down to 22 percent in 2005 but set a new record in 2009, at 29 percent. As Graham White notes in Chapter 12 (this volume), due to the low numbers of legislative positions, the three territories show no clear patterns. Electing one more or one fewer woman can make a huge percentage difference. That said, Yukon, where women's electoral success has seesawed, posted a record high for women in 2011, at 32 percent.

The second pattern is best described as a "lost peak" (see Figure C.2). In six legislatures, a peak was followed by an overall decline, such that the record number of women elected during the high point has yet to be repeated.

FIGURE C.2
The "lost peak" pattern

Mean percentage of women elected by jurisdiction at five-year intervals, 1980-2012

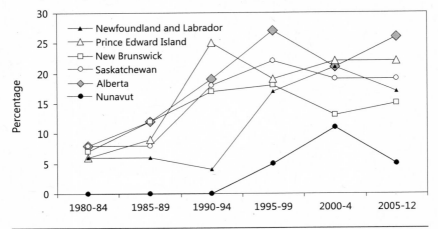

This pattern is evident in Alberta, Saskatchewan, Newfoundland and Labrador, Prince Edward Island, New Brunswick, and Nunavut. In Newfoundland and Labrador, women were elected in small numbers until 1996, when women's share of the seats finally increased, then stalled at 21 percent, then declined as a result of the 2011 election to 17 percent. In PEI, women's representation reached 25 percent in 1994, dipped to 19 percent, and then took three additional elections to rebound. However, the most recent election showed another drop, from 25 percent to 22 percent. Saskatchewan hit 22 percent in the mid-1990s then declined in recent elections. New Brunswick and Alberta also achieved record highs for women's representation in the mid- to late 1990s, only to see the numbers fall dramatically. Only Alberta has recovered to approximately the previous high-water mark. New Brunswick remains near the bottom of the pack, with women holding just 15 percent of the seats in that province.

The third trend can be called the "plateau pattern," and it illustrates an uncertain future for the electoral project (see Figure C.3). In the Northwest Territories and in Quebec, as well as with Senate appointments, numbers have stalled since the mid-2000s. Quebec is one of the few places where women's share of the seats has increased fairly steadily since the 1980s, but

FIGURE C.3
The "plateau" pattern

Mean percentage of women elected by jurisdiction at five-year intervals, 1980-2012

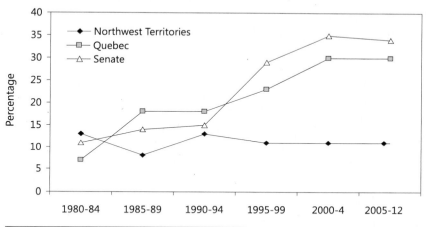

it hovered around 30 percent until the most recent election, held in 2012, which brought the number up slightly to 33 percent. Yet even with that small increase, Quebec's numbers show a plateau when averaged in five-year intervals. The Northwest Territories has too few seats for percentages to be particularly meaningful, but it remains the case that women's share of the seats in this territory has never risen above 15 percent. Appointments of women to the Senate have slowed of late, with the current prime minister less likely than his predecessors to nominate women.

Candidates

Women cannot win office if they do not seek nominations or stand for election, thus a key part of the story about women's electoral representation is candidacy. All the authors have noted a clear relationship between the percentage of seats contested by women nominated by competitive parties (particularly the winning party) and the percentage of seats won. Table C.2 displays the numbers from the most recent elections in jurisdictions with party systems to illustrate this point. The crucial role of recruitment by governing parties is confirmed by these data. In six jurisdictions (the House of Commons, British Columbia, Alberta, Saskatchewan, Manitoba, and

Newfoundland and Labrador) the percentage of women elected is either the same as, or within plus or minus four percentage points of, the percentage of female candidates offered by the winning party.

In other jurisdictions there is a noticeable gap between the percentage of women candidates who ran for the winning party and the percentage of women elected. The ability of opposition parties to recruit female candidates often shapes electoral outcomes for women, especially when minority governments are elected and opposition party members win more than half of the legislative seats. Even when the governing party wins a majority, the ability of other parties to recruit women to safe, or winnable, seats can make a difference to the outcome. For instance, women now hold 33 percent of the seats in Quebec's National Assembly despite the fact that women comprised only 27 percent of the candidates for the winning party, the Parti québécois. The election of a minority government and the higher percentages of women candidates offered by competing parties boosted the number of women elected in Quebec. In contrast, in Ontario and Nova Scotia, opposition parties are responsible for the percentage of women elected being lower than the proportion presented by the winning parties. For example, Ontario's recent election produced a Liberal minority government, with the Progressive Conservatives forming the Official Opposition. Only 22 percent of the PC candidates in Ontario were female, thus reducing the number of women elected overall. Similarly, in Nova Scotia, while the winning New Democratic Party boasted a large number of women candidates (33 percent), the opposition parties ran significantly fewer women (19 percent for the Liberals and only 13 percent for the PCs). New Brunswick is the outlier as women comprised 27 percent of the candidates in that province's 2010 election but won only 15 percent of the seats. As Everitt explains (Chapter 5, this volume), the NDP is weak in that province, typically winning very few seats, and women who are nominated by the Liberal and Progressive Conservative parties tend to run in "unwinnable" ridings.

Table C.2 also indicates differences between political parties in their willingness to nominate female candidates. Overall, parties on the left are more likely to nominate women, with the NDP averaging 34 percent across jurisdictions in the most recent elections and other left-leaning parties posting similarly high numbers (e.g., the BQ at 32 percent and the PQ at 27 percent). Notably, one of Quebec's new parties, Québec Solidaire, has offered equal numbers of women and men candidates in the last three elections. However, in a few cases, the NDP does not set the bar when it comes to recruiting women. In Saskatchewan, the NDP is competitive and indeed has formed

TABLE C.2

Percentage of women candidates in most recent elections, by jurisdiction and party

| Jurisdiction | Year of election | Political party | | | | Overall % of women candidates | % of women legislators |
		Liberal	PC/ Conservative	NDP	Other		
CANADA	2011	29	**22**	40	32[1]	31	25
British Columbia	2009	**29**	–	48	–	39	29
Alberta	2012	23	**24**	47	13[2]	29	21
Saskatchewan	2011	–	–	22	**17**[3]	20	19
Manitoba	2011	25	21	**30**	–	25	28
Ontario	2011	**39**	22	36	–	32	29
Quebec	2012	38	–	–	27[4]	34	33
					22[5]		
					50[6]		
New Brunswick	2010	22	**25**	33	–	27	15
Nova Scotia	2009	19	13	**33**	–	22	23
Newfoundland and Labrador	2011	35	**13**	25	–	24	17
Prince Edward Island	2011	**22**	26	43	–	30	22
Yukon	2011	15	–	19	25[7]	20	32

Note: Percentages for winning parties are in bold type.

1 Bloc Québécois
2 Wildrose Party
3 Saskatchewan Party
4 Parti québécois
5 Coalition Avenir Québec
6 Québec Solidaire
7 Yukon Party

the government four times in the past six elections, but since 1991 it has made few efforts to recruit more women, and the numbers have languished between 18 and 22 percent for the past twenty years. In Newfoundland and Labrador, the New Democrats lagged well behind the Liberals in securing female candidates in the 2011 election, possibly because the party is not electorally competitive in that province.

The centrist Liberal Party is close to the 30 percent "critical mass" point for nominating women, with women averaging 27 percent of the party's candidates in eleven jurisdictions. However, as Table C.2 shows, the Liberals are out-paced by the NDP in all but two jurisdictions, Ontario and Newfoundland and Labrador. Women are generally much less likely to be nominated by conservative parties as they are selected for just under a fifth (21 percent) of the candidacies in jurisdictions in which these parties are active. Other right-leaning parties register even lower levels of recruitment. Only 13 percent of Alberta's Wildrose Party's candidates and 17 percent of the Saskatchewan Party's candidates were women.

Party Leaders

Trimble and Arscott (2003, 70) identify 1993 as a high-water mark for women and political party leadership. At that point, ten women led competitive parties, defined throughout this volume as parties with at least one elected representative in the parliament or legislature. Two women were at the helm of national parties – Kim Campbell (PC) and Audrey McLaughlin (NDP) – and eight women led parties in the provinces and territories. However, this record level of representation for women in the party leader role was short-lived. The electoral misfortune of Kim Campbell, whose six-month stay in the Prime Minister's Office was followed by a dramatic defeat at the polls, coupled with the resignation of Canada's lone female premier, Catherine Callbeck, signalled a downward spiral for women in leadership roles from 1997 to 2002, followed by a long period of stagnation. Between 2003, when Alexa McDonough stepped down from the leadership of the federal NDP, and 2008, there were only three women leaders. With the exception of BC NDP leader Carole James, these women led third-place parties.

It has taken eighteen years for women to better the record of ten women party leaders set in 1993. As of February 2013, there are eleven female party leaders across Canada. Elizabeth May, who leads the Green Party of Canada and holds the party's lone seat in the House of Commons, is the solitary woman leader at the federal level. But ten women head competitive provincial and territorial parties, as indicated in Table C.3. Moreover, while the

TABLE C.3
Current women party leaders, by jurisdiction

Jurisdiction	Name	Political party	Period of service
CANADA	Elizabeth May	Green Party	2006 to present
British Columbia	Christy Clark	Liberal	2011 to present
Alberta	Alison Redford	PC	2011 to present
Alberta	Danielle Smith	Wildrose Alliance	2009 to present
Ontario	Kathleen Wynne	Liberal	2013 to present
Ontario	Andrea Horwath	NDP	2009 to present
Quebec	Pauline Marois	Parti québécois	2007 to present
Prince Edward Island	Olive Crane	PC	2010 to present
Newfoundland	Kathy Dunderdale	PC	2010 to present
and Labrador	Lorraine Michael	NDP	2006 to present
Yukon	Elizabeth Hanson	NDP	2000 to present

overall number of female party leaders is only slightly higher than it was in 1993, the parties of these women leaders are significantly more competitive, and thus more of them are in, or are poised to enter, the "premier's club" (Gillis 2011, 18). Competitiveness refers to their likelihood of holding or gaining power through an electoral victory.

In 1993, only two women led competitive parties (Ontario's Lyn McLeod and PEI's Catherine Callbeck). Those remaining were at the helm of governing parties headed for certain defeat (Kim Campbell), electorally decimated parties (e.g., Sharon Carstairs in Manitoba), or parties with traditionally low levels of electoral representation in their jurisdiction (e.g., Elizabeth Weir, NDP leader in New Brunswick). The picture as of February 2013 is much brighter. In addition to Nunavut, which has a woman premier but no political parties, five women are serving as heads of government, including three who brought their parties to victory in a general election: Alison Redford (Alberta), Kathy Dunderdale (Newfoundland and Labrador), and Pauline Marois (Quebec). Moreover, NDP leaders in Ontario, Newfoundland and Labrador, and Yukon produced a strong showing for their parties in recent elections.

First Ministers
With the election of Kathleen Wynne as Ontario Liberal leader and premier-elect in January 2013, women governed six of Canada's thirteen provinces and territories. Women are now more likely to hold the office of premier (46 percent of premiers are now women) than to be elected as

TABLE C.4
Women first ministers to date

Jurisdiction	Name	Political party	Period of service
CANADA	Kim Campbell	PC	June 1993 to November 1993
British Columbia	Rita Johnston	Social Credit	April 1991 to November 1991
	Christy Clark	Liberal	2011 to present
Alberta	Alison Redford*	PC	2011 to present
Ontario	Kathleen Wynne	Liberal	2013 to present
Quebec	Pauline Marois*	PQ	2012 to present
Prince Edward Island	Catherine Callbeck*	Liberal	1993-96
Newfoundland and Labrador	Kathy Dunderdale*	PC	2010 to present
Yukon	Pat Duncan*	Liberal	2000-2
Northwest Territories	Nellie Cournoyea	n/a	1991-95
Nunavut	Eva Aariak	n/a	2008 to present

* Elected in a general election.

member of a federal, provincial, or territorial legislature (25 percent of legislators are women). With this recent surge of women into the "premier's club" pundits declared that "women's time in politics has come" (Wente, 2013). Perhaps it has, but even when these newly minted women premiers are included in the tally, very few women have served as government leader in Canada's federal and provincial legislatures. Only eleven have made it to the top political job in Canada as prime minister or premier (see Table C.4). To date, Canada has had one woman prime minister and ten female premiers. Even fewer women – only five – have secured the first minister's job by winning an election (see Table C.4). PEI's Catherine Callbeck, Yukon's Pat Duncan, and, most recently, Alberta's Alison Redford, Newfoundland and Labrador's Kathy Dunderdale, and Pauline Marois in Quebec won office through a general election victory.

Women have been successful in ascending to the premier's role in Canada's territories, as each of the three territories has selected a female first minister. In the Northwest Territories and Nunavut, there are no parties, and premiers are chosen by vote of the members of the territorial assembly. Nellie Cournoyea and Eva Aariak were selected in this fashion. At the federal and provincial level, women's fortunes are tied to the fates of their political parties. Until quite recently, women tended to win the leadership roles of parties in decline. In fact, a "glass cliff" phenomenon, whereby women are chosen for leadership positions that are risky or precarious (Ryan and Haslam 2005, 81), was evident in the track record for the early female first ministers, and none lasted very long in the first minister's post. For example, two women stepped into the role just before their party careened over the edge of the electoral abyss. Forced to call an election shortly after her leadership victory, Kim Campbell had insufficient time to resuscitate the Progressive Conservative Party's electoral fortunes, and her stint in the Prime Minister's Office was over after four months. British Columbia's Rita Johnston, who took over the leadership of the scandal-ridden and extremely unpopular governing Social Credit Party just before it went to the polls, lasted only six months in the top job. Canada's newest women government leaders have the potential to hold power for much longer than their predecessors. Neither Alberta's Alison Redford nor Newfoundland and Labrador's Kathy Dunderdale faced a "glass cliff" as both were selected to lead popular governing parties and both won majority terms in office through successful election campaigns. Redford and Dunderdale could be among the first female heads of government to win re-election in Canada.

So, does the fact that half of Canada's provincial premiers are women mean, as *Globe and Mail* columnist Margaret Wente (2013) insists, that "the highly exclusive club for Canadian premiers will have to start considering affirmative action for men?" Not yet. Gender parity in leadership of provincial governments may well be a fleeting phenomenon, as only two of the five women premiers enjoy relative job security. Both Dunderdale and Redford were selected by governing parties and won resounding victories in recent general elections. In contrast, Quebec's Marois and Ontario's Wynne lead minority governments that could be brought down by a motion of non-confidence at any time. Moreover, the glass cliff phenomenon may yet befall BC's Christy Clark, who assumed the mantle of an unpopular government and must go to the polls in May 2013.

Appointing Women: Senate, Crown, and Cabinet

Women fare better in appointed positions because of the power of the prime minister or premier to correct women's under-representation in elected office through strategic appointments. As Chapter 14 (this volume) indicates, women's representation in the appointed Senate exceeds their representation in the House of Commons by ten percentage points. Premiers and prime ministers have also shown an inclination to appoint women to represent the

Crown in Canada. Three women have served as governor general, and all provinces except Newfoundland and Labrador have had at least one female lieutenant governor. In six of the ten provinces (Alberta, British Columbia, Ontario, New Brunswick, Nova Scotia, and PEI), two women have held the post, and Saskatchewan now boasts its third female lieutenant governor. However, in 2012 all but two of the eleven representatives of the Crown were men, including the governor general.

Representatives of the Crown are important symbols of the state and are constitutionally powerful, but by convention they act on the advice of the first minister. In practice, then, the roles of the governor general and lieutenant governors are ceremonial. Senators play a significant legislative role, especially with respect to legislative investigation and oversight, but the Senate's power has also been muted by convention because of the importance of democratic norms. Thus while senators correct and refine legislation, they do not make policy, and rarely do they challenge the policy initiatives of the elected House of Commons.

The true locus of power in the Canadian system is the political executive – the first minister and her or his cabinet. The executive sets and enacts the legislative agenda of government. Cabinet, therefore, is a crucial avenue for representation as it is the decision-making body of Canadian legislatures. Individual chapters show a modest tendency to over-represent women in cabinet positions; in other words, women have held a higher percentage of cabinet posts than of legislative seats. For example, in the House of Commons, since the 1984 election there has been a slightly higher percentage of women in cabinet than there have been female MPs. However, this trend may be waning as more women are elected.

Table C.5 enumerates the numbers and percentages of women in cabinet positions across Canada as well as the overall percentage of women in each legislature for the most recent elections. It shows three patterns. The first pattern is most prevalent, evident in seven legislatures, including the House of Commons, and it is one of congruence between women's presence in the legislature and their percentage of the cabinet positions. In each jurisdiction, women's share of the cabinet seats is within plus or minus four percentage points of their overall percentage of seats in the legislature. For instance, women hold 25 percent of the seats in the House of Commons and 29 percent of the cabinet positions. The second pattern, shown by Manitoba, New Brunswick, and Nova Scotia, is marked by over-representation of women in cabinet relative to their presence in the legislative assembly. The gaps are wide, with women holding a much higher percentage of the cabinet

TABLE C.5

Women in cabinet according to appointments made after the most recent election, by jurisdiction

Jurisdiction	Year of election	Governing party	Number of cabinet members[1]	Women in cabinet N	Women in cabinet %	% of women legislators
Pattern 1: A close match[2]						
CANADA	2011	Conservative	38	11	29	25
British Columbia	2009	Liberal	25	7	28	29
Saskatchewan	2011	Saskatchewan	18	3	17	19
Ontario	2011	Liberal	22	6	27	29
Quebec	2012	PQ	24	9	33	33
Newfoundland and Labrador	2011	PC	16	4	25	23
Prince Edward Island	2011	Liberal	11	2	18	22
Pattern 2: Over-representation in cabinet[3]						
Manitoba	2011	NDP	17	7	41	28
New Brunswick	2010	PC	16	5	31	15
Nova Scotia	2009	NDP	12	4	33	17
Pattern 3: Under-representation in cabinet[4]						
Alberta	2012	PC	19	4	21	26
Yukon	2011	Yukon	8	1	13	32
Northwest Territories	2011	n/a	7	0	0	11
Nunavut	2008	n/a	8	1	13	5

1 Includes the prime minister and first ministers.
2 Women's representation in cabinet is within +/- 4% of their share of the seats.
3 Women's share of the cabinet seats is more than 4 percentage points higher than their share of the legislative seats.
4 Women's share of the cabinet seats is more than 4 percentage points lower than their share of the legislative seats.

positions than of the legislative seats. Women's representation in the New Brunswick and Nova Scotia cabinets, for instance, is 16 percentage points higher than their representation in the legislative assembly. Finally, there are four jurisdictions – Alberta and the three territories – in which women are under-represented in cabinet. Yukon is particularly striking in this regard, with women holding 32 percent of the seats in the assembly but only one cabinet position (13 percent). Nunavut and the Northwest Territories have a different method of cabinet selection, whereby a substantial minority of the elected members oversees ministries, and those who are not in cabinet hold the government accountable by asking questions in a spirit of collaboration in the public interest. White (Chapter 12) points out that women figure prominently at the executive level in the bureaucracies of territorial governments.

Some of the chapters in this volume go beyond the numbers of women in cabinet to explore the importance and policy influence of the positions they tend to hold. However, authors use different approaches to weighing the relative significance of different cabinet portfolios. Everitt (Chapter 5, this volume) finds that women are much more likely to be appointed to junior portfolios such as community and social services and status of women than to senior ministries such as finance or economic development. White (1998) distinguishes between "important," "middle range," and "junior" portfolios (see also Moncrief and Studlar 1996). Bittner and Goodyear-Grant (Chapter 6, this volume) find that women are more likely to hold "middle-range" or "junior" portfolios in Newfoundland and Labrador, though a recent, albeit modest, shift towards appointing women to "important" portfolios has occurred, notably in the most important post of all, that of premier. Tremblay (Chapter 10, this volume) distinguishes between junior and senior portfolios in Quebec, where the distribution of women has been more or less balanced since 1976. However, women continue to be appointed to ministries that oversee policies of a cultural, social, or economic nature. Parti québécois governments in particular have appointed women to "royal prerogative" portfolios such as justice, finance, and international and intergovernmental affairs.

Explanations

Contributors to this collection have identified several explanations for the continued under-representation of women within municipal councils, the Parliament of Canada, and provincial and territorial legislative assemblies. Three sorts of causes emerge: cultural, socio-economic, and, political. These causes are frequently organized in an economics-inspired supply-demand model for political candidacies. On the supply side, women may decide not to put forward their candidacies because they perceive politics as a confrontational environment antithetical to their socialization (a cultural cause), or because they lack the financial resources to run their electoral campaign (a socio-economic cause), or because they regard themselves as lacking the essential supports within the parties needed to win a nomination contest (a political cause). On the demand side, party selectorates may reject a prospective female candidate on the assumption that the electorate is not ready to elect a woman representative (a cultural cause), or because they think that no woman has the socio-economic assets required to run a competitive electoral campaign in a given riding (a socio-economic cause), or because the incumbent plans to run again, with the result that there is no space for new blood since each party can run only one candidate (a political cause). The chapters in this volume illustrate that political causes – political parties, the electoral system, and rules governing the candidate recruitment process – provide the key explanation for women's under-representation in Canadian politics. Political institutions offer the formal framework within which political agents act in response to cultural, socio-economic, and political factors.

Cultural Explanations

Culture remains an elusive notion because it refers to both everything and nothing. Basically, culture evokes the broad belief system (e.g., values, attitudes, and opinions) supporting any society, its institutions, and the population's ways of being, thinking, and living. The processes of socialization and acculturation as well as religion, the educational system, and gender roles are formidable vehicles by which the culture becomes the cultural – that is, "processes of meaning-making in contexts of power" (Dhamoon 2006, 371).

Several contributors have pointed out cultural factors in order to explain the relative absence of women in Canada's Parliament, provincial and territorial assemblies, and municipal councils. One such argument concerns history – that is, the collective memory and roots. Sampert (Chapter 4, this volume) suggests that Manitoba's glorious legacy regarding women's rights obscures what appears to be its current complacency towards women's legislative under-representation. Regionalism constitutes an important marker of Canadian politics, and some studies have shown that women's legislative representation continues to be influenced by it (Arscott 1997; Carbert 2002, 2009; Vickers and Brodie 1981). For instance, Young (Chapter 13, this volume) comments on women's uneven legislative representation across Canada, as British Columbia and Quebec exceed the national average and the Atlantic provinces fall below it. However, there is little consensus about the role culture plays in explaining the unequal percentages of women legislators across Canada. For instance, Bittner and Goodyear-Grant reject the entrenched idea that a more traditional political culture is responsible for the low proportion of women MLAs in Newfoundland and Labrador. Yet Berdahl (Chapter 11, this volume) considers that a more traditional political culture may discourage women from getting into Saskatchewan politics. The urban-rural split is another component of culture that is expressed spatially. The studies show that women are more likely to be candidates and to be elected in urban electoral constituencies (Moncrief and Thompson 1991). Yet this is not always the case: Sampert's chapter on Manitoba shows that a woman wearing the colours of a non-competitive party in an urban riding (e.g., a Progressive Conservative in a city riding) has a very good chance of losing.

As the supply-demand model puts it, to be elected is the result of both supplying her candidacy and responding to a demand of electorates for female candidates and representatives. Several authors in this collection argue that the electorate does not discriminate against women who seek to sit in the federal Parliament or in provincial and territorial legislatures. Moreover, Praud (Chapter 3, this volume) argues that public acceptance of women candidates has put pressure on political parties to encourage them to select more women.

The "women in politics" field frequently points to the challenges that family responsibilities pose for women's political careers. Basically, family responsibilities are said to limit women's capacity for engagement in politics. In fact, caring for children is seen as a primary but time-consuming role for women – one that constrains their opportunities to develop the assets necessary for electoral success, such as building up a social network and being actively involved in a political party. Nevertheless, this general reading of the dynamics surrounding the family-politics balance needs to be nuanced. First, as Praud notes, family duties do not prevent women from eventually being elected, but they may delay women's entry into politics. Second, the "family responsibilities" explanation does not illuminate why women who are not mothers do not enter politics. In one of the first studies on women in politics in Canada, Brodie (1985) calls for a more critical analysis of the impact family has on women's political careers. According to her, it is a biological fallacy that motherhood "limits or delays" women's availability for political careers since "not all women are mothers." Accordingly not all women's political careers are affected by either motherhood or child-rearing. Such assumptions reproduce gender-role socialization by suggesting "that women should stay home until their children have matured" (79).

Moreover, might it be possible that the "family" argument diverts attention from the simple fact that fewer women run compared to men and that they run less often? Chapters in this collection identify various cultural reasons why women eschew candidacy. Berdahl, Tremblay, and Young observe that women are less likely to express political ambition than men. However, as Tremblay and Mévellec note, women also receive less encouragement than men to aspire to political office. The chapters on British Columbia, the House of Commons, and Saskatchewan point out that the confrontational nature of Westminster-style parliamentary debate may dissuade some women from running for office. The lack of role models and the perception that politics is a man's game may also diminish women's interest in political careers (as noted in the New Brunswick and Prince Edward Island chapters). Even worse, overt sexism against political women has a definitely repellent effect on women's engagement with politics, as is illustrated by the experiences of women politicians in Manitoba. To sum up, the cultural explanations help us to understand the enigma of women's low presence in politics. However, as the chapters in this volume show, the socio-economic explanations appear to be much less convincing.

Socio-Economic Explanations

Like cultural explanations, socio-economic factors refer to the supply side of the supply-demand model for political candidacies described above. However, these latter factors provide much less convincing evidence to explain why there are now fewer women in politics than there were before (Tremblay 2008). Socio-economic factors drive the pipeline theory, which holds that increased numbers of women in occupations that lead to political careers are likely to produce more political candidates. Women in these professions are perceived to have the "objective qualifications and economic autonomy" needed to be credible as candidates (Lawless and Fox 2010, 30). Thus, as women's level of education and occupational attainment increases, so should the numbers of women in electoral politics.

Two chapters in this collection (i.e., those on Newfoundland and Labrador and on Saskatchewan) assess the role of socio-economic factors on the proportion of women legislators. Their conclusions highlight the need to consider the continued relevance of these factors, particularly for Aboriginal and ethnic minority women. Indeed, while women are increasingly educated and involved in the workforce market, education and employment in Canada remain highly gender-segregated (see Statistics Canada 2011).

Berdahl notes a clear gender-based educational segregation in Saskatchewan: while seven out of ten female postsecondary graduates hold a degree, diploma, or certificate in education, health, public administration, or management, about half of their male counterparts have academic qualifications in engineering, agriculture, and natural resources. It is not surprising that this phenomenon extends to the labour force, leading at the same time to a marked gender-based discrepancy in income, which is likely to diminish women's political ambitions (as Bittner and Goodyear-Grant note occurs in Newfoundland and Labrador). Money remains a serious challenge for women running for a political position even in municipal politics, where the costs of candidacies are lower, leading to the assumption that they are more accessible (see Tremblay and Mévellec, Chapter 1, this volume). White makes a similar argument about territorial politics. Clearly the pipeline theory needs to be revisited, as increased levels of education and higher occupational achievement do not necessarily position women in the "pipeline" for political office. Moreover the socio-economic differences between women should be considered when measuring the increased presence of women on the traditional pathways to electoral success.

Political Explanations
Institutional factors remain particularly significant in explaining the under-representation of women in Canadian legislative and municipal politics. This book presents evidence challenging conventional wisdom about why the Canadian parliamentary system appears inhospitable to women. First, both Raney (Chapter 8) and Young (Chapter 13) contest the argument that a high rate of electoral turnover is a barrier to women's success; as these authors show, low incumbency rates have contributed to the feminization of the membership of the federal Parliament and the Ontario legislature. As Tremblay and Mévellec demonstrate, the rate of turnover in municipal politics is lower than it is in legislative politics, and the "long-standing power of incumbency" prevails. These factors help to explain why municipal politics seems to be no more sympathetic to women's descriptive representation than Ottawa and the capitals of provinces and territories: because municipal positions seem to offer fewer open seats than other levels of government.

The chapters by Tremblay and Young cast doubt on another long-standing assumption – that female candidates tend to be relegated to lost-cause ridings. There are, of course, some women who run in unwinnable ridings, as do some men (see the Nova Scotia and New Brunswick chapters). However,

Raney qualifies this position: not only does the electoral success of women depend on the nature of the ridings in which they run, but incumbency candidacies are apparently not as safe for women as was previously thought. After examining the 1995, 1999, 2003, and 2007 Ontario elections, Raney points out that, when winning parties have women in winnable seats and maintain power in successive elections, women incumbents benefit at least as much if not more than their male counterparts when it comes to retaining their seats.

Several chapters in this collection point to the electoral system (and notably the voting system) as largely responsible for the under-representation of women in Canadian politics. The single-member plurality voting system prevailing in Canada is of the first-past-the-post type: following a single round of voting the candidate who obtains the highest number of votes is declared the winner, without a requirement for an absolute majority. Since each political party nominates a single candidate in each riding, the local riding association will strive to choose the person it perceives as the "winning candidate." Yet that determination is not neutral since the very qualities deemed appropriate for a career in politics tend to privilege certain types of candidates: "As a result women, working-class candidates and those from the ethnic minorities will tend to be consistently disadvantaged" (Norris and Lovenduski 1989, 94). Thus, since the voting system shapes parties' strategies for selecting candidates, it is responsible in large part for the low presence of women, and the even lower presence of Aboriginal and racialized women, in politics. Clearly, the voting system stands between the political parties and the proportion of women in politics (Tremblay 2008). Farrell (2001, 167) captures this dynamic when he argues: "It is not the electoral system which is at fault [for the under-representation of women in parliaments] so much as the party selection committees."

As has been the case historically, political parties continue to bear a heavy responsibility for the under-representation of women in Canadian politics. A number of contributors to this volume, including Berdahl (Saskatchewan), Bittner and Goodyear-Grant (Newfoundland and Labrador), Crossley (Prince Edward Island), O'Neill (Alberta), Raney (Ontario), Sampert (Manitoba) and Young (House of Commons), note political parties' lack of enthusiasm for recruiting and supporting women candidates. But, once again, this general observation needs two qualifications. The first is based on the premise that political parties pose serious barriers to women's political careers. Women, arguably, are no better represented when parties are uninvolved in electoral contests, as is the case in much of municipal politics and in two of Canada's territories (the Northwest Territories and Nunavut). As White convincingly argues: "The territorial experience suggests that the *absence* of parties may play a role in women's under-representation. Parties can and do recruit, encourage, train, and support candidates. A party committed to – or even open to – having women as its standard-bearers can thus be a structural support rather than a structural barrier to women's participation." At the same time, Young notes: "When a party's leadership in a constituency is largely male, informal recruitment efforts may not yield potential female candidacies." Here she echoes the conclusions of Cheng and Tavits (2011) and Tremblay and Pelletier (2001), who argue that the presence of women in the upper echelons of local party executives may contribute to the selection of women as legislative candidates.

The second qualification is that there are exceptions to the general rule that parties on the left side of the political spectrum (which sometimes are also less competitive) do appear more willing to increase the number of women among the ranks of their candidacies than their counterparts on the right. Berdahl points out that the NDP in Saskatchewan has not always been supportive of women who were seeking to be candidates in an election. Everitt observes that, in New Brunswick, women have led non-competitive parties on the electoral scene, which is also true of Françoise David, the current co-leader of the left-oriented Québec Solidaire. In British Columbia, the conservative-leaning Social Credit Party opened its doors to women when it was fairly clear the party was headed to the "electoral slaughterhouse." Taking the opposite stance, Young puts forward a very interesting hypothesis that deserves to be explored in greater depth in the future: "The number of women running as Conservative candidates and being elected as Conservative MPs has increased markedly over the past three elections ... It is possible that the party has made some behind-the-scenes efforts to encourage this trend in order to address a potentially embarrassing absence of women from its caucus." O'Neill supports this reading: she notes that most of the female Conservative nominees in the 2012 Alberta election won, suggesting that the party and/or the leader had recruited women to winnable ridings. As O'Neill concludes, the "one-party dominant system ... hinders but does not eliminate the possibility of representational gains." The impact of first ministers and/or party leaders on women's legislative representation appears clearly in the Senate, the members of which are appointed. Mullen notes that the feminization of the Senate requires not only a prime minister who is willing to appoint women but also a women-friendly director of appointments who builds and promotes a list of female potential senators.

One of the reasons parties give to justify the lip service they seem to pay to having more women in their pool of candidates is that nomination processes tend to remain decentralized, rendering any coordinated approach on this terrain difficult. This argument is also used to excuse their reluctance to implement positive action measures. However, exceptions to this trend include the New Democrats (and sometimes the Liberals), who have adopted such measures (see the chapters on British Columbia, the House of Commons, Newfoundland and Labrador, Nova Scotia, Ontario, and Saskatchewan). Québec Solidaire has achieved gender parity since its inception, illustrating that it is possible to implement a policy of equality in representation. As well, certain provinces have set up public-funded activities to promote women's political leadership (see the Nova Scotia and Quebec chapters). Nevertheless, grassroots women's movement activism remains crucial to improving the feminization rate of Canadian politics.

Conclusion: Prospects for Gender Parity

The gender composition of legislatures remains a significant measure of the health of democracy and of the effectiveness of representational practices in Canada and around the world (Arscott and Trimble 1997, 16). International organizations such as the World Economic Forum (Hausman, Tyson, and Zahidi 2011, 4) and the OECD (2011, 2) are developing more complex indicators of women's empowerment with a view to closing gender gaps. One of the largest and most persistent disparities is that of women's presence in formal institutions of political authority. Internationally, women remain unable to gain access to decision-making structures and economic opportunities at the rates as do most men, at least according to Saadia Zahidi, one of the lead researchers on the World Economic Forum's annual gender gap study (Lederer 2011; Hausman, Tyson, and Zahidi 2011, 23). While gender parity in legislatures is by no means the only step necessary in order to achieve gender equality, it is certainly an important one. Only roughly equal numbers of women and men representing the electorate at all levels of governance will eliminate the gender gap in legislative representation. However, as this volume demonstrates, gender parity in Canadian politics remains a remote possibility.

This collection presents an updated and thorough accounting of women's political progress in Canada by broadening the scope of analysis to include the Senate and the municipal level, and by tabulating the number of women candidates, party leaders, cabinet ministers, first ministers, and representatives of the Crown. Overall, the results are discouraging. The addition of a few more women in the decision-making bodies of political representation positions Canada only halfway to gender equality in electoral politics. If women were to hold half of the seats in the House of Commons, for example, their numbers would need to double. Given that women's representation in the House of Commons has increased by only seven percentage points since 1993, gender parity will certainly not be achieved within the lifetimes of the editors of this volume. Moreover, as the chapters in this book document, the road to gender parity is riddled with potholes, detours, and delays. In fact, there is evidence to suggest that the modest progress that has been made over the past two decades may not be sustained in the next round of elections.

The chapters in this volume also show that a concerted and systematic effort to recruit and appoint women can produce dramatic results. In British Columbia, the New Democratic Party adopted an affirmative action program that led to the nomination of virtually equal numbers of women and men candidates in the 2009 election (48 percent women, 52 percent men). In Quebec, women were appointed to 48 percent of the cabinet posts after the 2008 election. Canadians are certainly ready to see women in positions of political power. A majority of Canadian women surveyed in an Angus Reid Public Opinion Poll (2011, 1) expressed the belief that the federal government should do more to improve gender equality, and a majority of all respondents supported the establishment of quotas to mandate a minimum level of representation in the House of Commons, the Senate, and on corporate boards. While quotas are used in several countries, and tend to be effective, they are not likely to be adopted in Canada. In lieu of legislated quotas to boost the number of women in political office, what can be done?

Public awareness and education undertaken by organizations such as Equal Voice contribute to the demand that governments do more to improve gender equality, but it will take determined and concerted efforts by political parties and governments to realize the goal of gender parity. Active recruitment of women candidates by party leaders must be coupled with clear commitments to place those women in winnable ridings and to support their campaigns. Election laws can provide incentives for parties that promote women to more than 30 percent of the candidacies. First ministers can appoint women to positions of political authority, including Senate seats and representatives of the Crown, but especially to the cabinet, where policy decisions are made. Electing a few more women every decade or so is a move in the right direction; however, to realize gender parity in Canadian politics, many more women will need to be recruited and nominated at all levels of decision making.

References

Angus Reid Public Opinion Poll. 2011. "Gender Equality: Two-in-Five Canadians Want More Action to Improve Gender Equality." Available at http://www.angus-reid.com/.

Arscott, Jane. 1997. "Between the Rock and a Hard Place: Women Legislators in Newfoundland and Nova Scotia." In Jane Arscott and Linda Trimble, eds., *In the Presence of Women: Representation in Canadian Governments*, 308-37. Toronto: Harcourt Brace and Company.

Arscott, Jane, and Linda Trimble. 1997. *In the Presence of Women: Representation in Canadian Governments.* Toronto: Harcourt Brace and Company.

Brodie, Janine. 1985. *Women and Politics in Canada.* Toronto: McGraw-Hill Ryerson.

Carbert, Louise. 2002. "Historical Influences on Regional Patterns of the Election of Women to Provincial Legislatures." In William Cross, ed., *Political Parties, Representation, and Electoral Democracy in Canada*, 201-22. Don Mills: Oxford University Press.

–. 2009. "Are Cities More Congenial? Tracking the Rural Deficit of Women in the House of Commons." In Sylvia Bashevkin, ed., *Opening Doors Wider: Women's Political Engagement in Canada*, 70-90. Vancouver: UBC Press.

Cheng, Christine, and Margit Tavits. 2011. "Informal Influences in Selecting Female Political Candidates." *Political Research Quarterly* 64(2): 460-71.

Dahlerup, Drude, and Lenita Freidenvall. 2005. "Quotas as a 'Fast Track' to Equal Representation for Women: Why Scandinavia Is No Longer the Model." *International Feminist Journal of Politics* 7(1): 26-48.

Dhamoon, Rita. 2006. "Shifting From 'Culture' to 'the Cultural': Critical Theorizing of Identity/Difference Politics." *Constellations* 13(3): 354-73.

Farrell, David M. 2001. *Electoral Systems: A Comparative Introduction.* Houndmills: Palgrave Macmillan.

Gillis, Charlie. 2011. "Premier Club for Women." *Maclean's Magazine*, 14 March, 18-19.

Hausman, Ricardo, Laura D. Tyson, and Saadia Zahidi. 2011. *The Global Gender Gap Report 2011.* Geneva: World Economic Forum. Available at http://www3.weforum.org/.

Lawless, Jennifer L., and Richard L. Fox. 2010. *It Still Takes a Candidate: Why Women Don't Run for Office.* Rev. ed. Cambridge: Cambridge University Press.

Lederer, Edith M. 2011. "Gender Equality in Politics Still a Long Way Off." *Globe and Mail*, 1 November. Available at http://www.theglobeandmail.com/.

Moncrief, Gary F., and Donley T. Studlar. 1996. "Women Cabinet Ministers in Canadian Provinces 1976-1994." *Canadian Parliamentary Review* 19(3): 10-11.

Moncrief, Gary F., and Joel A. Thompson. 1991. "Urban and Rural Ridings and Women in Provincial Politics in Canada: A Research Note on Female MLAs." *Canadian Journal of Political Science* 24(4): 831-37.

Norris, Pippa, and Joni Lovenduski. 1989. "Pathways to Parliament." *Talking Politics* 1(3): 90-94.

Organisation for Economic Co-operation and Development (OECD). 2011. *Interim Report on the Gender Initiative: Gender Equality in Education, Employment and Entrepreneurship.* Meeting of the OECD Council at the Ministerial Level, Paris, 24-25 May. Paris: OECD. Available at http://www.oecd.org/.

Ryan, Michelle K., and S. Alexander Haslan. 2004. "The Glass Cliff: Evidence that Women Are Over-Represented in Precarious Leadership Positions." *British Journal of Management* 16: 81-90.

Statistics Canada. 2011. *Women in Canada: A Gender-Based Statistical Report.* Available at http://www.statcan.gc.ca/.

Tremblay, Manon. 2008. "Conclusion." In Manon Tremblay, ed., *Women and Legislative Representation: Electoral Systems, Political Parties, and Sex Quotas,* 233-47. New York: Palgrave Macmillan.

Tremblay, Manon, and Réjean Pelletier. 2001. "More Women Constituency Party Presidents: A Strategy for Increasing the Number of Women Candidates in Canada?" *Party Politics* 7(2): 157-90.

Trimble, Linda, and Jane Arscott. 2003. *Still Counting: Women in Politics across Canada.* Peterborough: Broadview Press.

Vickers, Jill, and M. Janine Brodie. 1981. "Canada." In Joni Lovenduski and Jill Hills, eds., *The Politics of the Second Electorate: Women and Public Participation,* 52-79. London: Routledge and Kegan Paul.

Wente, Margaret. 2013. "You Go, Girls! Your Political Time Has Come." *Globe and Mail,* 29 January. Available at http://www.theglobeandmail.com/.

White, Graham. 1998. "Shorter Measures: The Changing Ministerial Career in Canada." *Canadian Public Administration* 41(3): 369-94.

Contributors

Jane Arscott is an associate professor at Athabasca University. She co-authored *Still More Counting: Women and Politics across Canada* (1997) and co-edited *In the Presence of Women: Representation in Canadian Governments* (2003) with Linda Trimble.

Sylvia Bashevkin is a professor in the Department of Political Science at the University of Toronto. Best known for her research contributions in the field of women and politics, Bashevkin is the author most recently of *Women, Power, Politics: The Hidden Story of Canada's Unfinished Democracy* (2009) and the editor of *Opening Doors Wider: Women's Political Engagement in Canada* (2009).

Loleen Berdahl is an associate professor of political studies at the University of Saskatchewan and project leader for the survey and focus group research facility at the University of Saskatchewan's Social Sciences Research Laboratories. Her research interests include Canadian federalism and regionalism, public policy, and public opinion.

Amanda Bittner is an associate professor in the Department of Political Science at Memorial University of Newfoundland. She studies public opinion and voting, and her main research interests include the effects of knowledge and information on voters' decisions, as well as the institutional and structural incentives affecting voting behaviour.

Naomi Black is professor emerita of political science and women's studies at York University (Toronto). She is the author of *Virginia Woolf as Feminist* (2004) and co-author of the third edition of *Canadian Women: A History* (2011). She is currently working on a study of contemporary feminism in Canada.

Louise Carbert is associate professor of political science at Dalhousie University. She is the author of *Agrarian Feminism: The Politics of Ontario Farm Women* (1995) and *Rural Women's Leadership in Atlantic Canada* (2006). Her current work tracks women's candidacy and election to public office.

John Crossley was a member of the Political Studies Department at the University of Prince Edward Island from 1987 to 2002. He is currently the vice president, academic, for Yorkville Education Company, which operates Yorkville University in New Brunswick and the RCC Institute of Technology, Academy of Design, and Toronto Film School in Ontario.

Joanna Everitt is a professor of political science and dean of arts at the University of New Brunswick in Saint John. She specializes in Canadian politics and political behaviour with a particular focus on gender differences in public opinion, media coverage of male and female politicians, and voting behaviour in Canadian elections.

Elizabeth Goodyear-Grant is an associate professor of political science at Queen's University. Her research focuses on Canadian and comparative politics, especially electoral politics, news media, and the political representation of women. She has a forthcoming book that examines the role of news media in the political under-representation of women in Canadian federal politics.

Anne Mévellec is an associate professor in the School of Political Studies at the University of Ottawa. Her research focuses on urban politics and especially on the sociology of local elected officials in Quebec and Ontario.

Stephanie Mullen is a part-time professor in the School of Political Studies at the University of Ottawa. She is currently researching legislative interactions between women MPs and Senators, and the gendered nature of Senate appointments.

Brenda O'Neill is head of the Department of Political Science at the University of Calgary. Her research examines the political behaviour and opinions of Canadians, with a particular focus on women and youth.

Jocelyne Praud teaches political science courses at Simon Fraser University. Her research focuses on gender parity, democracy, and quotas in European and Canadian politics. She co-edited (with Sandrine Dauphin) *Parity Democracy* (2010).

Tracey Raney is an associate professor in the Department of Politics and Public Administration at Ryerson University in Toronto. Her research interests and publications include work on the political representation of gender and ethnic minorities, Ontario politics, and national identity in Canada outside of Quebec.

Shannon Sampert is an associate professor in the Department of Politics and the associate chair for the Joint MPA Program at the University of Winnipeg. Her research areas include Canadian politics, women's representation in politics, and mass media studies.

Manon Tremblay is professor at the School of Political Studies at the University of Ottawa. Her research interests are gender/women in politics, electoral studies, social movements, and notably the lesbian and gay movement. Her most recent publications include *Quebec Women and Legislative Representation* (2010).

Linda Trimble is a professor in the Department of Political Science at the University of Alberta. Currently she is researching gendered media representations of Canadian national party leadership candidates and Canadian, Australian, and New Zealand prime ministers.

Graham White is professor of political science at the University of Toronto. He has been researching and writing about the North since the 1980s and is currently completing (with Jack Hicks) a book on the creation of Nunavut. A former president of the Canadian Political Science Association, he is currently English co-editor of the *Canadian Journal of Political Science*.

Lisa Young is professor of political science and vice-provost and dean, graduate studies, at the University of Calgary. She has authored/co-authored several books, articles, and book chapters examining political party organization, political finance, and women in politics.

Index

Printed and bound in Canada by Friesens

Set in Segoe and Warnock by Artegraphica Design Co. Ltd.

Text design: Irma Rodriguez

Copy editor: Joanne Richardson

Proofreader: Frank Chow